P.F.M. FONTAINE

THE LIGHT
AND
THE DARK

A CULTURAL HISTORY OF DUALISM
VOLUME VI

J.C. GIEBEN, PUBLISHER
AMSTERDAM

THE LIGHT AND THE DARK

P.F.M. FONTAINE

THE LIGHT AND THE DARK
A CULTURAL HISTORY OF DUALISM

VOLUME VI

DUALISM IN THE HELLENISTIC WORLD

J.C. GIEBEN, PUBLISHER
AMSTERDAM 1991

To the memory of
my beloved brother Bert,
who died in Brooklyn, New York,
December 18, 1989, 61 years old

No part of this book may be translated or reproduced in any form, by print, photoprint, microfilm, or any other means, without written permission from the publisher.

© by P.F.M. Fontaine / ISBN 90 5063 076 6 / Printed in The Netherlands

"For all things are called
light and darkness"

Parmenides

CONTENTS

Preface		xiii
I	**DIADOCHICA**	1
1.	What if Alexander had lived on?	1
2.	The sad fate of the Macedonian dynasty	2
	a. The claimants	2
	b. One year of peace	3
	c. Antipater the new regent	4
	d. The extermination of the Macedonian royal house	4
3.	Vain attempts to keep ambitions in check	6
	a. Perdiccas' arrangements	6
	b. Antipater's reshuffle	6
	c. The Diadochi	7
4.	The Wars of the Diadochi	8
5.	Thrace	8
6.	Macedonia	10
	a. The ruthless King Cassander	10
	b. The bloody fight over the succession	11
	c. King Demetrius of Macedonia	12
7.	Antigonus and Asia Minor	13
	a. The 'loyalist' Antigonus	13
	b. The no less 'loyalist' Eumenes	14
	c. A 'separatist' coalition against Antigonus	15
	d. The end of the imperial idea	16
8.	Demetrius' invasion of Asia	17
9.	A separatist on principle	17
10.	The Seleucid Empire	18
11.	The revival of Greek particularism	19
12.	Before the Romans came	20
	a. The Parthian menace	20
	b. Separatism in Asia Minor	21
	c. Antiochus III beaten back by the Romans	22
	d. The decay of the Seleucid Empire	23
13.	The remnants	24
	a. No Egyptian imperialism	24
	b. The Macedonian mother country	24
14.	What remained of Graeco-Macedonian power	25

15.	Greek dissensions		26
	a. Philip II imposes unity on Greece		26
	b. Anti-Macedonian movements in Greece		27
	c. Polis autonomy long dead		28
	d. Polyperchon's bid for Greece		29
	e. Demetrius in Greece		30
	f. Pyrrhus the liberator		32
	g. What Greece meant to them		33
	h. Enter Ptolemy II		33
	j. Hellas a Macedonian apanage		34
16.	When the Romans came		34
	a. Roman intervention in Greece		34
	b. Macedonia in Roman hands		36
	c. Egypt an imperial possession		37
	d. The Seleucid monarchy abolished		38
	e. The Romans get hold of Asia Minor		39
	f. Postlude		39
Notes to Chapter I			40
II	HELLENISTICA		44
1.	The diaphragm of the world		44
	a. On the older maps		44
	b. Revision after Alexander's expedition		45
2.	Hellenism or Hellenization		46
	a. Philosophical cosmopolitanism		46
	b. The Alexandrian conquests and the dualism of Europe and Asia		48
	c. What is Hellenism?		49
3.	Alexander's declaration of intent		50
4.	Alexander's ecumenical policies		51
	a. Alexander's monetary policy		51
	b. Alexander's marriage policy		51
	c. The Greek idea of the pure		53
	d. A mixed army		54
	e. The veterans' reaction		55
	f. Alexandrian and Diadoch city foundations		56
5.	What happened to Alexander's plans after his death		57
	a. Transfer of populations		57
	b. The 'koinê' language		58
	c. A syncretistic religion		64
6.	The impact of Hellenism		67
7.	The Indo-Greeks		68
	a. The Indian satrapy		68

	b.	Bactria, an outpost of Hellenism	70
	c.	First Indian interlude	73
	d.	Second Indian interlude	74
	e.	The end of the Graeco-Bactrian and the Graeco-Indian kingdoms	75
8.	The fate of the Greek presence between the Euphrates and Bactria		77
9.	The chances of Hellenism in Asia Minor		79
	a.	Hellenism and the northern territories	79
	b.	The Hellenistic kingdom of Pergamum	80
	c.	The four non-Greek kingdoms	82
	d.	Hellenism in the southern half of Asia Minor	83
10.	Hellenism in Syria		84
11.	The Jewish revolt against Hellenism		85
	a.	Persian, Macedonian, and Egyptian rulers and Judaism	85
	b.	Antiochus III and the Jews	86
	c.	Hellenizing by King Antiochus III	87
	d.	The internal hellenizing movement	88
	e.	A Hebrew protest	91
	f.	Antiochus IV and his anti-Jewish policy	92
	g.	Some main points	96
	h.	The implementation of the king's policy	97
	j.	Antiochus' 'evil decrees'	98
	k.	From guerilla to open war	99
12.	Resistance to Hellenization in Egypt		102
13.	Conclusion		106
Notes to Chapter II		108

III	PHILOSOPHICA	121
1.	The early successors and folowers of Plato	121
	a. Eudoxus	121
	b. Speusippus	123
	c. Xenocrates	125
	d. The Epinomis	130
2.	The Stoa	133
	a. The founders	133
	b. The primary element	134
	c. The cosmos	136
	d. Monistic or dualistic?	137
	e. The Stoic solution	139
	f. Are the Stoic archai dualistic principles?	139
	g. Fate and necessity	141
	h. The dualism of the wise and the unwise	143
	j. 'Knowledge'	143

		k. The Stoics' low idea of life	144
		l. Evil in Stoic philosophy	145
		m. The folly of mankind	147
		n. The origin of evil	149
		o. An assessment	150
3.	Hellenic Atomism		150
		a. Some thoughts on Atomism and the atomic theory	150
		b. What is Atomism?	152
		c. Pluralism, monism, and dualism	152
		d. Leucippus	154
		e. Democritus	154
		f. Being and change	155
		g. The problem of the void	156
		h. The main outline of Atomism	157
		j. Psyche and matter	159
		k. Death	160
		l. The fate of the gods in Atomism	160
		m. Summing up	161
4.	Epicureanism		163
		a. The life and the school of Epicurus	163
		b. Epicurean dogmatism	163
		c. The esoteric character of the School of the Garden	165
		d. Ridding mankind of fear	167
		e. Epicurus' 'All'	168
		f. Epicurus' Atomism	169
		g. Epicurus on the soul	169
		h. Epicurus and the gods	170
		j. The problem of evil	171
		k. Why Epicurus needed gods	172
		l. Epicurean epistemology	174
		m. Epicurean pleasure	175
5.	Scepticism		176
		a. What is a 'Sceptic'?	176
		b. Pyrrho	177
		c. Timon	178
		d. Greek forerunners of scepticism	178
		e. Pyrrhonic apatheia	180
		f. How to be wise	181
		g. Neither truth nor probability	181
		h. Resignation	182
		j. The Pyrrhonist method	183
		k. The happiness of not knowing	183

6.	The Middle Academy	184
	a. Arcesilaus, the trustee of Scepticism	184
	b. The impossibility of notional assent	185
	c. The withdrawal of reality	186
	d. Arcesilaus' popularity	188
7.	The New Academy	188
	a. Carneades, the founder	188
	b. The demolition of the notion of the divine	189
	c. The attack on justice	191
8.	The tendency of eclecticism	193
9.	The Middle Stoa	195
	a. Boethus	195
	b. Panaetius, the mainstay of the Middle Stoa	196
	c. Posidonius, traveller, historiographer, philosopher	198
	d. Conclusion	204
Notes to Chapter III		204

IV PRAECURSORIA GNOSTICA   225

1.	How the Greeks profited from Alexander's triumphs	225
2.	The reverse of the coin	226
3.	The demise of the polis	227
4.	The rise of individualism	228
5.	The complacency of Hellenistic comedy	230
6.	Individualism in Hellenistic philosophy and science	231
7.	Following the trail to the Gnosis	232
8.	The influence of philosophy	233
9.	A new goal for life	234
10.	The problem of Evil	235
11.	Hellenistic theology	235
12.	Mysticism, esoterism, and elitism	237
13.	The fate of objective Truth	238
14.	The issue of knowledge and wisdom	239
15.	A short overview of the mental situation	239
16.	Dualistic elements	241
17.	What to do with the Olympian gods?	241
18.	Euhemerism	243
19.	The ruler-cult	245
20.	Tychê, the new goddess	247
21.	Faith in the stars	249
22.	Astrology as a pseudo-religion	249
23.	Occultism	250
24.	Conclusion	251

Notes to Chapter IV 252

Appendix A 255
Appendix B 256

Bibliography 259
General Index 275

Genealogies of the Alexandrian Royal House, the House of Antipater,
    and the Antigonid House   opposite p. 4

Map I	The Hellenistic World in 301 B.C.	opposite p. 16
Map II	The Hellenistic World ca. 200 B.C.	opposite p. 22
Map III	The Hellenistic World ca. 140 B.C.	opposite p. 26

PREFACE

This volume is the sixth in the series 'The Light and the Dark'. Deo volente, the work will be continued with a volume on the first stages of the Gnosis. Just as the foregoing volumes, the present one can be read independently of the others. I wish to emphasize, however, that the series forms a unity; every volume, every chapter, and every section is centered around the theme of dualism. Although I can hardly require of my readers that they peruse all these volumes, nevertheless, somebody who really wants to know what it is all about, should consult the whole work. Much to my chagrin, it already happened more than once, that reviewers concentrate on the chapter that deals with their own field of study and dispatch the rest in one and a half sentence or even neglect it completely.

I must also draw attention to the subtitle of this work, 'A cultural history of dualism'. This means that dualism is studied in the context of the prevailing general situation in some country. In effect, this work is meant as a critical analysis of the political, social, moral, and intellectual climate of, as far as these six volumes go now, the ancient world - studied, that is, from the viewpoint of dualism. I must, therefore, ask my readers , and in particular my reviewers, if they have no time to peruse the whole work, at least to consult the contents of every volume, in order to get an idea of my approach, of the variety of subjects, and of the cohesion of the whole, and, anyhow, to study carefully the prefaces to each volume, in particular that to Volume V which contains a declaration of intent.

Every preface presents the formula of dualism as used by me throughout the series. So far I have found no reason for altering it. The term dualism, in my opinion, refers to two utterly opposed conceptions, principles, systems, groups of people, or even worlds, without any intermediate terms between them. They cannot be reduced to one another; in some cases they are not even dependent on each other. The opposites are considered to be of different quality - so much so that one of them is always seen as distinctly inferior, and hence must be neglected, repudiated, or, if needs be, destroyed. This same definition will serve as a premise for the discussions in this volume.

I often pride myself on the idea that this formula is sufficiently clear. But pride will have a fall. I am frequently surprised by two misunderstandings. The first is that the words 'without any intermediate terms between them' go unnoticed; this is often the case in conversations I have with people on my work. Dualism is all too often thought to mean every kind of opposition. As soon as two things are opposed there obviously is dualism. What these people do not see is that not only the term dualism then loses all significance but, still more, that it would be absolutely impossible to write a work on it. For there are far more oppositions that are connected by means of intermediate terms than irreducible oppositions. Oppositions of the first kind are extremely frequent; we use them hundreds of times a day, warm and cold, old and young, strong and weak, and so on, and so forth. Most of these have shifting meanings. A young man may find some person old whereas this person finds himself not old at all. Furthermore, it is impossible to say when young becomes old, or when it is no longer cold but warm. There is always a whole scala of gradations between such oppositions. This shifting and nuanced character does not make a fit subject for a scholarly work. It is impossible to get a grip on it.

The second misunderstanding is of a more serious character and less easy to refute. It is the widespread idea, especially among scholars, that dualism is a philosophical concept not occurring outside the field of philosophy, with the exception, perhaps, of the history of religions. If the reader should want to know why this is a misunderstanding, and how it came into the world, I must ask him or her to follow me patiently through the following disquisition.

1. A precursor

Until a short time ago I never knew that, as an historian of dualism, I had a precursor. And an eminent one at that, for he is Plutarch, the well-known Greek author who lived from ca. 45/50 to 125 AD. As a priest of the sanctuary of Apollo at Delphi he was interested in religion; as a scholar he was intrigued by religious phenomena. For this reason many of his seventy-eight essays that go by the collective name of 'Moralia', are about divination, oracles, and mysticism. One of them, 'On Isis and Osiris', written ca. 100 AD and perhaps the best-known of the series, is a treatise on Egyptian religion. Its widely travelled author had become personally acquainted with the country of the Nile and its priesthood.

Plutarch was at once struck and fascinated by the antagonistic element in Egyptian religion and mythology [*]. In his view the essential conflict is between Isis, the protectress of life, and Typhon, a mythological monster, with Osiris, the god of fertility and the brother and husband of Isis, as the victim of their strife. By a curious quasi-etymological trick the author connects the word 'Isis', a Greek word according to him, with the verb 'oida' = to know, thus turning Isis into a goddess of (divine) knowledge. "The name of her shrine", he says, "promises knowledge and comprehension of reality." It is a remarkable thing that for 'knowledge' he uses the term 'gnosis'. He explains the name of Typhon as 'being puffed up', from the verb 'tuphoo', "because of his ignorance and self-deception".

Now there does not exist an Egyptian mythological being that goes by the name of 'Typhon'. He must be seen as identical with Typhoeus, the offspring of Gaia (the Earth) and Tartarus (the underworld). This Typhoeus was a horrifying monster, 'fire burning from his hundred heads as he glared"; he lived underneath the earth and below the surface of the Ocean and was responsible for the fiery eruptions of the Etna [**]. In

---

[*]   For the relevant texts see Appendix A.
[**] Hes., Theog. 820-855.

effect, Typhon is identical with the Egyptian godhead Seth whose name, according to Plutarch, "being interpreted, means 'overmastering and compelling' ".

Plutarch's treatise is entirely dominated by the fierce strife between Isis and Typhon/Seth. Typhon who, just as Macduff in Shakespeare's 'Macbeth', was not 'of woman born' - for "with a blow on his mother's side he leapt forth" -, "tore to pieces and scattered to the winds the sacred writings which the goddess (Isis) collects and puts together". He reveals himself as an inveterate enemy of superior wisdom. He kills and dismembers Osiris, who later was restored to life by Isis. In general, Typhon "wrought terrible deeds, and, by bringing utter confusion upon all things, filled the whole Earth, and the Ocean as well, with ills".

At this point Plutarch pauses in order to ponder. The direct significance of the myth is obviously somewhat too simple to his taste. He will lend his ear to those Egyptians "who have a reputation for expounding matters more philosophically". These scholars interpret Osiris as the Nile, the fount of life in Egypt, Isis as the Earth with whom Osiris/the Nile consorts, and Typhon/Seth as the sea "into which the Nile discharges its waters and is lost to view and dissipated, save for that part which the earth takes and thereby becomes fertilized". In this way the author turned the old mythological lore into an geological allegory.

However, there are still wiser men. Some Egyptian priests "simply give the name of Osiris to the whole source and faculty creative of moisture, believing this to be the cause of generation and the substance of life-producing seed; and the name of Typhon they give to all that is dry, fiery and arid in general and antagonistic ('polemion')" . This is a still more encompassing interpretation in which Isis, Osiris and Typhon no longer are mythological beings; instead they are identified with fundamental and antagonistic forces in nature, such as generation and decay. These opposed and inimical forces are basic for the entire cosmic process, for "the terrestrial universe ... is never completely exempt from dissolution or generation". Thus Plutarch ends up with changing the old tale into an all-comprising cosmological explanation.

Having arrived at this point with his disquisition on Egyptian religion, Plutarch now interrupts himself in order to place the antagonisms which evidently intrigued him mightily, into a still wider perspective. Had he known the term 'dualism', he would have used it here; however, it would last another sixteen centuries before this term was coined. Nevertheless, Plutarch came very near to it where he speaks of 'two opposed principles and two antagonistic forces' in nature and in the universe. For he uses the Greek grammatical form of the dualis to indicate these forces : 'apo toon enantioon archoon kai duoin antipaloon dunameoon'. I remark in passing that Plutarch himself was a convinced dualist since he makes the universe come forth form two opposed principles or 'archai'.

We must not understand him wrongly, he says; we should not compare these two archai to the two great vases that stand next to the throne of Zeus, one filled with success, and the other with failure, from which the Allfather deals out banes and boons to mankind [*]. No, what Plutarch means is something far more drastic. There is not one Reason (Logos) that governs the universe; "Nature brings nothing which is not combined with something else". And since "nothing comes into being without a cause, and if the good cannot provide a cause for evil, then it follows that Nature must have in herself the source and origin of evil, just as she contains the fount and mainspring of good. The great majority and the wisest of men hold this opinion : they believe that there are two gods, rivals as it were, the one the Artificer of good, and the other of evil".

To assess now what Plutarch posited in this first theory of dualism, we must start from his statement that in his days the great majority, and in particular the more intelligent, thought along dualistic lines. We must not forget that this Apollo priest lived in the heyday of the Gnosis, a

---

[*] Il. XXIV 527-533; see Vol. I, p. 184.

dualistic system if there ever was one. This Gnosis came pretty near to become a world religion instead of Christianity. Dualism, of whichever kind, never was an isolated phenomenon, although in some periods it occupied a much stronger position than in others.

A second notable point is that Plutarch did not trace back dualism to the Zoroastrian religion of Iran. It is important to take note of this, since it is 'fable reçue', even among scholars, that it all began with the doctrine of Zoroaster[*]. On the contrary! He literally states that "it can be traced to no source" and explains it as a generally human, so to speak anthropological, phenomenon, occurring in many places, "among barbarians and the Greeks alike", that is everywhere.

Nor does he, as almost all modern scholars do, restrict it to the fields of religion or philosophy or both but says that we find it "in story and tradition but also in rites and sacrifices" which seems to make religious dualism into a somewhat secondary phenomenon. There is no mention of philosophy in this passage. Dualism, in this Greek author's opinion, is not something religious or exclusively philosophical but definitely something of a really universal nature. It causes "this terrestrial universe ..." to be "irregular and variable and subject to all manner of changes". This means that every existing opposition may be or become dualistic and is linked up with the basic dualism of good and evil.

Finally, I must emphasize that Plutarch did not give his dualism a religious origin. It is true that, according to him, wise men hold that there are two rival gods but he himself does not use religious terms, Nature having in herself the forces of Good and Evil. His rendering of the most comprehensive of the antagonisms between Osiris and Typhon, that of dissolution and generation, is thoroughly dedivinized.

Plutarch then proceeds with a short history of dualism. He describes Iranian Zoroastrianism as based on the opposition of Light and Darkness (and Ignorance). His is, by the way, the best ancient report on this

---

[*] I combated this opinion in Vol. IV, Ch. IV.4.

creed. According to him, the Babylonians oppose two benevolent and two malevolent planets. The Greeks "make the good part belong to Zeus, and the abominated ('apotropaion') part to Hades ... The philosophers are in agreement with these (legends)".

He then quotes a number of philosophers, first of all Heraclitus with whom "all things originate from strife and antagonism". For Empedocles, the "beneficent principle (is) friendship or friendliness ('philotēta, philia') ..., the worse principle is 'accursed quarrelling' and 'bloodstained strife' ". He gives the Pythagorean list of dualistic oppositions, and mentions Anaxagoras' opposition of Mind and Infinitude ('nous kai apeiron'). Aristotle's dualism is characterized by the contrast of Form and Privation ('eidos kai sterēsis').

He winds up his short history with Plato, on whose doctrine, quoting from the Laws [*], he dwells somewhat longer. "When (Plato) had grown considerably older, he asserts, not in circumlocution or symbolically (as he had done thus far - F.), but in specific words, that the movement of the Universe is actuated not by one soul, but perhaps by several, and certainly not less than two, and of these the one is beneficent, and the other is opposed to it and the artificer of things opposed. Between these he leaves a certain third nature ('phusin') ..., desiring the better always."

Plutarch concludes with giving his own opinion on the matter in the following terms. "The fact is that the creation of this world is complex, resulting as it does, from opposing influences, which, however, are not of equal strength. but the predominance rests with the better. Yet it is impossible for the bad to be entirely eradicated, since it is innate, in the body and likewise in the soul of the Universe, and it is always fighting a hard fight against the better."

Let us sum up by paying attention to the most important elements in this learned Greek's disquisition. The first is that, in his view, dualism has no starting-point in history. It has no specific source and is found

---

[*]   Plato, Laws 896D sqq.

everywhere among mankind. A second point is that it forms an integral part of the universe since its beginning as the inexorable and eternal opposition of Good and Evil. It is, therefore, also an integral part of human nature because man is the microcosmos in the macrocosmos.

Thirdly, we should not think that dualism is about the normal vicissitudes of life in which the bad things not rarely prove to be blessings in disguise, and in which failures and successes alternate. No, Good and Evil are the result of radically opposed principles in the cosmos.

The next element is that Plutarch does not see dualism as a specifically philosophical position. Otherwise he would not have said that it was 'in circulation among barbarians and Greeks alike'; according to the general conviction of the Greeks, barbarians had no philosophy. Finally, originally it is not a tenet of religious doctrine either. When he has related the myth of the deadly enmity of Isis and Typhon, he tells us that the wiser Egyptians explain it in a cosmological manner.

It seems to me that Plutarch gave a far more comprehensive definition of dualism than present-day scholars do who, with depressing monotony, keep repeating that it is either a philosophical or a religious concept or both at once.

2. A story told by Xenophon

We discover the same breadth of vision in an unexpected author, in Xenophon. In his 'Cyropaedia', a biography of the emperor Cyrus I of Persia, he relates a fascinating story that, even if the reader would not find it convincing, nonetheless might amuse him or her.

Panthea was an Assyrian lady made prisoner by the army of Cyrus, king of Persia. She was married to a certain Abradatas who, at the moment of the capture of his wife, happened to be away on an mission to Bactria. This Panthea, said to be the most beautiful woman in all Asia, was destined for the king himself. But he, without having set eyes on her, placed her in charge of a Mede, Araspas, his close friend.

This Araspas came to the king telling him how unbelievably beautiful Panthea was, and asked him to come over and see her. The king, however, refused, arguing that he might perhaps neglect his royal duties simply by gazing at her. His friend found this ridicilous because he could not believe that female beauty would be able to compel a man against his will. "It is a matter of free will, and each one loves what he pleases".

Cyrus contended that it is not that easy to remain master of one's erotic impulses. He had seen too many people become the slaves of their love. And while they prayed to be delivered from it, they proved nonetheless "fettered by a stronger necessity than if they had been fettered by shackles of iron". In the eyes of Araspas such an attitude was contemptible. "The high-minded and the good ... have the power to let all that (= money and attractive women) alone so as not to touch anything beyond the limit of what is right."

However, having returned home, the high-minded Araspas found the lady in his keeping so beautiful and so good and so noble that, in spite of himself, he fell desperately in love with her. The good judge of people that Xenophon was adds that "this was perhaps not at all surprising". No longer able to control himself, the guardian approached his charge with amorous proposals. But wanting to remain faithful to her husband she repulsed him. Finally, when Araspas threatened to use force, as Osmin did to Blondchen in 'Die Entführung aus dem Serail', she sent a servant to the king in order to lodge a complaint.

On hearing the story Cyrus burst into laughter. The remorseful Araspas had a private talk with him, very much fearing to be severely punished. But Cyrus forgave him easily, holding himself responsible to some extent for what has happened, since he had his friend shut up with this irresistible being - thus binding the cat to the pork, as my father used to say. He even selected Araspas to go on an important mission.

"But", he asked, "will you be able to give up the beautiful Panthea?". This is what Araspas answered. "Yes, Cyrus, for I have evidently two souls ... For if the soul is one, it is not good and bad at the same time, neither can it at the same desire the right and the wrong, nor at the same time will and not will to do the same things. But it is obvious that there are two souls, and when the good one prevails, what is right is done; but when the bad one gains the ascendancy, what is wrong is attempted"[*]. This reminds us of Goethe's Faust who complained of the two souls in his breast, or of the apostle Paul who confessed that he felt caught between two opposed impulses. "What I do not is not what I wish to do, but something which I hate"[**]. Both Xenophon and Paul, being eminently practical men, did not look for the origin of dualism in religion, philosophy, or cosmology, but in human nature, in the human psyche. To them dualism, to use a modern term they did not know, is something definitely anthropological.

3. The origin of the term 'dualism'

After Plutarch sixteen hundred years had to go by before the term 'dualism', or rather 'dualist, was coined. We find it in a work by Thomas Hyde, a professor of Hebrew in Oxford University; his book, published in 1700, described the religion of the ancient Persians[***]. He stated that the Persians acknowledged two principles, one eternal, the other created, which Zoroaster dubbed the Light and the Dark. The first principle worked the Good, the other Evil. Hyde called the Persian Magi, and later adherents of this doctrine, like the Manichaeans, 'dualists'; this was the very first time that this word was used.

It is highly deplorable that the term began its career in the context of the Iranian (Zoroastrian) religion. For this gave rise to the ineradicable myth that dualism has an historical origin, and that Zoroaster is the father of it.

---

[*] Xen., Cyr. 4.6.11, 5.1.2-18, and 6.1.31-41.
[**] Rom. 7:15.
[***] The reader will find the relevant texts for this section in Appendix B.

4. The subsequent history of the term

Perhaps Hyde's opinion might have gone unnoticed but for the fact that his book fell into the hands of that voracious reader, Pierre Bayle, who inserted an entry 'Zoroaster' into the second edition (1702) of his dictionary; in this article he quoted Hyde at length and mentioned the word 'dualist'. Bayle's dictionary was an authoritative work that was widely consulted and went through numerous editions. Thus the word 'dualist' began its career.

The next one to take it up was Leibniz in his 'Theodicy' of 1710. He was still more famous than Bayle and was considered the most learned man of his time, sometimes called the last 'homo universalis'. He took his cue form Hyde and Bayle. He, therefore, only spoke of Zoroaster's opposed principles and called the Iranian prophet 'the first author of duality'. In this way the 'fable convenue' of the Persian origin of dualism, and the idea that it had originated in the religious sphere, became firmly underscored.

Thus far we have not yet met the term 'dualism' proper. The very first time that it occurred happened a quarter of a century after Leibniz's 'Theodicy'. In 1734 Christian Wolff published a work called 'Psychologia rationalis' in which he not only spoke of 'dualists' but also of 'dualism'. Although this is a significant development since henceforward we have to do with an -ism, there is in his work something of still greater importance. Wolff broadened the notion of dualism beyond the meaning that was given to it by Hyde. So far it had been used to denote a religious doctrine of Iranian origin. But Wolff transferred it to the realm of philosophy by stating that the spiritual and the corporeal, the immaterial and material, are substantially different. From then on the study of dualism followed two lines, one in the history of religions, the other in philosophy, sometimes separately, sometimes in one context.

5. Why the term 'dualism' was introduced

Having arrived at this juncture in the history of ideas, we may well ask ourselves why it is that a phenomenon which has existed since the dawn of times and that was well-known to ancient authors, only got its name in the early eighteenth century. As a result of the Reformation Europe had become roughly divided into two spheres, one mainly Protestant, the other predominantly Catholic. The difference between these two denominations was felt to be more radical than it is nowadays. The Wars of Religion of the sixteenth and seventeenth centuries gave this difference a still more absolute and even highly aggressive character. This caused the German scholar Koselleck to speak of the 'pathogenesis' of the bourgeois world [*]. As a consequence the field became prepared for an upsurge of dualism. This found a vigorous and highly influential expression in the way Descartes opposed body and soul.

It was yet another consequence of the Wars of religion that theology became discredited as a source of strife and an incentive to civil and interstate war. Its place as the leading discipline was taken by philosophy with its corollary, mathematics. The fount of wisdom no longer was God but human reason. So the era of rationalism was ushered in. Philosophical ideas got pride of place and were considered to have practical, mainly political consequences. This was especially the case with the thinkers of the eighteenth-century Enlightenment. 'Ideologies' were born (let me characterize an ideology as a philosophical idea that is worked out in practice). The age of the -isms had begun. It will not surprise the reader than one of the very first -isms to appear was dualism.

---

[*] Reinhart Koselleck, Kritik und Krise. Ein Beitrag zur Pathogenese der bürgerlichen Welt. Freiburg/München, 1959.

6. The progress of the term dualism during the eighteenth century

To return now to Christian Wolff, this scholar was highly instrumental in creating new terms. He not only coined dualism, but also 'monism, dogmatism, teleology', and others, called by Rudolf Eucken 'Latin artificial expressions ... that soon enough found their way into the German language and from there came into general circulation"[*]. Wolff separated philosophers into 'scepticists' and 'dogmatists, and then the dogmatists into 'monists' and dualists. The monists he divided into 'idealists' and 'materialists'. In this way he made the notion current that monism and dualism are opposed ideologies. Obviously taken for an infallible statement it has since been reiterated continuously up to the present day.

In the course of my volumes I have repeatedly combated this notion (as I shall do in this volume too), arguing that monism and dualism come from the same stock. Monism can very easily give rise to dualism since, because of its exclusiveness tending to one-sidedness, it always leaves a residuum that finds no place in the prime concept and cannot be explained by it. This residuum sometimes reasserts itself by opposing itself to the monistic concept, even to such a degree that a dualistic opposition originates. Many dualistic systems have a monistic starting-point; dualism then begins one stage lower.

The only philosopher, as far as I know, who understood that monism and dualism really are chips of the same block, is Ludwig Stein. He expressed this in the following terms. "Monism and dualism are two types of thought that both have their foundation in man. But, in the antithesis 'monism-dualism', the issue is not that they are contradictorily opposed but rather that they are a contrasted pair of concepts connected with each other in the manner of correlation"[**].

---

[*] Rudolf Eucken, Geschichte der philosophischen Terminologie im Umriss dargestellt von --. Leipzig, 1879 (re-edited Hildesheim 1960).

[**] Ludwig Stein, Dualismus oder Monismus. Eine Untersuchung über die doppelte Wahrheit. Berlin, 1909. P. 14.

The progress of the term 'dualism' during the eighteenth century was slow but sure. Samuel Johnson, in his famous 'Dictionary of the English Language' (1755), makes an entry of 'dualis' but not of 'dualism'. David Hume, in his 'Natural History of Religion' (1757), mentions Hyde's book, and also Zoroaster, his disciples, and the Magi, but does not use the word 'dualism'. It obviously did not strike his attention forcefully enough.

Whereas the 1765 and 1778 editions of the dictionary of the Académie française carry no entry 'dualisme', we find it in the first edition (1755) of the more famous 'Encyclopédie' of Diderot. Since this work was widely used and considered supremely authoritative, I shall quote what it said, s.v. 'dualisme ou dithéisme', verbally. Dualism is "a theological opinion that opposes two principles, two gods, two beings that are independent (of each other) and not created, of which one is considered the principle of Good and the other the principle of Evil ... The first origin of this system results from the difficulty of explaining the existence of Evil in the world"*. The supposed religious origin of the concept was particularly emphasized because the term 'dithéisme' was used as the equivalent of 'dualisme' (this term soon fell into disuse). This statement presents the history of religions as the field of origin of dualism. Another unpleasant sequence of the popularity of this encyclopaedia is that once again dualism was provided with an historical point of departure.

A somewhat later comprehensive work, the 'Encyclopédie ou Dictionnaire universel raisonné des connoissances humaines', composed by M. de Felice, in 1778 literally repeats the text of its predecessor. Another popular work of half a century later (1828-1832), the 'Encyclopédie moderne', under the editorship of M. de Courtin, although calling dualism 'a philosophy', nevertheless says that it originally is "the

---

* The author of this article stated that he had drawn his information 'from the papers of M. Formey, historiographer of the Royal Academy of Prussia'.

doctrine of two coeternal principles, the sources of Good and Evil, moral as well as physical".

In his 'Kritik der reinen Vernunft' of 1781 Kant gives yet another turn to the meaning of dualism. He introduced the opposition of the real objects and the perceptions we have of them, or, in technical terms, of the 'phenomenon' and the 'noumenon'. He believed that real objects cannot be perceived directly. We only have a notion of them, and, starting from this notion, we conclude that the objects are the cause of our observations. "In consequence the existence of all objects is dubious"[*]. The current idea that objects exist outside ourselves, independently of our thoughts, was called by Kant 'transcendent dualism'[**]. He rejected this meaning of dualism and said he wanted to enlarge the concept making it into that of phenomenon and noumenon, of things in themselves and our perceptions of them[***].

As far as I know Kant did not speak of religious dualism. In his view dualism obviously was an essentially philosophical concept. Such it also was to Hegel who, in his 'Encyclopädie der philosophischen Wissenschaften im Grundriss' of 1817, par. 95, did not mention the opposition of (the gods or principles of) Good and Evil but only spoke of the, in his eyes invalid, opposition of finite and infinite.

7. Inappropriate uses of the term

Since Hegel dualism has become a well-known concept, not rarely used indiscriminately for any kind of opposition, whether unbridgeable or not. Allow me to cite the following example of improper use of the term.

In my country, the Netherlands, Montesquieu's 'trias politica' is still honoured as the most sacrosanct element of the constitutional

---

[*] Kritik A 367.
[**] Kritik A 389.
[***] See Morris Sockhammer, Kurzes dualistisches Wörterbuch. Archiv für Begriffsgeschichte, Band 4, 1663 (1959), s.v. 'Dualismus'; and Simone Pètrement s.v. 'dualism' in Dictionary of the History of Ideas II, 41 (1973).

system. Legal prudery even goes so far that, in contrast to the custom prevailing in Britain, ministers of the Crown are not allowed to be members of the States-General (parliament) at the same time; a representative who becomes a minister or a 'secretary of state' (vice- or deputy minister) has to give up his seat in parliament. This separation of the legislative and the executive is called 'political dualism'.

If it, according to my terminology, really were dualism, then parliament and cabinet would always be radically opposed; no collaboration would be possible between them. True enough, hard battles may be fought between executive and legislative. The cabinet can dissolve one or both of the chambers of the States-General (which rarely happens), whereas the representatives can bring down the cabinet (which is done more frequently). But this so-called 'dualism' is already mitigated by the fact the head of state (Queen Beatrix) forms part of both executive and legislative. In effect, cabinet and parliament are complementary forces and have to work together closely. Most of the time things go smoothly indeed. So in this context the term 'dualism', however much current, is actually inappropriate.

8. Dualism in modern lexicography

I have looked through a great number of modern dictionaries and encyclopedias, specialized and non-specialized, Dutch, English, French, German, Italian, and Spanish. Nearly all of them carry an entry 'dualism', although sometimes the subject is to be found under the heading 'monism'. In going over those numerous articles, long and short, two things catch the eye.

Very often monism and dualism are seen as contrasted concepts. In the 'Reallexikon für Antike und Christentum', Bd. IV (1959), J. Duchesne-Guillemin writes that "the whole history of western philosophy appears to be continously varying between dualism and monism". The Grand Larousse, Vol. 4 (1983), adds that "philosophies have been classified into monisms and dualisms". This obviously is a current and accepted opposition that "has found numerous applications in religions". There are "those that oppose Good and Evil, as moral alternatives, and/or as constitutive elements of the world". But "it is in philosophy that historians have found their favourite field in which the opposition dualism/ monism is best applied."

A second common element is that dualism most of the time is seen as a philosophical concept and/or as a religious one. Simone Pétrement, in the Dictionary of the History of Ideas, Vol. II (1973), categorically states that the word 'dualism' "has two different meanings : 1. religious, 2. philosophical". To cite a few instances, the Lexikon für Theologie und Kirche, 3. Bd. (1959), deals with dualism in three sections, viz. dualism in the history of religions, in theology, and in philosophy. In the Encyclopedia of Philosophy, Vol. 5 ,s.v. 'monism and dualism' (w.d.), Roland Hall understands by dualism "any philosophical system that divides the world into two categories or types of thinking, or uses two types of ultimate explanation, or insists that there are two substances or kinds of substance".

In the Philosophisches Wörterbuch, Bd. 1 (Leipzig, 1974 10), Manfred Buhr states that "philosophical dualism essentially is a secularized form of religious dualism, in particular the bipartition of the world into a natural and a supernatural one by the Christian religion".

In the Encyclopedia of Religion, Vol. 4 (1987), Ugo Bianchi obviously disagrees with this opinion since he writes that "the simple contrasting of good and evil, life and death, light and darkness, and so on, is in fact coextensive with religion itself and cannot be equated with the much more specific phenomenon of dualism". This is a sensible caveat against the slipshod way in which the term dualism is so often used by applying it to every kind of opposition. But even this eminent scholar is sinning by defining dualism "as a category within the history and phenomenology of religion", which in my opinion is much too restrictive. He does not even speak of dualism in philosophy.

A third element that will cause no surprise after the foregoing is that dualism is usually indicated as a doctrine, a philosophical position, an opposition of principles, a category of thought, a theory, a system, a concept, or an idea. Without exception these are terms normally used by scholars, in particular by philosophers. This terminology lends additional force to the opinion that dualism predominantly occurs in the realm of thought, as an abstract idea, from which it is tacitly thought to follow that it occurs nowhere else, above all not in the sphere of the concrete. There are, however, also scholars who do not see dualism as a philosophy proper. So for instance Marcel Deschoux in the Dictionnaire des grandes philosophies (1973) who writes that "dualism is not a philosophy but a characteristic of certain philosophies who oppose themselves ... to monistic doctrines".

8. Some interesting side-remarks

Sometimes an intriguing side-remark is made in such entries. In the Encyclopedia of Religion and Ethics, Vol. V (1912), Rudolf Eucken writes that "dualism in virtue of its precise definition of concepts, acts as a corrective to that confusion into which monism so often lapses". I for one find myself unable to understand why the erection of unbridgeable oppositions may serve as a corrective; it can only make things worse. It seems to me that Eucken vaguely realized this since he adds that it is "impossible that dualism should constitute the final phase of human thought; but in view of such consummation, it has an important function to perform, viz. to put obstacles in the way of a premature synthesis, and to insist upon a full recognition of the antitheses present in human experience".

I wonder what the 'final phase of human thought' would look like! Anyhow, I detect a certain tendency here to dub all kinds of (philosophical) antitheses 'dualistic' which, indeed, would only increase the confusion Eucken mentioned. Even Franz Austeda's Wörterbuch der Philosophie (1975 2) makes itself guilty of such confusion by stating that dualism in general means the positing of a duality.

Another striking remark is one made by Roland Hall in his already quoted article; he writes that dualism has been, "so to speak, the expression of a failed monism". This author adds, sensibly enough, that "the dualistic position is inherently unstable and puzzle-generating" which is exactly the reverse of Eucken's opinion.

9. Somewhat more generous views

I must say that the view taken by almost everyone of dualism is rather narrow. However, a few scholars come much closer to the much wider conception of Plutarch. Olof Gigon, writing in the Lexikon der alten Welt (1965), makes the notable remark that "dualism originated from the experience of the contradiction in the structure in the human self and from the observation between constructive and destructive (forces) in the universe, secondarily from the ontological thesis that the (process of) becoming is only triggered of by an opposition that is found below the one that is sufficient to itself" (I hope that this is a tentatively adequate translation of "dass erst der Gegensatz diesseits des in sich ruhenden Einen das Werden im Gang bringt"). For Gigon the ontological (=metaphysical, philosophical) sphere is secondary, whereas the cosmological (I would have preferred 'nature' to 'universe'), and still more psychological, or anthropological, factors get pride of place.

A similar view is taken by Giovanni Semprini in the Enciclopedia filosofica, Vol. 2 (1967). Dualism, he writes, "in a large sense, is every doctrine that, not only in the universality of reality, but also in the more specific fields of reality, and not only in metaphysical questions but also in whatsoever question, has recourse, as to an explicative principle, to two entities that between themselves are irreducible". He adds that the use of our term in metaphysiscs is more restricted. Although taking exception to his term 'doctrine', I agree with what Semprini is saying.

10. Helpful discussions

In his already twice quoted article Roland Hall sighs that "helpful discussions on monism, dualism, and pluralism are rather few in number". This is true. I do not pretend that I have seen every disquisition on these subjects but my quest through scholarly literature took me far and wide without yielding very much. Ugo Bianchi published a number of essays on dualism most of which I listed in the Bibliography of Volume I. However, he limits himself to the history of religions.

Then there is a profound and highly intriguing study by Simone Pétrement, Le dualisme dans l'histoire de la philosophie et des religions. Introduction à l'étude du dualisme platonicien, du gnosticisme et du manichéisme (Paris, 1946 3). As her title and subtitle indicate, she restricts herself thematically as well as with regard to the chosen periods. She first speaks of religious dualism, then of philosophical dualism, thus making the division that has been in use since the days of Hyde and Wolff. She proceeds with chapters on the place of dualism in the history of philosophy and that in the history of religions.

Next comes a chapter on 'some characteristics of dualism'. I give these as succinctly as possible. Dualistic thought is more subjective than monistic thought, being more inseparable of the subject. Contrary to what some other scholars feel, she thinks that dualistic thought is largely negative and critical. Speaking from the viewpoint of the historian of religions, she states that dualism is a search for salvation; what is thought after is a firm fundament for knowledge. I would modify this in so far that dualism in itself is not a search for salvation but engenders this search and makes a firm fundament for knowledge necessary.

This quest for sure knowledge, Pétrement continues, is still more pregnant in dualistic religions than in dualistic philosophies. The salvation that is found is something new and unknown. The key-words of (religious) dualism and salvation are subjectivity, solipsism, refusal of outside help, profound doubt concerning received truth, total negation, and then revelation, discovery, conversion and final decision. In my foregoing volumes the reader will have been confronted with telling examples of all this, in particular in Iranian and, still more, in Indian religions.

In a chapter on the meaning of dualism, Pétrement says that monism believes in unity, in the harmony of all things, in the possible satisfaction of our reason that asks for unity. Pluralism believes that this is a vain effort and that it is damaging to rally everything into unity. Beings are diverse and innumerable; principles too are innumerable. Each separate thing must have its own life. Dualism sustains that principles are neither unique nor innumerable but dual. It seems to be less difficult to reduce a great many principles to a duality than a duality to a unity. In the effort to make a synthesis something is excluded; we are, in our present condition, not able to make a total synthesis. It is not possible to consider all oppositions surmounted.

I can go a long way with this statement if only I am allowed to make a reservation. Where there is talk of monism, Pétrement's scope is wide indeed since monism is said to comprise all things. But as soon as we hear of dualism her emphasis imperceptibly shifts to the more limited domain of philosophy because then only principles are mentioned.

Pétrement continues as follows. Dualism, she says, is no gratuitous refusal of unity. A dualist too searches for unity. There is, however, a rupture in his quest for unity, since division and inner combat are thought to be indispensable to the life of the spirit. There exists a subjective condition that limits metaphysics. Metaphysics essentially is a search for unity. But at the same time it is an effort, an action. Unity necessarily remains unachieved because the thinking subject's action is inseparably bound up with action.

This action or effort appears forcibly in dualism. Dualism is only an imperfect, a limited metaphysics that is subordinate to ethics and to method. Perhaps it fundamentally is a negation of metaphysics; it keeps to what is certain, that is, to the fighting that is imposed on us. Going further or wanting more would suppress the fighting.

I must confess that I find this an astonishing and confused paragraph. To be quite honest, some of it seems abacadabra to me. I will not say once again that dualism is equated with metaphysiscs here. But it is presented as being at once a limited metaphysics and a negation of metaphysics. The existence of dualism seems to be justified and deemed even necessary because the only thing we may be sure of is the fighting, the turmoil, the effort. But all this exertion is hopeless since apparently unity is not possible. Nevertheless we are not allowed to stop fighting since there is nothing beyond the struggle.

Seen from this viewpoint it is no surprise that Pétrement does not believe in contemplation. True enough, unity could be reached in contemplation. But such pure contemplation (that is contemplation of the whole) would be monistic and never anything else than illusion and sleep. I wonder what Pythagoreans, Platonists, Hindus, Catholic monks and contemplative nuns would have to say of this. And was it not Hegel for whom the essence of philosophy is that all oppositions can and will be dialectically surmounted?

It seems to me that Pétrement's words re-echo the battles of this tumultuous century in which we stumble from one catastrophe to another and are continuously confronted with ever new world-historical events without being able to make sense of them. I do not deny that we, as human beings, will never be able to surmount really all oppositions. We simply have to live with them. But it should not be forgotten that nearly all oppositions are perfectly innocuous. Do we experience existential problems with night and day, warm and cold, old and young, and so on, and so forth? Those oppositions that are really insuperable are made so; they are man-made. As I said somewhere else, dualism, like beauty, is in the beholder's eye. In my opinion Pétrement's basic error is that she confuses the fruitful contrasting of oppositions with the negative and often destructive relationship of a dualistic pair. My conclusion is that we have every reason for sorting out and refining our basic notions on monism and dualism.

Ludwig Stein whose work on monism and dualism I have mentioned already, is more precise. For him monism and dualism are two sides of the same coin. He does not think that dualism is basically a philosophical concept. Already in time immemorial people knew of the contrast of the self and the outer world. Furthermore, there is the difference of heaven and earth which, says Stein, is the symbol of all dualism. This leads to what he calls a dualistic mirroring in the human person.

Among the primary impulses to thinking we should count the opposition of light and dark, of day and night, of sun and moon, of lightning and thunder, of rain and storm, in general the antagonism in the forces of nature. The shamans carry into effect the split between the visible body and the invisible soul. Still remaining far from any philosophical concept, Stein states that already the oldest mythologies contain the division of being and becoming, of a constant and unchanging principle and a variable factor in the events of this world, of a blessed afterlife that is lasting and a wretched life on earth that is subject to constant change.

Stein is one of the very few scholars, if not the only one, who detects the impulse for dualism in the human person itself, in human identity.

11. Why occupy oneself with dualism?

Having arrived at this juncture, the reader will probably ask if the author of this work is himself a dualist. The answer to this question is a categorical no. I am not a dualist. Neither am I a monist. If I must define my mental stance, I would describe myself as a Thomistic realist. But if I am not a dualist, why then do I occupy myself so extensively and so intensively with this subject? An answer that would seem satisfying to scholars is that it has never been much explored. Originally, I was contemplating to write the 'world-history of the Gnosis' of which Quispel once spoke. But the Gnosis is by no means a virgin subject; whole libraries have been written on it. I would have to compete with the most eminent scholars in the world.

Dualism is a constitutive and essential element in Gnostic doctrines; so my choice for dualism proper was only natural. I cannot remember when this term caught my eye for the first time. I became acquainted with the phenomenon as such in 1958 when I was studying the origins of the Reformation. Not feeling satisfied with the rather facile explanation that Luther's reason to act was to be found in the absuses in the late medieval Church, I explored his intellectual and religious development before 1517. The great Reformer was educated in the so-called 'via moderna', the nominalistic version of scholastic theology. Luther had to fight a hard battle within himself to free himself from this nominalism.

The basic tenet of nominalism is that there are no 'universalia'. When we see an oak and a fir and a poplar and an elm, we group them together under the heading 'trees'. This suggests a general entity called 'tree'. But no, the nominalists objects, what exists is the fir in your garden and the elm in your street and the poplar on the square and the oak in the park, all of them observable and identifiable objects. But you will never observe a 'tree'. 'Tree' is nothing more than just a name ('nomen') to which no actual reality corresponds. For Luther it became a painful problem whether 'God' was only a name too and whether it is possible to know which reality is connected with it.

It will be evident that nominalism is a form of dualism. There is a dualistic opposition between the existential world, the world of objects, of concrete things and beings, and the universalia, the world of the concepts, the conceptual world, between the 'names' and what they are supposed to denote. This became my starting-point. But it was only in May 1977 that I decided to write the 'world-history of dualism'.

However, the fact that a subject is disposable is not in itself a 'ratio sufficiens' for spending so much time on it. It is more than fourteen years now that I am working on it, the last eight years full-time. Another and more compelling motive is that dualism is one of the main elements in human thought and action. To avoid misunderstandings I must repeat here that from the fact that I am writing a world-history of dualism it does not follow that I derive world-history from the existence of dualism. To me, the history of the world is not the history of dualism. But, as the foregoing disquisition may have proved, dualism is a much neglected and often carelessly treated phenomenon, in spite of the fact that it is omnipresent. We find it in all times and in every civilization.

Although, true to their nature, dualistic phenomena usually appear in dispersed order, they sometimes gather into compact systems and movements. The first of these is the Gnosis which will the subject of the forthcoming volume(s). Later, in the fourth and fifth centuries, there was Manichaeism, and still later, in the thirteenth century, Catharism. Let us bear in mind that this radically dualistic movement was considered so dangerous that it had to be fought down by armed force.

But even in our modern age dualistic and also Gnostic phenomena are not rare. Goethe whose Faust was utterly dissatisfied with received wisdom and scholarly knowledge and frantically desired a wisdom that would unite him with the All, was near to the Gnosis [*]. Hegel who also wanted Absolute Knowledge may be considered a Gnostic [**]. We are equally entitled to apply this term to Rudolf Steiner and his anthroposophy, and probably no less to Carl G. Jung [***].

Perhaps scholars and scientists wil shrug their shoulders and say that this is all mysticism and not the field of interest of modern science. But Raymond Ruyer, in a book that is significantly called 'The Gnosis of Princeton" [****], describes modern science as a kind of Gnosis; his subtitle is 'scientists in search of a religion' which speaks volumes. Modern science is about highly specialized knowledge about the arcana of the universe and of mankind expressed in signs and symbols that remain a secret to the general public. The apprenticeship for this knowledge lasts as long and is as difficult as for admission into esoteric societies. In most modern societies compulsory education lasts about nine years; still, a boy or girl of about fifteen is only considered fit for simple jobs. The highest qualifications can only be attained after another fifteen years of study and training.

---

[*] Andreas Burnier, Faust en de Gnosis. In : Gnosis. De derde component van de Europese cultuurtraditie. Ed. G. Quispel, 205-233. Utrecht, 1985.

[**] J. Verseput. G.W.F. Hegel en de Gnosis. O.c., 225-242.

[***] Christja Mees-Henny and Rudolf Mees, Gnosis en antroposofie; Pety de Vries-Ek, De betekenis van de godservaring - het conflict Martin Buber-C.G.Jung. O.c. 245-254 and 255-269.

[****] Raymond Ruyer, La Gnose de Princeton. Des savants à la recherche d'une religion. Paris (1974).

The strongly dualistic urge in modern culture is perfectly exemplified in the macabre novel of Robert Louis Stevenson, 'Dr. Jekyll and Mr. Hyde' (1886), an attractive motive for several movies. The reader is for a long time induced to think that Jekyll and Hyde are two different persons till it proves that they are only the good and the bad sides of one and the same man, although dualistically split. Is it Stevenson's own credo when his Dr. Jekyll states that "man is not truly one but truly two", and when he hazards "the guess that man will be ultimately known for a mere polity of multifarious, incongruous, and independent denizens"? Still, the good aspect finally triumphs over the bad.

The reverse is the case in a novel of only five years later, Oscar Wilde's 'The Picture of Dorian Gray' (1891). Young Dorian had a painting made of himself on which he was pictured as beautiful as an Adonis, so much so that he became jealous of it. He wanted to stay just as he was, whereas the unavoidable changes for the worse had to occur in the picture. Gray gave himself up to every kind of profligacy, but whilst he himself remained serenely beautiful, his picture, that was safely tucked away, grew more and more ugly. In the end Gray could not withstand the temptation to look at his portrait. The confrontation shocked him so severely that he stabbed himself. When the horrified servants entered, "they found, hanging upon the wall, a splendid portrait of their master as they had last seen him, in all the wonder of his exquisite youth and beauty. Lying on the floor was a dead man, in evening dress, with a knife in his heart. He was withered, wrinkled, and loathsome of visage. It was not till they had examined the rings that they had recognized who it was."

Perhaps the reader will object that I am luring him or her into the realm of the fantastic, without a connection with real life. But what about President Reagan who in the early eighties said that the Soviet-Union was the Evil Empire? Nothing could be more dualistic. True enough, Reagan soon found out that the Soviet-Union was less demoniacal than he had thought.

However, a far more horrible example is at hand. I myself would not hesitate to call Adolf Hitler a neo-Cathar. Unfortunately, I have not the time to expatiate on this. But one aspect must be highlighted. In Hitler's ideology (which must not be equated with National-Socialism!), there were two 'nations'. One was the luminous 'Aryan race' (which is not to be identified with the German people), still something of the future, because it had to be created by means of special eugenic measures. Opposite this there was a people of darkness, bad, malevolent, vicious, and ugly. The luminous race could never triumph before the dark race was destroyed. This dark race was more real than the somewhat illusory Aryan race, since the Jews and the Gypsies belonged to it. But Hitler had no high idea of blacks and Asiatics either; they need not be destroyed but could fulfil a useful purpose by serving the dominant race. That he was quite serious about this is proved by what he did to the Jews and the Gypsies.

Let me summarize what I am doing by saying that I am looking at world-history, political, social, mental, and intellectual, from an unexpected angle, askance or from the backside, which, I hope, will yield unexpected results. I am well aware that I am deviating from the usual paths of the historian. Historiography is "especially well suited to the notions of continuity, wholeness, closure, and individuality that every 'civilized' society wishes itself to see as incarnating against a merely 'natural' way of life", so Hayden White [*].

In this study I am not presenting an harmonious picture of continuity and wholeness, quite the contrary! I consciously take the risk that my work, voluminous though it is, will, to some extent, fall on the blind spot of scholars. True enough, "it is part of our human condition to long for hard lines and clear concepts. When we have them we have to either face the fact that some realities elude them (i.e. the concepts), or else

---

[*] Hayden White, Droysen's Historik. Historical writing as a bourgeois science. The Content of Form. Narrative Discourse and Historical Interpretation. The John Hopkins University Press. Baltimore and London (1987), 87.

blind ourselves to the inadequacy of the concept"[*]. But such blinding ourselves is not really scholarly.

Although I wish to bear the responsibility for this volume, for its contents, wording, and typography solely myself, I could never have completed it as it stands without the help of many persons. Chapters I and II I entrusted to the judgment of Dr. F. Meijer, lecturer of ancient history in the University of Amsterdam. Chapter III has been critically read by Dr. P. Meijer (no family, Meijer being a rather common name in this country), teacher of classical philosophy in Leiden State University. As usual both scholars had to go out of their way to comply to my wishes which they kindly enough did saving me from a number of mistakes, errors, and inadequacies. For the short Chapter IV I trusted to my own devices. I must emphasize that in this volume I am following a double track, although not so twofold as it may seem, the usual one of dualism, and that of the elements leading up to the Gnosis.

For the sixth time in succession, Dr. J.R. Dove, a retired associate professor of English and American literature living in Amsterdam, carefully checked the infelicities of my home-spun English, discussing many other aspects with me 'over coffee', as he expresses it. Dr. A. Budé, a classical scholar, and my daughter Dr. Th.A.M. Smidt van Gelder-Fontaine, a philosopher, as always served as general readers providing me with many a useful remark and putting some penetrating questions to me.

The task of my dear wife Anneke was lightened since, on July 18, 1990, a word processor with printer was installed in my study. After a period of indescribable suffering I learned to handle the thing; it greatly facilitates my work. But when all is said and done, some final corrections remain to be done, and this my wife did with her usual accuracy. She had, however, to take her courage into her hands to go through a hundred pages of Hellenistic philosophy. As my son Filip, my cartograph-

---

[*] Mary Douglas, Purity and Danger. An Analysis of the Concept of Pollution and Taboo, 162. Ark Paperback. London, 1984 (1966 1).

er, was just moving house, my wife drew the maps this time. I am deeply indebted to all those who so kindly helped me. My thankfulness also includes my friendly publisher Mr. J.C. Gieben who saw this book through the press.

Piet F.M. Fontaine
Amsterdam NL

CHAPTER I

DIADOCHICA

1. What if Alexander had lived on?

What would have happened if Alexander had remained alive for three or four more decades? We know one thing for certain. After his return from India he would not have stayed in Babylon for long since, like 'the great Meaulnes' at the end of Alain Fournier's magnificent novel, he would have 'departed for new adventures'. I am deeply convinced that Alexander was a brilliant military commander, an excellent strategist, and an equally good tactician. He was expert at handling great masses of troops, in efficiently combining the most different sections of his army, and in guessing the plans of the enemy and their weak spots. Never sparing himself in battle he was adored by his soldiers; by the sheer force of his personality and his evident genius he kept his generals, eminent soldiers themselves, in check.

But would he have made as good as a politician? First of all, he would have left the realm he had conquered sword in hand soon enough in order to subdue North-Africa and, who knows, Europe. In that case he would have inevitably appointed some lieutenant who would have to rule the former Persian Empire in his stead, just like Antipater had been installed as governor of Macedonia. Very probably he would have awaited the birth of his child before leaving, hoping that it would prove to be a son. But anyhow, it would a matter of eighteen years at least before that prince could be entrusted with governmental tasks. So we may well ask what would have become of Alexander's grand design in his absence, the fusion of East and West and the creation of one common civilization, to replace the age-old dualism of Europe and Asia [1].

Who of his generals would have fully understood his mind and would have been wholly up to this immense task? The events after Alexander's death proved that his most daring and original plan was not uppermost in their minds; what each wanted was a monopoly on power. But even if Alexander had lived and had returned soon enough to take things in his own hands, we cannot be certain that he would have succeeded. Able though he was, it would still have to be demonstrated whether he possessed the necessary political qualities. Perhaps he was too much of a military man to be a 'political animal'; we know that he could be rash and impetuous, sometimes even imprudent. Some might point to Napoleon as a successful combination of a military and a political genius. But then we should not forget that this French emperor's grand design, namely to unify Europe under his leadership, ended in failure, not to say in a catastrophe in which hundreds of thousands of human lives were sacrificed.

2. The sad fate of the Macedonian dynasty

a. The claimants

For just over one year after the death of Alexander the Great at Babylon on the evening of June 10, 323 B.C., perfect harmony reigned among his generals. Under the surface, however, trouble was brewing. In particular, there was the problem of the succession. In spite of the fact that Alexander had married more than once and had had several concubines, he had left no undisputed adult successor. Two of these women, daughters of the Persian emperors Darius III and Artaxerxes III respectively, had no children. A Persian concubine, Barsine, whom he had made prisoner after the Battle of Issus in 333 B.C., had given him a son, Heracles, a year after that event. His lawful wife Roxane was a Bactrian princess, said to be the loveliest woman of the empire after the consort of Darius III. Posthumously she gave birth to a son, Alexander IV Aigos; as the only legitimate heir of the great king he had the best claim to the throne of Macedonia. There however existed another claimant, a half-brother of Alexander, Arrhidaeus; as a son of King Philip II he could be put forward. What pleaded against him was that he was dim-witted [2]. He also had a deadly enemy in the person of Olympias, the widow of Philip II, an unscrupulous woman who wanted to safeguard the rights of her grandson Alexander IV by any means.

b. One year of peace

In the first days after Alexander's death the man on the spot was Perdiccas, the king's second-in-command to whom he had given his signet ring. This man virtually acted as a kind of Grand Vizir for the Asiatic part of Alexander's domains. He succeeded in realizing his ambition of obtaining the regency of the kingdom. Together with the Macedonian cavalry and royal bodyguard he considered the then still to be born baby of Roxane the lawful heir. But since the birth had not yet taken place, and since it was of course by no means certain that the child would be male, the infantry favoured Arrhidaeus, the more so because he was genuinely Macedonian. The claim of the nine year-old Heracles was weak and found little support, as Alexander had not recognized him as legitimate [3]. After much wrangling and some hard blows - a prelude of what was to come - Roxane's son, Alexander IV Aigos, born just in time, became king, with Perdiccas as his regent. But Arrhidaeus also assumed the royal title, henceforward calling himself Philip III [4]. Very probably he did not realize what was going on, but he was manipulated by his wife Eurydice, hardly more than a girl but highly ambitious. As a daughter of a half-sister of Alexander the Great she too belonged to the royal family; she was married to her half-uncle in fact.

c. Antipater the new regent

In the autumn of 322 B.C. it had become abundantly clear that Perdiccas wanted either to be the new king or to rule in the name of the boy-king. This the other Macedonian satraps were not disposed to tolerate. He was murdered by his own soldiers near Memphis in Egypt while marching against Ptolemy, the governor of that country, whom he considered his most dangerous enemy [5]. This re-opened the question of the regency and the problem of what to do with the two kings neither of whom ever became more than a mere pawn in the pitiless power game.

The man who now took things in hand was Antipater, who had been appointed governor of Macedonia by Alexander when he departed for Asia. During a congress at Triparadisus in the north of Syria he tried to impose himself on the others but got into considerable trouble with Eurydice. As a scion of the royal family herself she had considerable influence with the troops at Triparadisus whom she aroused against Antipater, who barely escaped with his life. Having restored order and after frightening Eurydice sufficiently to keep her out of the way, he made himself regent of the infant king. After the congress he returned to Macedonia taking both kings and Eurydice with him [6].

d. The extermination of the Macedonian royal house

But this second regent too soon disappeared, for he died in the autumn of 319 B.C. On his death-bed he appointed another veteran, Polyperchon, as regent of the boy-king, thus by-passing his own son Cassander [7]. This was a most unfortunate choice. The new regent (the third in succession), an old man already, was much given to heavy drinking and often acted imprudently [8]. He not only had Cassander against him but surrounded himself with other enemies, among them Ptolemy. However, the ever scheming Olympias thought it safer to side with the regent of her grandson. She deeply feared Cassander who was eager for power and believed that he too had a claim since he was married to another half-

THE MACEDONIAN ROYAL HOUSE

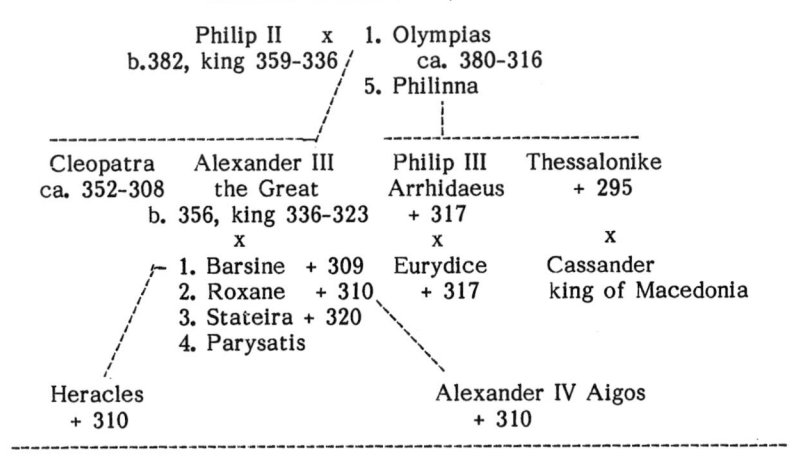

Philip II x 1. Olympias
b.382, king 359-336 / ca. 380-316
/ 5. Philinna

Cleopatra	Alexander III	Philip III	Thessalonike
ca. 352-308	the Great	Arrhidaeus	+ 295
	b. 356, king 336-323	+ 317	
	x	x	x
	1. Barsine + 309	Eurydice	Cassander
	2. Roxane + 310	+ 317	king of Macedonia
	3. Stateira + 320		
	4. Parysatis		

Heracles   Alexander IV Aigos
+ 310   + 310

THE HOUSE OF ANTIPATER

Antipater 397-319

Cassander   x   Thessalonike + 295
b. ca. 350, king 301-297   daughter of Philip II

Philip V + 297   Alexander V + 294   Antipater + 294

THE ANTIGONID HOUSE

Antigonus I Monophthalmos x Stratonike

Demetrius I Poliorcetes x Phila
ca. 327-283

Demetrius II x Phthia
ca. 278-229

Philip V x Polykrateia
237-179

Perseus x Laodicea
king 181-168   + 150
+ ca. 164

sister of Alexander, Thessalonike. It is after her that Thessalonika, now Salonika, a town founded by her husband, was named.

In the armed conflict that soon developed between Cassander and Polyperchon, the last named had the worst of the fighting. Cassander's hand was considerably strengthened by the fact that Eurydice who completely dominated her invalid husband, made him (Cassander) regent instead of the now powerless Polyperchon [9]. Olympias, mother of Alexander the Great, now showed her hand. She engineered the murder of Philip III Arrhidaeus in 317 B.C. and drove Eurydice to suicide [10]. For a year or two later, at the instigation of Cassander the Macedonian army assembly condemned Olympias to death and had her executed; she died the royal way not asking for mercy [11]. Because of his own aspirations the claim of his pupil Alexander IV and his mother Roxane was of no real concern to Cassander; he virtually held them both in captivity. Henceforward he acted as the guardian of what remained of the royal house of Macedonia.

In 310 B.C., when the boy-king was thirteen years old, the troops began to murmur that he should be raised to the throne. Out of fear for his own position Cassander had both Alexander IV Aigos and Roxane murdered in that same year [12]. Another Macedonian general who had Heracles, the last surviving son of Alexander, in his power, and who wanted to favour Cassander, ordered the killing of the young man, then only twenty-three years old, in 309 B.C. [13]. The last one to disappear was Cassander's wife Thessalonike; after the death of her husband in 297 B.C., she too was murdered two years later [14].

In this pitiful way the House of Macedonia found its final end. It had lasted two and a half centuries since it had been founded by Amyntas I ca. 540 B.C. It is characteristic of the bloody strife in this period that all Alexander's wives and concubines, both of his sons, his half-brother and his wife, his mother Olympias, and the four surviving children of Philip II all fell to the knife of the assassin. The great prize of this period was Alexander's heritage but it proved a death-trap. All those who had a claim, or were related to candidates, lost their lives. The power game that, ironically enough, had begun on the pretext of preserving the unity of the empire under the leadership of an offspring of the House of Macedonia resulted in the ruthless extermination of the whole dynasty. Power corrupts but it also destroys.

3. Vain attempts to keep ambitions in check

a. Perdiccas's arrangements

In contrast to rebellious movements among the Greeks in Hellas herself and in Bactria there was not the slightest sign of a revolt among the indigenous population of the empire when they heard of the untimely decease of the King of Asia. The whole situation seemed to spell peace. This greatly facilitated the task of Perdiccas who was in charge at Babylon; the arrangements made in the week after the king's death were presided over by him. The only real problem was the quarrel between the soldiers over the question of who should be the new king. For the rest the Macedonian soldiers only desired to return home with their booty. Most of the satrapies of the former Persian Empire remained in the hands of Persian satraps who had been installed or re-instated by Alexander himself. But five of the satraps, those of the most important provinces, were Macedonians, one of them being Ptolemy in Egypt, another Lysimachus in Thrace, the home of Alexander's most devoted troops. All the plans for further expansion of the empire were immediately given up; the leading idea was that the Macedonian Empire should remain one and undivided.

b. Antipater's reshuffle

The first sign of serious trouble to come appeared in the autumn of 322 B.C. As already related, Perdiccas, knowing that the others were not willing to submit to his ambitions, marched against Egypt to find his end there. Now came the turn of Antipater. In 321 B.C. he summoned the congress of Triparadisus where he reshuffled Perdiccas's arrangements to some extent. Ptolemy kept Egypt for, as Diodorus states, "it was impossible to displace him, since he seemed to be holding then by reason of his own prowess as if it were a prize of war" [15]. The foundation of a separate Ptolemaic kingdom in Egypt was already laid. Seleucus went to Babylon. With his instalment as the satrap of Babylonia the structure of the coming political situation was already predetermined. For from the ensuing wars between the satraps three great kingdoms would arise, Macedonia, Egypt, and the Seleucid Empire (together with some smaller ones in the northern half of Asia Minor). For the time being, however, another general, Antigonus, was invested with great power, for this man got the command of the army in Asia [16].

c. The Diadochi

On the surface of it, all this looked harmless enough. But "a mere redistribution of satrapies was", as Kincaid writes [17], "not enough to stay the ambitions of the generals. Each of them felt himself fit to wear the mantle of Alexander". Even the great authority of the veteran general Antipater could not keep them in check, and anyway, he died soon after. The great king had surrounded himself by a great number of uncommonly forceful personalities, in such a number, to quote Wilcken, as was only found during the Italian Renaissance [18]. They are called the Diadochi, the successors of Alexander. Diodorus sums up the situation as it was after the disappearance of the last scion of the Alexandrian House in the following terms. "Henceforward, there being no longer anyone to inherit the realm, each of those who had ruled over nations or cities, entertained hopes of royal power and held the territory that had been placed under his power as if it were a kingdom won by the spear. This was the situation in Asia and in Greece and in Macedonia" [19].

Actually, those in power, the Diadochi had acted since the death of Alexander as though no heirs of his were in existence. They themselves were the real successors, each wanting to be the sole one. They had been the king's comrades during the great campaign, colleagues of one another but hardly friends; soon after that unexpected event in June 323 B.C. each of them ruthlessly pitted against all others. So, at the very moment that the King of Asia expired, it was obvious that a dualistic situation of all or nothing would soon arise.

4. The Wars of the Diadochi

The dissensions between Alexander's ambitious generals soon led to hostilities which were to last for thirty years and are known as the Wars of the Diadochi, the successors of the dead king. Not everyone of those who, in the first instance, had a stake in the power game would live to see the final dénouement, because it was partly the successors of the successors who acquiesced in the definitive splitting up of Alexander's heritage after the Battle of Ipsos in 301 B.C. The first to disappear, as we saw already, was Perdiccas. I do not feel that my subject requires a treatment of the Wars of the Diadochi in great detail. But the main lines must be sketched.

5. Thrace

Let us first concentrate on Thrace, a country that seems to bring out the blind spot of classical scholars, as my compatriot, the Thracologist Jan Best, is always complaining. Lysimachus [20] (ca. 360-281) got it in the first division of satrapies by Perdiccas, and kept it in the rearrangement by Antipater. This governor of Macedonia not only was his neighbour but also became his father-in-law since he married Nicaea, Antipater's daughter [21]. That he more or less fell under the sway of his father-in-law who was commander-in-chief in Europe did not please Lysimachus at all.

No friend of centralization of power in the empire, Lysimachus first of all participated in the campaign against Perdiccas, and then in that against Polyperchon. His next enemy was the commander-in-chief in Asia, Antigonus, whom he fought in alliance with others, amongst them Ptolemy and Cassander. Antigonus tried in vain to stave off Lysimachus by inciting his subjects to rebel against him. The plan misfired, and the Thracian satrap proved able to extend his sway still more, along the west coast of the Black Sea south of the Danube where all the Greek towns came under his rule. The only exception was Byzantium that, in Cary's words, pursued a "policy of friendly neutrality all round, and generally contrived to stand outside the conflict of Alexander's successors" [22]. However, while Byzantium remained in undisputed control of the Bosporus, Lysimachus secured his hold on the Hellespont by founding a city there, Lysimacheia, in 309 B.C. [23].

The war against Antigonus brought Lysimachus conspicuous successes. He penetrated deeply into Asia Minor, captured Sardes, and finally, after Antigonus had fallen in the Battle of Ipsos in 301 B.C., controlled all Asia Minor as far as the Taurus; he cemented his friendship with Egypt by marrying Arsinoe, daughter of Ptolemy (Nicaea very probably was dead by then) [24]. Already in 306 B.C. Lysimachus had assumed the royal title; in doing so he severed his own realm from Alexander's theoretically still undivided heritage [25]. His whole career was one long demonstration of that old dualism of unity and particularity in Greek history.

Having successfully disposed of Antigonus the indefatigable Lysimachus now turned against Demetrius, the son of Antigonus, who proclaimed himself king of Macedonia in 306 B.C. [26]. This title could mean a claim to the whole extent of the Macedonian kingdom including Thrace. Lysimachus who, as we have seen, never liked the idea of a unified empire, saw a dangerous enemy in the Macedonian king. He therefore joined forces with King Pyrrhus of Epirus (a region more or less coextensive with present-day Albania) who had just then begun a great career as a conqueror. Attacking Macedonia jointly they succeeded in dividing it between them in 287 B.C. But soon enough Lysimachus turned against his ally who, with Thessaly too in his hands, had grown much too powerful for his taste. By conducting a guerilla warfare against Pyrrhus he soon enough made him lose interest in Greek affairs. In 286 B.C. Lysimachus was master of the whole of Macedonia and of Thessaly proper; only Hellas proper did not come under his sway [27].

6. Macedonia

a. The ruthless King Cassander

After this allusion to Macedonia we should shortly review the affairs of this country. After all, it was there that Alexander's great dream of the unification of Europe and Asia had originated. To a certain extent the aged Antipater (397-317 B.C.) may be seen as the real trustee of the dead king's heritage. To him, the friend of his father Philip II and the man who had assisted Alexander in acquiring the succession, the king had entrusted his home country to rule in his absence. He was, as we have seen, commander-in-chief in Europe, and after Perdiccas' death, the regent of the realm with both kings under his guardianship. The future of the monarchy lay in his hands. Without any doubt this experienced and moderate man exercised a stabilizing influence. The fact that he appointed Polyperchon as the new guardian of the boy-king proves that he cared for the future of the empire rather than for the interests of Macedonia. His disappearance in 319 B.C. was one more blow for the dead king's master plan [28].

After Antipater's death his son Cassander (358-297 B.C.), a man far more ruthless than his father had been, became commander-in-chief in Europe [29]. This man was highly displeased with the arrangements that had been made since he considered himself perfectly capable of acting on his own initiative [30]. He neither felt any attachment to the surviving members of the monarchy, nor was he interested in the unity of the empire [31]. Acting in unison with Ptolemy and Antigonus he soon succeeded in driving back his rival Polyperchon into the Peloponnese; the kings remained in his hands. Polyperchon, now no more than a mere mercenary general, soon disappeared into nothingness; even the date of his death is unknown [32].

With Polyperchon out of the way and with the greater part of Greece safely in his power Cassander, from 315 B.C. onwards, could concentrate on what interested him most : the fight against Antigonus who, as commander-in-chief in Asia, considered himself the one and only successor of Alexander and the guarantee of the coherence of the great king's domains. Cassander allied himself with all the other 'particularists', like Ptolemy and Seleucus, against Antigonus. After several years of inconclusive warfare the allies made a peace treaty with Antigonus in 311 B.C. Antigonus recognized Cassander as commander-in-chief in Europe but only till the coming of age of Alexander IV Aigos, then twelve years old. Cassander played safe, as already related, by having the young king and his mother assassinated [33]. The foreseeable consequence was that he now proclaimed himself king of Macedonia in 306 B.C. [34].

The peace of 311 B.C. proved no more than a truce. Soon enough hostilities were resumed, with Antigonus trying to divest Cassander of Greece. The new Macedonian king again allied himself with Ptolemy and Seleucus; in 301 B.C. the death of Antigonus in the Battle of Ipsos freed him of his most dangerous opponent. But he did not enjoy his happiness for long, since he died in 297 B.C. Cary writes that "he left behind him a bad reputation, for the Greeks remembered him as the ruler who held them down with garrisons, and the Macedonians as the murderer of Alexander's kin" [35].

b. The bloody fight over the succession

After the death of King Cassander, his son Philip IV ascended the throne but being consumptive like his father, he died in the same year [36]. Seeing that her two surviving sons, Antipater I and Alexander, were coming to loggerheads over the succession, their mother Thessalonike set aside the Macedonian rule of primogeniture and divided the kingdom between the two, Antipater, the firstborn, receiving western Macedonia and Thesssaly, and Alexander, the younger one, the eastern part of the country [37]. This was a most imprudent move that plunged the country into confusion. The Queen Mother paid for it with her life, for her son Antipater who saw his rights to the throne thwarted by his mother, killed her with his own hands although she cried for mercy [38].

After this horrible deed he began a civil war against his younger brother who had been his mother's favourite. As he felt that his brother

Antipater's claim was the stronger one, Alexander V turned to Pyrrhus of Epirus whom I mentioned already as intervening in the affairs of Thrace, and to Demetrius, the son of Antigonus, who was married to Phila, the daughter of the senior Antipater. Thus Demetrius was the brother-in-law of the two Macedonian kings which made him interested in the succession; apart from that, he was every inch an adventurer [39]. Alexander V's alliance is one of those highly imprudent moves of which this whole history abounds, for Demetrius was a most unreliable person.

Pyrrhus was the first to act. He made peace between the two brothers and was remunerated with some Macedonian territory [40]. When Demetrius arrived there remained nothing for him to do. Naturally, inaction did not satisfy this impetuous man; he invited Alexander V to a pretended farewell supper during which he had him killed by the men of his bodyguard [41]. By telling the Macedonian army assembly that Alexander V had been plotting against him, and playing on his kinship with Antipater's family through his wife Phila, he persuaded the soldiers to proclaim him king of Macedonia in 294 B.C. Antipater the younger then fled the country to his father-in-law Lysimachus of Thrace. The reader will be deeply convinced by now that family connections counted for nothing in this endless struggle for power. Wanting for the moment no quarrel with his powerful neighbour Demetrius, Lysimachus gave the order to kill Antipater [42]. With his death the House of Antipater came to an end, and Demetrius was freed of all fear for competition.

c. King Demetrius of Macedonia

Born in 336 B.C. as son to Antigonus, the now fifty year-old King Demetrius "was always a conqueror rather than a ruler and age had taught him no wisdom" [43]. In his younger days he had been the helper of his father campaigning far and wide but not always successfully. As his father had been the faithful trustee of imperial unity, Demetrius assumed that the mantle had now fallen on him. The fact that he had become king of Macedonia, the historical starting-point of Macedonian imperialism and its real power-base, did not make him think less of himself. The military forces at his disposal were very considerable. But being at bottom no more than a condottiere, he had no stamina. "In the politics of his day", concluded Cary, "he was merely a disturbing factor, and the Greek world could never again regain its equilibrium so long as he lurched out of one adventure into the next" [44].

What worked against him was that the Macedonian population was thoroughly wary of war. But their new king was by no means willing to desist from warfare. In the years between 294 and 289 B.C. he campaigned in Greece, not without success. Obviously comparing himself favourably with Alexander the Great now that Macedonia and Greece were in his power, he made plans for conquering Asia. Having got wind of this scheme, Pyrrhus, Lysimachus, and Ptolemy, "knowing that he inherited his father's grasping ambition" [45], and none of them wanting a new emperor, tried to forestall him by invading Macedonia. When the enemy appeared, a large part of Demetrius' army, angered by his constant levies, deserted to his opponents [46]. Lysimachus and Pyrrhus now divided Macedonia between them; their agreement seemed to spell the end of Macedonia as a separate kingdom [47].

7. Antigonus and Asia Minor

a. The 'loyalist' Antigonus

We must retrace our steps to the time that Antigonus was commander-in-chief in Asia; we shall meet with Demetrius again because this man was Antigonus' son and assistant. Antigonus, the 'one-eyed' (ca. 380-301 B.C.), who in the foregoing paragraphs has been mentioned more than once already, doubtless was a most remarkable man [48]. He was an able commander in the field who had a strong army at his disposition; the greater part of Asia Minor was in his power. "Above all", says Cary, he "recalled Alexander himself in his unflagging energy and breadth of vision. Of all the dead king's officers Antigonus was best qualified to reunite his empire" [49]. Nevertheless, we may hesitate a little in deciding whether he acted wholly in the interests of the Alexander's son or whether his own position was slightly more important to him. After having related the murder of the young king, Diodorus remarks that "Cassander, Lysimachus, and Ptolemy, and Antigonus as well, were relieved of their anticipated danger from the king ... there being no longer anyone to inherit the realm" [50].

b. The no less 'loyalist' Eumenes

Although Antigonus was commander-in-chief in Asia, he did not control the whole of Asia Minor, since her north-eastern provinces, Cappadocia and Paphlagonia, and the southern littoral of the Black Sea, had been given by Perdiccas to Eumenes [51] in the original arrangement. Now this Eumenes [52], a former secretary in Alexander's chancellery, was the only Greek in a high position; as such he was despised by all those haughty Macedonian nobles in whose eyes he was only a bourgeois upstart.

Eumenes too was a great champion of the unity and indivisibility of the empire, the more so because in his view the imperial interests coincided with those of his own. He knew that he had nothing to expect from all those would-be Macedonian monarchs [53]. The first he had to confront was Antigonus who was no less 'loyalist' than he himself. Although being an able general, Eumenes proved no match for Antigonus' superior forces. However, he escaped to the Aegean coast and rose there to new glory. The new regent, Polyperchon, Olympias, and King Philip III Arrhidaeus, entrusted him with the interests of the dynasty in Asia, made him the tutor of the boy-king Alexander IV Aigos, and provided him with a large part of the royal treasure to enable him to wage war against Antigonus [54].

But once again Eumenes had to retreat before Antigonus' well-trained troops; from the coastal region he steadily retired eastward, deeper and deeper into Asia, always with Antigonus at his heels. Receiving no help whatsoever from the Macedonian satraps, he finally found himself at Susa despairing of the loyalty of his own Macedonian officers [55]. Then, in the spring of 316 B.C., he had to face Antigonus in a battle near Susa. In spite of his competent generalship Eumenes had the worst of the fighting. One of his best Macedonian commanders simply left the battle line; his own men surrendered and delivered their commander-in-chief to Antigonus. Against the wishes of Antigonus himself the Macedonian army assembly condemned Eumenes to death and had him executed [56].

c. A 'separatist' coalition against Antigonus

Eumenes' defeat and death greatly fortified the position of Antigonus, But of course the 'separatist' generals, as Thompson Griffith calls them [57], coalesced against him. They greatly feared him since he not only was in command of the strongest army in Asia and had many provinces under his control, but perhaps still more because he seemed to assume the airs of a king. Ptolemy, Seleucus, Cassander, and Lysimachus all combined against him and desired of him that he would redistribute the provinces of the empire. This would have left him with no more than part of Phrygia [58]. Antigonus rejected this ultimatum out of hand. Now a period of warfare began that would last for fifteen years.

There is not the slightest need to relate all the military moves of this period. Antigonus, a highly experienced commander, on the whole stood his ground rather well, with this proviso that Seleucus, the Macedonian satrap of Babylon, made himself master of all the satrapies between the Tigris and the Indus [59]. The peace treaty of 311 B.C., that has already been mentioned, left Antigonus in the undisputed possession of Asia Minor [60]. Of course, all dreams of reunification of the empire by then had melted into thin air but the hyenas did not cease feeding on the corpse. Soon enough hostilities were resumed, for, says Diodorus, "they (the Diadochi) did not abide by their agreements but each of them, putting forward plausible excuses, kept seeking to increase his own power" [61].

For several years Antigonus fought his enemies one by one, campaigning in turn against Ptolemy, Cassander, and Seleucus. In 306 B.C. Antigonus proved as successful against Ptolemy that it seemed possible for him to succeed where Perdiccas had failed, viz. in the conquest of Egypt. In the usual grand royal manner he founded a new capital on the

Orontes in northern Syria named Antigoneia after himself [62]. And when he had heard that his son Demetrius had conquered Cyprus from the Egyptians, Antigonus, "elated by the magnitude of his good fortune ... assumed the diadem and from that time on he used the style of a king". He made sure of his succession by appointing Demetrius as his crown prince [63]. However, he had reckoned without his hosts for his enemies were not all inclined to accept Antigonus as the new emperor; each forestalled the new king's ambitions by assuming the royal title, Ptolemy as well as Cassander, Lysimachus and Seleucus not remaining behind [64].

d. The end of the imperial idea

The fact that the Alexandrian heritage suddenly became divided among no less than five independent kings sealed the fate of the imperial idea; it was not formally abolished but had actually been dead for many years already. This did not mean that the Diadochi now stopped campaigning against Antigonus. The man himself was eighty years old now but his son Demetrius won many a victory for him. Finally, Seleucus, always Antigonus' most inveterate enemy, joined hands with Lysimachus of Thrace; in 301 B.C. their combined forces met those of Antigonus and Demetrius near Ipsus in Phrygia, both armies counting about seventy thousand men. Father and son were defeated and Antigonus fell, mainly, it is said, because Demetrius handled his part so clumsily [65].

One can easily agree with Cary's verdict that "after the Battle of Ipsus the reunion of Alexander's empire passed out of the sphere of practical politics, and the only task that appeared to remain for his successors was to consolidate the separate kingdoms which they had created out of its ruins" [66]. Nevertheless, the imperial idea had a short aftermath in which the last possibilities of combining Alexandrian imperialism and Macedonian particularism were briefly combined in the person of Demetrius.

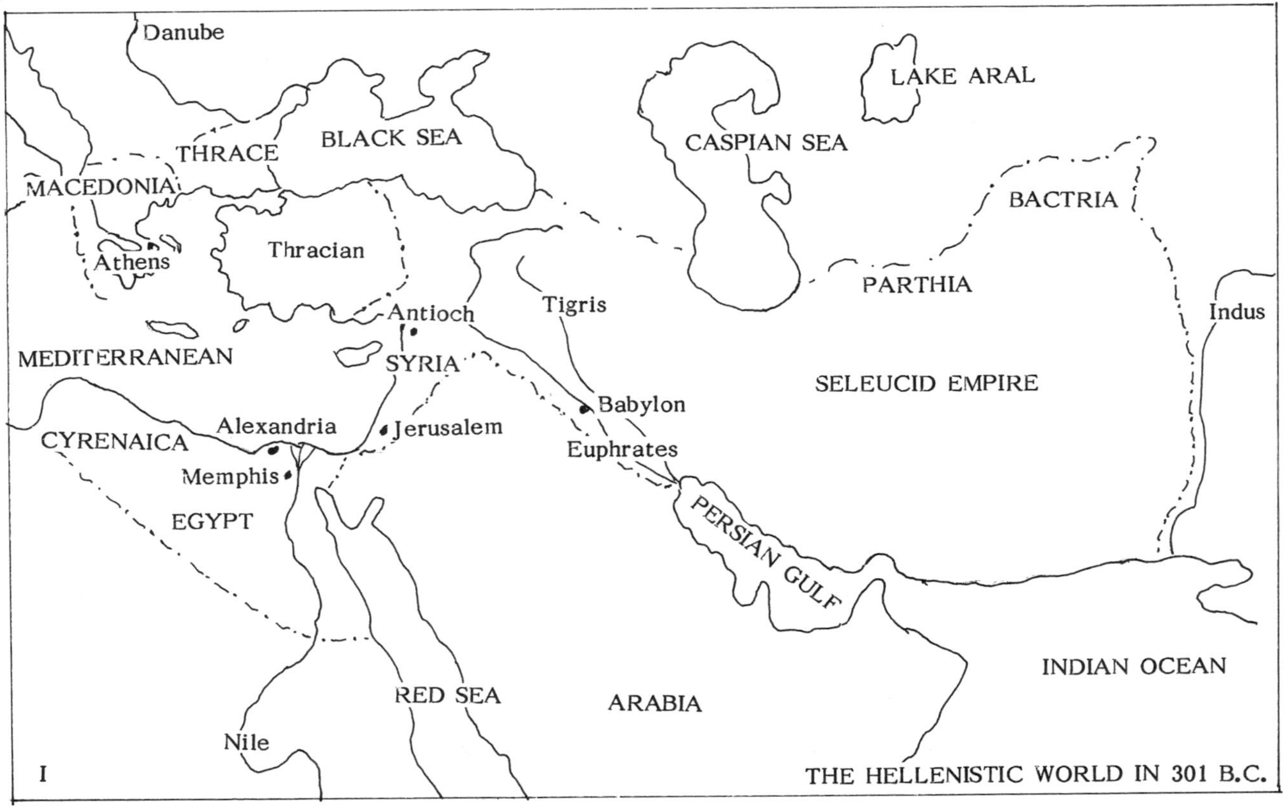
Danube
LAKE ARAL
CASPIAN SEA
BLACK SEA
THRACE
MACEDONIA
BACTRIA
Thracian
Athens
PARTHIA
Antioch
Tigris
Indus
MEDITERRANEAN
SYRIA
SELEUCID EMPIRE
Babylon
Alexandria
Jerusalem
CYRENAICA
Euphrates
Memphis
PERSIAN GULF
EGYPT
INDIAN OCEAN
RED SEA
ARABIA
Nile
I
THE HELLENISTIC WORLD IN 301 B.C.

8. Demetrius' invasion of Asia

Demetrius, never giving up, assembled a large army in his remaining Greek possessions and set out with it, not to reconquer Macedonia but to invade Asia Minor, thus treading in the footsteps of Alexander the Great [67]. Initially he was successful capturing first Milete and other Ionian cities, and then even Sardes in 287 B.C. But then he committed the same mistake as the Greek army in its campaign against the Turks in 1921 : meeting with but little resistance he pushed on and on through the interior of Asia Minor. During the difficult march hunger and sickness cost the army a great many men while the survivors were angrily asking where they were being led. Finally, having arrived in Cilicia, Demetrius capitulated to Seleucus who, wanting to be King of Asia himself, with great misgivings had seen him coming [68]. This happened in the spring of 285 B.C.

Living in custody did not suit this restless man; he began to drink heavily and to play at dice. Perhaps, says the wise Plutarch, "he had convinced himself that this was the real life, which he had long desired and striven to attain, but had foolishly missed it by folly and empty ambition" [69]. It was from drink that he died in 283 B.C.; thus the last images of the imperial dream vanished in alcoholic vapour.

9. A separatist on principle

In the settlement of 323 B.C. Ptolemy, one of Alexander's most trusted generals, became the satrap of Egypt. He had no ambition to become the new emperor, although he did not remain content with the possession of the country of the Nile. So from the very first he was a 'separatist on principle', thus conforming with the Egyptian national tradition; Egyptians had never felt at ease in the Persian Empire and were only too glad to be led out of the imperial magic circle. It therefore is no wonder that in 306 B.C. he was the second of the Diadochi to proclaim himself king, thus making his country into an independent realm. King, or rather Pharaoh, Ptolemy I became the founder of the Ptolemaean dynasty in which, the one following the other, fifteen Ptolemy's occur, the last one being Ptolemy XV Caesarion who, in 30 B.C., was executed at the command of Caesar's successor Octavian.

10. The Seleucid Empire

In the reshufflement of 321 B.C. Seleucus was invested with the Babylonian satrapy. Of all the Diadochi he was by far the most successful. He became the founder not only of the Seleucid dynasty but also of a large empire that comprised the major part of Alexander's Asiatic conquests. As I have already described the vicissitudes of the Seleucid Empire in Vol. V, Ch. I.1, I can cut it short here. Having secured himself of the Median and Persian satrapies to the east of the Tigris, Seleucus made himself king in 305 B.C. Actually, the Seleucid Era had begun earlier, on October 7, 312 B.C., according to the Macedonian calendar. His great opponent in the west was, of course, Antigonus. The two fought many a battle without making any headway against one another. When Antigonus' attention was diverted to then, Seleucus marched eastward, conquered all the territories up to the Indus and beyond, and even invaded the kingdom of Chandragupta Maurya in India [70]. But he was back in time to take part in the Battle of Ipsus in 301 B.C. that was to free him from the competition of Antigonus.

When the victors of Ipsus divided the spoils, Syria, with Phoenicia and Palestine, fell to Seleucus. In honour of his son Antiochus (I) he gave Syria a new capital in 300 B.C. calling it Antioch. Now the possession of the coastal roads and of the Phoenician harbours had long been a bone of contention between the Pharaohs of Egypt and the eastern emperors; Ptolemy I disputed Seleucus' claims, and a long series of wars was fought between them and their successors.

After Ipsus, Lysimachus of Thrace acquired western and central Asia Minor, thus providing Seleucus whose main thrust remained directed towards the west, with a new rival. In 282 B.C. Seleucus I was in the position to stage a major offensive against his Thracian competitor. Discontent among Lysimachus' governors and officers had prepared the way; Seleucus' arms did the rest. The two kings met in the Battle of Corupedium in 281 B.C. in which Lysimachus was killed, leaving Asia Minor in the hands of his enemy. However, when Seleucus in 280 B.C. crossed the Dardanelles to lay hands on Macedonia, he was treacherously murdered.

11. The revival of Greek particularism

For decades endless wars had been fought by everyone against everyone by all the successors and by the successors of the successors. All of them showed themselves incredibly tough in their attempts to secure their own rights; all of them proved without merciless in their relations with their rivals. None of them was above murdering even their nearest relatives when these stood in their way. They also ruthlessly sacrificed thousands of human lives in their often fruitless campaigns and battles. In the context of this treatise, however, the main victim was the idea of unity, the imperial idea.

About sixty years earlier, in 338 B.C., Philip II of Macedonia on the battlefield of Chaeronea had crushed Greek resistance to his rule and made an end of the unceasing internecine Hellenic wars [71]. His son Alexander had succeeded in combining under his sceptre Greece, Macedonia, and the Persian Empire, thus founding an empire the like of which the world had never seen before. But as soon as Alexander was dead, his generals, disregarding their supreme commander's lofty imperial ideas, showed themselves worthy successors of Greek particularism and started to fight the same fratricidal wars, although now on an immensely larger canvas.

One could even argue that they exported the dualistic strife that had infested Greece for over one century and a half after the retreat of the Persian invaders to Asia [72]. Just as the Greeks had been at each other's throats in Hellas herself and just as every move towards unity had been smothered by a particularist backlash [73], they now, in that limitless war theatre between the Aegean and the Indus, indefatigably tried to throttle one another - in these regions that had known peace and unity under the Persian Emperors. The dualistic character of the struggle - the issue at stake being all or nothing - is amply demonstrated by the incredible number of those murdered and still more by the fact that the idea of a unitarian empire was definitely and completely disposed of to make place for separatist kingdoms.

Overviewing the situation as it was about 275 B.C., we can state that at least some balance of power had appeared. There were then three principal successor-states, Macedonia, Egypt, and Syria or the Seleucid Empire, this last one being by far the largest of them all. No king, however, had ever become Alexander's true successor. The Alexandrian Empire had been only short-lived, and its throne remained vacant. But at the same time it proved impossible to banish every form of imperialism from the east where, thousands of years earlier, it had first originated [74]. In the end a great part of Alexander's heritage would pass under the aegis of the imperial power of the future, Rome.

12. Before the Romans came

a. The Parthian menace

The Seleucid Empire soon shrivelled up. Its Indian possessions proved untenable. About 250 B.C. the Graeco-Bactrian kingdom, roughly in what is now Afghanistan, made itself independent. Somewhat later every inch of land between the Tigris and Bactria was lost to the new Parthian Empire. It would certainly have served the interests of Egypt too had the Ptolemaeans assisted the Seleucids against the growing threat from Parthia. For although the Arsacid rulers of that country later used to dub themselves 'Philhellenes', they rose to power on a wave of anti-Hellenistic reaction [75]. The Pharaohs, however, were constantly at loggerheads with their Seleucid colleagues, the apple of discord being as always Syria. In fact a venerable pattern of history repeated itself, for ages before this Pharaohs and Babylonian Emperors had already come to blows over this issue.

During the third century B.C. five bitter wars were fought over this province between the Egyptian rulers and their Seleucid counterparts. The Ptolemaeans finally had the worst of it. After the disastrous Battle of Panium, near the sources of the Jordan in (about) 200 B.C., Ptolemy V ceded southern Syria to Antiochus III. It is not important but notwithstanding intriguing that Antiochus married off his daughter Cleopatra to his Egyptian rival. Thus this name - one of the very few historical names that everybody knows - was introduced into Egyptian history and into the memory of the world [76].

b. Separatism in Asia Minor

Asia Minor was of great importance to the Seleucid Empire because it connected them with the harbours on the Aegean coast and with the Macedonian motherland. However, Alexander had never set foot in the northern half of it, south of the Black Sea. Formally all these lands fell under the competence of Antigonus but no sense of loyalty either to him or the imperial idea was found there. Local rulers in those parts adroitly took advantage of the fact that there were so many candidates for supremacy over Asia Minor - Antigonus, Demetrius, the Seleucids, the Ptolemaeans, and even Lysimachus of Thrace, to say nothing of Eumenes.

In the north-west, south of the Sea of Marmora, Pergamum by 263 B.C. was virtually an independent country. A petty Macedonian officer who skilfully shifted his allegiance from one Diadoch to the other, laid the foundations for the later sovereignty. Under the kings of the Attalid House the capital, Pergamum, became a resplendent centre of Hellenistic culture. To the east of the Bosporus the Kingdom of Bithynia, with its Thracian rulers and population, survived Alexander and the first Diadochs, keeping its end up against all its rapacious neighbours. Although open to Greek influence Bithynia was not a typically Hellenistic country, and still less was Pontus on the south coast of the Black Sea. As an independent kingdom it was founded around 300 B.C. by a certain Mithridates, a Persian, the first of six kings of that name.

In the interior of Asia Minor the western half of the upland plain, east of Pergamum, was lost to all rivals in an unexpected way. Since about 400 B.C. the Celts were on the move again; they sacked Rome in 390 B.C. An eastern branch of them made steady headway towards the Danube; in 279 B.C. they appeared in force in Thrace and Macedonia. Greek authors called them 'Galatians', etymologically the same word as 'Celts'. Having satisfactorily filled their knapsacks to the north of Greece they descended on Hellas where they wanted to plunder the rich sanctuary of Delphi; however, stubborn resistance made them retrace their steps. Some of them settled in Thrace but the main body, invited by the Bithynian king to help him in his wars, finally found homesteads in Phrygia, henceforward to be called 'Galatia' (about 270 B.C.). The new inhabitants did not become hellenized and continued to speak Celtic; they never founded a united kingdom but formed a loose federation of three tribes. Finally, there was Cappadocia, occupying the eastern half of the central plateau, the old heartland of the Hittite Empire. Ca. 300 B.C. this too became an independent kingdom under oriental rulers.

Summing up we must state that the northern half of Asia Minor in the third century B.C. became fragmented into five different political entities. This was due to two historical facts, the first one being that Alexander himself never made an impact here, and the second the mutual rivalry of the Diadochi. The antagonistic relationships of the three great powers are mirrored in those of the smaller potentates of this region who were constantly fighting one another. So here too the imperial idea petered out in what the Germans call 'Kleinstaaterei" and incessant warfare.

c. Antiochus III beaten back by the Romans

All this meant that only the southern half of Asia Minor, between the harbours of Ephesus and Milete in the west and Cilicia in the east, remained in the possession of the Seleucids. But even here their claims were disputed by the Ptolemies. Sometimes we find the Pharaohs

THE HELLENISTIC WORLD CA. 200 B.C.

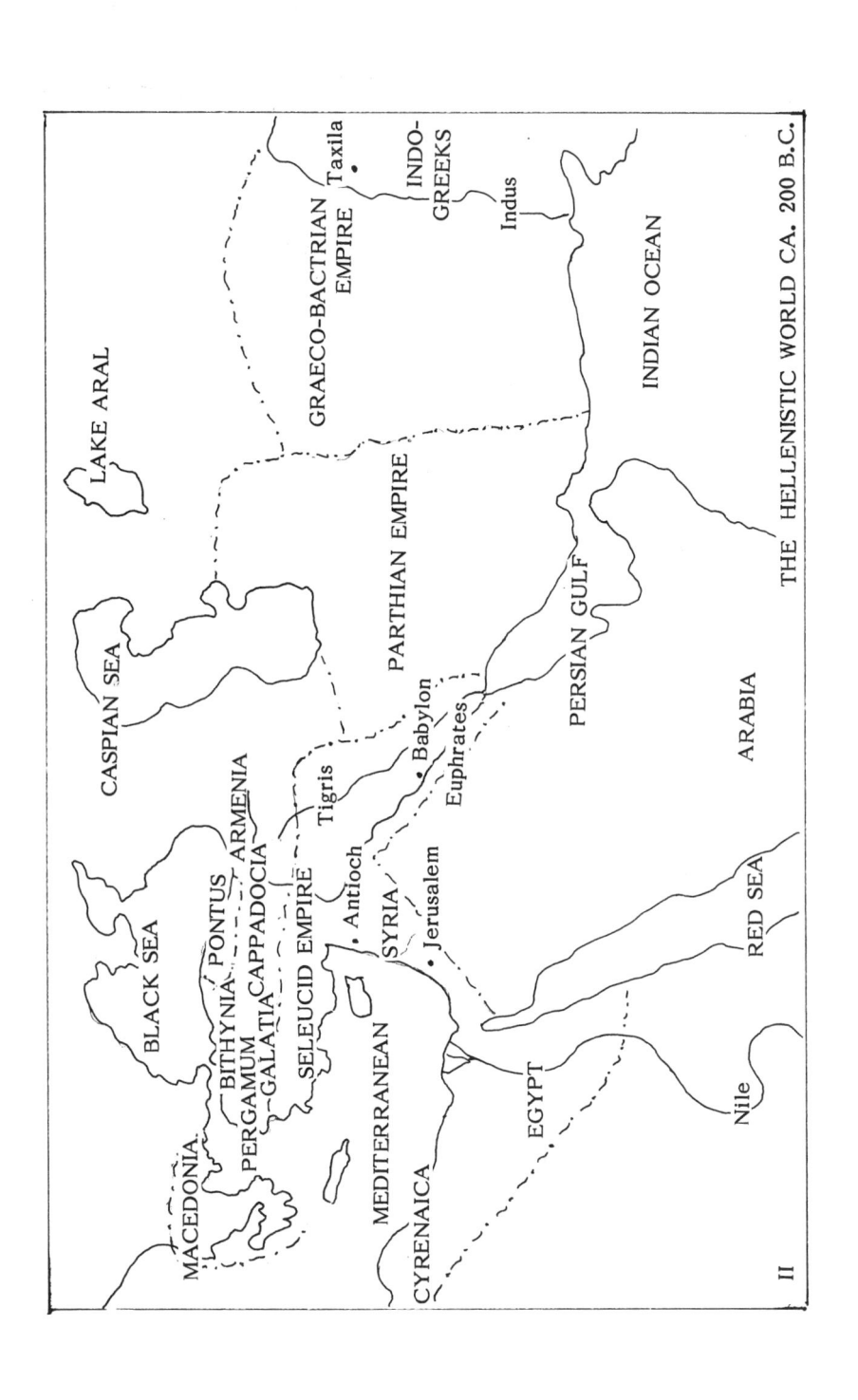

occupying large parts of the southern seabord; it was not before 197 B.C. that Antiochus III definitively wrung these possessions from the Egyptians.

It was this same Antiochus III, the last really powerful Seleucid king, surnamed 'the Great' (ca. 242-187 B.C.), who triggered off the events that in the long run would restore imperial unity in the east. Having been extremely successful everywhere, having even cowed Parthia and Bactria, and defeated his Egyptian rival, he got it into his head to 'liberate the Greeks', as the long since outmoded terminology expressed it. In the autumn of 192 B.C. he landed in Hellas but within a year he was back in Asia without his army. He had reckoned without the Romans who already were deeply interested in the Balkans. Although at that moment they were not yet intending to conquer the Balkan peninsula, they surely were not waiting for a rival. They quickly chased Antiochus from Greece, routing his whole army in the Battle of Magnesia. In this forceful way Rome made it abundantly clear that south-eastern Europe was her affair.

Roman troops did not actually follow him to Asia Minor but already their mighty shadow began to fall over Antiochus' western domains. In 188 B.C. he was forced to sign the Peace of Apamea; as a consequence of this treaty he had to resign every strip of country west of the Taurus. What Antiochus lost in Asia Minor was divided between the island of Rhodes that was then an independent kingdom, and the Kingdom of Pergamum, both of whom enjoyed the favour of Rome.

d. The decay of the Seleucid Empire

After the death of Antiochus III in 187 B.C. the decay of his empire continued. The disastrous outcome of the king's Hellenic campaign incited the Armenians to sever their country from the Seleucid Empire and to set up an independent kingdom. Worse was to follow. In 141 B.C. the Parthians conquered Mesopotamia; all Seleucid influence east of the Euphrates was now lost. The Seleucid Empire henceforward only comprised Cilicia, Syria with Phoenicia, and Palestine. The history of the last decades of the Seleucid kingdom makes sorry reading. There was civil war in Syria between claimants to the throne; the cruel way in which Antiochus IV treated the Jews led to the establishment of an independent Jewish kingdom in Judaea (about 160 B.C.) [77].

13. The remnants

a. No Egyptian imperialism

The overall result of nearly three centuries of strife in the Middle East was that only remnants of Graeco-Macedonian power precariously clung to the coasts of the Mediterranean, the Aegean, and the Black Sea. The re-emerging political entities of the East had pushed them back. The largest and most solid power block doubtless was that of Ptolemaic Egypt. Attempts were made by the first three Ptolemies to extend the Egyptian sway over Palestine and Syria, (parts of) Asia Minor, the Aegean, and the southern Balkans. But in the long run unrest among the local population along the Nile convinced the rulers that there was no popular basis for Egyptian imperialism.

During his later years Ptolemy III (246-221 B.C.) gave up all attempts at expansion; his grandson Ptolemy V Epiphanes saw the loss of nearly all outlying Egyptian possessions. After 200 B.C. his successors had to remain content with the country of the Nile itself. However, there were two exceptions. Cyprus always was an integral part of the Ptolemaic kingdom, while Cyrene (the eastern half of what is now the Republic of Libya) also belonged to it (except for a short period of independence in the third century B.C.).

b. The Macedonian mother country

In Europe there was Macedonia. When Demetrius ingloriously disappeared from the Graeco-Macedonian scene in 287 B.C., never to return, he left behind his son of around thirty-three years old whom he had by his wife Queen Phila. This man was made of a far more solid mettle than his mercurial father. Having assembled an army in Greece he knew how to bide his time and to make use of opportunities. Then, in 277 B.C., he succeeded in ridding Macedonia of the marauding Galatian bands which, with one stroke, made him immensely popular in this country. As a consequence the Macedonian army assembly proclaimed him king in 276 B.C. as Antigonus II Gonatas. He reigned till 239 B.C. warding off attacks by the Epirotes.

He was succeeded by his adoptive son Philip V (238-197 B.C.) who tried to expand Macedonian influence far and wide but was finally driven back into Macedonia by the Romans in 197 B.C. Cary writes that he "most nearly recalled the giants of Alexander's generation". He displayed the same indomitable energy and resilience, the same ambitions and the same 'autocratic arrogance' [78]. The most fateful element in his policy was that he underrated the Romans. Quarreling with the Greeks all the time, he made himself incapable of taking the lead of a Graeco-Macedonian anti-Roman alliance. Instead, his shortsighted policy lured the Romans always deeper into the Balkans. His son Perseus (179-168 B.C.), paid the price for his father's and his own ambitions. After his defeat against the Romans in the Battle of Pydna in 168 B.C. the populace of the imperial city saw him walk through her streets in the triumphal procession of his victor, Lucius Aemilius Paullus. Thus ended the existence of the country of Philip II and Alexander the Great as an independent kingdom.

14. What remained of Graeco-Macedonian power

Seen in an historical perspective, the Macedonian conquests may seem a short interlude in the long-standing dualistic conflict between Europe and Asia [79]. The east indeed had fallen an easy prey to Alexander's mighty blows; however, in three centuries time it seemed to have reasserted itself very powerfully. But were the gains of Macedonian imperialism politically really so trifling as may seem on the surface? True enough, a great part of the conquests was irretrievably lost but what remained, in the period just before the Roman conquests, was impressive enough.

The extent of Hellenic political power was even then immensely much larger than it was before Alexander set out to subdue the world. Two powerful kingdoms, Egypt and Pergamum, were governed by Hellenic dynasties, while a third, Syria, although less successful, was still ruled by a descendant of Seleucus the Macedonian general. Shortsighted as we are, even as historians, we tend to forget that remarkable Graeco-Macedonian Kingdom of Bactria, whose Hellenic kings ruled over Afghanistan and a large part of Pakistan (to use the modern indications). Their supremacy over this country remained virtually unimpaired till 140 B.C., when they were confronted with Sako-Scythian and Yue-Chi invasions. Some small Graeco-Bactrian kingdoms, however, managed to subsist in Afghanistan and in the Punjab till ca. 40 B.C. [80].

15. Greek dissensions

a. Philip II imposes unity on Greece

We must now go back in time to review the Greek political scene; after all, Greece was the cradle of the particularist movements I have described which were fatal for the unitarist idea. In Volume II, Chapter II, I discussed the history of the relationships between the Greek poleis in the fifth and fourth centuries B.C. as a dualism of structure and antistructure. The Greeks of the period after the Persian invasions were viscerally unable to restructure their collection of independent cities into anything like a common national organism. Instead they preferred the antistructure of every town for itself. Doubtless there were repeated attempts to conclude a lasting general peace but they all failed dismally in the shortest possible time.

Then Philip II of Macedonia swooped down on Greece like an eagle from the north, crushed Greek resistance on the field of Chaeronea in 338 B.C., and dissolved the existing leagues of poleis. All Greek poleis

THE HELLENISTIC WORLD CA. 140 B.C.

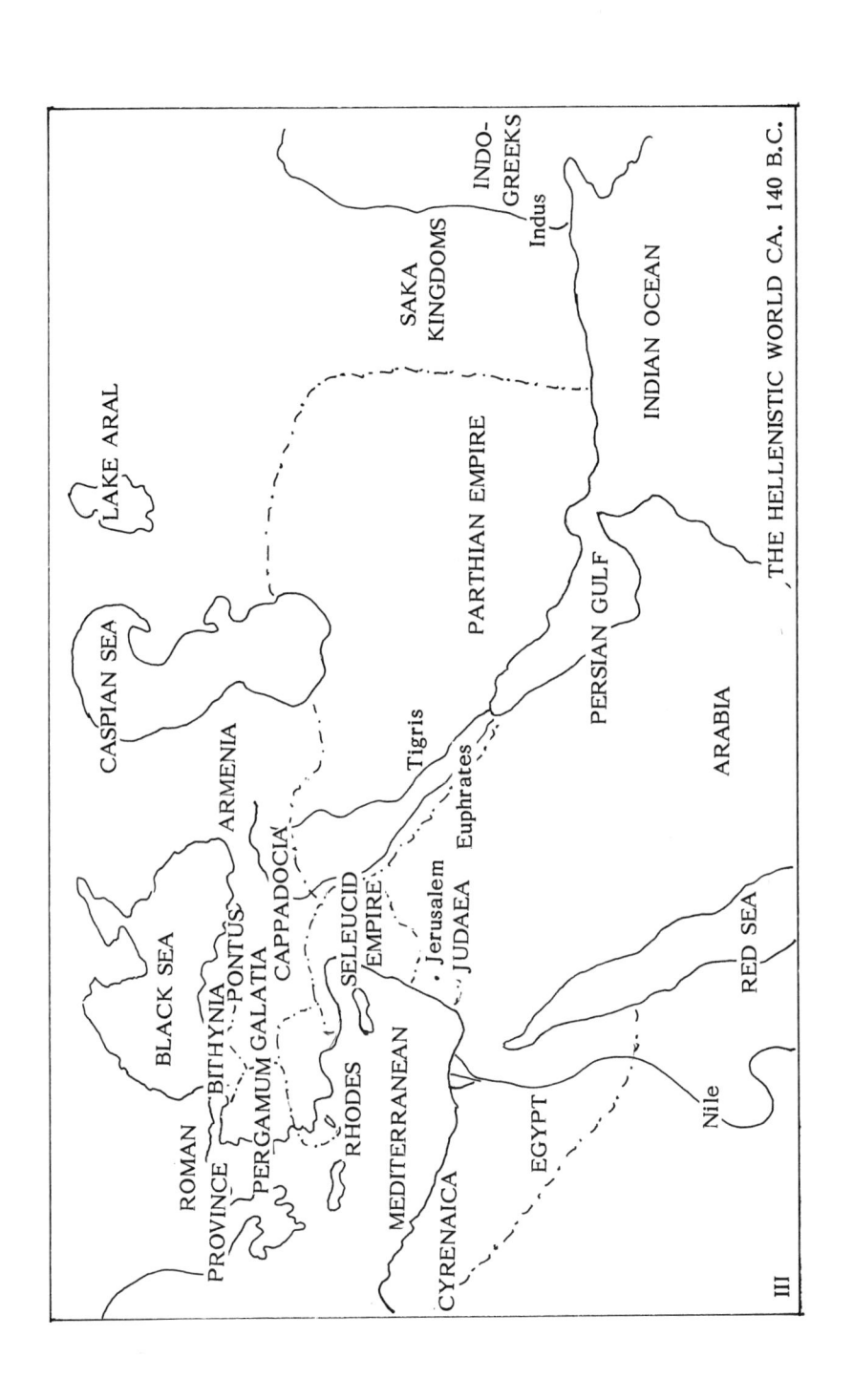

crop up again and again in the subsequent two centuries. A 'general peace' was imposed on the Greeks in 337 B.C.; all the poleis now formed a new confederation, the 'Corinthian League', which choose King Philip as it supreme commander. So there was peace now, there was quiet, there was unity and leadership. How long would this idyl last? It would have been a miracle that only would have happened if the Greeks had now desisted for good and all from their special brand of political dualism.

b. Anti-Macedonian movements in Greece

When Alexander left Macedonia for his invasion of the Persian Empire, he installed Antipater as governor of Macedonia and, by the same token, as his lieutenant in the command of the Corinthian League. The Greeks, in general, had no liking for the Macedonians; they did not consider Alexander's war against Persia their affair. Athens in particular fretted at the situation that deprived her of every chance of supremacy. The Macedonian king even had to leave part of his fleet behind to keep an eye on the Athenians (and on the Greeks) in order to forestall the Persian navy to make contact with them. This danger was not imaginary for King Agis III of Sparta, assisted by Persian money and ships, succeeded in organizing an anti-Macedonian coalition, without including Athens. He saw his army crushed by Antipater in 331 B.C. in the Battle of Megalopolis in which he himself was killed.

As soon as they had heard that Alexander was gone, the Greeks, now under the leadership of Athens, rose in revolt and tried to throw off the Macedonian yoke. At first they were fairly successful in this 'Hellenic War' [81] but then the Macedonians fell on them with their full weight. Beaten on land and at sea in the summer of 322 B.C. the Greeks were forced to dissolve their coalition; the Athenians saw a Macedonian garrison march in. Demosthenes then, as ever, the staunch opponent of Macedonia, fled the town, and, seeing no escape, ended his life by taking poison. Other victims of this episode were Aristotle who, as pro-Macedonian, was forced by the Athenians when they still were triumphant, to go into exile, never to return, and the Corinthian League that was dissolved by the Greek allies and was not revived by the Macedonians after the war [82].

c. Polis autonomy long dead

Antipater abolished the democratic constitution of Athens and many other Greek cities and imposed oligarchic regimes on them in order to keep them dependent on Macedonia. But, as Tarn writes, Antipater "attempted no comprehensive system" [83]. One could argue that with the dissolution of the Corinthian League and the (anti-Macedonian) Hellenic League, a state of perfect Greek antistructure had been reached. To the Greeks comprehensive political organization had always been identical with or conducive to tyranny; they saw this embodied in the Persian Empire. Their own history had been deeply moulded by their dualistic struggle against its enormous weight. Their dislike of the Persian system was so great that they did not want to have any similar kind of structure in their own country.

But the dualistic system of structure and antistructure had never been absolute. There always had been some league or other and often even more than one at a time. The Peloponnesian League under the leadership of Sparta dated back into the sixth century B.C. The designs of Xerxes I on Greece had caused the creation of the Isthmian League in 481 B.C. which united for the common struggle many, but by no means all, Greek states. The fifth century B.C. saw the First Athenian Sea League, the fourth the second of that name. In that period we detect a tendency to create large federal states, which meant that the idea of polis autonomy was dead and buried. In the period before the Macedonians came there were five of them. Then the Macedonians forced the Corinthian League upon the Greeks, the first one to unite all the poleis in one common bond.

Now, in 331 B.C., there was nothing of all this left; Hellas had reverted to complete general autonomy - a situation that in practice had never occurred before. But a prize had to be paid for this unexpected realization of a Greek dream; this prize was utter dependence on a Macedonia that many Greeks saw as a non-Hellenic, even a barbarian state.

d. Polyperchon's bid for Greece

When Polyperchon in 319 B.C. was contending with Cassander for the mastery of Macedonia, he tried to win over the Greek poleis to his side by issuing a proclamation in which he restored the democratic constitutions of the cities; this proclamation was formally signed by 'his' king Philip III Arrhidaeus [84]. Those who had been exiled after the Battle of Megalopolis were permitted to return. The exiles who in 318 B.C. returned to Athens revenged themselves on the friends of Antipater in this city. They used their influence on the assembly to have them condemned to death and executed because "these men had been responsible for the enslavement of the fatherland and the overthrow of the democratic constitution and laws" [85]. What they conveniently forgot was that they themselves were just as obsequious to Polyperchon as their opponents to Antipater.

With this sad event the dualistic party strife that always had been the corrolary of the Greek love for antistructure [86] seemed to have returned. Diodorus expresses himself in a way that reminds one of Thucydides' bitter words of a century earlier in similar circumstances : "When hatred that in prosperity finds no utterance, after a change of Fortune breaks out in adversity, it loses all human semblance in its rage against its opponents". The executed men were all thrown unburied beyond the frontiers of Attica [87].

Polyperchon by no means succeeded in rallying all the Greeks under his banner; soon enough his sole stronghold was the Peloponnese where he made Corinth into his fortified headquarters. Athens came under the supervision of Cassander, who installed a hard-handed governor there in 317 B.C. Polyperchon's cause seemed irretrievably lost, especially when 'his' king Philip III was murdered by order of Olympias. He was then hardly more than a mercenary general in the Peloponnese where many soldiers could be hired.

e. Demetrius in Greece

Now Antigonus, commander-in-chief of the armies in Asia, appeared on the scene. In his bid for the empire he issued a proclamation in which he declared Cassander a public enemy; all the Greek poleis were to be free and autonomous and would not have to tolerate foreign (= Macedonian) garrisons (315 B.C.) [88]. It is remarkable that all those who wanted to enlist the Greeks for their cause tried to catch them with the same bait. For the ink on Antigonus' decree was hardly dry when Ptolemy I of Egypt who had thrown himself across the path of Antigonus' imperial ambitions, issued a similar one. "Each of them, indeed, perceiving that it was a matter of little moment to gain the goodwill of the Greeks, rivalled the others in conferring favours upon this people" [89].

In all probability such promises of freedom had no greater value than the paper on which they were written. However the struggle between Antigonus and the coalition against him might turn out, Greece would always have a master. Another telling point is that none of the competitors, although being great admirers of polis autonomy, believed that he could do without some form of Hellenic confederation. Already Ptolemy, when campaigning in Greece, had tried to revive the Corinthian League in some form or other 21 [90]. In 307 B.C. Antigonus sent his son Demetrius with a strong army to Greece. Athens fell into his hands and once again got back her democratic constitution [91]; he had orders from his father to convene a congress of Greek cities to "consider in common what was advantageous for Greece" [92], doubtless meaning by this that again a general league should be organized. But nothing came of it for soon enough Demetrius' strategic capacities were needed elsewhere.

He came back in the autumn of 304 B.C by order of his father Antigonus and secured the larger part of the Peloponnese. He also captured Corinth, got hold of Athens, and pushed on as far as the Thermopylae. The tenderness with which Greek affairs were handled then is exemplified by Demetrius' cruelty against Polyperchon's garrison-commander of Orchomenus and eighty of his adherents who were crucified in front of this city [93]. He then convened a general assembly of Greek poleis on the Isthmus of Corinth - which reminds one of the foundation of the Isthmian League in 481 B.C. -, and forced them to revive the Corinthian League of 338 B.C. He himself was proclaimed commander-in-chief of the Hellenic forces, "as Philip and Alexander had been proclaimed before him", says Plutarch. And he continues : "and to these he considered himself in no slight measure superior, lifted up as he was by the good fortune and power he then enjoyed" [94]. But although Demetrius had now manoeuvred himself into the position of Philip II and Alexander the Great, the enemy to be fought was not the Persians but Cassander of Macedonia and Lysimachus of Thrace. Soon after Antigonus recalled his son to Asia Minor where together they fought the disastrous Battle of Ipsus in 301 B.C.

After Demetrius' departure for Asia in 302 B.C. the Greeks suddenly were relatively free. "His (Demetrius') garrisons were expelled everywhere" - with the exception of the strong body at Corinth -, "and there was a general defection to his enemies", according to Plutarch [95]. This situation was the great opportunity for the Greeks to take things into their own hands by converting the Corinthian League into their own instrument of power. But they did nothing of the kind allowing the League to crumble away once again [96]. They always preferred antistructure above structure.

Some years later, in 297 B.C., Demetrius, having assembled a big fleet, threw himself on Greece for the third time; he succeeded in capturing Athens and Thebes but failed in bringing down Sparta [97]. But already in 293 this quixotic man disappeared to Macedonia where he became king and from where he began his campaign in Asia Minor to find his end there.

f. Pyrrhus the liberator

Demetrius' son and successor in Macedonia, Antigonus II Gonatas, just like his predecessors since Philip II had done, considered Greece to fall under the suzerainty of Macedonia. This king who was more or less able to control Greece by the number of garrisons he had there, was highly unpopular in Hellas because of his constant levies of recruits. In 280 B.C. a widespread Greek rebellion broke out led by King Areus of Sparta. For a moment another Hellenic ghost was revived, the Peloponnesian League. The initial successes were impressive enough, and perhaps the Greeks would have fought themselves free had not Athens remained neutral. True enough, there was a Macedonian garrison in the adjoining Piraeus but the old jealousy of Athens against Sparta may have played a role too [98]. Gonatas in fact considered Athens his Greek capital [99]. Thus another attempt to make Greece autonomous evaporated.

In 274 B.C. King Pyrrhus of Epirus, one of the great condottieri of this period, returned to the Balkans (he had been away for six years campaigning in Italy), invaded Macedonia, and chased Gonatas to Greece [100]. This forced the Epirote king to follow him there; in 274 B.C. he landed in force in the Peloponnese. Again the banner of Greek freedom was raised; the story of the relations between Greece and Macedonia in this whole period is a tale of a dualistic relationship. Many Greek cities, one of them being Athens, defected to Pyrrhus the liberator but this time Sparta kept aloof [101].

The king stormed this city but failed and then turned to Argos which he found in the possession of Gonatas. In the middle of the night his troops managed to enter the city through a gate opened by a friendly hand. This led to a horribly confused battle in the narrow streets during which a woman from a housetop threw a tile on Pyrrhus' head; the benumbed king was finished off then by an enemy soldier. His head was brought to Gonatas [102]. Antigonus II Gonatas experienced no difficulties now in recovering Macedonia.

g. What Greece meant to them

We may well ask why one ruler after the other took so much trouble to get Greece into his power. First of all, the possession of Hellas would have given them the authentically cultural background which all those Macedonians and Epirotes sorely felt they lacked. Secondly, once being the hegemon of an Hellenic League, they would have a considerable army at their disposal. And thirdly, using Greece as a jumping-off board, they might be able to subdue Macedonia; if, moreover at one and the same time it was possible to combine the Macedonian crown with the role of hegemon of Hellas, they would find themselves in the original position of Philip II and Alexander the Great. All the candidates were foreigners; no Greek ever tried to win the supremacy over his country.

h. Enter Ptolemy II

The next aspirant was King Ptolemy II Philadelphus of Egypt (285-246 B.C.), a monarch with an insatiable lust for power. Lavishly spending the rich king's money his envoys first succeeded in bringing about yet another Peloponnesian League in 267 B.C. with Sparta as its leader, and then even luring Athens into it. This feat of diplomacy must have caused a mild sensation in Greece since the two cities had not joined hands for two hundred years [103]. The theoretical aim of the league was the liberation of the Greeks - the old battle cry once again; its direct goal to wrest the country from Gonatas' hands. It was the last time that Athens acted in the anti-Macedonian spirit of Demosthenes.

There were two adverse circumstances : many poleis did not join the League, and Ptolemy II by no means gave them the military assistance that was needed. So the initiative was left to Gonatas; Sparta was defeated, King Areus fell in battle; a starved Athens had to surrender in 262 B.C. The city got a Macedonian governor, a Macedonian garrison, and an autocratic constitution. For the next thirty years, as Wilcken writes, she was no more than a Macedonian provincial town [104]. Finally,

Egyptian sea power was crushed in the Battle of Cos in 261 B.C. What the Greeks needed in this period was a national hero with the prestige of a Themistocles (but then, they had ostracized even him).

j. Hellas a Macedonian apanage

For this and the subsequent periods sources are scarce or no longer existent. Greece now sank away into endless civil strife. There was an Achaean League, founded already in 280 B.C., but brought to greater glory by one Aratus who obviously wished to play the role of the leading and, self-evidently, anti-Macedonian statesman. This brought him into conflict with Sparta who saw her hegemony over the Peloponnese threatened. Being brought into dire straits, Aratus now completely reversed his policy and asked the Macedonian regent, Antigonus Doson, for help. This man duly came, defeated the Spartans [105], and founded the umpteenth Hellenic League with Macedonia as one of its members, graciously permitting the Achaeans to join it. This was in 224 B.C. Once again Macedonia had affirmed that Greece was her apanage.

16. When the Romans came

a. Roman intervention in Greece

Not all Hellenic cities joined the Hellenic League, and the internecine war of pro- and anti-Macedonian poleis relentlessly went on. The historrical significance of this is that it gave the Romans an opportunity to intervene. King Philip V of Macedonia (238-179 B.C.), a highly ambitious man, was much feared for his high-handedness, especially when he had joined forces with Antiochus III of Syria in order to divide the outlying provinces of Egypt between them. The anti-Macedonian allies in Greece, Egypt, Rhodes, Pergamum, all appealed to Rome for help - not foreseeing that Rome would come to stay for centuries. This call for help, says Justinus, was welcomed by the Romans because Philip V had assisted

Hannibal against them, and because they feared that he, like Pyrrhus, would come to campaign in Italy too [106].

Athens was the first city to declare war on Macedonia. As Livius writes, " the Athenians seemed especially suitable for the purpose, on account of the dignity of their state" [107]. The days of before Chaeronea seemed to have returned. Philip's terroristic treatment of the free city of Abydos which he conquered in 200 B.C. [108] incited the Romans to land an army of twenty thousand men in Illyria [109]. In the two campaigns of the now following 'Macedonian War', Philip V suffered one defeat after another; after the Battle of Cynoscephalae in Thessaly in 197 B.C. against Rome and her Greek allies, he was forced to conclude peace. This cost him his whole fleet and his non-Macedonian possessions; from then on he operated more or less under Roman guardianship [110]. "A Macedonian hegemony (over Greece - F.) had ceased to be within the range of practical politics" [111].

A period of one hundred and forty one years of Macedonian ascendancy in Hellas had now come to an end. Was it to be replaced by a Roman supremacy? Not yet! At the Isthmian Games of 197 B.C. where Flamininus, the victor of Cynoscephalae, was personally present, a herald in his name and that of the Roman Senate proclaimed the freedom of the Greeks. Such a din arose that the herald had to repeat his message. But when at last everybody had understood what he said, "a shout of joy arose, so incredibly loud that it reached the sea". If we may believe Plutarch whom I am quoting here, there was such a whirl made in the air by the shouting that "ravens which chanced to be flying overhead fell down into the stadium" [112]. To make this promise true the Romans withdrew their troops from Greece in 194 B.C.

Soon enough another candidate for the supremacy over Hellas presented himself, Antiochus III of Syria. The Aetolians, in the north of Greece, chafed at the way in which Flamininus had treated them - the Romans could be very high-handed too!; in 192 B.C. they invited the Syrian king to cross over and liberate Greece. But the Romans, of course, were not disposed to tolerate a new foreign intervention in Greece. As already related earlier in this chapter, the Romans defeated Antiochus at Magnesia and forced to him to leave Europe.

b. Macedonia in Roman hands

Again the Romans withdrew their troops from Hellas but they remained spiritually present. In many a dispute the Hellenic poleis appealed to the Roman Senate for a verdict. Some of its judgments caused misunderstandings and made the hypersensitive Greeks nervous. Another factor that kept the Romans entangled in Greece and Macedonia was that they mistrusted Philip V of Macedonia. Not wholly without reason, for although Philip was much too prudent to provoke the Romans, he nevertheless made military preparations [113]. His son Perseus (179-168) pursued this policy which made the Romans ever more suspicious and finally, in 171 B.C., saddled him with a war with Rome.

Macedonia's fate was sealed on the battlefield of Pydna in 168 B.C. For the last time the famous Macedonian phalanx was deployed; the Roman commander, Lucius Aemilius Paullus, later said that he never had seen anything more terrifying than its onslaught [114]. But the Romans did not meet their adversary in battle for the first time; by now they had learned how to deal with the shock. The fate of the Macedonians was decided within an hour [115]. Perseus was captured some time after the battle and, as related earlier, brought over to Rome. He was the last of the Antigonid dynasty.

The Romans dissolved the Macedonian kingdom and replaced it by four quasi-independent republics. In Greece the victorious Romans made an extensive purge of all those who were supposed to have been pro-Macedonian; the Achaeans alone had to send a thousand hostages to Rome, one of them being the famous historian Polybius. It did not make the Romans more sympathetic to the Greeks.

The Romans still desisted from garrisoning Greece and Macedonia. But in 149 B.C, a daring Macedonian adventurer tried to reunite his country. The Romans hastily moved in, defeated him, and in 148 B.C. made the country into a province, which meant that it was occupied by Roman troops and got a Roman admistration. In 150 B.C. the surviving Achaean hostages returned home filled with hatred against Rome. Soon enough the old enmity between the Achaean League and Sparta flared up for the last time. In 146 B.C. the Achaean federal assembly decided for war against Sparta which meant war with Rome too. There was only one big battle, on the Isthmus in the same year, where the federal army was thoroughly beaten by Roman legions.

Now the Romans made it unambiguously clear that no Greek city or league would ever again act on its own initiative; this virtually meant the end of that time-honoured concept of polis autonomy but also of all the internecine dualistic strife it always had implied. Corinth was completely destroyed and her inhabitants sold into slavery. The official excuse for this barbarity was that Roman envoys had been insulted there; the real reason, however, was that the Roman capitalists were not disposed to tolerate a successful commercial competitor. The Achaean League was dissolved of course.

Administratively Greece became dependent on Macedonia; some parts of her were even annexed by that province. So the toughfisted Romans decided the old dualistic dispute between Greece and Macedonia in favour of the last; the irony of history willed that Macedonia triumphed only when she no longer existed as an independent country. Athens and a number of cities and small leagues remained autonomous; at last, for the first time in history, there was lasting peace in Hellas. It was only in 28 A.D., that she was converted into a Roman province.

c. Egypt an imperial possession

On Egypt too the Romans threw a covetous eye since the rich cornfields along the Nile provided enough grain to feed the ever growing population of the eternal city. Dynastic rivalries in the second city B.C. gave them an opportunity to intervene because several pretenders to the throne appealed to Rome for help. In 154 B.C. Ptolemy VIII Euergetes even went so far as to make the Romans his heirs by testamentary disposition in case he were to die childless. As he later begot offspring this came to nothing, but Rome concluded that she might have a legal claim on Egypt. Anyhow, from this period onward Egypt's foreign policy virtually was under Roman supervision. This cost the country the island of Cyprus, made into a Roman province in 58 B.C. The Pharaohs of the last century B.C. were hardly more than protégés of different Roman potentates.

The history of independent Egypt ends in a romantic glow. In 69 B.C. Cleopatra VII became queen, with her brother-husband Ptolemy XIII as king. According to Bradford Welles she was one half Greek, three-eighths Macedonian, and one-eighth Iranian, obviously an highly successful recipe for physical beauty. Far from being a 'dumb blonde', she was intelligent and the first Ptolemaean to speak Egyptian. She only failed to become the first Roman empress because her lover Julius Caesar was murdered in 44 B.C.

In the civil war that followed the death of Caesar she took the wrong side, that of Antony. His rival Octavian, the later emperor Augustus, followed him to Egypt where Antony as well as Cleopatra committed suicide. Augustus abolished the Egyptian monarchy and thus in 30 B.C. another Diadoch kingdom passed out of existence. The country did not become a Roman province but remained a personal estate of the emperors [116].

d. The Seleucid monarchy abolished

Since the Peace of Apamea in 188 B.C. the Seleucid Empire remained restricted to Syria with the adjoining regions of Cilicia and Palestine. Under the leadership of Judas the Maccabee Judaea fought herself free around 160 B.C. On the outskirts of Syria proper many principalities made themselves independent, while in the country itself Seleucid claimants contested the throne. In 64 B.C. Pompey appeared; he was campaigning against the pirates that infested the eastern Mediterranean and against anti-Roman potentates in Asia Minor. Without much ado, he abolished the Seleucid monarchy and turned Syria into a Roman province. The Jews too became dependent on Rome.

e. The Romans get hold of Asia Minor

In Asia Minor the Romans gained a first foothold in 133 B.C., when the Romanophil King Attalos III of Pergamum died and bequeathed his country to Rome; it became the province of Asia. Perhaps the Romans believed that they would have a walk-over in the rest of Asia Minor but then they had reckoned without Mithridates VI, king of Pontus (120-63 B.C.). He succeeded in carving out for himself a large kingdom reaching ever farther into Asia Minor where fierce hatred against the rapacious Romans made him welcome as a liberator. He claimed to be a descendant of the Persian Achaemenids as well as of the Seleucids; this meant that he combined in his person all the imperialist aspirations since the days of Sumer. This man of genius and limitless ambitions - the last exceptional statesman of this whole history - must inevitably have seen in Rome his great and dangerous competitor.

In 88 B.C. he attacked the province of Asia and gave orders for all Romans and westerners residing there to be killed - an order that was joyously executed. Even Athens now hoped to be able to free herself and Greece, but she was conquered by Sulla who had arrived with an army in 86 B.C. Mithridates was defeated, and had to surrender his fleet and his conquests. The province of Asia was restored.

In 65 B.C. Bithynia became a Roman province by testamentary disposition of her last king. It was Pompey who succeeded in liquidating the kingdom of Pontus and in combining it with the province of Bithynia. When he left for Rome in 62 B.C. the interior of Asia Minor had become a Roman apanage; sooner or later its regions were converted into Roman provinces.

f. Postlude

Does all this mean that at last Alexander the Great as King of Asia had found a worthy successor in the Roman Empire? Only partly. True enough, the Near East, together with Macedonia and Greece, had become united again under one single ruler. But this ruler was neither

Greek or Macedonian nor Asiatic; he resided far away in the west. There was to be no other independent Asiatic realm; the fate of Greece and the Near East henceforward was decided in Rome. Furthermore, the old cradle-land of imperialism, Mesopotamia, fell beyond the pale of the Roman Empire. It had fallen into the hands of the "new Persians", the Parthians. The Euphrates had now become 'the frontier of Europe"; for centuries the dualistic battle for the Middle East would rage between Rome and Parthia. However, that other dualism, that between unity and particularism which had bedevilled the history of the whole region for so long, had been resolved in favour of unity.

NOTES TO CHAPTER I

1. I described this dualism in Vol. II, Ch. III.2.
2. Diod. 20.2.2.
3. Diod. 20.20.1 and 28.1.; Marmor Parium, FrGH IIB.239.18.
4. Appian 52.
5. Diod. 18.33-36; Arrian, FrGH IIB.156F9.29.30.
6. Diod. XVIII.39.
7. Diod. XVIII.48.
8. Ath., Deipn. 4.155c., on the authority of Duris of Samos, FrGH IIA.76.12, who calls the man Polysperchon.
9. Just. 19.5.
10. Paus. 1.25.6.
11. Diod. XIX.51.
12. Diod. XX.104.
13. Diod. 20.28.
14. Paus. 9.7.3.
15. Diod. 18.39.
16. Arrian, FrGH IIB.F9.30-38.
17. Kincaid, Succ. 17/18.
18. Wilcken, Gr.Gesch. 208.
19. Diod. 19.105.4.
20. As far I know the only biography on him is by G.B. Possenti, Il re Lisimaco di Tracia (Turin, 1901). I could not consult this work. See F. Geyer s.v. 'Lysimachos', PW 27 (1928), 1-31. See also Paus. 1.9.5-10.

21. Cary, Hist.Gr.World 13.
22. Cary, Hist.Gr.World 118.
23. Destroyed 144 B.C. See Der kleine Pauly III.838.1 s.v. 'Lysimacheia'; Diod. 20.29.1.
24. Cary, Hist.Gr.World 43; Diod. 20.53.41.
25. Cary, Hist.Gr.World 36.
26. Cary, Hist.Gr.World 35.
27. Cary, Hist.Gr.World 53/54.
28. Kaerst s.v. 'Antipatros', PW X (1919), 2501-2508. As far as I know, there is no monograph on Antipater.
29. Stähelin s.v. 'Kassandros', PW X (1919), 2293-2313.
30. Diod. 18.9.1.
31. Stähelin s.v. 'Kassandros', PW X (1919).2295.
32. Lenschau s.v. 'Polyperchon', PW XXI (1952), 1798-1806.
33. Diod. XIX.105.4.
34. Diod. 20.53.3-4.
35. Cary, Hist.G.r.World 45. Fortina, Cass. 120 defends him by stating that he, for personal reasons, had no particular motive to be devoted to the Macedonian royal house. It is certainly true that Alexander has treated him badly (see Paus. 1.9.5 who relates that the king had him once locked up in a closed room together with a lion, but that he killed the beast singlehanded. Henceforward the king held him in the highest regard.) But is this possible antipathy of Cassander against the king a sufficient reason to murder a boy of twelve years old and his mother?
36. Paus. 9.7.3.
37. Cary, Hist.Gr.World 46.
38. Just. 14.4 does not excuse him saying that there can be no motive for matricide.
39. Just. 15.5-6; Plut., Demetrius 36.1-2.
40. Plut., Pyrrhus 6.2.
41. Related in some detail by Plut., Demetrius 16.3-6.
42. Just. 14.2.1-4. Diod. 21.7.1 incorrectly states that he was assassinated by Demetrius.
43. Thompson Griffith s.v. 'Demetrius', Oxf.Class.Dict. 325.
44. Cary, Hist.Gr.World 52; one might ask whether the Greek world had ever known political equilibrium.
45. Paus. 10.9.1.
46. Just. 16.2.1-3.
47. Plut., Dem. 44.2.
48. Kaerst s.v. 'Antigonos', PW I (1894). 2406-2413.

49. Cary, Hist.Gr.World 22.
50. Diod. 19.105.3-4.
51. Diod. 18.1; Arrian, FrGH IIB.151F1.5.
52. A monograph on Eumenes is A. Vezin, Eumenes of Kardia (1907); I did not see this book.
53. I. Kaerst s.v. 'Eumenes', PW VI (1909)(1083-1090), 1084.
54. Plut., Eumenes 13.1.; Diod. 18.57.3-4.
55. Diod. 18.73.
56. Plut., Eumenes 16-19; Diod. 19.39-44.
57. Thompson Griffith s.v. 'Antigonos' in Oxf.Class.Dict. 69.
58. Diod. 19.57; Appian, Syrian Wars 53.
59. As related in Vol. V, Ch. I.1.
60. Diod. XIX.105.
61. Diod. 19.105.1.
62. Diod. 20.47.5.
63. Diod. 20.53.1-2.
64. Diod. 20.53.3-4.
65. Diod. 20.113; Plut., Dem. 28-29.
66. Cary, Hist.Gr.World 42.
67. Plut., Dem. 46.2.
68. Plut., Dem. 46.4-49.5.
69. Plut., Dem. 52.
70. Vol. V, Ch. II.4b.
71. Vol. II. Ch. II.5b.
72. Described in Vol. II, Ch. II.
73. See Vol. II, Ch. IV.1.
74. See Vol. IV, Ch. III.2.3.
75. Wilcken, Gr.Gesch. 221/222.
76. Cary, Hist.Gr.World 93/94.
77. Vol. IV, Ch. II.7b.
78. Cary, Hist.Gr.World 199/200.
79. See for the origin of this dualism Vol. II, Ch. III.2.
80. Vol. V, Ch. II.4d.
81. Also called the 'Lamian War'.
82. Wilcken, Gr.Gesch. 209; Diod. 18.9-13; Paus. 1.25.3-6.
83. Tarn, Greece. CAH. VI.459.
84. Diod. 18.56.
85. Diod. 18.66.5.

86. See Vol. II, Ch. IV.2.
87. Diod. 18.67.5-6.
88. Diod. 19.61.3.
89. Diod. 19.61.1.
90. Suidas no. 431, Adler II.41.
91. Diod. 20.46.1.
92. Diod. 20.46.5.
93. Diod. 20.103.5.
94. Plut., Dem. 25.3.
95. Plut., Dem. 31.1.
96. Cary, Hist.Gr.World 44.
97. Plut., Dem. 33-40.
98. Just. 24.1-2; Pol. 2.41.11; Cary, Hist.Gr.World 126/127.
99. Scott Ferguson, Hell.Ath. 162.
100. Plut., Pyrrhus 26.2-7.
101. Plut., Pyrrhus 26.9-11.
102. Plut., Pyrrhus 30-34.
103. Cary, Hist.Gr.World 133.
104. Wilcken, Gr.Gesch. 221.
105. Plut., Aratus 46.1.
106. Just. 30.3.1.
107. Liv. 35.32.7.
108. Pol. 30-32; Liv. 31.16-17.
109. Liv. 31.14.3.
110. Livius relates this war in Books 31-33.
111. Cary, Hist.Gr.World 193.
112. Plut., Titus Flamininus 10.3-6.
113. Cary, Hist.Gr.World 196-200; Wilcken, Gr.Gesch. 226.
114. Plut., Aemilius 19.1.
115. Plut., Aemilius 18-22; Liv. 44 (part of the description missing).
116. Bradford Welles, Hell.Welt 515.

CHAPTER II

HELLENISTICA

1. The diaphragm of the world

a. On the older maps

On the oldest Greek map, that drawn by the Ionian Anaximander at some time between 600 and 550 B.C., the world, encircled by the Oceanus and grouped around the Mediterranean, was divided into two halves : the northern Europe, the southern Asia. In the second half of the sixth century B.C. Hecataeus, a Milesian, drew another map on which the circular disk of the earth was again divided into two parts, the northern Europe, the southern Asia, with the Mediterranean separating them. Thus already in these early days the Greeks became accustomed to the idea that a 'diaphragm of the world' existed, a line running from west to east with different worlds on either side. From ca. 400 B.C. rectangular maps instead of circular ones became the vogue. Yet this had little effect on the idea of bipartioning the world, while the notion that the earth is a globe [1] only became common to scholars after Aristotle who was, indeed, the first to express it.

b. Revision after Alexander's expedition

The first great geographer of the Hellenistic period was Dicaearchus, a Sicilian from Messina who lived from ca. 326 to 296 B.C. [2]. He undertook the revision of the maps made necessary by Alexander's expedition [3] and the fresh geographic insights resulting from it. It was this many-sided author who established the notion that the globe consisted of two halves, one to the north and one to the south. His diaphragm, however, took another course. Called by him 'eutheia', it began at the 'Pillars of Heracles', i.e. at the Straits of Gibraltar, ran through Sardinia, Sicily and the Peloponnese, but then branched off through Asia Minor along the Taurus and farther east to the Hindu Kush [4]. As we possess only fragments of Dicaearchus' main geographical work, we do not know how he envisioned the difference between the two halves.

The greatest geographer of this period was doubtless Eratosthenes (286-200 B.C.), born in Cyrene in North-Africa. His principal claim to fame is his fairly exact calculation of the circumference of the earth which he saw as global [5]. He too drew that dividing line from the Straits of Gibraltar through the Straits of Messina and along the southern tip of the Peloponnese and Attica, via Rhodes to the Taurus and then on to India [6]. Berger makes the remark that this meridian, running along a west-easterly line through the Mediterranean and entering Asia Minor in Cilicia, changes its direction there by turning to the north-east along the range of the Taurus and then along the mountain chains that separate Iran, Afghanistan, and India from the steppes of Central Asia [7].

This would signify that Eratosthenes assigned Asia Minor to 'Europe', and the region beyond the Taurus and the Euphrates to 'Asia', a view which soon enough would become political reality. What seems to support this idea is that this ancient geographer criticizes Aristotle for having divided mankind into Greeks and barbarians, and other scholars for having advised Alexander to treat the Greeks as friends and the barbarians as enemies. The real difference, he says, is that between those with good and those with bad qualities. And he praises Alexander for not having paid heed to this Aristotle's simple dichotomy [8].

2. Hellenism or Hellenization

a. Philosophical cosmopolitanism

Already some Sophists of the fourth century had proclaimed that all human beings are born free and equal, Alcidamas, for instance, who held that "God has created everybody equal; nature made nobody into a slave" [9]. It was, of course, in character that pure intellectuals like the Sophists gave precedence to culture over nature. Since nature was not the determining factor - once a barbarian, always a barbarian -, this made it possible, or at least conceivable that barbarians could be turned into Hellenes by means of education.

We know that Aristotle did not agree with Sophist views on equality but we also know that Alexander did not follow his master in this. The opening of the east by the Macedonian conquerors and the subsequent introduction of Alexandrian policies meant a severe blow to some cherished Greek convictions : the perfection and sovereignty of the polis, class-rule as a matter of course, and the inequality of nations as ordained by nature. Some later philosophers were to adopt a stance very different indeed from the ingrained prejudices of Hellas.

The leading mind of these scholars was Zeno, a Cypriote [10]. He probably was born about 350 B.C. [11]. The town where he came from, Kition on Cyprus, though a Greek polis, had a very mixed population. He himself had a dark complexion and a small stature; he was slightly handicapped because he had a twist to his neck. It was said that he was of Phoenician descent. Perhaps this background predisposed him to the cosmopolitan ideas of Alexander by whom he is said to have been inspired [12]. He was to become a rich merchant like his father. However, after settling in Athens as a result of a shipwreck on the coast of Attica, he gave up trading after having read part of Xenophon's memories of Socrates in an Athenian bookshop. He studied philosophy at the Academy and later became a lecturer there. He used to walk up and down a portico, or 'stoa', when teaching : hence the name of his philosophy, Stoicism. He lived to an extremely old age, probably more than ninety years, and died, we may guess with some plausibility, in 262/261 B.C. The teaching of Zeno and his school have become proverbial since we still use the term 'stoical' for someone who is not be perturbed by anything.

Stoics believe that we live in the best of worlds, in a rational cosmos in which everything is pre-ordained. The law of the universe is also the law of nature and of mankind; the only thing people can reasonably do is to conform to this law. Who does so is wholly virtuous and has no reason at all to be confused by the vicissitudes of life. He practises impassiveness, or 'ataraxia'. Enthusiasm is to be avoided just as much as despair. One of the consequences of this impassive attitude is that a Stoic remains indifferent to forms of government or the organization of society, although his sense of duty will compel him to play his role as a citizen. Probably this is the reason why Zeno never developed a political programme.

Several historical circumstances fostered Zeno's cosmopolitanism. The polis no longer was the ideal; the new towns in the east were not city-states. Then there was the appearance of a universal form of Greek speech, the 'koinè,' which made ecumenical conversation and discussion possible as well as common understanding [13]. Zeno's philosophical but not very practical or political cosmopolitanism, which also may be considered as his particular rendering of Alexandrian universalism, is contained in the summary of his 'Republic' by Plutarch. Here we find the follwoing. "All the inhabitants of this world should not live differentiated by their respective rules of justice into separate cities and communities; we should consider all men to be of one community and of one polity, and we should have a common life and an order common to us all, even as a herd that feeds together and shares the pasturage of a common field".

Plutarch adds that "it was Alexander who gave effect to this idea" of cosmopolitanism. The king, however, did not know Zeno since he was dead before the philosopher began to teach. We may well ask whether Zeno, had he been the king's adviser, would have been of much use to him. For, to quote Plutarch once again, his ideal was no more than a dream, or 'a shadowy picture of a well-ordered and philosophic commonwealth' [14]. Anyhow, it will be evident that Zeno's dream was a refutation of the polis ideal as well of Plato's class-ridden, hierarchical, and elitist society in his 'Republic' [15]. Ferguson at this point argues that "the political theory of the Greeks leaped at one bound from the reality of the polis to the vision of 'the universe of men', the oecumene ... It was, however, a leap of the imagination alone". For, as this scholar remarks, this leap was made "without deigning to set foot in passing on the territorial monarchy and the federation" [16]. Instead of Alexander's universal empire, these forms of government did become the reality of the day.

b. The Alexandrian conquests and the dualism of Europe and Asia.

In my Volume II I wrote about 'Europe and Asia contrasted' and about 'the earliest phase of east-west dualism' [17]. Greek historiography of the classical period tended to equate 'Europe' and 'Hellas'; I remarked there that the extension of the notion 'Europe' to the whole continent is possibly an after-effect of the Persian Wars. In Greek public opinion Greece and Asia, or rather, perhaps, Hellas and the Persian Empire, were so entirely different and so strongly contrasted that we may speak here of a dualistic opposition.

The final result of the Alexandrian conquest was that the whole of Asia Minor, up to the Euphrates, now fell within the Hellenic ambit. This 'annexation' of Asia Minor to Europe was first of all a military and political event. At the moment that Alexander died the Persians and other orientals had become subjects of the new Macedonian Empire. But culturally and mentally they still were just as different from Greeks as they had always been. The question was whether or not the new rulers would try to erase the differences and to bring about an organic unity of nations and civilizations, if, indeed, they really intended to inaugurate such a policy of amalgamation.

c. What is Hellenism?

The Dutch scholar Allard Pierson [18] opens his study of Hellenism with the remark that it is unnecessary to date this phenomenon from the days of Alexander the Great. He defines Hellenism as a civilization in which Hellenic and non-Hellenic are blended to such a degree that they henceforward may be considered one single civilization. We shall have to see whether this really was the case, and if so, whether it happened in all regions of the entire empire.

Pierson goes on to state that from the earliest times Greek culture spread far beyond the confines of Hellas proper. "To hellenize barbarians is as old as Hellas herself." Greeks and barbarians have always influenced one another. But the civilization we refer to as 'Hellenism' is the first of which we know how far its influence went. Whereas we can only guess whether and in what way Graeco-barbarian cultural relationships before Alexander took shape, the concrete forms of Hellenistic culture are on the contrary well known [19].

Before we proceed it must not escape our attention that Pierson, when introducing his notion of Hellenism to us, probably unwittingly lets slip in another word, viz. 'hellenizing'. He spoke of 'hellenizing the barbarians'. 'Hellenization' could also be a meaning of Hellenism. If the idea of Hellenization - 'hellenizein', making Hellenic, really is a Greek word -, was to make sense, the notion that the inhabitants of Asia Minor were barbarians, had to be abolished. In practice this would mean that there would be no question of fusion but of one culture, the Hellenic (considered superior) superseding the others, the oriental ones (considered inferior), and this would be a dualistic process. And if Hellenization were to be adopted as the official policy, it would very probably result in a new dualistic contrast, viz. between those who had become hellenized and those who were not.

3. Alexander's declaration of intent

Our first great question is whether Alexander the Great wanted to 'hellenize' the inhabitants of the former Persian Empire. Did the idea of 'Hellenism' originate with him [20]? Very probably not [21]. The problem, of course, is that the new King of Asia himself never published a 'programme' for his future imperial policy; he never said in as many words that his aim was to fuse the Hellenic and the 'barbarian' civilizations [22]. We shall have to remain content with what Arrian said, viz. that he was unable to "determine with certainty what sort of plans Alexander had in his mind" [23].

However, as the ruler of an enormous empire with very different ethnic groups ranging from Greeks to Indians, the king doubtless wished to base his realm on a common sense of unity which would imply some measures conducive to uniformity and conformity. That he really had these in his mind is proved by a prayer he uttered at a banquet given at Opis on the Tigris in the summer of 324 B.C. His guests were his own Macedonians, and then Persians, Greeks, and non-Persian orientals, in that order of precedence. Greek soothsayers and Persian magi initiated the ceremony, and then gathered around the king all drank and poured libations from the same bowl. In his prayer Alexander expressed the wish that "Macedonians and Persians should enjoy harmony as partners in the same government" [24].

The first conlusion from this episode is that in Alexander's view the unity of his empire should rest on the good partnership of the two leading nations, Macedonians and Persians. The fact that he told all those present, Greeks and non-Persian orientals too, to drink from the same cup signifies that he saw all the nations of his realm as co-equals. Finally, this banquet was also a religious occasion as is proved by the initiation by priests, by the king's prayer - although it is not said to which gods! - and by the blessings invoked and the libations. I believe - that Alexander desired to base the political unity of his realm on a religious foundation with an ecumenical character (he obviously put Greek soothsayers and Persian magi on a par). It, therefore, is not without reason that Lauffer dubs this prayer Alexander's political testament [25].

4. Alexander's ecumenical policies

a. Alexander's monetary policy

What the intentions of Alexander were becomes evident by his acts. First of all, he tried to turn his empire into one great economic unity, a kind of 'free trade-zone'. One of the most important elements of this economic policy was that he gave his domains a uniform monetary system. According to Beloch the monetary situation of the Persian Empire had been chaotic. Whereas the issuance of gold coins had been the monopoly of the emperor, every satrapy and city possessed and made use of the right to mint its own silver coins. Alexander made the emission of any sort of coin a royal monopoly, and replaced the Persian coinage by the unitary Alexander-coin; this new monetary system was so successful in Asia as well as in Macedonia that two centuries later the Romans adopted it [26].

b. Alexander's marriage policy

A still more important element of unity was Alexander's marriage policy. Perhaps the idea of a fusion of civilizations was too abstract a notion for him - if it was in his mind at all -, but bringing the nations nearer to each other by making them intermarry seemed a far more down-to-earth and efficient measure. Alexander himself gave the example by marrying the Bactrian princess Roxane. According to Arrian, the king fell in love with this renowned beauty in the spring of 327 B.C [27], but Plutarch says it was during a banquet, where she, like Salome, took part in a dance [28].

Classical scholars are obviously more romantic than modern ones since they unanimously agree that the marriage was a love affair, whereas present-day scholars squabble over the question whether the erotic or the political element was more important [29]. However this may be, there surely was a political side to this love marriage [30]. This is proved by the fact that he married Roxane instead of making her into a concubine. By marrying her he raised her to the position of a queen and that of the mother-to-be of the successor. This successor, therefore, would be a European-Asiatic half-breed. Attention should be paid to the fact that Alexander's wife was not a Persian but a Bactrian, that is, a non-Persian oriental. This means that he did not consider the Persian nation, the hitherto leading one in that area, unconditionally privileged. To justify his marrying her Alexander declared that he intended to stabilize his realm by making Macedonians and Persians intermarry; only thus the vanquished could be freed from their sentiment of shame and the victors of their pride. During the marriage ceremony he had a loaf of bread brought to him which he cut into two with his sword; he and his spouse ate from it. This act symbolized their union [31].

This incipient policy of intermarriage was further intensified by the massive ceremony held at Susa in 324 B.C. The occasion was the solemn conclusion of the Persian campaign; the war was over now, henceforward peace would reign. The fusion of Macedonians and Persians was cemented first of all by a second marriage of Alexander, this time with Statira, a daughter of the deceased emperor Darius III [32]. It is evident that by marrying a member of the Achaemenid House the new emperor wanted to strengthen his claim to the throne of Asia. At the same occasion he also married a third woman, Parysatis, the younger daughter of the Persian emperor Artaxerxes III Ochos, a predecessor of Darius III [33]. She too had been made captive after the battle of Issus; there resulted no offspring from her alliance with Alexander [34].

He did not restrict himself to his own person, for he made about eighty of his nearest collaborators and generals marry oriental women. His bosom-friend Hephaestion married Drypetis, another daughter of Darius III; in this way the king and his friend became brothers-in-law. The famous general Craterus wedded Amastrine (or Amastris), a niece of the last Persian emperor [35]; so this general too became related to the royal family. Others, like Perdiccas and Eumenes, were given in wedlock to daughters of Persian satraps, while Seleucus married a daughter of Spitamenes, a Bactrian, one of the most stubborn opponents of Alexander.

The wedding solemnities lasted five days and were celebrated in the Persian style. Alexander told those of his Macedonian soldiers who had oriental concubines - there were about ten thousand of them - to marry these women and to have these marriages officially registered. Acting as a marriage-broker on a grand scale, the king gave all of them a wedding gift [36]. Alexander of course wanted to bind some of his nobles closer to his person by making them his relatives. But there is more to it. His overriding aim was to melt Macedonians and Persians together, in high society as well as on the level of the common soldiers. It was a grandiose attempt to abolish the time-honoured dualism of Hellas and Persia, of Europe and Asia.

c. The Greek idea of the pure

Did generals and soldiers wholeheartedly follow their king in his marriage-policy? Were they as eager as he was to triumph over this dualism? Diodorus says that he 'persuaded' [37] his nobles to take oriental wives; very probably they obeyed without much enthusiasm. Apart from the fact that many bridegrooms, like Perdiccas, soon enough fell in battle, and that Hephaestion died in October 324 B.C. of an illness, most of them seem to have repudiated their oriental spouses shortly after Alexander's death. For instance, not long after the decease of the king, Craterus married Phila, the eldest daughter of Antipater, an alliance that, politically, was far more profitable to him than that with Amastris; in 322 B.C. Amastris divorced him [38]. The only one of these marriages to last was that of Seleucus I and Apame, Spitamenes' daughter; she became the mother of Antiochus I and the ancestress of the Seleucid dynasty [39]. We may well ask how many of the Macedonian soldiers took their foreign wives with them on repatriating.

As far as I know, none of the Diadochs of Alexander pursued his deliberate policy of intermarriage. Of course, the Greek colonists who swarmed out over the east in the decades that followed Alexander's death often took orientals to wife and had a mixed offspring from them. However, we must state with Walbank that "Alexander's notion of a Greco-Persian ruling class never took hold. From the outset the newcomers formed the governing minority in the areas where they settled" [40]. The old idea of 'the pure' was too deeply ingrained for the Hellenes to shed it easily once they lived amidst a 'barbarian' population. To Strabo, for example, even the Hellenic element in Alexandria seemed questionable since it "was not distinctly inclined to civil ('politikon') life and adherence to the customs of the polis", that is, to the most essential characteristics of being Greek. But, Strabo adds, these Alexandrians were 'a mixed people', which obviously explained their political backwardness [41]. Greeks did not accept barbarians as their equals as long as they were not thoroughly hellenized [42].

d. A mixed army

Another instrument of fusion was the admission of oriental elements into the Macedonian army, even in large numbers. Already the army with which Alexander invaded Asia was not purely Macedonian in its composition; he took with him Thracian cavalry and detachments recruited among Balkan tribes, Greek mercenaries, and, finally, the contingents put at his disposal by the members of the Corinthian League [43]. No sooner had the army set foot on Asian soil when the recruitment of indigenous soldiers began, although for a long time these were merely used in a subordinate position as auxiliaries.

During the extremely long and hard campaign there was of course an enormous wastage of military manpower. Recruits from the home country were regularly sent on, but the Macedonian reservoir was not inexhaustible. When the army arrived in the difficult terrain of Afghanistan, the practical need of specialized forces, in particular of cavalry and mountain-troops arose. From then on, Persian and Iranian troops were recruited. Later, the recruitment was extended to the infantry too; for instance, many Bactrians were enrolled. The ancient authors say that the eastern satraps brought the king thirty-thousand boys, all of the same age and 'comely in their looks'; Alexander had them dressed in Macedonian uniforms and trained in the Macedonian way. Indigenous soldiers were either incorporated into Macedonian regiments or drawn up in formations of their own [44].

e. The veterans' reaction

Since Alexander had succeeded Darius III as King of Asia he desired to have a really imperial army at his disposal. It was not only, not even in the first place, for practical reasons that he accepted large Asiatic contingents into his forces. He wanted to cement the unity of his realm by making all its nations responsible for its defense. For the time being he was prudent enough to restrict himself to Persians and Iranians, members of the hitherto ruling nations which he wished to gratify; Semitics and Egyptians were not enrolled as yet.

But notwithstanding this prudence he profoundly irritated his Macedonian veterans. Many of them showed themselves discontented because he dressed and behaved in the Persian way [45], just as they found his pretension that he was of divine origin ridiculous [46]. This tension between the veterans and their commander-in-chief became aggravated by the insertion of indigenous elements into the army. They did not relish the idea of having to fight side by side with 'barbarians'. In 324 B.C., at Opis, they even called on the king to discharge them; they had got it into their heads that their king now no longer needed them and henceforward would only rely on Asiatic troops. The army was on the verge of mutiny; Alexander had the greatest difficulty in quelling the incipient revolt [47]. Whatever plans the king himself may have had, the Macedonians could not get over their ingrained Hellenic habit of considering all Asiatics equally barbaric. In other words, they stuck to the old dualism of Europe and Asia.

f. Alexandrian and Diadoch city foundations

It had been an old habit of the Greeks to found colonies - the word is not used here in the modern sense but means 'Greek cities outside Hellas proper'. In the archaic and classical periods we find them abundantly on the shores of the Black Sea, the Aegean, and the Mediterranean. Nearly always the colonists clung to the sea that connected them with the motherland; they remained purely Greek in everything. The population of the hinterland with whom they traded were in their eyes barbarians; they did not mix with them. All these colonies were 'daughters' of individual mother-poleis way back in Hellas.

Alexander and his Diadochs founded hundreds of towns on the territory of the former Persian Empire, far beyond the confines of the original Greek colonization. Those most remote from Hellas were to be found in Afghanistan and in the southern Soviet-republics, the most famous of them being Alexandria in Egypt; in all twenty new cities bore the name 'Alexandreia'.

The situation of these new colonies was entirely different from that of the older ones. Nearly all of them lay far inland and, for that reason, had no maritime connection with the motherland that often was hundreds of miles away. Furthermore, they were founded directly by the king and his successors and had, therefore, no special link with any Hellenic city. Some of the new towns began their existence as military colonies with a Macedonian garrison where sick and disabled soldiers could be left behind. Others were peopled with Greeks from the motherland. Another difference with the older colonies was that the new ones were not, like the poleis in Hellas, sovereign states; although often enjoying autonomy, the Hellenistic cities formed part of a kingdom and were not independent [48].

In spite of all this, the cities founded by Alexander and his successors remained in existence; not a few of them even flourished. We may assume that Jouguet is correct in saying that they had a distinct Hellenic colouring [49]. True enough, they were far apart, and their potential was in all probability not strong enough to bring about either the

Hellenization of the entire Orient or the fusion of nations and civilizations - whichever may have been their aim. Still, they will have contributed, at least to a certain extent, to the realization of that ideal of the post-classical authors, namely that of hellenizing the barbarians.

5. What happened to Alexander's plans after his death

a. Transfer of populations

Diodorus relates that immediately after the king's death Perdiccas read his 'hypomnemata' or 'last plans' to the troops [50]. One of these plans was the foundation of cities and the transfer of populations from Asia to Europe and from Europe to Asia "in order to bring the largest contingents to common unity and to friendly kinship by means of intermarriage and family ties". But together with all other projects that were presented to them, the army assembly found this plan too "extravagant and impracticable and decided to carry out none of those that had been mentioned" [51]. Once again the disgruntled veterans put themselves in the way of their king's lofty plans. A massive transfer of 'barbarians' to Hellas? That never [52]!

What, however, really took place was some transfer of Hellenes to Asia, that is to the newly founded cities. Did these cities function as centres of radiation of Hellenic culture? Plutarch proudly states that Alexander "sowed all Asia with Grecian magistracies, and thus overcame its uncivilized and brutish manner ... By the founding of cities in these places savagery was extinguished and the worst elements, gaining familiarity with the better, changed under its influence" [53]. Is it possible to imagine a more telling dualistic text?

But the reverse is also true. The orientals in their turn influenced the immigrants so that there was some measure of reciprocity. Many of the new towns took in a fair proportion of Asiatics; otherwise they would have remained exiguously small. The most remote Alexander-town, Alexandria Eschatê, in southern Russia, received a mixed population of Greek mercenaries and local tribesmen, together with a number of disabled Macedonians [54]. In the Caucasus foothills the king founded cities where he settled three thousand campfollowers, seven thousand natives, and a number of volunteers from among the mercenaries [55]. Other colonists were prisoners of war who were given their freedom on condition that they were willing to settle in the towns.

Whereas the Macedonian veterans and discharged soldiers seem to have made the best of it, the Greek mercenaries in the cities of the eastern satrapies remained restless. Diodorus says that "they longed for the Greek customs and manner of life (but) were cast away in the most distant part of the kingdom". They therefore rose in revolt as soon as the king was dead [56]. One of them, a certain Athenodorus, proclaimed himself king but, says Diodorus, with no other aim than to conduct his men home. Although he was killed by a rival, the mercenaries abandoned their cities and marched back to Hellas [57].

b. The 'koinê' language

So the prospects for Alexander's universalism were none too bright. Greeks and Macedonians loathed the barbarians just as much as ever before, while his hard-boiled successors were interested in nothing but power. His only support came from some woolly-headed and impractical philosophers. But perhaps there were still other instruments of policy to bring about the desired uniformity, for instance language, a 'lingua franca', or religion, in the form of a syncretistic religion. Let us see.

Those of us who had Greek in grammar school know that it is impossible to speak of the one Hellenic language. The authors we read expressed themselves in their several dialects, like Herodotus who wrote in Ionic, or Thucydides who used the Attic variant. When studying the great epics we had to memorize special Homeric words and turns of speech that we could look up in our 'Homer glossary'. The Homeric language seems to be a mixture, probably artificial, of Aeolic and Ionic [58]. How the Greeks stuck to their dialects is shown by the fact the official documents of every polis even of the great classical period were phrased in the local dialect; scholars explain this as the expression of the proud selfconsciousness of even the smaller towns [59].

But already in the fifth century B.C. the road to a common Hellenic language was taken. The first serious candidate for such a tongue was the Ionic dialect, that of Herodotus and Hippocrates. For the Asiatics the Ionians were the Greeks tout court, called Yauna in Persian, Yawana in Indian, Javan in Hebrew; the remark has been made that several Asiatic words are still known to us in their Ionian form, like 'Persian, Median, or Indian' [60]. Such Ionian pretensions were frustrated by the rise of Athens that, in the fifth century B.C., became the cultural capital of the Hellenic world; subsequently the Attic dialect superseded the Ionian one as having the best claim for becoming a common Hellenic tongue.

Attic we mainly know as a literary language, written by the tragedians, by Plato, and other famous authors; in its written form it spread over the whole Greek world. Therefore, the orator Isocrates could proclaim Athens about 354 B.C. as 'a school for the education of able orators and teachers of oratory'. It is supposed, he says, "and not without reason, that all clever speakers are the disciples of Athens" [61]. Attic, perhaps, came nearest to becoming 'standard Greek', just as there also exists a 'standard Dutch' [62].

This Attic, however, was, as a literary language, not without a strong touch of artificiality, perfectly suited to become the common speech of scholars all over the Hellenistic world but far less capable of developing into a general vulgar speech. Only the latter could become the linguistic and mental instrument for uniting all the inhabitants of the wide Hellenistic orbit; only so it would serve as a weapon to break down the dualism of east and west. But the triumph of the Attic dialect really was the expression of an ideology that is called 'Atticism' and that is dubbed 'conservative-classicistic' by Jüthner, as opposed to 'internal-cosmopolitan Hellenism' [63]. The term 'Atticism' is normally used for the imitation of the stylistic example presented by the classical authors of Athens. Its élitist connotation lives on in our expression 'Attic salt' for witticism.

Protests arose against this pretended superiority of literary Attic. The comic author Posidippus, a Macedonian or Thessalian who published in the first decades of the third century B.C., states that the Athenians spoke or wrote Attic whereas the Hellenes spoke 'Hellenic' [64]. This means that he opposed some (hypothetical?) Greek speech against what he considered the purely local, Attic dialect. A later scholar, Heraclides, in the beginning of the second century B.C. and very probably also a Thessalian, by quoting this text of Posidippus, protested against the tendency of equating Athens with Greece. 'Hellenizein', he declared, did not mean 'speaking correctly' but 'speaking Greek', thus turning himself against Attic pretensions [65]. In this way, by assuming such an élitist character, Attic disqualified itself from becoming the common tongue of the Hellenic ecumene.

In the two texts I mentioned we have a twofold suggestion that, in opposition to Attic, there existed something like a common Hellenic speech in comparison to which Attic only was a dialect. Somewhat paradoxically we may locate the beginnings of a possible ecumenical language in that selfsame city of Athens. An unknown author of about 430 B.C., writing on the Constitution of Athens and, ironically enough, reputed for his bad Attic, says that all Greeks are distinguished by their own dialect, way of life, and type of dress, but that the Athenians are a mixture of both Greeks and non-Greeks [66]. It certainly is a remarkable thing that non-Greek, i.e. barbarian, elements were willingly received. However, how a vulgar tongue replacing the established dialects developed in the Greek world is not very well known. Anyhow, on the brink of the Greek conquest of Asia, the idea of a common Hellenic language, whether in a literary or in a more popular shape, was about to be realized. Alexander's expedition exported this idea eastward and southward.

Such a common Greek tongue we call 'koinê' ('koinos' signifies 'common'). The linguistic fundament of the speech that was introduced into Asia was literary Attic. The Macedonian court and the royal chancellery thrived on Athenian culture. King Archelaus (ca. 413-399) was a 'Philhellen' and brought Euripides to his court. King Philip II's chancellery used the Attic linguistic forms. Alexander's mentor Aristotle very probably spoke Attic. The king himself might have said "I am an Athenian more pertinently than President Kennedy who said "Ich bin ein Berliner" - not that he had visited the city but he was imbued with its culture. The conclusion of Hoffmann and Debrunner is : "The language that Alexander exported to the east and used as the imperial speech was Attic" [67].

But this imperial Attic was too sophisticated a language to serve the needs of every life. It was the developing koinè that was more fit to play this role. The climactic question in the context of this work is whether this koinè-Greek would succeed in piercing the dualistic barrier between Europe and Asia. Such would only be the case if all the inhabitants of the new Hellenistic kingdoms were to adopt koinè as their vernacular.

Wilamowitz modifies the notion of koinè-Greek somewhat by stating that we may dub it thus if we want so but that he would prefer the term 'Hellenistic' to mark off this whole period from previous ones. In his opinion the word 'koinè' often is connected with a value judgment with the result that it is seen as a debased form of Attic. True enough, says this great scholar, the Attic of the classical authors underwent some changes; he even writes that those who speak of 'decay' are not wholly wrong. Hellenistic Greek adopted elements from this later Attic but also from tongues spoken in Asia Minor so that it slowly but certainly became a real 'koinè'; through it the old opposition between the language of the educated and the uneducated speech was conquered [68].

But koinè's triumph never became complete. First of all, there were those who nostalgically looked back to the days that the purest Attic was spoken and who heartily loathed that plebeian Hellenistic. In the second century B.C. a reaction developed against what was called 'Asianic', a term denoting a certain florid rhetorical. It flourished in the Greek cities along the Aegean littoral of Asia Minor; for this reason it was called 'Asianic', which means un-Hellenic! These opponents of 'Asianism' are called 'Atticists' since they were admirers and imitators of Attic rhetoric.

It is really curious that those persons among whom Cicero became a leading figure later were not Greeks at all but Romans [69]. When we hear that the rhetor Caecilius Calactinus, an authentic Greek this time, wrote a treatise 'against the Phrygians' (by whom the Asiatic Greeks are meant) [70], we know that the time-honoured dualistic opposition between Greece and Asia had not yet disappeared and now enveloped even those Hellenes who had adapted themselves somewhat to Asian ways. The name 'Phrygians' was all the more insulting since the Greeks saw the Phrygians, like the Thracians, as a very barbaric people. It will be clear that such a campaign damaged the chances of koinê becoming the ecumenic language of the Greek world.

Did the Hellenistic language, or koinê, which was a new form of Greek, replace the national idioms, like Babylonian, Egyptian, Iranian, or Hebrew, and did it relegate them to the position of unimportant dialects? This, of course, did not happen. The position of the Asiatic languages, many of them far, far older than Greek, was too strong. We may compare the situation of koinê-Greek in Asia to that of English in British-India (and even to that of English in the Indian Union of to-day) : it was and is used as an official language and as that of the civilized. In the same way the Hellenized top-layer spoke and wrote Greek. With this language one could make oneself understood everywhere from southern Egypt to the valley of the Indus and from the Caucasus Mountains to the frontiers of Arabia. In so far it really was a binding element of great importance. But at the same time there remained countless others who at best had a few words of Greek and often none at all.

True enough, we possess a great many texts in Greek written by non-Greeks; many Romans spoke and wrote Greek, and a great number of scholars preferred this language for their works to their vernacular. The native language of the apostle Paul who so proudly calls himself a Hebrew from the tribe of Benjamin and a child of Abraham [71] was Greek; he wrote his letters in koinê. But the Greek of non-Greeks was very different in quality. Whereas some of them wrote it very purely, the best-known example of it, the Greek translation of the Old Testament by the Seventy, the Septuagint, is characterized by Wilamowitz as 'stammering translators' work'[72]. Even the official documents of the cities, he says, though written in Greek, nearly always wear 'a local garb'[73]. Koinè, therefore, shows a slow gradient, beginning at pure Greek and ending in a bastard mixture of Greek and Asiatic. This too weakened its claim of becoming the language of the ecumene.

Far too few Greeks emigrated to the east to transfuse this whole world with Greek culture and language. In the far east of the Macedonian empire, in the limitless area between the Tigris and the Indus, the influence of the Hellenes always remained exceedingly small. The oriental nations as such did not prove interested in Greek culture. Very few traces of Hellenic civilization are to be found there. In Syria and Egypt Greek was spoken in the cities by cultured circles; in Egypt it was the official language of the state. But the agricultural population, the great mass that is, continued to speak Egyptian or Aramaic. Jesus, when addressing his Jewish audiences, spoke Aramaic; to all intents and purposes he did not know Greek.

Asia Minor became the most hellenized country by far. There the Greek towns, old and new, were very numerous. The proof of this successful Hellenization is that many indigenous tongues totally disappeared. The non-Greek Paul wrote to the equally non-Greek Galatians in koinè; there are no translations of the Bible into any language of Asia Minor[74].

Summarizing we can state that the regions beyond the Euphrates, Syria, Palestine, and Egypt remained what they were : fundamentally non-Greek countries. This means that in the larger part of the Macedonian Empire the influence of the Greek language varied from not unimportant to minimal. We shall study this subject in some more detail in the following sections. However, the Greek linguistic area became extended to the Euphrates and now involved most of Asia Minor (which did not signify that Greek now became everybody's vernacular). Our overall conclusion must be that the Greek language, even in its adapted and simplified Hellenistic form, did not succeed in becoming the instrument of unity that should have triumphed over the dualism of Europe and Asia, in particular with regard to the regions beyond the Euphrates.

c. A syncretistic religion

There is still another aspect of the question to be discussed. Religion too could be turned into an instrument of unification, with an even greater impact than language or politics. Did there originate in the Hellenistic world something like a common, a syncretistic religion? We do not know what was in Alexander's mind in this respect, but it is an extremely important fact that he considered himself divine. All his life he honoured the gods of Hellas and sacrificed to them. It had been a very fundamental tenet of Greek religion that human beings could never become divine; gods and men always were two totally different categories. But during the fourth century things had begun to change somewhat. Kings might become divinized after their death, as heroes had been divinized long before, and later even when still living. There is no doubt that Alexander, as Wilamowitz says, felt that he was more than human, and that he had an exceptional, a superhuman mission. Was not his ancestor Heracles who also performed unbelievable deeds a son of Zeus? And did he not become a god after his death [75]?

When in Egypt Alexander paid a visit to the oracle of Ammon in the Siwah oasis. In itself there was nothing strange in this since the Greeks saw this oracle as the equivalent of that of Delphi. But the fact that the king undertook the laborious expedition through the desert to this temple proves that he expected something special. He was greeted there as the 'son of Ammon' which again is a natural thing since all Egyptian Pharaohs were sons of the sun god; being a son of Ammon must have seemed to Alexander equivalent to being a son of Zeus. He went inside alone to put questions to the oracle; he did not disclose what he had heard but said that he was pleased with it [76]. In my opinion this event strengthened his already strong conviction that he was no common mortal.

That Alexander's own religion was quickly becoming syncretistic is shown by the fact that he brought a sacrifice to the sacred Apis bull [77]. It has, of course, been brought forward that he did so as Pharaoh of Egypt. But this is by no means self-evident, for we know that the

Persian king Cambyses who also was Pharaoh not only refused to sacrifice but, horrified at the thought that he should pay divine honour to an animal, killed it. After this Alexander gave the Greek side its due by organizing games at Memphis which also were religious occasions [78].

For several years Alexander observed silence on this issue. When the army was campaigning in Bactria, Callisthenes, a Greek philosopher and a relative of Aristoteles, who accompanied the expedition, began to make propaganda for the idea that the king was of divine origin; perhaps Alexander secretly prompted him in. The philosopher wrote an embellished account of the king's visit to the Ammon temple adding 'sensational details', as Strabo disapprovingly wrote [79]. But the king himself was pleased with what he wrote; it found its way into Greek historiography [80].

If Callisthenes really was trying to pave the way for a general acceptance of Alexander's divine character, then with the Macedonian generals his message fell on deaf ears. Relations between the king and his veterans had become increasingly strained, what with the king wearing Persian dress and adopting Persian court ceremonial. When he wanted to introduce the 'proskynêsis', things came to a head. The prostration with which the Achaemenid emperors had always been honoured did not mean that the ruler was a god since Persian emperors were not considered divine. But Greeks and Macedonians suspected that their king positively felt that he was a god. When, during a banquet, they were invited to go down on their bellies, there was laughter and mockery, and many downright refused to do so [81]. Henceforward Alexander no longer required this ceremony from the Macedonians [82]. This incident proves that the Greeks clung to their old religious tenets with regard to the divinity of human beings. Perhaps they would not have objected to his being divinized after his death, but consorting daily with a more than human being was too much for them.

Was Alexander sincere when he pretended to be more than human and of divine origin, even divine himself? It is very often stated by modern historians that his aim was political : having become Pharaoh and Great King of Asia he was forced, in order to be credible in the eyes of his oriental subjects, to present himself in this guise. But, with Kern, I believe that "we inflict a bitter injustice on Alexander when we deduce his veneration of oriental godheads" - like Marduk, Astarte, and Ammon - "only from practical, political reasons". His ideal must have been 'a religion above religions' [83].

However, his very first attempts at establishing this religion already proved him being at loggerheads with his national background. Generals and soldiers were quite willing to serve their king as long as he restricted himself to his military purpose; they also readily accepted the destruction of the Persian Empire and the foundation of a Graeco-Macedonian one. But when it came to Alexander's fundamental aims that were not military nor even political in the usual sense of the word, they disagreed with him in every respect. They rejected the transmigration of populations, the fusion of the Greek, Macedonian, and oriental nations, his plans to put these nations on an equal footing (which would imply the abolishment of the notion of 'barbarian'), his favouring of Persian and other oriental nobles, his marriage policy, and perhaps most of all, his idea of making the former Persian Empire into a new universe with a godlike ruler at its apex.

This disgruntlement foreboded ill for the future of Hellenism. For what would it come to mean? Would it become an amalgama of the Hellenic, Macedonian, Egyptian, Persian, and oriental civilizations? Or would it only become the repetition of an old pattern, that of the superior Hellene and inferior 'barbarian'? In other words, would Hellenism be no more than 'Hellenization', an attempt to spread a veneer of Greek culture over Egypt and the east? Whatever success this attempt might have, in the last resort it would be based not on the superiority of Greek civilization but on that of the Macedonian arms.

However, the idea of a syncretistic religion was not so impossible as it may seem at first sight. A number of divinities from Asia Minor had already found a niche of their own in the Hellenic pantheon; I need only mention Dionysos [84] and Adonis. As Ferguson explains, there were two possibilities for the development of Hellenistic syncretism. The first was to rationalize theology so that the idea of the godhead became more abstract; in this way divinities that originally were individual beings might be combined. A practical consequence of this was that it also made possible the fusion of temples, rituals, and priesthoods. The second possibility - the more general tendency and the more crude kind of syncretism, says Ferguson - was that of giving Greek names to foreign gods as if they were all identical. The next and logical step then was to raise one of the gods to the position of universal and all-embracing supreme power. Thus we find the combination of the Greek Zeus, the Egyptian Ammon, the Hebrew Yahve, the Iranian Ahuramazda, and later, the Roman Juppiter, into one single Highest God, usually called 'Zeus' in the Greek 'lingua franca'. At a lower level, rituals and cults were exchanged, exported and imported freely [85].

More often than not, the inhabitants of the empire took easily to this second kind of syncretism. Jonas writes that its first appearance dates from centuries before Alexander; he cites the example of the Samaritans who were transplanted by the Assyrian rulers to the northern kingdom of Israel : "They venerated the Lord (Yahve) and at the same time served their carved statues. And their children and grandchildren do so to the present day like their fathers did" [86]. And he continues to say that "this religious syncretism would become the decisive characteristic of Hellenism but then on a world-embracing scale" [87]. How great the success of this syncretism would be and whether it would really triumph over the older religions would depend largely on the resilience of the national creeds. That there would be resistance will already appear from the circumstance that the whole thing had an unmistakably Hellenic flavour. Think only of the name of the new supreme godhead, Zeus.

6. The impact of Hellenism

It is time now to examine in some detail how great the impact of Hellenism was on the several non-Hellenic nations of the east and on Egypt. In the context of this work the main question will be whether the divergence of East and West, the discrepancies, the misunderstandings, in short the dualism of Europe and Asia, would be overcome and make place for a universal civilization. I have already stated that under the Seleucids and under the Romans the Euphrates became the 'frontier of Europe'. Let us, therefore, study first of all the fate of Hellenism in the vast regions beyond that river.

7. The Indo-Greeks

a. The Indian satrapy

The Far East of the Macedonian Empire was the Indian satrapy, along and beyond the Indus. Here, in the Punjab and in Sind, Alexander mainly relied on Indian princes whom he had made into his allies. This formed part of his design to associate Indians, along with Greeks and Macedonians in the government of the empire. Of course, Greek and Macedonian garrisons were stationed in the regions where Greek cities were founded.

Alexander seems to have intended to turn the Indus valley into 'a Hellenistic centre' [88], but nothing came of it. First of all, the rivalry between the Macedonians and the Greek mercenaries proved insuperable; they exported their old dualistic antagonism to regions where cooperation was a vital necessity. Immediately after the departure of Alexander, the Indians became active, fighting the westerners with guerilla tactics. Already in 316 B.C. the Macedonians evacuated the Punjab and retired to the western shore of the Indus. In Sind, on the lower Indus (now Pakistan), where several Greek cities had been founded, one after the other succumbed to Indian pressure. "We hear nothing more of them" [89]. A number of Hellenic colonies east of the Indus, however, were not obliterated, although they soon came under the sway of Indian princes.

When in 312 B.C. Seleucus I took hold of Babylon, he considered himself the lawful ruler of all the satrapies east of the Euphrates, even of those east of the Indus. In 306 he marched eastward with his army, crossed the Indus, and then saw his path blocked by the forces of the Mauryan emperor Chandragupta; this Indian prince is said to have had nine thousand war elephants at his disposal. We know very little of this campaign [90]; whether there was a battle or not remains uncertain. But finally there was a treaty by which Seleucus ceded the satrapies east of the Indus to the Mauryans [91].

This did not yet mean the end of the Greek presence in India since the Greek colonies in Gandhara and in Taxila remained in existence; they were even favoured by the Emperor Açoka who showed a predilection for 'Yavanas'. This presence would be of importance to our theme only if the influence of the Indo-Greeks on Indian thought and culture had been so great that India perhaps would have been hellenized. But this was not the case. During Açoka's reign some Greeks became Buddhists, but Woodcock thinks it is "hard to estimate ... how much influence Greek thought ... may have had on the development of Buddhism" [92]. Probably very little. Perhaps the Greeks had some more influence on Indian art and architecture [93]. But on the whole the Greek presence caused no more than a slight ripple on the surface of the ocean of Indian history.

One reason for this ineffectiveness doubtless is that the Indo-Greeks only were a small minority in the vast mass of Indian nations. But there also is a clearly dualistic factor that plays its part. The Brahmans were inexorable opponents of everybody and everything that was 'Yavana". Ancient authors relate that 'a city of the Brahmans' was desperately defended by them; they fought with poisoned arrows one of which nearly killed Ptolemy, the future king of Egypt. When the town was stormed by the Macedonians, a number of Brahmans put their houses on fire and perished in the flames; most others died fighting, and only a few were captured [94].

Tarn believes that those Brahmans loathed the Greeks "not of course on religious but on patriotic grounds" [95]. Why 'of course not on religious grounds'? There was no 'Indian fatherland' at that time. The Brahmans who were the leading element in the Hindu religion were no shining models of religious tolerance; they must have seen in the Greeks a people with a very inferior religion. What also played a role was not patriotism but class consciousness. The Hindu population was divided into four varnas or 'colours' [96]. The highest and most important varna was that of the Brahmans who looked down on the three others. Lower down came the Kshatriyas, the varna of the warriors. In the eyes of the Brahmans the Yavanas who had fought their way into India were also Kshatriyas but of a different kind (they did not speak Hindi), perhaps mixed with Shudras - these being the most inferior and most despised of the varnas. An additional religious consideration may have crept in because the Greeks (who could never become Brahmans) readily took to Buddhism [97].

b. Bactria, an outpost of Hellenism

In several places of this work I have already spoken of Bactria, the most remarkable chip of the Hellenistic block. Even those of us who have had a classical education very probably have never heard of the Graeco-Bactrian kingdom in Afghanistan and along the Indus [98]. But even professional authors either pay scant attention to it or none at all [99]. Perhaps Rostovzeff unconsciously gave the real reason for this neglect by stating that "Bactria, a half-Greek country, broke away from the Seleucid main body" [100].

This 'breaking away' is obviously seen as a kind of treason which is explained by the fact that Bactria was only 'half-Greek'. This reminds me of the way Dutch historians and the general public have treated Belgian history for a long time. Belgium too 'broke away', in 1830/1831, from the United Kingdom of the Netherlands; it was also seen as only 'half-Dutch' since the southern half of that country speaks French. This 'treason' made the Belgians unworthy of further attention [101]. Admittedly Bactria almost escapes our attention from the time around 250 B.C., when the Parthian Empire was founded; its policy was anti-Seleucid and anti-Roman to a degree. This empire shoved its mighty bulk between Asia Minor and Bactria and thereby obscured the view of westerners of what remained of Greek influence still further east.

George Woodcock calls Bactria 'the Siberia of the Persian Empire' [102]. Alexander arrived there in 327 B.C. and conquered this ruggedly mountainous country, now Afghanistan, in several years of hard fighting.

To the north of Bactria, the Macedonians conquered Persia's most northeastern satrapy, Sogdiana (in southern Russia). The Graeco-Bactrian kingdom was not founded by Alexander but by a satrap of the Seleucid king Antiochus II in Bactria and Sogdiana, called Diodotus. By degrees - probably there never was an open rebellion [103] - he loosened the bond that tied him to his suzerain in Babylon; in this he was helped by the rise of the Parthian Empire in the same period, ca. 250 B.C., that interrupted the direct connections between Bactria and Babylonia. Justinus says that he assumed the title of king [104]. Diodotus I was followed by his son Diodotus II of whom too very little is known - except that "the Diodoti laid the foundations of the Greco-Bactrian kingdom" [105].

The rise of a Diodotian dynasty was nipped in the bud by the coup of Euthydemus. This man, 'a stern, humourless and ambitious individual' [106], was a native of a Greek city in Lydia. He led a revolt of the Greek military aristocracy in Bactria against Diodotus II, whose policy of allying himself with Parthia (barbarians!) they opposed. Not much is known of these events except that Euthydemus took the crown as Euthydemus I, probably about 235 B.C. and killed Diodotus and his offspring [107]. He extended his realm in several directions, in particular to the west and northwest in order to push back the Parthians.

Then, in 209/208 B.C. the Seleucid king Antiochus III appeared, intent on reconquering his far-eastern dominions. With a strong army he invaded Bactria and after fierce fighting drove Euthydemus back into his capital called Bactra [108], the 'mother of cities' and a main centre of Zoroastrianism with a great fire-temple. Antiochus laid siege to the capital and sealed it off for the next two years. In 206 B.C., with Bactra still resisting, the two kings compromised. Antiochus paid a peaceful visit to the Indus valley and then returned to his own country [109]. This meant that he left Euthydemus in the undisputed possession of Bactria. This king now was able to extend his sway northward over Fergana and into Chinese Turkestan in order to forestall nomad incursions [110].

Woodcock warns us that we must not compare ancient Bactria to modern Afghanistan with her wastelands and blowing sands. Bactria was well irrigated and the soil was extremely fertile. Apollodorus of Artemisia, a Greek historiographer, says that the power of the Bactrian Greeks was based on the excellence of the soil [111]. Furthermore, Bactra was situated on the famous Silk Road from China to the west [112]. Not only horse raising and agriculture but also commerce made the country prosperous [113]. Thus the infrastructure of Bactria which was extended and developed by the Greeks was capable of supporting a large Hellenic population that might have made the country into an authentic Greek kingdom.

But did Bactria really carry an extensive Hellenic population large enough to hellenize the country thoroughly? The fact that in Antiquity Bactria was commonly called the land of 'the Thousand Cities' may make us think so [114]. However, only very few of the Greek towns of Bactria are known by name; Tarn believes that there cannot have existed more than fifty real cities. Next to these there were military colonies - most of them fortified villages -, the first of them having been founded by Alexander which was followed by many additions by later Bactrian rulers; they were mainly intended to stave off incursions by nomad tribes. The Greek population was increased during the third century B.C. as a result of immigration from the west. Military campaigns undertaken by Euthydemus and his successors prove that the Greek population must have been considerable. But it is impossible to state what the ratio was of the number of Greeks to that of the natives. It is highly improbable that the Greeks were in the majority [115].

Anyhow, we are impelled to believe Ghirshman when he writes that in Bactria, and only in Bactria, Greeks and Iranians got on well together and formed a real community, albeit with two different ways of life. Not even here, where conditions were so favourable, did the two races fuse into one [116]. Hearing of 'walled towns' and 'military colonies' (for the Greeks) and of 'fortified villages' (for the Bactrians) we are not surprised because of this mutual aloofness. Neither of the two nations really desired to fuse. We must also not forget that the Greeks in Bactria were military men and the descendants of Alexander's mercenaries who saw the defense and the conservation of the country as their primary task rather than the diffusion of culture. We must agree with Ghirshman's verdict that, even after the arrival of the Greeks, Bactria remained 'an Iranian country with a feudal society' ; the newcomers brought little more than 'greater security to the frontiers' [117].

I feel that we should speak of dualism here. Two nations, two civilizations in one country that did not come together, that did not want to come together, that restricted themselves to 'friendly intercourse' but in reality carried on as though the other part did not exist, what else is this than dualism [118]? In one respect, however, Greeks and Bactrians must have cooperated, for Euthydemus and later Demetrius cannot have undertaken their conquests without the active support of the Bactrian military aristocracy [119].

In modern works on the history of Bactria one will find very little on her culture; even Tarn in his bulky volume has hardly anything to say on this subject; the same applies to Altheim in his chapter on the Greeks in Bactria [120]. The reasons for this absence is not that these authors would be uninterested in cultural matters but that the sources tell us next to nothing about Graeco-Bactrian culture. I suppose that with the Greeks in Bactria we do not find ourselves in the highlands of Hellenic civilization. This does not mean that there was nothing at all, for, after all, the Greek presence in Bactria was powerful enough to radiate into Central Asia and India [121].

c. First Indian interlude

At some moment between 200 and 190 B.C. Euthydemus was succeeded on the Bactrian throne by his son Demetrius I [122]. For Tarn this was the man who successfully invaded India. Later authors disagree with this and believe that this Demetrius held no more than the so-called 'white India', that is Arachosia, once a Persian satrapy well to the west of the Indus. Both Woodcock and Narain assume that there were two Demetrii, one the already mentioned King Demetrius I who, so they say, never crossed the Indus, and another Demetrius whom Woodcock calles Demetrius II and considers him a son of King Antimachus I, a rival of Demetrius I ruling in the same period over Bactria [123]. Woodcock states that this Demetrius II "was the first Greek king of whom we have unimpaired evidence that he occupied parts of India east of the Khyber pass"; this evidence is based on the fact that coins with his stamp "have been found in Gandhara as far as Taxila" [124].

I find it impossible to take issue on this thorny question. But one thing is certain, and let this console us : it is beyond doubt that some King Demetrius ruled part of India at some time between 190 and 150 B.C. [125]; Justinus calls him 'King of India' [126]. Was it this Demetrius in whom Alexander, as the conqueror of India, found a worthy successor? Demetrius seems to have modelled himself after his great predecessor of one and a half centuries earlier. His coins show him as a man with a thick-set face, wearing a head-dress with an elephant's trunk and tusks [127]. This was a symbol of imperial power, and one that pointed in the direction of India, the homeland of the elephant.

In some way or other - we do not know how or when - the Greeks established themselves in the Punjab and ruled there. The successors of Demetrius enlarged the Greek area in India which for some time included Taxila, obviously the Indo-Greek capital; a new city was built there [128]. Perhaps realizing how precarious their position was the Greeks of the Punjab made no attempt at hellenizing the Indian population; here too the Hellenic element remained an isolated minority.

d. Second Indian interlude

Then came King Menander, the 'Milinda' of Buddhist tradition, the only Greek king to be mentioned in Indian sources [129]. He began his reign as King of Taxila but intent as he was on conquest he extended his realm in many directions; coins from his mint are found far and wide. In the period around 150 B.C. he struck south-eastward from the Punjab with a large army, followed the course of the Ganges, and seems even to have reached Pataliputra (Patna), the capital of the Mauryan Empire, which the Greeks stormed and sacked. Several Buddhist texts mention this feat of arms.

These sources also state that the Greeks soon retired because they began to fight one another. It will also have been a point of consideration for Menander that he was a thousand miles distant from his own capital. So "Menander loaded the spoils of battle into one of those baggage trains which customarily followed the Greek armies of Asia, and retired to the natural frontier formed by the Jumna" [130].

Did this second presence of the Greeks in the Punjab (the first being the arrival of Alexander) usher in an era of demographic and cultural fusion between Greeks and Indians? By no means! The same peacefully dualistic situation as in Bactria prevailed in India. Menander himself probably wanted to bring his two kinds of subjects nearer to each other; this is, for instance, proved by the fact that his coins are bilingual. It seems, however, that he slowly evolved from a purely Hellenic ruler into a more Indian one. He favoured Buddhism and is said to have become a Buddhist himself. Whereas to his Greek subjects he simply was 'basileus'= king, for his Indians he was "Maharaja' = Great King, and 'Dharmaraja' = King of Justice [131]. But his Indian subjects underwent his rule just as passively as that of all other rulers. Woodcock speaks of "two separate ways of life : the Indians fenced off by their own cult and caste rules, and the Greeks largely remaining within their own cities and military colonies" [132].

e. The end of the Graeco-Bactrian and the Graeco-Indian kingdoms

The dynastic ties between Bactria and the Punjab kingdom were severed when about 175 B.C. the usurper Eucratides seized the throne of Bactria. An attempt by a certain king Demetrius to dislodge him failed dismally. Eucratides even crossed the Hindu Kush and conquered the western half of Gandhara. So even in these far eastern regions the Greeks manifested their inveterate tendency to fight one another instead of their common enemies. In that period Bactria was subject to increasing pressure from the side of the Parthians, while nomads from the north threatened the Indo-Greek domains.

About 165 B.C. Bactria proper was overrun by a nomad tribe that made an end of Greek rule there. It is commonly thought that they were Scythians, or 'Sakas' in Persian, who were chased from their grazing-lands in the south of Central Asia by the Yuezhi [133]. These Sakas also occupied parts of western India such as Gujarat and Malwa. Thus the Indo-Greeks saw themselves threatened from the west and south. This did not prevent them from carrying on with the favourite pastime of the Greeks : fighting one another. After the reign of Menander his kingdom was split up in several smaller ones the rulers of which were constantly at each other's throats.

Steadily Greek territory was lost to nomads from 150 B.C. onward. Shortly after 100 B.C. the important Greek town of Taxila fell into the hands of a Saka conqueror. Around 40 B.C. there still remained one small Greek kingdom in the Indus valley under King Hermaeus; he had to surrender his realm to the rulers of the Kushan Empire that in the meantime had replaced the Sakas in Bactria and western India [134].

As Woodcock remarks, the fall of the last Hellenistic kingdom at the far eastern end of Alexander's conquests coincided in time with Cleopatra's suicide, which marked the end of political Hellenistic power in Africa [135]. Thirty-nine Greek kings and two queens had mounted the throne during the history of those remarkable Indo-Greeks [136]. The downfall of the last political Greek entity in the east did not mean that all Hellenistic influence was now over. On the contrary, elements of Greek cultural influence are discernible in the decades and even centuries that were to follow. Nowhere were the Greek settlements massacred or their inhabitants expelled [137]. But living in the midst of the Indian masses they slowly but certainly became indianized themselves. Woodcock estimates that about 200 A.D. the Greeks had disappeared 'as a self-contained and identifiable minority in India' [138]. That there was some Hellenic influence on Indian craftmanship and architecture is an established fact.

The overall conclusion, however, must be a negative one. In the Hellenistic regions of Bactria, Punjab, Gandhara, and the Indus valley where the Greeks were politically dominant for a considerable time the old European-Asian dualism was not surmounted. In the long run it was the Indo-Bactrian Greeks who succumbed to the east, first through their political demise, and then because of their demographic and cultural extinction. Was there ever any chance of a successful merger of the autochthonous Bactrian and Indian civilizations on the one hand, and of Hellenic culture on the other?

I feel that we must rule out India. The Indo-Greeks, never more than a tiny minority in only a small part of India, did not stand a shadow of a chance against the far older and powerful Hindu culture. But in Bactria it might have been possible. However, neither there nor in India were the two necessary conditions fulfilled, viz. that the Greeks would stick together as one man, and that they would conduct a vigorous policy of cultural amalgamation. Neither of the two happened. I have already said enough of the internecine warfare of the Greeks in this part of the world. Furthermore, they were primarily soldiers and who later became merchants, members, in other words, of two social groups not particularly interested in cultural policy [139]. That east is east and west is west and never the twain will meet, as Kipling put it, was confirmed in the case of the Greeks, the Bactrians, and the Indians. And thus a promising enterprise faded into nothingness [140].

8. The fate of the Greek presence between the Euphrates and Bactria

Let us now, with the Seleucids, retreat westward. As already stated, Parthia made herself independent ca. 250 B.C. The Seleucid emperors never succeeded in recovering Iran. On the contrary, always pushing westward the Parthian emperors drove the Greeks steadily further back. The great conqueror and the real founder of the Parthian Empire was Mithridates I (163-138 B.C.). His conquests reached as far as the Euphrates which became, and for centuries would remain, the 'frontier of Europe' [141]. In this way a very large section of Alexander's conquests fell into the hands of a non-Greek nation.

The paramount question now confronting us is what happened to the Greek presence between the Euphrates and the western frontier of

Bactria. We know that the Seleucid Emperors had not pursued a deliberate policy of cultural and demographic fusion in these areas; we can hardly expect that their Parthian successors would execute such a policy. But then we are reminded of the fact that they used to call themselves 'Philhellenes' [142]. What did this mean?

When the Seleucids retired they left behind a well-organized Greek presence. There was a great number of Greek cities and of Greek colonies in Iranian towns; part of the Iranian upper class had become hellenized [143]. But on the whole, the Greeks kept to themselves. Altheim says that, in contrast to their Graeco-Bactrian counterparts, the Seleucid rulers never succeeded in establishing a friendly relationship with their Iranian subjects. They did not hold Persian art and religion in esteem. The Iranian and Graeco-Macedonian sections of the population always remained separate entities. In the countryside everything stayed as it had been for ages. "This", Altheim concludes, "had as a consequence that Macedonian rule had no real foothold in the countryside. Only in this way the rapid and stupendous success of the Parthians in those regions of Iran that fell under Seleucid sway can be understood" [144].

Although the Parthian conquerors were hardly more than uncouth nomads, they knew how to value Greek civilization. The Greek presence was left unmolested; the Greek cities saw a new prosperity that is vividly exemplified by the famous archaelogical sites like Dura-Europos [145]. To quote Momigliano : "The Greek subjects of the Arsacics (= the Parthian Emperors) took an active part in the intellectual life of the country in which they lived, explored the land and wrote down its history" [146]. Some Graeco-Parthian authors might also be mentioned such as these Apollodorus of Artemisia although only a few fragments remain of his work.

The Parthian rulers left the Greeks in peace. They themselves coined in Greek, spoke Greek, wrote Greek, favoured Greek art and artists, and employed Greeks in high offices. Some of the Hellenic cities, like Seleukeia on the Tigris, continued to exist for centuries. But what does this add up to? With regard to the Hellenization of the east to very little. The Parthian and Hellenic societies subsisted side by side in 'mutual understanding', although not always harmoniously [147]. But in the long run the Greek presence east of the Euphrates succumbed to oriental pressure. In spite of the Philhellenism of the Arsacid rulers, the foundation of their empire signified, as Eduard Meyer remarks, 'the beginning of an ongoing reaction against Hellenism'. The connections with the Greek world in the west were severed, new Greek immigrants no longer arrived. The Greek cities slowly dwindled away [148]; in Sasanian times little was left of Hellenic culture. In this part of the world too 'Asia' finally reasserted herself.

9. The chances of Hellenism in Asia Minor

After the destruction of the Graeco-Bactrian kingdom and the advance of the Parthians to the Euphrates, this river became the dividing line between non-Greek territories and what remained of Alexander's conquests in Asia. The difference with the situation that prevailed before Alexander invaded the Persian Empire is that now not only the Aegean coastal strip but the whole of Asia Minor was included in 'Europe'. For centuries to come the frontier would remain where it lay in about 150 B.C. We now must see whether Asia Minor could rightfully claim to belong to Europe.

a. Hellenism and the northern territories

On the death of King Alexander, Asia Minor was, as a Macedonian conquest, included in the Macedonian Empire. During the third century B.C., however, as already related in Chapter I, the whole northern half of the peninsula became divided into five separate states, these being from west to east along the southern shore of the Black Sea : Pergamum, Bithynia, and Pontus, and to the south of these in the interior Galatia and Cappadocia. Of these states only one, Pergamum, had Hellenic rulers. So the great question is, what had taken place in Asia Minor? How had it fared with the ideals of Alexander? After his death, we may talk of three possibilities. First, a fusion of nations and cultures.

Second, a Hellenization so thorough that all that was oriental would have been reduced to a memory. Or third, with the exception of the coastal strip, Asia Minor might have remained as oriental as it had always been. We shall see that none of these possibilities was fully realized.

b. The Hellenistic Kingdom of Pergamum

In the north-west of Asia Minor, bordering on the Sea of Marmora and the northern Aegean, lay the Kingdom of Pergamum. Since 263 B.C. it was an independent state under the Macedonian House of the Attalids. The glory of sovereign Pergamum lasted till 133 B.C., when the last prince ceded his rights to Rome. The capital of the state was also called Pergamum, some twenty miles inland from the northern Aegean coastline. It was not a big city situated as it was on the top of a 333 m high mountain. The royal palace, the famous library, and the residential quarters, were skilfully spread over well designed terraces. The agora, that indispensable element of every Greek town, was at the foot of the mountain, with a second agora higher up the slopes. A big theatre, yet another indispensable element, was almost perched on the steep western mountain-side [149]. The most famous monument of the Attalid period is not to be seen on the site but in the Pergamum Museum in Berlin; it is the 'Pergamum Altar' dedicated by King Eumenes II to Zeus between 180 and 160 B.C.

It will be evident that in Pergamum we visit one of the great centres of Hellenistic civilization, together with Athens, Antioch, and Alexandria [150]. The Attalids were great patrons of learning. "The gymnasium of Pergamum, the largest and most complete of its kind known from Antiquity, is in itself a monument to the Attalids' interest in education" [151]. That this education bore fruit is proved by the fact that Galen (129-199), together with Hippocrates, the most famous doctor of the ancient world, was a born Pergamese. From everywhere in the Greek oikumene scholars came to the Pergamese court. Scholars and students could rely for their work on the well-stocked library, one of the largest in the Hellenistic world. The town was also a great centre of art; I mentioned the Pergamum Altar. Famous statues like that of the Dying Gaul and of a Dead Amazon testify to the excellence of Pergamese sculpture. And even to-day we can admire the graceful lines of the temples.

But it is not my task to describe the history of Hellenism in general nor that of Pergamum in particular. The great question in the context of this chapter is whether this country, with its resplendent Hellenistic capital and court, did indeed become a region in which the difference, the opposition between Asian and European had disappeared. Certainly, if anywhere, it should be here because of the powerful radiation of a brilliant Hellenistic centre on a modestly sized country. But very probably, here as elsewhere, Greek influence remained restricted to the cities, and in Pergamum these were scarce. The kings were Hellenizers, no doubt, but, as Petit writes, they were not disinterested.

After having defeated the Celts, they enrolled them into their army to fight with them against their neighbours, the Hellenic ones not excluded; this enlarged the already dominant barbarian element in the country. In their predilection for colossal buildings, the enormous Pergamum Altar, for instance, that covers a surface of 1200 m2, they seem influenced by the megalomania of oriental rulers. With regard to their subjects they showed themselves as cruel and merciless as any indigenous prince [152]. The kingdom only too frequently seethed with rebellion, and indeed revolts sometimes actually broke out [153].

If we could for one moment stop being obsessed with 'the glory that was Pergamum' (the town's, I mean) [154], we find that the not so numerous cities in the hinterland were military colonies rather than cultural centres. It is a reasonable guess that outside the capital there was no more than a thin veneer of Hellenic culture, and that by far the larger part of the indigenous population was not affected by it.

c. The four non-Greek kingdoms

This applies all the more to the other kingdoms and regions of the northern half of Asia Minor. They were all of them non-Hellenic countries with non-Hellenic rulers. The kings of Bithynia, a Thracian country on the southern littoral of the Black Sea, were far from anti-Hellenic, on the contrary. Yet Greek colonies were rare here, and post-Alexandrian foundations were not numerous either, the later so famous Nicaea being one of them. Whatever Hellenistic influence there was must have been restricted to the court at Nicomedia, the capital [155].

To the east of Bithynia, and equally along the southern coastline of the Black Sea, lay the kingdom of Pontus. Here still fewer Greek colonies of the first period, like Trabizonde (Trebzond), or even new ones, like Nikopolis, were to be found. The Greek towns were mainly on the coast. Inland we can trace little more than villages, while barbarian tribes lived in the mountains. It is not be expected that we shall detect much Greek influence in Pontus.

Her kings are described as a mixture of Persian and Hellenistic; the court was hellenized, spoke Greek, and favoured Greek art [156]. It, nevertheless, was a country in which 'all degrees of human culture' were represented 'from the most profound barbarity to the most refined civilisation' [157].

That, nonetheless, Greek influence was not wholly negligible is proved by the fact that one of the most famous Hellenic geographers, Strabo (64/63 B.C. - ca. 21 A.D.), was born in the Pontian town of Amaseia. It should be added that this was in Roman times. Strabo was of mixed Greek and oriental descent. Reinach pays homage to King Mithridates VI Eupator who died in the year that Strabo was born, as a ruler who strongly favoured Hellenism; he, this scholar states, was "the symbol of a great historical event, viz. the fruitful union of two cultures, Persism and Hellenism", and in this respect he must be thought of as a late follower of Alexander [158]. But Tarn scornfully remarks that this king "was only a barbarian varnished"; the gods he worshipped were oriental ones 'with Greek names attached' like Mithras [159]. When everything is taken into consideration, even the Philhellenism of the Pontian kings, Pontus must be seen as an oriental country with a feudal structure; large stretches of it remained impervious to Greek culture.

Cappadocia was almost devoid of Greek cities; her rulers were hellenized to some degree, but the country itself remained as Asiatic as it had always been. Galatia, the country of the Asiatic Celts, was nearly impregnable to all forms of Hellenism. The Galatians were "a foreign body camped in a strange land, living in strongholds whence they raided and plundered, and ruling over the native peasantry who cultivated their fields" [160].

In conclusion we must state that the cultural situation of the entire northern half of Asia Minor in Hellenistic times was not much different from that under the Persian emperors. On the whole orientalism most successfully resisted the impact of Hellenic culture in this part of the eastern world.

d. Hellenism in the southern half of Asia Minor

Let us now see whether Hellenism stood a better chance in the southern half of Asia Minor. Along the Aegean and Mediterranean coasts the Greeks had been present for an incredibly long time. The western and southern littorals were richly studded with numerous Hellenic cities of ancient date; in post-Alexandrian times many new ones were added to these, not a few of them situated deep in the interior. But on the other hand, the map of Greek city foundations shows a large void in the central part around and to the south of Lake Tatta. This part of the Hellenistic world was constantly under the sceptre of Graeco-Macedonian rulers, whether Seleucid, Ptolemaic, or Rhodian. So, on the surface of it, if Hellenism could be successful, it would be here.

Petit believes that the Seleucid kings, although they always were closer than others to Alexander's intentions, did not aim at a 'fusion of races' [161]. What cemented their realm together were the Greek cities; these enabled the Greeks to live in their own style on foreign soil. At the same time, as Petit also writes, they offered an inspiring model to the indigenous population. If this is true - and who would doubt it -, then the Seleucid kings must have deemed Hellenic culture and life the real thing, in contrast to autochthonous civilization. This would mean that the term 'Hellenism', in Allard Pierson's sense, would be inappropriate to Seleucid policy; we should rather talk of Hellenization, which signifies, of course, making Greek. This would also mean that Seleucid policy was essentially dualistic.

Did it work? Partly. Hellenization had some success in southern Asia Minor and in Syria, although not everywhere. The well-to-do and the upper classes began to speak Greek and to adopt forms of Greek culture. But, as Michael Grant states, "they rarely took on the Greek spirit ...; the success of the Seleucid colonizing (= hellenizing - F.) effort (was), after all, only partial". He lays the blame for the final failure at the door of the Graeco-Macedonian settlers who "for the most part still passionately practised linguistic and cultural apartheid". This author even speaks of an 'antagonism between Greeks and natives' the first living in the cities, the others tilling the land [162]. The Graeco-Macedonian class formed an elite that did not want to share its power, and the spoils of it, with the 'barbarians' whom, with only few exceptions, they kept at their proper distance. It has been calculated that no more than 2 1/2 % of the natives ever acquired positions of authority; hardly anybody rose higher than commanding a local unit [163]. Nowhere in the Hellenistic world did the Greeks ever surmount their deeply ingrained prejudices; they imported these wherever they went.

10. Hellenism in Syria

This rather negative picture does not become much altered by the fact that on the Orontes yet another brilliant Hellenistic centre stood, Antioch, the capital of the Seleucid Empire after the loss of the east, one of the few Hellenistic cities that still exist. At first sight it was a purely Hellenic city with its chess-board ground-plan, its resplendent public buildings, its temples, theatres, shaded porticoes, and with Greek spoken at every streetcorner. The first inhabitants were 5300 Athenians and Macedonian veterans [164], later joined by many newcomers.

But when we had wondered enough at this Hellenic splendour we would perceive oriental perfumes in the city's air. Perhaps something went wrong with it right from the start. The town had been inaugurated with the cruel oriental custom of using the bones of a human being as a foundation stone, as it were. In the early morning of May 12, 300 B.C., at sunrise, a girl called Amathe was sacrificed by Amphion, the high-priest [165]. Apart from the Greek quarters there was also a Syrian quarter and a large Jewish community; many orientals flocked to the prospering town. The city was aptly called 'the great' and 'the beautiful' but "the spirit of authentic Greekdom failed there" [166].

The unavoidable result was that the Greek inhabitants became orientalized to some extent. "Nowhere the oriental element was suppressed by the Hellenic one." It is therefore that a sixth-century Byzantine author could refer to Antioch as 'mixo-barbaros' [167]. The traveller who left the town and passed along the fine Greek villas surrounding it, soon enough found himself in purely Syrian country. With regard to Graeco-Syrian civilization Pierson asked : "Is this still Hellenism or should it rather be called Hellenistic Semitism?" [168].

11. The Jewish revolt againts Hellenism

a. Persian, Macedonian, and Egyptian rulers and Judaism

In the foregoing paragraphs I referred to the dualistic elements in the policies of Hellenization. The Hellenes, with their supercilious denigration of 'barbarians', tried to hellenize them, to make them Greek, but with little enthusiasm or fervour. The overall results were meagre; the larger part of the autochthonous population resisted all efforts to make them live, think, and speak in other ways than they were accustomed. There was, however, within the Seleucid orbit one case of active resistance which developed into open war. At the same time, the pattern of dualism was reversed, for instead of Hellenes trying to impose their culture on others, we see a nation trying to stamp out every spark of Hellenism within its bounds. It will be clear that I am speaking here of the Jewish nation and of the Wars of the Machabees.

Perhaps the autochthonous civilizations of Syria and Palestine were still more impervious to Hellenic culture than other parts of the Hellenistic world. While koinê-Greek was the language of the court and of officialdom, the local population continued not only to speak but even to write in Aramaic, a Semitic language akin to Hebrew. Not much was changed in this situation when the Seleucid emperors, forced out of Mesopotamia by the Parthians, made Antioch their brilliant capital. On his way to and from Egypt Alexander had passed through the Jewish country; from then on the Persian rulers of Judaea had been replaced by the Hellenic Seleucids.

The Persian emperors had always adopted an attitude of cool benevolence with regard to the Jews, leaving them as much as possible to their own devices. At first the coming of the Macedonians brought no change in this; some authors say that Alexander granted the Jews permission to live 'according to their ancestral Law', but there exist no ancient texts to warrant this [169]. During the decades after Alexander's death the Diadochi fought each other for the possession of Syria and Palestine. Since the roads and passes of their country formed the strategic connection of Egypt with Syria and Asia Minor, the Jews saw armies tramping through their cities and fighting in their fields. The Ptolemaic Pharaohs were highly interested in Palestine as a strategic asset but hardly in Jewish life. On the whole they too, when they were the masters of the country, left the local population in peace. Inevitably there was some degree of Hellenization; some people learned to speak Greek and adopted Greek names.

b. Antiochus III and the Jews

Whereas the Jews enjoyed a period of peace during nearly the whole of the third century B.C., at the end of this period trouble arose. The ambitious Seleucid king Antiochus III wanted to wrest Palestine from the hands of the Egyptians; after two decades of fighting during which the Jews again witnessed many a fierce battle, the Egyptians definitely left the country to the Seleucids. From then on, 199/198 B.C., the Jewish population fell under Syrian control. Already in 210 the Syrian army had made its appearance in Jerusalem. No resistance was offered; there seems to have been a pro-Syrian party in town that opened the gates of the citadel to Antiochus. According to Tcherikover, "this party was composed of the representatives of the upper stratum of the priestly class, of the Jerusalem aristocracy ... and of the wealthy". The fact that they were pro-Seleucid did not necessarily mean that they had also Hellenistic leanings [170]; it rather meant that they were anti-Egyptian.

Flavius Josephus prints a letter from Antiochus III to his governor of the region in which he shows himself highly pleased with his reception by the Jews (no wonder!). Wishing to be grateful, he orders his man on the spot to respect the religious customs of the Jews. He adds that this nation must be administered 'according to their ancestral laws' [171]. In a decree the king testified to his friendship for the Jews [172]. With these 'ancestral laws' not only the Mosaic Law would have been meant but, at the same time, the social and political institutions like the Jewish theocracy with the Jewish High Priest as the virtual head of community [173]. So the Seleucid era in Judaea began with a honeymoon.

c. Hellenizing by King Antiochus III

The benevolent attitude of King Antiochus III did not mean that Palestine remained out of the reach of Hellenization. How would this have been possible when the country in the north and south bordered on the hellenizing regimes of Egypt and the Seleucid Empire? Furthermore, Palestine was an important military and commercial transit road. This peculiar character was stressed by two strings of Greek cities, both lines running from north to south. The first line went along the Syrian, Phoenician, and Palestinian coasts, beginning at Alexandria - not the Egyptian one but the city near Asia Minor (now the Turkish town of Iskenderun) - and ending at the Egyptian border. Most of these were ancient towns, like Akko, Jaffa (Jafo, in Greek Joppe), or Gaza, that in the course of time became hellenized.

The second string of Greek towns ran more inland through the Orontes valleys. It began at Antioch in the north and ended near the Dead Sea in the south. Nearly all these towns were new Hellenistic foundations. In the north of Palestine lay a group of cities that was known as the Dekapolis [174]; it is mentioned in the New Testament. 'Dekapolis' means 'Ten Cities' because ten is a convenient number, although there were more than ten. One of these was the still existing Gerasa, now Jerash, a Jordanian frontier town, with magnificent Greek buildings the remains of which form a must for tourists. In Jewish territory proper there were very few Greek towns, probably no more than three. In the whole region there were perhaps thirty cities in all. On principle, these were instruments of Hellenization [175].

d. The internal hellenizing movement

So not only from the north and south but also from the east and west the Jews saw themselves hedged in by Hellenic elements. The question, however, is whether these two rows of towns really radiated Greek influence into Judaea. In this region there existed no great cultural and intellectual centre comparable to Pergamum or Alexandria. "Of the cultural activity of the Greek cities of Palestine we hear absolutely nothing", says Tcherikover [176]. Probably the cultural level of the Greek immigrants was not very high.

The threat to Jewish life did not arise from such uncouth settlers, it did come from inside, from hellenized Jews. About 170 B.C. we detect a group of Jews who were thoroughly hellenized. They looked down in scorn on Jewish tradition and on all those who still adhered to it. Diodorus, on the authority of Hecataeus of Abdera, says that "as a result of their (the Jews') mingling with men of other nations ..., many of their traditional practices became disturbed" [177].

The hellenizing movement was led by the members of a wealthy family, the Tobiads; we know them from Greek papyri found in Egypt.

Probably they were descendants of a certain Tobiah whom Nehemia around 440 B.C. refers to with much bitterness refers as an 'Ammonite slave' [178], a despised foreigner who was an enemy of the Jewish people. He married into a Jewish family and cemented valuable friendships with many Jewish nobles [179]. To all intents and purposes the wealthy sheik Tobiah of Ptolemaic days was his descendant [180]. His son Joseph made much money by acting as a tax-gatherer for the Egyptians. In the period we are speaking of the Tobiads were a large aristocratic clan of Ammonite origin. They were not priests but entertained close ties with the priestly caste. They are typical of the mentality of the new age, for they were 'modern', enterprising, internationally oriented money-makers and politicians, and none too scrupulous, nor were they either very civilized or conspicuously religious [181].

It goes without saying that people like the Tobiads were open to Hellenistic influences : they travelled widely, they frequently met with Greeks, they spoke Greek themselves. We must not see them as 'deliberate Hellenizers'; we may assume that their interests lay elsewhere [182]. As Tcherikover says, "their Hellenism was the outcome of imitation" [183]; it suited them in every respect to pose as being hellenized. Although one would expect otherwise, the larger part of the sacerdotal class went with them in their Hellenistic reforms. The priests were so closely connected with them, financially and by family ties, that they were in no position to defend the patriarchal Jewish tradition [184]. We even hear that Tobiad funds were deposited in the temple [185].

Backed by their wealth the Tobiads exercised considerable influence on the hellenizing process in Jerusalem and Judaea. Although Hellenistic influences had already been at work for a considerable period, we may date the beginning of the official campaign at the time of the deposition of the High Priest Onias in 275 B.C. He was replaced by his brother Joshua who suited the purposes of the Tobiads better than Onias; significantly he changed his Hebrew name into the Greek one of Jason. He paid King Antiochus a large sum for acquiring the office [186]; this made the High Priesthood "a normal official post and the High Priest a Seleucid royal official utterly dependent on the king's favor"

[187]. The Book of Machabees states that Jason 'straightway set about converting his countrymen to the Gentile (=pagan) way of living" [188]. What happened?

First of all, he was responsible for enrolling the men of Jerusalem as citizens of Antioch (for which favour he paid another large sum of money to the king) [189]. By this move, the Holy City became a polis in the Greek style, while the inhabitants were organized as a demos. In no Greek city all the inhabitants were automatically members of the demos; we may safely assume that here the measure favoured the members of the bourgeoisie and excluded the orthodox rank and file [190]. Furthermore, two constitutive elements of Grecity were introduced into Jerusalem, a gymnasium and an ephebeion [191]. The author of the second Book of Machabees probably read Jason's mind correctly when he wrote that it was the High Priest's aim to abrogate the customs of the Jews [192]. "Come", the Hellenizers said, "let us make terms with them (the Greeks) that dwell about us! Ever since we forswore their company, nought but trouble has come our way" [193]. Some of the Tobiads told Antiochus that "they wished to abandon their country's laws and the ways of life prescribed by these, and to follow the king's laws and adopt the Greek way of life" [194]. In the eyes of the orthodox this was the vilest possible treason since keeping apart from everything that was not Jewish had always been a fundamental trait of Jewishness [195].

With refined tact the Hellenizers situated the gymnasium on the Temple Hill just underneath the walls of the citadel. The boys went about with the broad-rimmed hat of their patron-god, Hermes. What was worse, the ephebes used to exercise in the nude - which was already utterly contary to Hebrew habits - thus exposing that they were circumcised. Ashamed of this, they had their circumcision removed (by a kind of plastic chirurgy?) "in order to be Greeks even when unclothed" [196]. The Machabee author relates this with obvious disgust since circumcision was the seal of the Covenant between Jahve and his people [197]. The gymnasium was highly popular; even priests went there forgetting their sacerdotal duties [198].

e. A Hebrew protest

It must not be forgotten that up to now we have been speaking of the upper section of Jerusalem society. Further down the social ladder, the artisans, shopkeepers, day-labourers, and peasants remained untouched by the process of Hellenization. They neither understood nor spoke Greek, remained faithful to the Law of Moses, read the Bible in Hebrew, and on Sabbath evenings gathered in the synagogues to listen to the scribes who explained the Torah to them [199]. We possess an echo of what moved these people in the Book of Ecclesiasticus, or the Wisdom of Jesus Ben Sirach. The original Semitic of this book was translated into Greek by the author's grandson and presumably published about 118 B.C. in Egypt [200]. Ecclesiasticus is an exceptional document since it is the only one text in which we find an opposition to Hellenizing.

Sirach was no friend of Greek philosophy; in veiled terms he warns his readers against it. "Seek not to know what is far above you; let your mind ever dwell upon the duty God has given you to do, content to be ignorant of all his dealings besides". He is pleading for an unsophisticated religious life guided by the Torah, and not by Greek teachers who, in fact, know no more than you do : "By such fancies many have been led astray, and their thought chained to folly" [201]. A plague on the renegades! "Woe to you, rebels that have forsaken the Law of the Lord, the Most High; (you are) born of an unholy birth, an unholy death (is) your destiny!" [202].

He is on the side of the poor and fulminates against the sacerdotal and commercial aristocracy. They are constantly after money but they will be punished for it : "Love money, and you shall be called to account for it; you quest corruption, of corruption you shall have your fill!" [203]. The poor are utterly helpless. The rich man will always find friends to help him out, "he has many to keep him in countenance ..., but the poor man in his ruin is driven from familiar doors". When he speaks, people ask who he may be [204]. Sirach sees the social situation of his day as dualistic : "What fellowship can there be between the rich and the poor? Poor man is to rich as wild ass is to lion out in the desert, his prey;

wealth hates poverty, as the proud heart scorns the humble rank ...; as well match wolf with lamb as rogue with whom lives honestly" [205] - the last named category of course being those who live according to the Law of Moses. It is true, as Tcherikover says, that there was as yet no 'class conflict" [206], but the explosion would come soon enough.

In the long run the Tobiads did not remain satisfied with Jason and replaced him by a stooge who suited them better, a certain Menelaus (another purely Greek name). The populace of Jerusalem hated Menelaus fiercely because he had 'a cruel tyrant's heart' and was 'more wild beast than High Priest' [207]. Whilst the new High Priest was at Antioch to serve his interests at the court, he left behind his brother Lysimachus as his governor. When asked for money by Menelaus, his brother took a large sum from the temple treasury. This treasure was considered national property. There was a popular outburst against this outrage. Lysimachus brought three thousand men under arms and began attacking the people, who, just like the Palestinians of to-day's intifadah, pelted them with a hail of stones. Lysimachus' men took to their heels; their commander was stoned to death [208]. Tcherikover admirably sums up the situation in this way : "Thus two strong forces confronted one another, ... the Jerusalem aristocracy, organized in the Hellenizing party, and the people who had not yet found their leaders and could only express their bitterness in risings and abortive demonstrations" [209].

f. Antiochus IV and his anti-Jewish policy

In the end, it was not the Tobiads but the Syrian king Antiochus IV who ran into serious trouble with the population of Judaea [210]. His 'Gezerot', or 'evil decrees', caused the big explosion which began as a rebellion and developed into open war, with the final victory for the Jews. What prompted this Seleucid king to attack religion, the dearest possession of a nation? Everywhere, just like the Romans in a subsequent age, the Diadoch rulers had practised general tolerance with regard to the religions and creeds in their realms. This seemed to them the safer policy; apart from that they were all of them politicians and strategists rather than religious innovators. Taking little interest in religion themselves, they considered all religions very probably as more or less identical and as useful instruments to keep the subjects in their proper place, in particular vis-à-vis their rulers. We must, therefore, seek an answer to the question why Antiochus IV fell upon the Jews since, I repeat this, this was the only occasion that Hellenization was not smothered in dumb and passive indifference but was met in a dualistic struggle.

The Israeli historian Victor Tcherikover has paid ample attention to the problem why Antiochus IV deviated from the traditional policy so significantly [211]. First of all, there was the character of the king. It will not surprise us that Jewish historiographers picture him the blackest terms. However, non-Jewish ancient sources are not really friendlier. It is not improbable that there was more than a streak of insanity in him. Polybius calles him 'Epimanes", the 'mad one', a quip on his official surname 'Epiphanes" = 'who manifests himself as a god' [212]. Some found him childish but others considered him 'unquestionably insane' [213]. Perhaps we may conclude with Radin that he was quite capable of acting normally in politics but that he "had periods of mental derangement" [214].

He is said to have often wandered about in Antioch with one or two companions visiting shops and discussing technical matters with craftsmen. At other times he burst in upon parties of young people accompanied by musicians. He lobbied in the market square for votes for some honorary office, visited public baths, sat sometimes drinking in obscure pubs with foreigners, and lavished unexpected gifts on many people. No wonder that "in consquence all respectable people were entirely puzzled by him" [215].

On the one hand, his character was quixotic, on the other, he often showed himself a 'Realpolitiker', fighting to keep the Seleucid heritage intact and even to enlarge it. Both sides of his character may have played a role in his Jewish policy. He did not feel inclined to suffer a dangerous rebellion, although at the same time he handled this affair very tactlessly.

Could a second motive for Antiochus' anti-Jewish policy have been his 'philhellenism'? It is a venerable tradition in European historiography that he brimmed with enthusiasm for Greek culture; he is seen as a fervent Hellenizer [216]. Let us for a moment concentrate on what Radin said : "(Antiochus IV) was a Greek. Hellenism was to him a real and profound enthusiasm" [217]. But he was no Greek, he was a bastard. His first ancestor was Seleucus I, a Macedonian, who mas married to an Asiatic woman. His mother, the wife of Antiochus III, was Laodice, a daughter of King Mithridates II of Pontus, a 'barbarian', that is [218]. The foregoing chapters on the Diadochs have amply shown that the Hellenistic rulers were only lukewarm promoters of Hellenization; most of them were hardly more interested in matters of civilization than in religion. There is very little concrete evidence to support the idea that Antiochus IV was an enthusiast for Greek culture. It is true that he favoured and patronized Greek cities, temples and festivals, but this is not the same as spreading Hellenic culture far and wide into the country-side. Many of his royal gifts were destined for cities and temples in Hellas proper, not so much in his own realm [219]. Shall we dub it spreading Hellenic culture when he presented the temple of Zeus in Olympia with a beautiful tapestry from Mesopotamia dyed in Phoenician purple [220]?

In my opinion he was a 'Romanizer' rather than a 'Hellenizer'. We must not forget that he had lived for fourteen years in Rome where he was sent by his brother Seleucus IV as a hostage; once a king he used to speak in the most laudatory terms of the treatment he had received in the imperial city, proclaiming himself 'a loyal and faithful ally' of Rome [221]. He proved deeply imbued with Roman values. The lobbying he did, clad in a white toga, was a Roman custom; when he sat up his 'sedes currulis', his ivory chair, in order to hear law-suits, he acted as a Roman magistrate [222]. He also held gladiatorial games [223]. To live in friendship with the Roman people was one of the overriding aims of his entire policy.

A third element in Antiochus' anti-Jewish attitude could have been a desire to unify his empire, with 'the establishment of one religion for all the people (as) part of his plan of reform' [224]. The author of the first Book of Machabees was convinced that such a plan existed. "A letter came from King Antiochus to all the subjects of his realm, bidding them to leave ancestral custom of this race or that, and become one nation instead". He interpreted this edict as meaning that the Jews should forgo their ancient Covenant with Jahve and "live by the law of the heathen round about" [225].

But if the Jews feared that Antiochus IV intended to replace Jahve by Zeus Olympios, or to identify their God with that pagan divinity, that would not imply that the Syrian king himself was trying to introduce a 'pagan monotheism' [226]. With, perhaps, the exception of the Zoroastrian cult of Ahura Mazda in ancient Iran (never an official state religion), there existed only one purely monotheistic cult in the ancient world, that of Israel. For the rest of the oriental, Greek, Hellenistic, and Roman world, monotheism was an idea that was utterly alien to the ancient mind. Therefore the Jewish War was not a struggle between two monotheistic creeds [227].

Yet another motive may have been "Antiochus' general policy of reconstituting the decaying power of his kingdom". There is no doubt that the king did his utmost to fortify the fabric of his tottering realm - in consequence of which he did not want the Jews going their own way. But, as Tcherikover rightly remarks, this does not explain why this policy led to religious enmity [228].

Up to this point I have followed Tcherikover's reasonings that have as yet proved inconclusive. Perhaps I may add another possible cause of the Syrian-Jewish opposition. This is that the king called himself 'epiphanes', in full 'theos epiphanes' = the manifest god. Whereas Alexander the Great had considered himself divine, his successors did not follow suit in this respect [229]. Surnames that imply their divinity were forced upon them by Greek towns [230]. The first to call himself 'epiphanes' was King Ptolemy V (210-180 B.C.) of Egypt [231]. Among the Seleucid rulers Antiochus IV was the first to name himself 'the manifest god'; as far as I know this title was not bestowed on him by a Greek town.

Did he, in contrast to his predecessors, see himself as deified? It is not improbable, for it would square with his slightly megalomaniac character. He venerated Zeus Olympios and promoted his cult throughout his domains; this was something new since the protecting deity of the Seleucids had always been Apollo [232]. Some scholars argue that the effigy of Zeus on the king's coins bears the royal features; if this is correct, then we have a clear case of identification. Did the king see a rival whom he wished to eliminate in the Jahve of the Jews ? We have no evidence of this. But he would obviously have been irritated by the uncompromising monotheism of the Jews with its implicit rejection of his claim to divinity.

The author of the Book of Daniel who wrote later in this period fostered no illusions about the royal pretension. "As for the king (doubtless Antiochus IV is meant - F.), he shall have his own way; in his pride, he will think himself a match for any god, even if that God (= Jahve) boast himself the rival who is above all gods ... What are his father's gods to him? ... Of gods he recks little that will set up himself over all" [233]. This might be a plausible reason why Antiochus IV and the Jews opposed each other so implacably.

g. Some main points

Before we proceed we must make a few things clear. Firstly, the attempts to hellenize Judaea did not originate with Antiochus IV. Secondly, as we saw, there was an influentiual hellenizing party among the Jews themselves. And thirdly, there had already been rebellious movements and even street-fighting in Jerusalem before the king published his anti-religious decrees [234]. On his return from an Egyptian campaign in 169 B.C., the king had already shown how little respect he had for what was sacred to the Jews. He then had visited Jerusalem and left the city with the plunder from the temple treasury [235]. The population of the town felt this not only as a financial catastrophe but still more as a sacrilege : "Loud mourning there was in Israel, mourning in all the country-side" [236].

h. The implementation of the king's policy

Encouraged by a (false) rumour that the king was dead the banished Jason tried his luck again; he stormed Jerusalem and captured it taking a bloody revenge on his fellow-countrymen [237]. But not long afterwards he had to flee for the second time and now for good (he died as an exile in Sparta [238]). The king who did not want to see the Hellenizing party in trouble sent a Syrian army that took the town by storm; the victorious soldiers were given a free hand to go around killing and slaughtering the citizens (the orthodox, of course) without sparing women and children; many thousands were afterwards sold as slaves [239]. The temple treasury was thoroughly robbed once again [240]. When the army marched away, a Syrian garrison was left behind under a Phrygian commander [241].

There is a hiatus in the story here, but it seems that, after the departure of the main body of the army, the rebellion flared up again. For it is related that a Syrian general, called Apollonius, came to the city with a large army, entered it (obviously without encountering opposition), and then, on a sabbath evening, fell upon the population. Striking left and right at those who were going to the synagogues, the ferocious soldiers once again butchered many people [242]. The Syrian reaction had now reached the stage of genocide. And if one thing is dualistic, it is genocide. All this happened in 168 B.C.

Apollonius, now undisputedly master of the Holy City, secured his position by turning the so-called 'David's city' into an impregnable stronghold [243]. It got regular garrison, and apart from that, was peopled with 'a godless crew of sinners' [244], 'people of a foreign god' [245], 'the sons of the aliens' [246]. To all intents and purposes this was the start of a policy of hellenizing Jerusalem, not only mentally but first of all demographically. This policy was unwittingly helped on by the Jews themselves who now began to flee the town; their 'leaving the city to strangers' [247] made it into 'a haunt of the Gentiles' [248].

j. Antiochus' 'evil decrees'

Literally speaking, Tcherikover is right in saying that at the end of the year 168 B.C. there still was no religious persecution [249]. However, the population of Judaea must have felt themselves persecuted, particularly in view of the immigration of pagan settlers who brought their hated idols, like Baal, with them and even wanted to venerate them on the Temple Hill. The real persecution of Jewish religion began in 167 B.C. with the decree of Antiochus IV that I have already mentioned. The king's new policy clearly aimed at eradicating the Jewish religion lock, stock, and barrel. The stubborn resistance of the orthodox to hellenization and the repeated risings had proved to the king that political and military measures were not sufficient to stamp out the simmering revolt. He must have reached the conclusion that the spiral spring of the resistance to him and his claims was the Jewish creed; without dealing this a deadly blow he would never be able to triumph over these rebellious subjects. The fact that he considered himself divine may have spurred him on to eliminate a rival. The dualistic character the struggle had assumed already was still more strengthened in this way.

A royal envoy was sent to Jerusalem to enforce the decrees. Filled with horror, pious Jews saw what the pagans did, helped by many of their compatriots [250]. The following measures were taken. The Temple was rededicated to Zeus Olympios; on the fifteenth of the month Kislev [251] his statue was placed on the altar [252]. The sacred precincts were defiled by the presence of temple prostitutes. The daily sacrifices no longer took place; instead an altar was set up in the forecourt on which the 'abomination of desolation' was placed, an idol that became the object of pagan offerings. The people shuddered at the idea that swine's meat was eaten in the Temple grounds, together with other proscribed food. Everywhere in Judaea shrines were set up and sacrifices brought. The holy books of the Torah were hunted up and burnt. Circumcision was forbidden on pain of death; sabbath might no longer be celebrated. Everything that was fundamental in the Jewish creed was to be abolished until, at last, it would be forgotten [253]. Can anything more dualistic be imagined?

Even for us moderns it will not be difficult how offensive this was to Jewish orthodoxy. In particular the setting up of an idol on the Temple's sacrificial altar must have appeared to the pious as the worst possible desecration of all that was holy to Israel. Tcherikover may be correct in asserting that 'Zeus Olympios' really was the Syrian 'Baal Shamim' = the Lord of the Heavens', and that Antiochus probably saw no great difference between the Greek, Syrian, and Jewish supreme gods [254]. But could he have misunderstood his Judaean subjects to such an extent that he did not realize how deeply he had insulted them by introducing a Graeco-Syrian deity into their sanctuary? If we remember that Antiochus in no small measure identified himself with Zeus Olympios, it will be clear that the Jews were supposed to adore Zeus Olympios, Baal Shamim, and their king in the same ritual.

The population of Judaea, especially that of the Holy City, now fell apart into two dualistically opposed groups. There were the Hellenizers, dependent on Syria, who complied with the king's wishes. And there were the orthodox, the mass of the common people who made the Law of Moses their 'war-cry', "just as Greek culture was the watchword of the aristocracy" [255]. The Books of Machabees have bloodcurdling stories to tell of how valiantly Jewish men, women, and children resisted the decrees, and how cruelly they were punished for this. The elderly scribe Eleazar, seven brothers and their mother were all martyred to death in the most sadistic way because they refused to eat swine's flesh [256]. Though such stories doubtless are embellished with fabulous elements, we should not dismiss them too glibly as pure legend [257]. Why doubt that some pious clashed with the authorities because of their faithfulness to Mosaic Law and that they paid dearly for it?

k. From guerilla to open war

Already before Antiochus' decrees had been issued, a party of ten men had taken to the hills, utterly disgusted as they were with the situation;

they lived there like hermits [258]. Their leader was Judas the Machabee (the Hebrew word 'makkabi' means 'hammer' [259]). This man was the third of the five sons of Matthatias who belonged to the Hasmonaean family, the descendants of a certain Hasmon [260]. Many other Jerusalemites fled to the desert too. The royal garrison of the citadel surprised them on a sabbath day; adhering strictly to the Law the Jews offered no resistance and were all butchered, a thousand people in all [261]. When this tragic news reached Judas' party, they resolved that they would fight for their lives, even on sabbath days [262].

Secretly visiting the villages of the country-side they rallied a small Jewish army of about six thousand men [263]. Their ranks were swelled by a number of Chassidim. These Chassidim were a party of strict adherents to Mosaic law, 'of great consequence in Israel, lovers of the Law one and all' [264]. Tcherikover calls them "the chief scribes and authoritative interpreters of the regulations and commandments of the Torah" [265].

It was in 166 B.C. that Judas with his men began the guerilla against the Syrians exterminating idolatry root and branch in the whole country-side [266]. Two Syrian generals who tried to stop him were successively defeated by Judas [267]. The Syrian government now became apprehensive [268]; Palestine was too important as a base for Egyptian campaigns against Syria to leave it in the hands of Jewish insurgents [269]. The Syrians came out in great force against the Machabaean army but suffered defeat in three successive battles [270]. Judas, now master of the whole country, stormed Jerusalem and took it, with the exception of the citadel [271].

What now followed was the Purification of the Temple, an event that is still commemorated annually by orthodox Jews (it is called 'Chanukah'). The polluted altar was demolished and replaced by a new one; in every respect the traditional cult of Jahve was restored (165 B.C.) [272]. With this restoration the first and purely religious phase of the War of Liberation ended.

The successes of the Jews did not spell much good for their co-religionists living in the Graeco-Syrian towns. The well-to-do of these cities came forward with large sums of money to buy Jewish prisoners-of-war as slaves [273]. After the restoration of the Jahve cult the temperature in the Hellenic cities rose quickly. "Great indignation had the Gentiles that lived round about, when they heard that altar and temple were standing as of old. Their first thought was to rid their own territory of Jacob's breed" [274]. In the Tubin country all the Jews who lived there were deported [275].

The predicament of his brethren in the Diaspora forced Judas to give his crusade a more political character. He consequently began to campaign far beyond the frontiers of Judaea, in Idumaea to the south, in the regions east of the Jordan, and along the coastal strip as far north as Ptolemais (= Akko), while his brother Simon fought successfully in Galilee [276]. The fame of Judas rose to the stars on account of these exploits; he might be compared now, says Tcherikover, with other daring men of his generation, like Mithridates of Pontus and Arsaces of Parthia who also fought the Seleucids sword in hand [277]. Judas' successes laid the basis for the royal rule of the Hasmonaeans over the country.

Of course the Syrian court was highly alarmed at the extension of Jewish power. When in 163 B.C. King Antiochus IV had died and had been succeeded by Antiochus V Eupator who still a minor, Lysias, the boy's guardian and the Grand Vizir, mustered an enormous army and marched southward. Confronted by forces that were far superior to his, Judas fell back on Jerusalem where he was beleaguered by the Syrians. But before Lysias could take the town, a rival turned up way in Syria. Suddenly feeling the need to fight this man, Lysias compromised with Judas [278]. A royal decree of 162 B.C. restored religious freedom to the Jews but did not grant them independence [279]. In this way the fateful hellenizing episode in Judaea ended. One sore point remained : a Syrian garrison was still posted in the citadel, and the Hellenizers lived under its protection.

Soon enough the war broke out again. Lysias, who did not trust the Jews farther than he saw them, appointed an Hellenizer, Alcimus, as High Priest [280]. This man was sent southward from Antioch with a big army under a Syrian general. Fighting was renewed in what was also a civil war, since part of the Jews were on the side of Alcimus. At first Judas was successful but later the Syrians became the stronger; Judas was defeated and fell (160 B.C.) [281].

The Syrians were in complete control now, but Judas' younger brother Jonathan carried on the struggle in the form of a guerilla [282]. Hiding in the hills and supported by the local population he stood his ground very well. Campaign after campaign was conducted against him till the Syrians finally became fed up with the affair. The Jewish cause was helped by the fact that pretenders to the Syrian throne sought Jonathan's assistance. In 152 B.C. the Syrian government at last realized that they could not lean on the isolated hellenizing faction. Jonathan was appointed High Priest; bedecked with the sacred vestments he officiated at the Feast of the Tabernacles in that same year [283].

The rest of the story can be told quickly. In 150 B.C. Jonathan became governor of Judaea by appointment of the Seleucid monarch; he now combined spiritual and secular power in his person. Under his successor and brother Simon the citadel was conquered at last [284]. The son and successor of Simon, Johannes Hyrcanus, definitively severed the Hasmonaean realm from the Seleucid Empire in 129 B.C.. Thus the long and dualistic struggle of the Jews against Hellenization ended with their complete triumph and the end of hellenizing policies. Palestine is the only region in the Hellenistic world where such a struggle was fought.

12. Resistance to Hellenization in Egypt

At first sight Egypt seems to make a convincing case for the success of Hellenization. For was there not the splendid city of Alexandria, founded by Alexander himself and laid out in the geometrical Greek fashion? And did not this town become one of the great centres of Hellenistic learning and culture? But on second thoughts certain qualifications spring to mind. The Egyptian civilization is one of the oldest in the world; Egyptians have always looked down on foreigners as being far less civilized than they themselves [285]. We may assume that, though they were subdued by these uncouth Greeks and Macedonians, they were not really impressed by their culture. To autochthonous and self-conscious Egyptians it must have seemed as though the times of the Hyksos had returned : foreigners were in complete control of the country. Eduard Meyer must be correct in stating that even the idea of an amalgamation of nations did not arise in Egypt; for such a policy the country was too isolated and its population too well aware of its peculiar character [286].

Add to this that an important element of Hellenization was almost completely failing in Egypt, viz. the founding of Hellenic cities. Of old Greeks had by no means been as numerous in Egypt as in other regions of the Mediterranean world. There existed only one pre-Alexandrian colony, Naucratis in the Nile Delta. Apart from the royal foundation Alexandria, there were perhaps three or four other Hellenic towns. Very probably there was only one (besides Alexandria) really Hellenic city in Egypt, Ptolemais, built on the site of ancient Thebes; this town possessed an authentic polis constitution [287].

And Alexandria? This town "was never an autonomous Greek city. (it) was founded as a Greek centre of government to ensure Greek control over the land, but this control was to be exercised ... by an autocratic satrap after the Prussian model". When this satrap later became the king-Pharaoh, Alexandria "developed into the city in which the Greek king of Egypt resided, and in which Greek and Egyptian lived on terms of equality" [288]. The population of the town consisted of several ethnic groups, composed of more or less cultivated Greek mercenaries, most of them a rough lot, and Egyptians who were 'hard to control', says Polybius [289]. The town also saw a large influx of Jews who became tax-collectors or engaged in commerce.

There were so many of them that the town became one of the great centres of Judaism. The wealthier section of the Jewish community spoke, wrote, and traded in Greek; this necessitated the translation of the Old Testament into koinè; it was in Alexandria that the Septuagint originated. The Jews of the town kept very much to themselves and isolated themselves from the other townfolk. As a consequence of this conspicuous aloofness there occurred anti-Jewish (but not necessarily anti-Semitic) riots in which Greeks and Egyptians for once put up a common front; from time to time the Jews repaid in kind [290]. All this means that this turbulent city should not be quoted as a model polis but rather as an example how difficult it proved to establish a mixed but harmonious society.

Of course, the existence of four Hellenic cities was not sufficient for hellenizing such a big country. Egypt had never been a land of cities; it was almost totally agricultural. When in the first centuries of Ptolemaic rule Greek mercenaries and Macedonian veterans had to be settled, and Greeks from the mother-country began to immigrate (not always the best elements), the kings diverted them to the countryside [291]. There these people were allotted land [292]; in the course of time a kind of Greek landed gentry came into being. After 200 B.C. the emigration from Greece stopped since the country was becoming depopulated.

The result of the arrival of the Graeco-Macedonians was the establishment of a new ruling class. As Walbank writes, "the Egyptians were at a disadvantage in so far as the new ruling class was entirely made up of newcomers". These formed "a single caste from which even the richer native Egyptians were excluded" [293]. It was only much later, in the second century B.C., that, because of economic developments, this sharp social dividing line became somewhat blurred. The difference between Greek and non-Greek was to some extent replaced by that of rich and poor, now that many Egyptians had grown wealthy and many Greeks had become destitute [294].

This should not be exaggerated, however. Rostovzeff gives a fascinating example of how Egyptian society was organized, even in later days. A governor travelling on a Nile boat arrives at a landing-place. The whole population turns out to welcome him. In front stand the high priest and the other priests; behind them the militarized Greek settlers. Then come the families of the soldiers and the clients of the governor, and next a number of people who happen to be present but do not reside there. The governor will certainly need a fairly high pedestal in order to detect the mass of the autochthonous population standing grouped behind all the others. So this author is justified in concluding that "the old division into a privileged class of 'Greeks' (which now comprised many hellenized Egyptians) and a subordinate class of natives remained as it had been" [295].

Although the two nations seem to have got on reasonably well with each other, there were nevertheless two races and not one; this occasionally caused friction, with the Egyptians complaining the loudest. In the middle of the third century B.C. we hear an important priest protesting that the Greeks "despise him because he is an Egyptian" [296]. For a long time the Greeks of Egypt, like their compatriots everywhere else, kept themselves apart from the indigenous population, although there was some degree of intermarriage. A special role was played by the Greek gymnasia. Here young Greeks received their cultural and physical education; the graduated formed associations of ex-students, a kind of old boys' network. Later 'culture-Greeks' were also admitted, Egyptians who had become thoroughly hellenized. Other Greeks organized themselves in the so-called 'politeumata', or 'nation groups' [297]. It will be clear that these Egypto-Greeks were not very keen on mixing socially or otherwise with the rest of the population.

Of course, the Egyptians had become used to foreign domination for centuries. They had already been subjected to Ethiopian, Assyrian, and Persian rule. But no Assyrian or Persian emperor had resided in person in the country nor had there been a foreign ruling class in those periods. But with the advent of the Graeco-Macedonians things changed considerably; the new ruling class, foreign as it was, fed on the country and appropriated many of its resources. The Egyptians, always a proud race with an incredibly old civilization, resented this. Justinus vaguely mentions a rising in Egypt that may have taken place in 241 B.C. [298]. A quarter of a century later there was trouble again. For the umpteenth time there was a war on between Egypt and Syria; being short of soldiers, Ptolemy IV Philopator had enlisted many native Egyptians, even providing part of them with heavy armament. Polybius calls this 'a mistake as regards the future'. After the Egyptian victory over the Syrians at Raphia in 217 B.C., these soldiers chose a leader of their own, and now were 'able to maintain themselves as an independent power' [299]. The result was a rebellion that was to last for many years; perhaps it was supported by a Nubian prince. Several cities, like Abydos, seem to have temporarily been in the hands of the insurgents; they had to be besieged and recaptured. The rebellion only ended when the last bulwark of the rebels, Sais in the Delta, was taken by a Greek general in 184/183 B.C.

The last century B.C. again saw a revolt; this too followed in the wake of a Syrian war. An Egyptian called Dionysios Petoserapis organized a popular revolt in Alexandria, possibly in 168 B.C.; according to Jouguet he wanted to bring down the monarchy. In this design he did not succeed; soon enough he somewhat mysteriously disappeared. Although the capital was pacified, the rising was not yet quelled. Thebes, the old capital, now became the main centre of resistance. Finally this town was captured by the royal army and partly destroyed in 86 B.C.

The history of internal Egyptian rebellions covers a period of one and a half centuries. The Egyptians did not get much out of this prolonged struggle. The royal Greek troops always proved the stronger [300]. On the whole, one could say that Hellenization in Egypt was successful in so far that there originated a class of 'half-Greeks', of (partly) hellenized Egyptians. But, as Jouguet exclaims, "what a distance between these half-Greeks and the veritable Hellenes". They had no poleis - and what is more authentically Greek than life in a polis? -, and living in villages they laid themselves open to oriental superstitions. They could read Greek but wrote it ever more incorrectly. Even official documents were written in bastard-Greek. Jouguet speaks here of a 'dishellenization of the Greeks in Egypt' [301]. It is a remarkable example of how conquerors become conquered by an older and stronger civilization.

13. Conclusion

At the beginning of this chapter I stated that the Macedonian conquest had shifted 'the frontier of Europe' to the Euphrates. The use of this term has an ideological implication, since it may mean that Asia Minor was thoroughly hellenized whereas all other regions, in particular those between the Euphrates and the Indus, were simply left to the orientals.

As we saw, neither alternative is correct. But the new rulers of Asia Minor had a far better chance of triumphing over the age-old dualism of Europe and Asia than the other Graeco-Macedonian kings.

East of the Euphrates, the autochthonous civilizations, Babylonian, Iranian, Bactrian, Indian, in the long run reasserted themselves and finally obliterated the Hellenic element. But it is a very remarkable thing that in Afghanistan and in the Indus valley pockets of Greekdom held out so long.

Active resistance against the policy of Hellenization only occurred in Palestine and in Egypt. In Judaea this resistance assumed a religious character; it was so successful that the Jews became independent from Syria. The rebellions in Egypt failed but there too the national culture slowly but certainly overcame the alien one. The existence of two brilliant Hellenistic cultural centres in these regions, Antioch and Alexandria, by no means proves that the policy of Hellenization had succeeded. Mixed civilization never arose while the success of Hellenization everywhere remained limited to a small part of the population. On the whole, all those regions remained as Egyptian or oriental as they were before Alexander came.

The picture is somewhat different in Asia Minor because this is the only region where Hellenization scored a partial success. From a political and military point of view it could be argued that 'Europe' had indeed been extended now to the Euphrates. In social and political respects, we see the country studded with Greek towns, one of which, Pergamum, became one of the great cultural centres of Hellenism; the Greek koinê was in wide use as lingua franca. But on closer inspection we see that the kingdoms on the south coast of the Black Sea, Pontus and Bithynia, and Galatia and Cappadocia in the interior, remained virtually untouched by Hellenic civilization.

Summarizing, we must state that Hellenism, as an official policy, never got off the ground if we understand by it the complete fusion of the Greek, Macedonian, Egyptian, and oriental nations and their cultures. A common identity transcending what was specifically Hellenic, Asiatic or Egyptian was nowhere to be found. The policy of Hellenization, as it was pursued with more or less success by the Graeco-Macedonian rulers, never really impaired the old dualism of Europe and Asia. There was much resistance on both sides. The Greeks in Egypt and Asia who either secretly or openly loathed the barbarians kept too much to themselves to really influence and change their surroundings. The orientals had mixed feelings about the situation; they often felt slighted by the foreign ruling class but at the same time realized that their own civilizations were far older than the Hellenic and even superior to it. Sometimes Hellenization was accepted rather on pragmatic grounds because it made orientals socially acceptable to the ruling class, or because speaking koinê often came in handy, but there is no evidence of a profound change of heart. Most of the time the orientals offered a dumb resistance to Hellenization, with a few violent outbursts. This whole curious episode of world history, starting with Alexander's invasion of Asia and ending with the coming of the Romans, resulted in a highly confused situation, with the old dualism as the enduring factor.

NOTES TO CHAPTER II

1. See Vol. II, Ch. III.2a.
2. See Martini s.v. 'Dikaiarchos', PW V (1905), 546-563.
3. Pédech, Géogr. 97.
4. FrHG II.251, Dic. fr, 55.
5. Knaack s.v. 'Eratosthenes', PW VI (1909), 358-388.
6. Geogr.Fr.Er. 170/171, Fr. IIIA2 (= Strabo 2.1.1-3).
7. Geogr.Fr.Er. 174.
8. Geogr.Fr.Er. 168, Fr. IIC24 (= Strabo 1.4.9).
9. Aristotle, Rhet. (schol.) 1373b18; text given in Aristotelis Ars Rhetorica, ed. Adolphus Roemer, Lipsiae, 1898, note 1018. See also Jüthner, Hell.u.Barb.
10. He is not to be confused with Zeno the Eleate who lived a century earlier.
11. His life in Diog.Laert. 7.1-158; this is the longest biography in Diog., even longer than that of Plato! See Kurt von Fritz s.v. 'Zenon von Kition', PW 2.Reihe, 19. Halbband (1972), 83-121.

12. Tarn, Greece, CAH VI, 437.
13. Haarhoff, Stranger 99/100.
14. Plut., De Fort.Al. 329B6.
15. See Vol. III, Ch. III.14.
16. Ferguson, Leading ideas, CAH VII 37.
17. See Vol. II, Ch. III.2c and 2f.
18. His name lives on in the Allard Pierson Museum on the Oude Turfmarkt at Amsterdam NL; this fine museum displays a rich collection of Egyptian, Hellenic, and Roman antiquities. It really is worth a visit!
19. Pierson, Hell. I, 1/2.
20. In its modern meaning the term 'Hellenism' was introduced into historiography by J.G. Droysen in the title of the first volume of his book 'Geschichte des Hellenismus' (1836 1); very soon it was in general use.
21. Lauffer, Al. 113.
22. In Diod. 18.4.4-5 we find the so-called 'Hypomnenata', or royal memoranda, that contain the last plans of Alexander. Some scholars consider these spurious and others authentic. This tricky question need not concern us since the Hypomnemata say nothing about a fusion of cultures. Baldry, Unity 113, writes ; "The view that Alexander was a man of vision as well as of action, and held a conscious and explicit belief in the unity of mankind, had its supporters in Antiquity as well as in modern times ... (that he was) the dreamer who envisaged a world of universal brotherhood, and so must be regarded as the creator and earliest champion of the idea of human unity." This thesis is in our own days strongly defended by Tarn. Baldry combats the view that the notion of a common and universal mankind was in Alexander's mind. He nevertheless admits that the king took an attitude to 'barbarians' that was not usual among the Greeks. He ascribes this first and foremost to the fact that "racial exclusiveness was not part of the Macedonian outlook".
23. Arrian, Anab. 7.14.
24. Arrian, Anab. 7.11.8-9; Strabo 1.4.9.
25. Lauffer, Al. 177/178; See for a thorough discussion of the whole subject of 'Brotherhood and unity', Tarn, Al. II, App. 25.
26. The still sovereign Greek poleis constituted an exception to this rule since they kept their right of minting coinage, but even in Hellas the Alexandrian coins came into general use, Beloch, Gr. Gesch. III.1.42/43.
27. Arrian, Anab. 4.19.5.
28. Plut., Al. 47.4; so Curtius too who usually has a negative judgment on Alexander, Curt., Hist.Al. 8.4.23-24.

29. Tarn, Al. II, 26 : "It is certain that he married her for political reasons"; Hampl, Al. 50 : 'an act of wild passion'.
30. Plut., Al. 47.4. even says that Roxane was the only woman the king ever loved.
31. Curt., Hist.Al. 8.4.27.
32. For Statira see Berve, Al.Reich II, nr. 722, 363/364. Arrian, Anab. 7.4.4. confuses her with Barsine whom Alexander also made prisoner after the Battle of Issus, Berve, Al.Reich II, nr. 206, 102/103. Alexander's first wife Roxane became so jealous of Statira that she, immediately after her husband's death, had her murdered and her corpse thrown into a well. Statira never had children, Plut., Al. 72.4.
33. Arrian, Anab. 7.4.4.
34. Nothing more is known of her, Berve, Al.Reich II, nr. 607, 306.
35. Berve, Al.reich II, nr. 50, 24; Craterus does not belong to the Diadochi since he fell in battle already in 321 B.C.
36. Arr., Anab. 7.4.4-8; Plut., Al. 70.2.
37. Diod. 17.6 : 'epeise'.
38. Diod. 18.7; Berve, Al.reich II, nr. 50, 24.
39. Berve, Al.reich II, nr. 98, 52; Tarn, Al. III, 111 calls this 'an honourable and politic exception', politic no doubt because Seleucus wanted to placate the nations beyond the Tigris. He called three cities 'Apameia'.
40. Walbank, Hell.World 63.
41. Strabo, 17.1.12.
42. Préaux, Monde hell. II, 546 and 550.
43. See for the composition of the invading forces Berve, Al.reich I 103-105.
44. Arrian, Anab. 7.6.1; Plut., Al. 7.1-2; for the indigenous troops see Berve, Al.reich I, 150-155.
45. Plut, Al. 45.1-3; Diod. 17.77 and 78.
46. Diod. 17.108.3; Arrian, Anab. 7.8.3.
47. Arrian, Anab. 7.8-11; Plut., Al. 71.
48. The first exhaustive survey of Alexandrian foundations was given by Droysen, Gesch.d.Hell. III. II.Halbband. Beilage I, 187-385; Berve, Al.reich I, 291-301; Tarn, Al. I, App. 8, 232-259; a good modern discussion of the role of the Hellenistic city by Préaux, Monde hell. II, 452-460.
49. Jouguet, Imp.Mac. 104.
50. Consult the book of Waldemar Heckel, The Last Days and Testament of Alexander the Great : A Prosopographic Study. Stuttgart, 1988 (Historia, Einzelschriften, Heft 56). This book came too late into my hands to make use of it.

51. Diod. 18.4.4-6.
52. Hamilton, Al. 156 finds it very difficult to believe that Alexander really wanted to transfer Asiatics to an already overpopulated Greece. But could he plan otherwise in view of his idea of the basic equality of rights between Hellenes and orientals?
53. Plut., Fort.Al., Moralia 328E and 329F. Plut. gives the number of Alexandrian city foundations as more than seventy; of these only thirteen have been recovered with certainty, and twenty others with some degree of probability, Préaux, Monde hell. II, 402.
54. Arrian, Anab. 4.4.1.
55. Diod. 17.83.2.
56. Diod. 18.7. According to this author the revolt took place after the death of the king. But Curtius has it that they rebelled when he was campaigning in India, Curtius 9.7. Their relations differ so much that they perhaps are speaking of two different occasions.
57. Berve, Al.reich I 298, II, nr. 29, 109 and nr. 219, 110.
58. Hoffmann/Debrunner, Gesch.Gr.Spr.I 65.
59. Hoffmann/Debrunner, Gesch.Gr.Spr. I 59.
60. Hoffmann/Debrunner, Gesch.Gr.Spr. II 27.
61. Isocrates, Antidotis (15), 295-296.
62. In Dutch 'Algemeen Beschaafd Nederlands', or ABN.
63. Jüthner, Hell.u.Barb. 39.
64. Com.Att.Fr. III 345.
65. Fr.Hist.Gr. II 261.
66. (Xenophon), Const.Ath.2.8. See Bowersock's introduction 461.
67. Hoffmann/Debrunner, Gesch.Gr.Spr. II 69.
68. Wilamowitz, Gesch.gr.Spr. 30/31.
69. Haarhoff, Stranger 238/239; Jüthner, Hell.u.Barb. 40/41.
70. Not a letter of this treatise has been preserved.
71. Rom.11:1; Phil.3:5; 2Cor.11:22.
72. Wilamowitz, Gesch.gr.Spr. 33.
73. Wilamowitz, Gesch.gr.Spr. 36.
74. Hoffmann/Debrunner, Gesch.Gr.Spr. II 76.
75. Wilamowitz, Glaube II, 264.
75. Arrian, An.Al. 3.4.5; Plut., Al. 27.3.4.
76. Arrian, 13.1.4.
77. Arrian 3.1.4.
78. Strabo 17.1.43.
79. Pearson, Lost.Hist. 33-35.
80. Arrian, An.Al. 4.10-12.

81. See also Tarn, Al., CAH VI, 399.
83. Kern, Rel.d.Gr. III, 56.
83. See for this subject Kern, Rel.d.Gr. III, Kap. IV, Einbruch und Umbruch.
85. Ferguson, Leading Ideas, CAH VII.5.
86. 2 Kings 17:33,34.
87. Jonas, Gnost. 29.
88. Woodcock, Gr.Ind. 41.
89. Woodcock, Gr.Ind. 42.
90. See Vol. V, Ch. II.4b.
91. Woodcock, Gr.Ind. 47.
92. Woodcock, Gr.Ind. 57; see for the relationship between Açoka and the Indo-Greeks his Chapter III, 'Ashoka and the Greeks'. Also Tarn, Gr.Bactr. 388/389 and 391/392.
93. Woodcock, Gr.Ind. 58/59.
94. Arr., An.Al. 6.7.4-6; Diod. 17.103.
95. Tarn, Gr.Bactr. 173.
96. See Vol. V, Ch. II.15.b and d.
97. Tarn, Gr.Bactr. 173/174.
98. For instance H. van Gelder's much used textbook of ancient history for Dutch grammar schools (Groningen, 1962 12 ed.) does not even mention it.
99. CAH VII, although having chapters on Hellenistic Syria and Egypt, has no chapter on Bactria; two books destined for a general public, Fischers Weltgeschichte, and Chester G. Starr, A History of the Ancient World (New York, 1974 2, 1965 first publ.) remains silent on this subject while in Berve, Gr.Gesch. II it is only mentioned as a conquest of Alexander.
100. Rostovzeff, Hist.Anc.World I, 259.
101. Since World War II, however, several combined Dutch-Belgian histories have appeared.
102. Woodcock, Gr.Ind. 62.
103. Tarn, Gr.Bactria 72; Sallet, Nachf. 19.
104. Just.41.4; this author calls him 'Theodotus'. That Antiochus II married his daughter to Diodotus I as Tarn, Gr.Bactr. 73 states, is combated by Narain, Ind.Gr. 18 as an unproved suggestion; her name is not known and of her existence. there is no evidence.
105. Narain, Indo-Gr. 19.
106. Woodcock, Gr.Ind. 70.
107. Pol. 11.39.

108. Pol., Hist. 10.49 calls it 'Zariaspa', very probably identical with the present-day 'Balkh', 336 km north-east of Kabul. The ancient town has not been excavated, see Tomaschek s.v. 'Baktra', PW II (1896), 2804/2805, and Tarn, Gr.bactr. 114-116.
109. Pol. 11.39.
110. Tarn, Gr.Bactria 83/84.
111. FHG IV (1851), 308/309, no. 5.
112. See Vol. V, Ch. III.10.
113. Woodcock, Gr.Ind. 63.
114. So for instance Just. 41.4.5, and Strabo 15.3 (686).
115. See for this passage Tarn, Gr.Bactria 118-122.
116. Ghirshman, Iran 222.
117. Ghirshman, Iran 222.
118. Altheim, Weltgesch. Asiens I, 296/297 : "Art and forms of life of the Bactrian Greeks do not give the slightest indication that they were prepared to create something like a Graeco-Iranian mixed culture ... The will of the indigenous Iranian population to preserve its own seems to have been not smaller".
119. Tarn, Gr.Bactria 124/125.
120. Altheim, Weltgesch.Asiens I, 323-353.
121. Ghirshman, Iran 222.
122. Not to be confused, of course, with Demetrius I Poliorketes, the son of Antigonus Monophthalmos and king of Macedonia; the date of the death of the Bactrian Demetrius I is unknown. There is considerable confusion in the ancient sources (which are scarce) on the question of who conquered what in India; there is this Demetrius, and perhaps yet another Demetrius, further an Apollodotus, probably a younger son of Euthydemus, and finally Menander. See for this problem Tarn, Gr.Bactr. 76, Narain, Indo-Gr. 34-37, Woodcock, Gr.Ind. 79 sqq.
123. There is no mention of Antimachus I in classical sources; he is only known from coin finds, Wilcken s.v. 'Antimachos I', PW I (1894), 2433.
124. Woodcock, Gr.Ind. 85.
125. Woodcock, Gr.Ind. 79.
126. Just.41.6.
127. See Plate 3 in Tarn, Gr.Bactria.
128. Now the ruins of Sirkap; the rectangular pattern is still visible, Woodcock, Gr.Ind. 89.
129. See Vol. V, Ch. II.4d. Narain, Ind.Gr. discusses these sources pp. 81-85. The name of a certain King Antialcidas is found in an inscription on a pillar, o.c. 118.
130. Woodcock, Gr.Ind. 103.

131. Woodcock, Gr.Ind. 104 and 113. There is an echo of this in Plut., Moralia 821 D, where he says that Menander ruled 'with equity'.
132. Woodcock, Gr.Ind. 103.
133. Vol.V, Ch. II.5. I say 'commonly' because Tarn, Gr.Bactr. 283-286, strongly combats the view taken by nearly all other authors that Greek Bactria was lost to the Sakas. He believes that Strabo's communication (11.8.4) "the Sakas ... occupied Bactria" does not refer to the second century B.C. but to the seventh century B.C., that is to the Achaemenid period. However, Tarn does not deny that the country was indeed overrun by nomads in the second century B.C.; according to him, however, the invaders were called Arsi or Arsii who formed part of the Yuehzhi.
134. See Vol. V, Ch. I.3b and Ch.II.5.
135. Woodcock, Gr.Ind. 128.
136. Narain, IndoGr. 164.
137. Woodcock, Gr.Ind. 129.
138. Woodcock, Gr.Ind. 131.
139. It is a significant thing that there never existed a Graeco-Bactrian or Indo-Greek literature.
140. Altheim, Al.u.As. 161-163 writes that the Graeco-Bactrian king Euthydemus did "what Alexander had planned and begun (and) what the Seleucids let slip", viz. the possibility of fusion, was actualized by this king. But on reading him carefully, I can only find that Greeks married Iranian women, that indigenous cavalry formed an important part of Euthydemus' army, and that the name of one native Bactrian governor is known. Is this sufficient to speak of a deliberate policy?
141. See Vol. V, Ch. I.2a.
142. We find this title on their coins, Ghirshman, Iran 226.
143. Ghirshman, Iran 266.
144. Altheim, Weltgesch.As. 268/269.
145. On the Euphrates midway between Aleppo and Baghdad; in 363 A.D. already in ruins, now Essalehiye.
146. Momigliano, Al.Wisdom 139.
147. Ghirshman, Iran 267.
148. Meyer, Blüte 70/71. Reprinted in Hell. in Mittelas. 19.
149. Its present successor is the Turkish town of Bergama. The attention of tourists is mainly attracted by the sanctuary of Asclepius, dating from 390 B.C., with the remains of the temple (ca. 170 B.C.). this does not belong to the urban area itself from which it is one and a half miles distant.
150. Just as writing on paper, 'papyrus' (a kind of cane or rush growing along the Nile), originated in Alexandria, writing on parchment was invented in Pergamum. As will be evident, the material 'parch-

ment' has the same name as the town. In Dutch this is still more evident, for there it is called 'perkament'. Curiously enough, scarcely any of the few monographs on the history of Pergamum has anything of importance to say on its culture : 1. Giuseppe Cardinali, Il Regno di Pergamo. Ricerche di storia e di diritto pubblico. Roma, 1906; 2. Joachim Hopp, Untersuchung zur Geschichte der letzten Attaliden. München, 1977; 3. Roger B. McShane, The Foreign Policy of the Attalids of Pergamum. Urbana, 1964. It seems that historians find it easier to write political history than the history of culture. It is only in the bulky volume of Esther V. Hansen, Attalids, that we find a hundred and thirty pages on art and learning. And then, of course, the eighty page-chapter in Kuiper, Hell. II.

151. Hansen, Att. 390; description of this building 253-259.
152. Kuiper in his eloquent and admiring essay on Pergamum in Hell. II does not say a word about this.
153. Petit, Civ.hell. 60-64.
154. W. Zschietschmann s.v. 'Pergamum', PW XIX (1938), 1235-1263, does not take one step beyond the city precincts.
155. Vitucci, Bitinia, Cap. VI.
156. Reinach, Mithr. 28-30.
157. Reinach, Mithr. 227/228.
158. Reinach, Mithr. 246.
159. Tarn, Hell.Civ. 149.
160. Tarn, Hell.Civ. 150.
161. Petit, Civ.hell. 52.
162. Grant, From Al. to Cleo. 55/56.
163. Walbank, Hell.World 65 and 125.
164. Strabo 16.2.10-30.
165. Joannes Malalas, Pausanias Damascenus, FGH, ed. Müller, IV 468/469.
166. W.Tomaschek s.v. 'Antiocheia', PW I (1894), 2443.
167. Tcherikover, Hel.Civ. 35. For once I was unable to spot the quotation.
168. Pierson/Kuiper, Hell. I 193.
169. Tcherikover, Hell.Civ. 49.
170. Tcherikover, Hell.Civ. 81.
171. Jos. Jew.Ant. 12.138-144.
172. Jos.Jew.Ant. 12.153. Many scholars doubt the veracity of the letter and the decree, considering them 'a Jewish forgery of a later period'; they were led into this by Jos. himself who states that in the days of Julius Caesar many persons expressed doubts with

regard to the authenticity of these documents, on the ground that nobody else had preserved them, Jos., Jew.Ant. 14.187. But I agree with Tcherikover that there is no reason why Antiochus should not have written this letter. It is in perfect harmony with the traditional policy of the Persians and the Egyptians, and he had good cause to be grateful to the Jews, Tcherikover, Hell.Civ. 82/83.

173. Tcherikover, Hell.Civ. 83.
174. Plin., Nat.His. 5.18.74.
175. Tcherikover, Hell.Civ. 105.
176. Tcherikover, Hell.Civ. 115.
177. Diod. 40.3.
178. Neh. 2:19.
179. Neh. 6:17,18.
180. Tcherikover, Hell.Civ. 64.
181. Will, Hist.pol. II, 278.
182. Tcherikover, Hell.Civ. 139/140.
183. Tcherikover, Hell.Civ. 139/140.
184. Will, Hist.pol. II, 278.
185. 2 Macc. 11:7-13.
186. 2 Macc. 4:7-8.
187. Tcherikover, Hell.Civ. 160/161.
188. 2 Macc. 4:10.
189. 2 Macc. 4:9.
190. Tcherikover, Hell.Civ. 161/162.
191. 2 Macc. 9 and 12.
192. 2 Macc. 4:11.
193. 1 Macc. 1:12.
194. Jos., Ant. 12.240.
195. Described by me as a sort of dualism in Vol. IV, Ch. II.15.
196. Jos., Ant. 12.241.
197. 1 Macc. 1:16.
198. 2 Macc. 4:14.
199. Will, Hist.pol. II, 278.
200. In the preface the translator says that he found the book somewhere in Egypt; there is also a terminus ante quem non since the author himself in 10:8 refers to a change of empire doubtless meaning the passing of Judaea from Ptolemaic to Seleucid rule in 197 B.C.
201. Eccl. 3:22-26.
202. Eccl. 41:11-12.

203. Eccl. 31:5.
204. Eccl. 13:26-29.
205. Eccl. 13:20-23.
206. Tcher., Hell.Civ. 147.
207. 2 Macc. 4:25.
208. 2 Macc. 4:39-42.
209. Tcherikover, Hell.Civ. 174.
210. See also Vol. IV, Ch. II.7.b.
211. Tcherikover, Hell.Civ. 175-185.
212. Pol. 26.1. Some modern authors find Polybius' judgment on the king biassed and partial. But Polybius had no reason at all to be severe on this truly Hellenistic king because of his Jewish policy. Furthermore, both Diodorus and Livy follow him in his judgment. Why should these ancient authors have been sympathetic to the Jewish cause? Ath.,Deipn. 10.10.438D also has to say strange things, partly on the authority of Antiochus' royal kinsman Ptolemy III Euergetes of Egypt.
213. Liv. 41.4
214. Radin, Jews 136.
215. Pol. 26; Diod. 29; Liv. 41.
216. To quote only two instances : "Vor allem war er begeistert Freund des Hellenentums ...; auch in seinem Reiche versuchte er nun das Hellenenwesen zu verbreiten", Niese, Gesch. 3, 94/95. He was a 'begeisterter Verehrer des Hellenentums', Wilcken s.v. 'Antiochos IV', PW I (1894), 2470.
217. Radin, Jews 138.
218. Pol. 5.43.1-4.
219. See for instance Pol. 28.22 and 29.13, and Liv, 20.6-9.
220. Paus. 5.12.4.220.
221. Liv. 42.6-12.
222. Pol. 26.6.
223. Liv. 20.11-12.
224. Tcherikover, Hell.Civ. 181.
225. 1 Macc. 1:43-52.
226. Tcherikover, Hell.Civ. 181.
227. Tcherikover, Hell.Civ. 182 argues that this supposed policy of 'religious unification' is 'only a theory held by modern scholars'.
228. Tcherikover, Hell.Civ. 182/183.
229. Nilsson, Gesch.gr.Rel. II, 148.

230. So for instance Antiochus II (287-246) who was given the title 'theos' by Milete because he had liberated the town from a tyrant, App., Syrian War 65; see Habicht, Gott-Menschentum 104.
231. This Ptolemaean Pharaoh was the first of his race to be crowned with the customary Egyptian ceremonial; this circumstance may account for his assuming a godlike surname, Egyptian Pharaohs always having been considered gods, Nilsson, Gesch.gr.Rel. II, 154 and 174.
232. Tcherikover, Hell.Civ. 181.
233. Dan. 11:36-37.
234. Nilsson, Gesch.gr.Rel. II, 160/161 blames the Jews for the outbreak of the war and speaks of the "unversöhnlichen Intoleranz der Juden, dass daraus ein erbitterter Religionskrieg entstand". This scholar seems to expect of the Jews that they would silently accept the introduction of pagan gods into their sanctuaries. Tcherikover, Hell.Civ. 201 says that "the persecution did not anticipate the uprising, but rather the uprising anticipated the persecution", implying that the king, the guarantee of law and order, simply had to retaliate. This is a fair example of how modern historians tend to disown the religious factor. For this is sheer nonsense : the rebellion began precisely because of the attacks on Jewish religion and the sanctuary.
235. 2 Macc. 5:21.
236. 1 Macc. 1:26-27.
237. 2 Macc. 5:6.
238. 2 Macc. 5:7-10.
239. 2 Macc. 5:11/14. It is a problem who stormed Jerusalem. 2 Macc. 5:11 says it was Antiochus himself. This would mean that he was in the city twice, in 169 and in 168 B.C. Many scholars doubt this since 1 and 2 Macc. both mention only one visit, although they may be speaking of two different events. However, the Book of Daniel clearly mentions two visits of the king who on both occasions raged against the Holy Covenant, Dan. 11:28-31. See Tcherikover, Hell.Civ. 186.
240. 2 Macc. 5:22.
241. 2 Macc. 5:22.
242. 1 Macc. 1:30-34; 2 Macc. 5:24-26. This reminds me vividly and tragically of what happened in Amsterdam on sabbath afternoon, Saturday February 22, 1941. Squads of the German Ordnungspolizei under a SS-commander, suddenly appeared in the Jewish quarter where hundreds of people were peacefully taking their sabbath walks. Hundreds of men were torn away from the arms of their wives and fiancées and dragged away. It is not known how many Jews were arrested that afternoon, but 389 were deported to Germany. They were put to work in the stone quarries of KZ Mauthausen. There were no survivors.

243. 1 Macc. 1:35-37.
244. 1 Macc. 1:36.
245. Dan. 11:39.
246. 1 Macc. 3:45.
247. 1 Macc. 1:40.
248. 1 Macc. 3:45.
249. Tcherikover, Hell.Civ. 195.
250. 1 Macc. 1:45; Dan. 11:39.
251. = December
252. 1 Macc. 1:57.
253. 1 Macc. 1:53-64; 2 macc. 6:1-9.
254. Tcherikover, Hell. Civ. 200.
255. Tcherikover, Hell.Civ. 197.
256. 1 Macc. 1:63-67; 2 Macc. 6:18-7:19.
257. Tcherikover, Hell.Civ. 200 " : 'hardly more than fables".
258. 2 Macc. 5:27. 1 Macc. 2:23-28 has the version that Matthatias the Hasmonian killed an apostate Jew and a Syrian official in his city of Modin when he saw them sacrificing to the false god, after which he and his sons, one of whom being Judas the Machabee, fled to the desert; there Matthatias soon died (166 B.C.), 2 Macc. 2:39-70.
259. He therefore was one of the two historical persons being called 'hammer', the other one being the Carolingian mayor of the palace, Charles Martel, the grandfather of Charlemagne.
260. According to Jos., Bell.Iud. 1.36 and Ioannes Antiochenes, FHG IV, fr. 58, pp. 558/559, Hasmon was the father of Matthatias, but according to Jos., Ant. 12.265 his greatgrandfather; this Hasmon is not mentioned in the pedigree of the Machabees in 1 Macc. 2:1-5. See Walter Otto s.v. "Hasmon", PW VII (1912), 2489-2491.
261. 2 Macc. 2:29-38; where Tcherikover, Hell.Civ. 204/205, gets it that these people were Chassidim is a mystery to me; there is not the slightest indication of this in the biblical text.
262. 1 Macc. 2:39-41.
263. 2 Macc. 2:41.
264. 2 Macc. 2:42.
265. Tcherikover, Hell.Civ. 197; he adds that the Chassidim joined the Hasmonaeans because Hellenization would make 'their entire class superfluous'; this led to 'the struggle of an entire class for its existence'. Apart from the fact that interpretation of the Law was not the means of subsistence of the scribes, is it not possible that they were really devoted to the Law and were ready to lay down their lives for it?

266. 1 Macc. 3:1-9; 2 Macc. 8:5-7.
267. 1 Macc. 3:10-14.
268. 1 Macc. 3:25-30.
269. Wolff s.v. 'Judas Makkabaios', PW IX (1916), 2462.
270. 1 Macc. 3:31-4:35.
271. 1 Macc. 4:36-41.
272. 1 Macc. 4:47-61; 2 Macc. 10:1-8.
273. 1 Macc. 3:41; 2 Macc. 8:11 and 34. However, there were no slaves to be bought, and the money fell into Jewish hands, 2 Macc. 8:25.
274. 1 Macc. 5:1-2.
275. 1 Macc. 5:13.
276. 1 Macc. 5:14-68.
277. Tcherikover, Hell.Civ. 223/224.
278. 1 Macc. 6; 2 Macc. 11:1-15.
279. 2 Macc. 11:22-33.
280. 1 Macc. 7:5-9; 2 Macc. 14:3-17; Jos., Ant. 12.387-388 and 20.235.
281. 1 Macc. 7:10-50 and 9:1-18; 2 Macc. 15.
282. 1 Macc. 9:23-31.
283. 1 Macc. 10:15-21.
284. 1 Macc. 13:489-54.
285. See Vol. IV, Ch. II.3.
286. Meyer, Gesch.d.Alt.Äg. II, 399/400.
287. Budge, Hist.Eg. VIII, 127.
288. Budge, Hist.Eg. VIII, 127/128.
289. Pol. 34.14.1:5.
290. Budge, Hist.Eg. VIII, 129/130.
291. Jouguet, Imp.Mac. 34.
292. Walbank, Hell.World 108-110.
293. Walbank, Hell.World 115.
294. Rostovzeff, Hist.Hell.World II, 883.
295. Rostovzeff, Hist.Hell.World II, 883/884.
296. Walbank, Hell.World 115/116.
297. Walbank, Hell.World 117/118.
298. Just. 27.1.9.
299. Pol. 5.107.2-4.
300. Jouguet, Imp.Mac. 386-390.
301. Jouguet, Imp.Mac. 397/398.

CHAPTER III

PHILOSOPHICA

1. The early successors and followers of Plato

a. Eudoxus

What happened to Plato's philosophy after his death, in particular to his Theory of Forms (or Ideas) [1]? Was it safe in the hands of his associates and pupils in the shaded haunts of the Academy in Athens? We know that Aristotle rejected his theory as untenable. Another close associate was Eudoxus who I referred to in Chapter I in his capacity as a geographer. He was also a brilliant mathematician and at the same time a philosopher; we should think of him, indeed, as of those many-sided scholars that the word 'Academy of Plato' calls to mind.

He came from Cnidus in the Dorian south-west of Asia Minor where he was born ca. 408 B.C. Having studied geometry with the famous Archytas, he lived the life of the wandering teacher for a long time till he finally settled in Athens. He was no great friend of Plato, although he seems to have acted as temporary head of the Academy when the great philosopher himself was off to Sicily for his first visit there. He died about fifty years old in 357 B.C. [2].

Although in some way or other associated with the Academy, he was no full-blooded Platonist, for he experienced the same difficulties with the Theory of Forms as Aristotle [3]. Of the philosophical works of Eudoxus only a few quotations remain, but they throw light on his problem with Plato. According to Zeller, the Theory of Forms was too imaginary and too nebulous for his liking [4]. He tried to remedy this by claiming that the Forms were wholly immanent in objects (which, of course, is an utterly un-Platonic thought). For instance, something is white because it is mixed with the Form of white [5]. By making the Forms immanent, Eudoxus rejected the most essential element of Platonic dualism, the so-called 'chorismos', the separation that exists between Forms and objects [6]. Very probably Eudoxus was more of a scientist with a somewhat materialistic turn of mind than a philosopher. This is a sign that the age of the great philosophers was nearing its end.

There was also a parting of the ways between Eudoxus and Plato since for Eudoxus the highest goal of the philosophical thinker was pleasure rather than the Good, although he probably identified this Good with pleasure [7]. Aristotle warns us not to misunderstand this since Eudoxus was a very sober man [8]. But nothing could have been farther from Plato's mind than equating the Good with pleasure [9]. Eudoxus gives us some very telling reasons for claiming that pleasure is the real Good. He introduces a dualistic element by saying that man's decision for pleasure results 'from opposition' [10] since all beings hate pain; hence the choice of the opposite is an existential necessity. All creatures, man and beast alike, are naturally drawn to pleasure as an end in itself [11]. This abhorrence of pain with the choice of pleasure as an obvious corrolary anticipates both Stoicism and Epucureanism.

This too is, I feel, a sign of the times. People were becoming fed up with all the 'sound and fury' of the great classical life-style, where superb and elevated ideas only too often gave rise to events marked by horror, tension, and tragedy. They were longing for a quieter, more pleasurable, and easy-going way of life. I suppose that Greek people of the metropolis were heartily glad that Alexander choose Asia, and not Hellas, as the theatre for the newest edition of Hellenic heroism. But it remains to be seen whether they would get rid of all their dualism by playing the ostrich. The fact that Eudoxus dualistically opposes pleasure to pain is an indication that the Greek mind remained as fundamentally inclined to antagonism as ever.

b. Speusippus

Pleasure must have been a favourite topic in the Academy. Plato, Aristotle, and Eudoxus all occupied themselves with it, and Speusippus too took part in the discussion. This philosopher, born ca. 407 B.C., was a nephew of Plato, being a son of his sister. When his uncle died in 347 B.C., Speusippus became his first successor as head of the Academy. He seems to have suffered from multiple sclerosis; he succumbed to it in 339 B.C. Diogenes says that he was 'easily overcome by pleasures' which perhaps explains why he was interested in the subject. Of the thirty treatises he wrote only a few fragments are extant [12]. He seems to have been searching for a sort of scientific 'philosopher's stone' since according to a certain Diodorus quoted by Diogenes, he was "the first to discern the common element in all studies and bring them into connexion with each other as far as this was possible" [13].

This shows that basically Speusippus was no dualist. Although Diogenes says that "he adhered faithfully to Plato's doctrines" [14], he deviated from the philosophy of his master by stating that the One is not identical with the Good. According to him, the Good is not a beginning but a result. All beings begin by being imperfect and only slowly and gradually come to perfection [15]. Well-being, he thought, is caused by living in accordance with one's nature; this is what everyone is striving after. But for those who are good, he said, happiness is identical with freedom from disturbance [16]. Once again we see a philosopher taking a step in the direction of Stoicism with its abhorrence of pain.

That he was not really a dualist is also shown by the fact that he invalidated the most important element of Platonic dualism, the chorismos. This he did by intercalating an intermediate term between the Forms and the objects. As soon as connecting elements between the two poles of a dualistic antithesis are posited, there no longer is dualism. Just like Plato, he 'divided the objects of cognition into intelligible and sensible' [17]. The intelligible were knowable by reason, the sensible by perception (by means of the senses). He then brought reason and sense-perception together by saying that both are 'epistemonic' [18], that is, conducive to knowledge. He literally stated that perception by means of the senses partakes of the truth of reason, or to put it into strictly philosophical terms, that perception and reason have the same epistemological value [19]. This is wholly un-Platonic; for Plato reason opened the way to truth, the senses, however, only produced 'doxa' = opinions (which could very well be erroneous). By the same token what Speusippus says is a far cry from Parmenides' iron ontology and even from the orthodox Platonic Theory of Forms.

In fact, Speusippus did not believe at all in his predecessor's Theory of Forms. He obviously considered the Forms fictitious, that is, a product of Plato's imagination. He replaced the Forms by numbers; he may even have said that the Forms are numbers. He agreed with Plato to that extent that numbers exist independently from objects, but in his view they have a mathematical rather than an ideal character [20]. Confronted with a Theory of Numbers, we think, of course, of Pythagoras who was the first to propose such a theory [21]. There is, however, one important difference between original Pythagoreanism and the notions of Speusippus : to Pythagoras the numbers were objects, but Speusippus considered, as we have seen, that numbers are separate from objects. In this way he saved something of the Platonic Theory of Forms, but for the rest he did away with such 'archai', or first principles, as the Good and the Forms. In his doctrine everything begins with numbers [22].

No real knowledge, Speusippus thought, is possible if we do not postulate a universal basis for all that exists. Zeller would call him a true-blue Pythagorean metaphysician were it not for the non-identification of numbers with things [23]. Yet I wonder whether the word 'metaphysician' is the appropriate term here. For there is a touch of mysticism discernible in Speusippus' philosophy. This mysticism is also apparent in original Pythagoreanism. If I may be permitted to quote myself : "Through cognizance of this theory (of numbers), by developing feeling and taste for it, the Pythagorean got into touch with the essence of things, with the foundation and model of the cosmos" [24]. The means to bridge the distance between the microcosmos that is man and the macrocosmos is not philosophy, most emphatically not that of the

Aristotelian brand, not even Platonic 'theoria', or contemplation, but music. There is a touch of such mysticism in Plato's later writings. Because Speusippus and other followers of Plato introduced 'arithmetical and theological mysticism' into their physics, they turned philosophy into 'an abstract dogmatism' which Zeller finds 'objectionable' [25].

But objectionable or not, this mysticism is a stage in the long line - I do not say straight or teleologically - from the Pythagorean movement to the Gnosis [26]. Two important characteristics of the Gnosis are indeed that it, if anything, is mystical, and that it is esoteric - organized mysticism in most cases leading to the foundation of closed societies. I must mention yet another element. Like all staunch dogmatics the Gnostics were self-confident people. Now Cicero, speaking of the Academic and Peripatetic Schools and mentioning Speusippus by name, says that they "framed a definitely formulated rule of doctrine, and this fully and copiously set forth, whereas they abandoned the famous Socratic manner of discussing everything doubtingly ('dubitanter') and without the admission of any positive statement" [27].

c. Xenocrates

As head of the Academy Speusippus was succeeded in 339 by Xenocrates who fulfilled this function until his death in 314 B.C. This man came from Chalcedon, on the Asiatic shore of the Bosporus, just opposite Byzantium [28]. Diogenes [29] has many charming anecdotes to tell about his grave demeanour, as for instance of the famous hetaere Phryne who did her utmost to seduce him but failed even when she was alone with him as he lay on his couch; afterwards she told everyone who wanted to hear it that Xenocrates was not a man but a statue [30]. However, since he did not squander his time on such activities, he could become a prolific author; Diogenes gives his total output as 224.239 lines [31]. But alas, of all this work only scanty fragments remain [32].

He is known as a systematizer of Platonic philosophy since he standardized the division of the field of philosophy into three separate departments, Logics (or Dialectics), Physics, and Ethics [33]. Now Plato, of course, was anything but a systematic philosopher, among else because he wanted to make his work accessible to the general reader. Dörrie considers it 'horrifying' that Xenocrates should apply this sort of schematism to Plato's teachings; 'Platonic orthodoxy' begins, he argues, with Xenocrates [34] whose general approach has the unfortunate effect that it places Platonic philosophyhy at a greater distance from the general educated public for whom Plato's dialogues were intended.

Xenocrates turned away from 'exoterism' in the direction of 'esoterism'. This is demonstrated by the near certainty that with the exception of a few dialogues, he confined his work to colleagues and students. Dörrie supposes that most of his work never left the library of the Academy (like the philosopher himself who rarely went to town). Perhaps all of it went up in flames, when Sulla set the Academy on fire in 86 B.C. to avenge the fact that Athens had dares to resist him [35].

That Xenocrates was the custodian of the Platonic heritage does not signify that he faithfully followed his master in everything. For Plato there were two kinds of beings, the intelligible (the realm of the Forms) and the sensible (the world of created beings and things); of the first we may have sure knowledge, of the second we have only opinion [36]. Xenocrates, however, discerns three modes of being, corresponding with three different modes of knowing. The first level of being is that of the world above, beyond the heavens, which can be known through the use of intelligence only; of these mode we may acquire true knowledge. Then there is a world below, our world, the sublunar one. This is known by means of perception through the senses. Yet since the senses are fallible, knowledge about our world is always partly true, partly false. These two worlds are interconnected by the heavens themselves. The celestial bodies and their movements can be observed by the eye but must also be interpreted by intelligence. Judgments about them, therefore, are true but not so true as judgments on objects beyond the heavens [37].

The fact that Plato's two modes of cognition have been replaced by three also points in the direction of esoterism - the use of the number three being one of the main features of esoteric movements. In this context it should be emphasized that Xenocrates confided his three spheres to three Moirai, or Fates, that beyond the heavens to Atropos, the heavens themselves to Clotho, and to Lachesis the sublunar world [38].

Far more than Speusippus, Xenocrates stuck to the Platonic Theory of Forms that to him were the divine cause of everything existing, in a paradigmatic way, that is separate from the objects [39]. Less Platonic it is that he equates Forms with Numbers : "Ideal number (= the number belonging to a Form) and mathematical number are the same" [40]. This equation makes it impossible to posit the Good as 'archê'. Xenocrates in fact posited two archai : the Monad, or One, and the Dyad (duality); both principles are considered gods.

It is a very curious thing that in Xenocratic metaphysics the cosmos from its very first incipience is dual. The One is male and has the function of a father; as such it holds sway in heaven. The philosopher called this principle Zeus, Mind (Nous), or Odd, and also the First God. The Dyad is even and female and fulfills the role of a mother; she is the soul (psychê) of everything, she is the World Soul. Being indefinite, she may be described as unlimited plurality from which everything flows [41]. Xenocrates himself does not call his second principle Matter but in all probability this is what he meant [42].

Three remarks are necessary here. First, although Xenocrates' dual ontology may easily give rise to a dualistic epiphenomenon, it is in itself not dualistic, since the two principles do not exclude each other. Next, the two principles are divine which is a step into the direction of a mystic world vision. Last, we are very close here to the Pythagorean Table of Oppositions [43].

Xenocrates needed a male and a female first pinciple because his cosmos is a generated and an evolutionary one; we have, however, no fragment showing how he imagined this. "He does assign everything its place in the universe", says Theophrastus, "alike objects of sense, objects of reason or mathematical objects, and divine things as well". He praises him for this, for, as he goes on to say, most philosophers "go to a certain point and then stop, as those do who set up the One and the indefinite Dyad". They are typical mathematicians, he sighs, for "after generating numbers and planes and solids they leave out almost everything else" [44].

We find ourselves here at a most important stage of the development of philosophy. For in all probability Xenocrates was the ancestor of one of the most fruitful of philosophical conceptions, that of the 'chain of being', the idea that created entities are hierarchically ranged on a scale that we conceive, metaphorically, as the ascending steps of a ladder [45]. We meet this all-embracing idea in Middle and Later Platonism, also in Gnosticism (although there the chain is broken), in medieval and later philosophy, and in our own time in the evolution theory [46].

The process of generation begins when the One poses a limit on the Indefinite Dyad. Now, when the One which is a principles of sameness and, therefore, of rest, and the Dyad which is a principle of difference and, therefore, of motion, have become commingled, the result is soul, the soul being at once something at rest and in motion [47]. The soul that is generated thus is the World Soul, or the Cosmos. In Greek thought, an unlimited cosmos would be a contradiction in terms. It is the One that introduces continuity into the universe, whereas the Dyad injects the principle of change in it. In accordance with his Theory of Ideal Numbers soul for Xenocrates was also a number but at the same time a moving and mobile one [48].

From the First Numbers all the geometrical figures come (point, line, surface, solids); once given these, the unbroken continuity of the physical world becomes possible [49]. In every new object or being, however low down the scale, the double principle of continuity and change recurs. But the farther we come from the cosmic origin the more imperfect the world becomes. Creation, in Xenocrates' eyes, is a descending series [50].

Of this physical world - our world, so to speak - Xenocrates takes a somewhat pessimistic view. It is the world of perception by the senses, and the senses easily lead to error and false judgments. He opposes it to the region beyond the heavens where truth prevails. There is a very curious Xenocratic passage about Zeus recorded by Plutarch. "Zeus (is) topmost (when) among things invariable and identical", that is in the heavens, but "nethermost (when) beneath the moon" [51]. What may the philosopher mean by this twofold Zeus, a celestial and a sublunar one? It is evident that with 'Zeus' he does not mean the personal Olympian godhead but a general divine principle. This principle obviously is twofold, so much so that we come very near to a dualistic bipartition of the cosmos.

Heinze supposes that Xenocrates did not observe here his division of all knowable things into three categories but simply clung to the popular belief in upper and nether divinities. Xenocrates, this same author says, shows "a curious propensity to combining arid schematism with phantastic speculation" [52]. The nether world (which in Xenocrates is not Hades) is peopled with demons. This brings us to his theology.

It will be obvious that for Xenocrates, as for Thales, "everything is full of gods". This does not mean that he professes belief in the traditional twelve Olympians. To him the One and the Dyad are divine; we saw how he 'generalized' Zeus (or the One). Lower down we find eight gods, five for the planets, one for the sphere of heavens to which the stars are fixed, one for the sun, and one for the moon [53]. The lowest of the astral godheads is the moon to which Xenocrates assigns the number nine as rightly belonging to her [54]. Perhaps he gave the last and least valuable number to the divinity that governs the changeable world.

In the space between the moon and the human world the demons live; Xenocrates nowhere speaks of a Hades, a subterranean world [55]. There is nothing new, of course, in his believing in demons; it was quite general in Greek popular religion. Plato too assumed their existence. In Xenocrates' theology the occurence of demons is necessary because human beings are incapable of conversing directly with the gods; the demons must intervene. The celestial beings are too far distant from us on the ontological scale; they govern the world only in a general way. Specific human wishes are better looked after by the demons, who are able to interfere in causal connections [56].

Plutarch, who says that Pythagoras and Plato and others have held the same view, writes that these demons were alleged "to be stronger than men and, in their might, greatly surpassing our nature, yet not possessing the divine nature unmixed and uncontaminated, with a share also in the nature and the perceptive faculties of the body, and with a susceptiblity to pleasure and pain" [57]. We detect here the opposition between 'body' and '(world) soul' but this is not absolute since the demons form the connecting link.

Xenocrates would have belied his mathematical mind if he had not expressed his idea in geometrical terms. He compared the gods to a equilateral triangle, men to a scalene one, and the demons to an isosceles [58]. The isometry of the divine triangle expresses the perfection and the power of the gods, the human scalene the imperfection of men, and the isosceles expresses the idea that demons are partly (two sides being equal) perfect, and partly (one unequal side) imperfect. In this vision gods and men find themselves at opposite ends of the chain of being. For Xenocrates this obviously was an embarrassing consequence of his theological ontology. But the question is whether this interposing of demons really was sufficient to bridge the gap. His rather forced geometrical simile proves that he did not feel wholly at ease with it. The way I see it is that his philosophy was hovering between his 'holistic' chain of being and a dualistic conception of the universe.

Xenocrates was a curious mixture of a rational, mathematical, even rigid mind, and of a mentality tending to fantastic speculations. He seems still farther distant from Aristotle's scientific rationalism than Plato was. I guess that, with him, we are moving a step nearer to the Gnosis that thrived on bizarre and far-fetched conjectures. Other elements too herald the Gnosis : the imperfection of mankind, the difference between the sublunar and supralunar spheres, the desinterestedness of the godhead in the world, the demonology, and, finally, the notion that the existence of evil may not be imputed to the supreme godhead.

d. The Epinomis

We must now turn to the pseudo-Platonic dialogue 'Epinomis' [59], the author of which is unknown; he must have belonged to the Platonic

School but was also a Pythagorean because of his predilection for numbers [60]. This dialogue contains a conversation between a Cretan, an Athenian, and a Spartan, with the anonymous Athenian as the one who presents the argument and leads the discussion. The three are considering the question of wisdom [61]. For 'wisdom' the author uses the Greek words 'phronêsis' [62] and 'sophia' [63]; a person who has acquired wisdom is called 'sophos' [64], and even 'sophotatos' = most wise [65]. Nowhere does the author utilize the word 'gnosis', either in its common colloquital meaning or in the sense of a special knowledge or wisdom.

Soon enough, however, it becomes evident that 'wisdom' in the Epinomis has a very special significance. The author began with calling it 'phronêsis' while making it clear that with this term he means something higher than just plain knowledge : the godhead is the cause of a greater understanding [66], for divine spirits partake of an extraordinary intelligence [67]. A person who has been initiated is in the possession of 'phronêsis' [68], perhaps best translated with '(deeper) insight'.

But we need not read far into the text to discover that the author prefers 'sophia' to 'phronêsis'. Whereas the dialogue opens with the term 'phronêsis', what is found at the end is 'sophia' [69]. "Existence is difficult for every live creature ... It is impossible for men to be blessed and happy, except a few" [70]. If we desire to live the right life, we need wisdom but this is extremely difficult to attain. Possessing a thorough knowledge of the sciences does not help at all; they do not make men wise [71]. "None of these seem worthy to be called by the title of wisdom." The author is speaking here of 'technai' (sciences) and 'epistêmê' (scientific knowledge) which he opposes to 'sophia'; 'phronêsis' too proves to be very different from 'sophia' [72]. Of course, there are many useful occupations like being a smith or a carpenter and so on, but these are not conducive to wisdom; even among artists, generals, sailors, or doctors it will be difficult to find somebody who is wise, although there are persons who believe they are [73].

Must this make us despondent? Is there really no science that can teach us wisdom? There is but it is not something that we can acquire all by ourselves; it is a gift from above, from Heaven. This gift is

Number, the source and origin of all good things [74] (the author evidently is a good Pythagorean). Who has received 'the gift of Numbers' will be able 'to explore the whole circuit (= the movements of the heavens) [75]. Being knowledgeable about numbers is the basis of all intelligence and understanding. A person who does not know about numbers (obviously ordinary counting is not meant) may be courageous and temperate but not wise. And without wisdom there is no perfect goodness nor happiness [76].

Let us lift up our heads and look at the dome of Heaven. It is from there that we receive 'the conception of one and two' [77]. The movements of the celestial bodies are orderly, which is a strong proof of their intelligence. They are "possessed of mind ... because they always do what has been decided long ago for an incalculable time, not deciding differently this way and that, and doing sometimes one thing and sometimes another in wanderings and changes of circuit" [78]. Clearly, the stars are either gods themselves, or 'images of the gods, creations of the gods themselves' [79].

The conclusion is that whoever wants to become wise should turn to the study of astronomy; the godhead himself will teach him [80]. Astronomy, basically a science of numbers, will include two other numerical disiplines, geometry and stereometry [81]. Only such a person will be deemed wise who has acquired this knowledge; only he will fully possess all spiritual gifts, only he will be fit to govern, only he will be entirely blessed and happy. But at the same time it must be reiterated that these gifts will come to a few only [82].

This exposition will have made it clear that the anonymous author's 'knowledge' is something highly specialized. Wisdom can only be acquired by means of a profound study of astronomy and mathemathics leading to veneration of the astral gods. The author is well aware that he finds himself at a great distance from Greek popular belief. There clearly is a dualistic difference between those who think like the author and 'the others'. But it is still more important that this wisdom is so utterly, so dualistically opposed to common knowledge and practical wisdom. It is esoteric to a degree since it is only given to a few. It has mystical connotations since it is the result of a divine gift, of a revelation.

In the beginning of this section I said that the unnamed writer does not employ the term 'gnosis'. However, what he describes as wisdom comes very close to what the Gnostics understood by it. In this context it is interesting to note that the author sometimes uses forms of the verb 'gignooskein' = to know. The astral gods, he says, "understand (gignooskein) the whole of our thought"; the godhead "has a share of intelligence and knowledge (gignooskein) in every sphere"[83]. Human beings must perceive (gignooskein) what is the right education[84]. A being who does not know (gignooskei) numbers is an irrational person[85]. In all these cases the meaning of 'to know' is enhanced and lifted to a higher level, that of more than human, even divine insight. This is not everybody's portion.

2. The Stoa

a. The founders

The founder of the Stoic School has already been mentioned in these pages and his life shortly described; he was Zeno of Kittion, a Cypriote who in 311 B.C. came to Athens. After having been grounded in philosophy by famous scholars he began to teach himself. His favourite haunt was the Stoa Poikilè, the 'multi-coloured portico' on the Athenian agora. From this Stoa the name of his school and the words 'Stoicism' and 'Stoics' have been derived. When he died in 262/261 B.C., he was succeeded by his faithful disciple Cleanthes. Born in 331 B.C. at Assos on the north-west coast of Asia Minor, just oppossite Lesbos, Cleanthes came to Athens with only a few pennies rattling in his pocket. As a student of philosophy with Zeno he earned his money by working during the night. He probably knew more about the practical and even the seamy side of life than most philosophers for having been a pugilist in his youth. As a student he worked as a journeyman baker and water drawer. He wrote many philosophical works of which only fragments remain, and some poems; the famous Hymn to Zeus has been preserved in its entirety [86].

Cleanthes was a conventional philosopher, devotedly true to what his master had taught. His authority was not great enough to keep the diverging tendencies in the Stoa together. Several members of it parted ways with him and with one another to found their own schools or teach independently [87].

When Cleanthes died in 232 B.C., he was succeeded by Chrysippus. Coming from Soloi or Tarsus in Cilicia (on the south coast of Asia Minor), where he was born ca. 281 B.C., he was one of the many non-Athenians who in this period enriched the intellectual climate of Athens. Originally an athlete, a long-distance runner, he was conquered by Stoic philosophy as taught by Cleanthes whom he succeeded as head of the Stoa. He was very popular as a lecturer and wrote an incredible mass of treatises, 705 in all, says Diogenes, of which, once again, we possess nothing but fragments. He died 73 years old, ca. 206 B.C. [88]. Considering how little has been left of the work of these philosophers, we can do no better than take them together as 'the early Stoics' [89].

b. The primary element

Nearly all philosophers of the great classical period, like Plato and Aristotle, had postulated that the primary element, the first principle or 'archê', was an incorporeal one, like 'the Good' in Platonic doctrine. This line of reasoning goes back to Parmenides who posited Being as the primary element. The Stoics deviated from this line and reverted to Heraclitus who had posited fire as his primary substance, that is to say, a physical or corporeal element [90].

To Zeno and his followers the universe was "an entirely physical system ... The starting point of physical philosophy had been the assumption that there was a perpetual store of some primary substance and that from this was formed the cosmos, that is the ordered system of this world in which men live and the heavenly bodies" [91]. "Zeno says that substance is the prime matter of all existing things and this in its entirety is everlasting, without increase or decrease" [92].

Now we might state, with Hunt, that since the Stoics acknowledged only one 'archê', their system was 'a form of monism' [93]. But perhaps it is not so simple as this. The Stoics called their prime matter 'ousia' which means 'being'. Now Being is by definition unchangeable, indestructible, everlasting, and constant in everything; in other words, it has near-divine properties. But the curious thing, as Diogenes already remarked, is that the terms 'substance' ('ousia') and 'matter' ('hulê') both have a double sense : they connote the whole, the universe, as well as the parts of the whole. While it is true that "the whole neither increases nor decreases", the parts do [94]. In other words, the parts are changeable and liable to temporality. In Latin terms it could be said that 'ousia' not only is 'essentia' but also 'substantia'. This means that the Stoic first principle has two different sides.

Furthermore, although "the Stoics are materialists throughout ..., more materialists than were the Presocratics" [95], they did not succeed in incorporating - here the term can be used also in its most literal sense! - everything into their physical universe. For there clearly are incorporeal things, to begin with the infinite void or empty space which needs must be located outside the cosmos. This 'infinite void' is the 'apeiron', the boundless that in Greek cosmology surrounded the spherical and bounded universe [96]. This evidently bothered the Stoics, for Chrysippus wrote a book 'On Void', and several others discussed it in their works [97]. And well they might, for the acknowledgment of the existence of the apeiron at least suggests that the so-called Stoic monism was by no means so monistic as is supposed.

'Place' ('topos') too is not corporeal [98] neither is 'Time' [99]. With his notion of time Chrysippus offers a nice problem to historians for whom time is the basic ingredient of their work. In his view Time possesses no proper reality, because it is a dimension of movement, a measure of speed and slowness. Time, like the Void, is boundless (apeiron) in both directions, for past and future are equally boundless. The past no longer is there, while the future is not yet there, which signifies that they don't exist. Does then the present moment really exist? Perhaps we might say so until we realize that this present moment is immediately submerged into the flux of Time [100]. Still more important, and still more destructive to the notion of complete corporality, is that 'what is thought' is not material either.

There is, of course, an unbridgeable opposition here between the fundamental materialism of Stoic philosophy, and the equally fundamental assumption that there exist incorporeal elements. Exist? The Stoic would protest. They do not 'exist', he says, they 'subsist'. 'Mere hairsplitting' (mikrologia), Galen called this subtle distinction [101]. Because of this distinction it proved impossible for the Stoics to posit 'being' as the most general species. Instead they used the philosophically rather flaccid term 'the something' ('ti'), since this could indicate corporeal as well as incorporeal elements [102].

c. The cosmos

Does the Stoic axiom that all is matter, and that everything proceeds from matter, mean that the cosmos is an inanimate mass of particles or corpuscles, perhaps with some semblance or order? On the contrary, the cosmos is utter perfection, 'the best of all possible worlds'. The universe is not "like a clod of earth or a lump of stone with only the natural principle of cohesion", but it is "like a tree or animal, in which there is manifest, not haphazard structure but order and a certain semblance of design" [103]. The Stoic conclusion, therefore, is that "nothing exists among all things that is superior to the world, nothing that is more excellent or beautiful ...; (even) nothing superior can be conceived" [104].

This naturally excludes the idea of a creating godhead who is outside the world but it strongly suggests a superior craftsman or designer who is at work within it. Although we must assume with Hunt that the Stoic universe is 'a self-directing physical system' [105], the question nevertheless looms up whether the ordering principle is something material or immaterial.

To explain how the inert material mass was made to move into an ordered structure, Zeno needed two 'archai' or first principles, which perhaps we should regard as aspects of the first principle 'matter'? "(The Stoics) consider that there are two principles in the universe, the active and the passive. The passive principle, then, is the qualityless substance, the matter, while the active is the Logos (reason) in it" [106]. Here we not only rediscover the already mentioned difference between matter as a whole, with its quasi-divine qualities, and the imperfect parts of matter, but still more important, we encounter a distinction between Matter and something else. "Matter lies inert, a substance ready for all things but destined to remain inactive if nobody moves it; but cause, i.e. Reason (logos), gives form to Matter' [107].

d. Monistic or dualistic?

Is this dualism? Copleston calls the Stoic doctrine 'a monistic materialism' - monistic "since the two principles are both material and together form one Whole". It is, therefore, 'hardly (sic) dualistic at all', although he admits that the Stoic materialistic position "is not consistently maintained" [108]. Expressions like 'hardly dualistic' and 'not consistently monistic' only serve to sow confusion. What is monism if it is not consistent? Hunt adds that "in Zeno's theory it was only by mental abstraction that the passive archè could be thought of separately" [109].

Let us see how the active first principle, or Logos, is referred to. In Stoic doctrine the Logos is god (theos), "for he is everlasting and is the artificer of each several thing throughout the whole extent of Matter" [110]. This eternal Creator is clearly distinct from the Matter on which he is working. His separateness is stressed by other quotations from Zeno; Stoics speak of 'god and matter' [111].

The problem with monism is that it never can be made true to itself. For if all is said to be mind or spirit, it becomes hardly possible to deny that there exist also material things. Very clever dialectical juggling-tricks will have to be performed to show that a stone after all is a spiritual thing or a direct manifestation of a spiritual principle.

Parmenides, for one, tried to extricate himself from this aporia by stating that concrete and material objects are no more than semblance. On the other hand, the thesis that everything is basically matter hardly squares with the obvious fact that there also exist spiritual phenomena. Karl Marx, with his dialectical materialism, coped with this problem by positing a cultural suprastructure on top of the material infrastructure of production and consumption. Classical behaviourists, like Watson, who are materialistic psychologists and worked on the premise that there is no such thing as soul or psyche, could not deny that people do think. They decided to ignore thinking because thoughts cannot be observed.

So every monism leaves a residue of elements that do not fit into the system. Therefore, as I have explained in an earlier work [112], it gives easily rise to dualism since a large existential or spiritual field is in fact excluded from the system. In my opinion modern commentators are profoundly mistaken when they see monism and dualism as opposites. Where there is monism, there is no dualism, or the reverse, so they believe. Quite the contrary, monism and dualism are blood-brothers generated by an imperfect conception of reality. It is perfectly possible that a system or an ideology is monistic on principle but that dualism sets in one level lower [113]. The real opposition, or rather negation, of both dualism and monism is the 'analogia entis', the 'analogy of being', that is the similarity (not the identity) of Creator and created.

The conspicuous inconsistency in Stoic materialistic monism was evident to many ancient commentators. In the second century AD Galen, while criticizing the basic position of the Stoics, remarked that according to this school god had made the cosmos and each of the things in it [114], and this, obviously, postulates two separate entities. About 200 AD the Christian apologist Tertullian in as many words wrote that Zeno "made a distinction between the matter of the world and god" [115]. Epiphanius, a bishop of the fourth century says that Zeno held that god and matter are contemporaneous ('synchronos') [116], and this makes them distinct from one another.

e. The Stoic solution

e. The Stoic solution

How did the Stoics resolve this problem? By means of what we may call pantheism. The godhead suffuses the whole cosmos. "God is an unseparable quality in matter as the seed in the organs of conception" but although the Stoics clearly equate god with matter - "god is what matter is" [117] -, seed and the organs of conception are two different things. "(God) absorbs himself into the whole substance" [118]; "God has run through matter as honey through the comb" [119]. Hunt does not find this last simile really fitting since honey and the comb are two different things". They are indeed, as is evidenced by a quotation from Epiphanius that he cites with approval : "The divine force spreads through all things" [120]; the divine force may spread as much as it wants to, it never becomes wholly identical with matter.

This is the old problem of pantheism : if the godhead is fully identical with the order of creation, it becomes indistinguishable from it; we may say then that all is matter, just as we are entitled to say that all is god. And if the godhead remains distinct from the created order, the pantheism is not complete. Anyhow, we are approaching here the notion of the 'cosmic god', a notion that was to cause much furore in the subsequent centuries [121].

f. Are the Stoic archai dualistic principles?

Finally, we should, in the context of this work, discuss the question that I have evaded up to now : whether Zeno's and his adherents' two 'archai', god and matter [122], must be regarded as dualistic. I do not believe that it really alleviates the Stoics' plight when they declare over and over again that their godhead is, like matter, corporeal. This is pithily expressed in this phrase : "Everything that is acted upon (= matter) and everything that acts (= god) is body" [123]. Galen bluntly stated that to Zeno god was body [124]. With this statement the dialectical dualism that is inherent in Plato's Theory of Forms is 'given its congé', says Moreau [125].

However, in Stoic philosophy this brand of dualism is not replaced by monism but by materialistic dualism, that of the two principles, the active and the passive. For although 'god' and 'matter' are corporeal, they could, nevertheless, not be more different : the everlasting and all-comprising, unnchangeable and indestructable divine archê, and the floating and ever changing matter that is always crystallizing into separate objects.

Furthermore, while it is stated that god works on and in matter, it is nowhere explained how he, or it, does this; in other words, how concrete objects are brought into being by the general first cause - just as in Plato's Theory of Forms it is never made clear how the Forms shape the things.

Moreau says that this dualistic materialism "must deny itself in order to remount to the source of being" (i.e. that there is nothing but matter); " this means that the Stoics try to confound what they had begun to distinguish, so much so that they seem to attach no more than nominal value to their dualism" [126]. It seems to me that this scholar is making the same conceptual mistake as Hunt when he said that "only by mental abstraction ... the passive archê could be thought of separately [127]. Dualistic attitudes without exception are mental or nominal; they originate in the human mind, and are then introduced into the existential world where they generate dualistic oppositions, i.e. by human action.

Let us see who this cosmic god is, or what it is. The godhead is postulated by the fact that matter of itself is inert and shapeless. To get it moving and structured a prime mover is needed, a force that is self-moving, divine, and invisible [128]. This sounds highly abstract and purely metaphysical, just like Aristotle's Prime Mover [129]. But differently from him, the Stoics defined their Prime Mover as Fire - moving in this way far closer to Heraclitus [130] than to Aristotle. "Zeno, like Heraclitus, says that Fire is the (first) element of all beings" [131]. Other ancient commentators hold that Zeno's godhead was air or the aether [132].

Just as the Presocratics had posited ethereal elements like fire, air, and aether, in order to edge away from the most blatant materialism, Fire, the most incorporeal of all elements, served Zeno and Chrysippus very well to solve the problem (for which they were much criticized and even derided) that body (for we must allow that their all-pervading god was a body) could pass through matter (which also is a body). Fire is a divinity considerably less abstract than Aristotle's cold and distanced Prime Mover, and much more of a cosmic god, since "a hot and fiery principle is interfused with the whole of nature' [133].

This fiery element is the cause of all movement. "Hence since all motion springs from the world-heat, and since that heat moves not by any impulse from something else but spontaneously, it follows that heat is soul; from which it results that the world is animate" [134]. Therefore, according to Chrysippus, " the cosmos (i.e. taken as a whole) is a living being, rational, and endowed with soul and mind" [135]. Because the divine principle is rational, the Stoics also called it Logos . "This Zeno defines as the maker who has formed all things in due order" [136].

"So the Logos, as the active archê proceeding rationally, acted with purpose in producing the cosmos, and nature planned with will and foresight every detail of the work" [137]. As a consequence, the godhead might as well be named Providence : he is, according to Zeno, "a craftsman whose foresight plans out the work to serve its use and purpose in every detail ... It can therefore be correctly be designated as prudence or providence (for in Greek it is termed 'pronoia')" [138].

g. Fate and necessity

However, Cicero, who is quoted in the above passage, adds something to it, viz. that "nature has an unchanging method and path to follow". This reeks of determinism since it seems as though nature is following a pre-ordained course. Not a few critics, Cicero being one of them, accuse the Stoics of leaving very little room for the freedom of the will [139]. This freedom evidently was replaced by 'necessity of fate'. The Stoics, says Cicero, consider even the future as unchangeable, with the inevitable consequence that there is an eternal series of causes; this means that man necessarily becomes deprived of his free will [140].

There is no certainty that Chrysippus actually used the expression 'necessity of Fate' [141], although we may be fairly sure that he spoke of 'necessity and fate' [142]. Perhaps the early Stoics made a distinction between Fate and necessity, in order to do justice to the fact that they look differently from a human standpoint. "The fated path is simply the path of what will be" [143]. To a wise man, to a Stoic that is, this is the ordained will of the world-soul that can act only rationally. "Fate is the reason (logos) of the cosmos", said Chrysippus, "... (it) is ordering everything in the cosmos in the most excellent way" [144]. The Stoic accepts this without demurring but to a non-Stoic what happens will look like brute and senseless necessity. "(Zeno and Chrysippus) hold that everything has been ordained by fate; they use the example that man is tied to a cart like a dog ...; if he does not want to follow, he will be drawn and follow" [145].

In Stoic philosophy very little room is left for moral freedom, for human beings to act as free moral agents. The following is a verse by the Stoic poet Cleanthes : "Lead me, Zeus, wherever you have ordained for me. For I shall follow unflinching. But if I become unwilling, I shall follow none the less" [146].

It may seem to us that this does not make much of a difference : whether or not one is willing, one has to follow, that is, to obey Fate. But the Stoics say that one who obeys Fate willingly and knowingly is a free person whereas the others are slaves, "freedom being power of independent action, whereas slavery is privation of the same" [147]. 'Freedom' and 'slavery' are understood here as resulting from an inner condition, not from social circumstances. The Stoics saw the wise as exceptionally privileged. They alone "are fit to be magistrates, judges, and orators, whereas among the bad not one is so qualified ... The wise is infallible, not being liable to error. They are also without offence; for they do no hurt to others nor to themselves ... Friendship ... exists only between the wise and good, by reason of their likeness to one another ... Everything belongs to the wise." In short, "the wise man does all things well" [148].

h. The dualism of the wise and the unwise

It will be evident that we are in the presence here of a dualistic distinction between two sets of people, the wise and the dull, the free and the slaves, the good and the bad. This must be dubbed an opposition rather than a distinction, for between virtue and vice there is nothing intermediate; the Stoics reject the possibility of moral improvement : "a man must be either just or unjust" [149]. We are coming very close to the Gnostic position that the great mass of mankind will be damned and only a few elect saved. But there is also a dualistic distinction between the godhead, or World-Soul, or Fate, or whatever it may be called, and mankind.

Did we ever before encounter in Greek history such a radical partitioning of mankind into two strictly separated groups? True enough, the Pythagorean fraternity was an élitist society too, keeping itself apart from the common run. But when all is said and done, it was possible to become a Pythagorean by studying the doctrine and living according to the precepts of the Master. Plato's philosopher equally is an exceptional kind of person, decidedly different from those who are lost in the darkness of their own opinions. But it is possible to become a philosopher by studying mathematics and dialectics. Being a Stoic, however, seems to be a fated effect of the preordained course of the world.

j. 'Knowledge'

When speaking about the Gnosis, it is important to note that in Stoic anthropology the real difference is between those who know and those who do not. "Freedom is knowledge of what is allowable and what is forbidden, and slavery is ignorance of what is allowed and what not", according to a Stoic author of the first century AD. He even gives a remarkable extension to the notion of freedom. "The wise are permitted anything whatsoever they wish" [150]. There is only one virtue of the soul,

to know about good and bad things [151]; such knowledge is to be found only in the wise [152]. It is the highest good [153].
In the cited quotations the Greek word that is being used is 'epistēmē'; sometimes it is equated with 'phronēsis' [154]. Does 'gnosis' also occur? Only in a negative sense : the ignorance of the unwise is called 'agnoia' [155]. Anyhow, the Stoics acknowledge a very special brand of knowledge.

k. The Stoics' low idea of life

However exalted a notion the Stoics may have had of themselves, in their philosophy humanity does not come off very well. That their ideas about freedom and Fate drove them into a very tight corner is proved by the fact that the one real freedom they acknowledged was to commit suicide. I know of course what Rist says, that "during the whole of classical Antiquity suicide was not only common but acceptable and justified by a variety of circumstances". But he is equally correct in saying that "justification of the practice has been regarded as an especially Stoic phenomenon. In the Roman period at least, a number of the more famous suicides were Stoics or would-be Stoics ... Seneca regards suicide is the ultimate justification of man's freedom [156], perhaps even as the only genuinely free act" [157]. But we need not turn to Seneca who committed suicide himself - the scene became a favourite subject for painters! -, for among the older Stoics Cleanthes and others voluntarily parted with life.

Now Rist argues in his chapter on (Stoic) suicide that no older text connects suicide with freedom; there is no ancient quotation showing that to the Stoics suicide was an act of ultimate freedom. Be this as it may, the question arises whether suicide can be anything else than taking one's fate into one's own hands? We did not give life to ourselves. Whosoever gave it us, God, our parents, nature, Fate, evolution, or whatever we may choose as the cause of our existence, it came to us from a source outside ourselves. It is for this reason that most people feel that in consequence we should not take our own lives. If we do, it is a free and deliberate choice. This is expressed by a phrase that frequently occurs in death-notices of persons who obviously died by their own hand : "We respect your choice". By putting it thus the relatives also take their distance from the act. Must we suppose that for the ancients suicide was not an act of supreme freedom?

This view is supported by the fact that, according to the Stoics, the unwise should be restrained from taking their own lives; it is obviously a privilege reserved for the wise alone. "The Stoics speed many sages from life on the ground that it is better for them to have done being happy, and restrain many base men from dying on the ground that they ought to live in unhappiness ... It behoves the latter to abide and the former to take leave of life" [158]. Chrysippus is quoted as having said that "the base ought to remain alive" [159]. The suicidal act should not performed arbitrarily but 'for reasonable cause', i.e. "on his (the Stoic's) country's behalf or for the sake of his friends, or if he suffers intolerable pain, mutilation, or incurable disease" [160].

l. Evil in Stoic philosophy

This brings us to another point that looks like yet another inconsistency in Stoic philosophy : the existence of evil. Although their fundamental belief was that the godhead had ordered everything for the best, the Stoics could not deny that there was evil in the world. They certainly were not unaware that this presented a problem, and they did not beg the question. Edelstein ranges what they had to say on this topic under 'Stoic self-criticism' [161].

Against the old slogan that re-echoes through world history to the present day : "If there were a Providence, there would be no evils", Chrysippus takes the following position in the fourth book of his (lost) work 'On Providence'. "There is absolutely nothing more foolish than these men who think that good could exist (only) if there were at the same time no evil. For since good is the opposite of evil, it necessarily follows that both must exist in opposition to each other, ... since as a matter of fact no opposite is conceivable without something to oppose it .... (For instance), how could there be wisdom, if folly did not exist as its opposite?" [162]. This subtle argument reduces itself to the proposition that evil exists for the good of good. But it is, true as Copleston says (he himself finds 'a great deal of truth in this contention') that the argument "that evil in the universe throws the good into greater relief" recurs later in Neo-Platonism, St. Augustine, Berkeley, and Leibniz [163].

Chrysippus in yet another curious way tried to escape from this problem. Sometimes, he said, Providence is negligent and overlooks something which would explain why unpleasant things happen also to upright and virtuous men, "just as in larger households some husks get lost and a certain quantity of wheat although affairs as a whole are well managed". Providence takes on in this passage the aspect of an overwrought housemother. Plutarch remarks that Necessity or Fate also "is involved in large measure" [164]. "The Stoics see Necessity as an invincible and coercive cause, and Fate as an ordered chain of causes with which our affairs too are connected, so that some are determined by Fate, and others not" [165].

But Plutarch, who was an opponent of Stoicism, continues, "if in events Necessity is involved in large measure" - he is referring to things that necessarily go wrong -, "then god does not control all things nor are all things ordered in conformity with his reason". Plutarch is laying his finger here on a sore spot in the Stoic theodicy. Furthermore, he says that he finds it highly insensible "to compare the horrible things that sometimes happen to the most irreproachable of men, like the death-sentence passed on Socrates, to the loss of a few kilograms of wheat from the store-room" [166]. But this insensibility is the inevitable consequence of the Stoic desire to belittle the problem of evil as much as possible.

No, Chrysippus did not after all "think that it was nature's original intention to make men subject to disease, for that would never have been consistent with nature as the source and mother of all things good" [167]. From this point of view, evil, as we saw, may be explained as a corollary or side-effect of the existence of the good. But Chrysippus also tries to find a way out of the quandary he finds himself in with regard to the existence and origin of evil. The following quotation will bring this out still more clearly. "Or is it because base spirits have been appointed over matters of the sort in which there really do occur instances of negligence that must in fact be reprehended?" [168].

So one of the leading spirits of early Stoicism saw himself forced to admit at least the possibility of malevolent spirits who can be made responsible for the existence of evil. Could he possibly have realized that, when carried to its extreme consequences (as the Gnostics did), this would mean the dualistic splitting up of the universe (and of mankind) into two halves, that of the good and that of evil.

Yet another line was followed by Zeno himself who declared that all those things that are not the result of our good or bad intentions but simply befall us, like life and death, good and bad opinions, well-being and misery, wealth and penury, health and sickness and the like, are 'adiaphora', indifferent things, neither morally good nor bad [169]. Does this really solve the aporia? Tell a man whose house has been swept away by a flood and who has lost his wife and children in the catastrophe that he should remain unmoved because what befell him was a '(morally) indifferent thing'.

m. The folly of mankind

The foregoing paragraphs speak of physical or material evils. But what about moral evil? We saw already that, according to early Stocism, mankind is divided into dualistically opposed parts, that of the wise and that of the unwise, and this view also embraces virtue and vice [170]. The reason for this is that virtue is considered to be a whole. Since fools by definition do not possess all of it, they have no virtue at all. "The Stoics ... will have it that nothing base can attach to virtue, and nothing good to vice" [171].

It is by no means easy to be wholly virtuous. Most people do not succeed in this, probably they do not even try. "Of men the greatest number are bad, or rather there are one or two whom they speak of as having become good men as in a fable, a sort of incredible creature as it were ...; and the others are all wicked and are so to an equal extent, so that there is no difference between one and the other, and all who are not wise are alike mad" [172]. So on the one side we have the immense massa damnata, on the other a few elect.

Is it possible to pass from one condition to the other? Certainly not by means of gradual progress. "The successive stages of his (man's) progress produce no abatement of his unwisdom, but, on the contrary, vice besets all progress" [173]. When a transition from one state to another - at any rate a rare event - takes place, it always is something sudden and abrupt. "Frequently the man who has got the virtue and happiness in question does not even perceive their presence but is unaware of having now become prudent and blissful when a little earlier he was most wretched and most foolish."

How ludicrous, says Plutarch whom I am quoting here, that a person should be wholly unaware of this essential change in his moral condition [174]. And never wanting to miss an opportunity for ridiculing the Stoics, he amuses himself with saying that "the sage of the Stoics, though yesterday he was most ugly and at the same time most vicious, to-day all of a sudden has been transformed into virtue and from being ... wrinkled and sallow ... has become of comely bearing, divine aspect, and beauteous form" [175].

It nowhere becomes clear what causes this change. At all events it is nothing within the scope of human action or will-power. It therefore must not be called conversion in the usual sense since one remains unaware of it. It is rather like redemption effected by some outside power or entity, although the idea of redemption does not occur in Stoic doctrine. So far as I know, we have not encountered this idea of sudden change before in Greek ethics. It seems to me to be yet another stepping-stone on the road to the Gnosis, an ideology which also thrived on the notion of an absolute division of mankind into the redeemed and the unredeemed and on the sudden and radical transition from one state to the other.

n. The origin of evil

What is the origin of evil? It cannot come from the perfect godhead. Here too we are allowed to think of the necessity of opposites, the idea of the good supposing the idea of a corresponding evil. But of course it is impossible to see this as a genuine origin. Probably we must look into another direction. Since the universe is perfect, all that materially forms part of it also partakes of this perfection. Therefore, there are no evil actions, only good ones. What makes a human action or deed morally good or reprehensible is the intention with which it is done. Since man is a free agent his intentions can be right as well as wrong [176]. Once again the doctrine of oppositions prevails : wrong opinion is coupled to right opinion. And wrong opinion is actualized in bad deeds. This would mean that the origin of evil is to be found in the human mind, for it is man himself who, by his intentions, gives the wrong colouring to his deeds.

This is not so plausible as it seems since it leaves the problem of the Stoic theodicy unsolved. However much it may be true that man has the possibility to do wrong, because the necessity of opposites, the question remains why it is that so few are good, or sage, and so many bad. The Stoic took a very low opinion of mankind considering that the overwhelming majority were doing nothing but evil. How does this square with the central part of Stoic philosophy that the World-Soul has ordered evrything for the best, and that human reason mirrors divine reason? How come then that human beings so easily and so massively make the wrong judgment? It seems to me that the Stoics, in spite of themselves - they never admitted as much because it conflicted with their basic idea of the one perfect world - nevertheless posited two human worlds that were irreconcilable. Anyhow, in their philosophy the problem of evil became more acute than it had ever been before.

o. An assessment

Finally, we must try to assess the place of Stoicism in Greek thought and life. Zeno, Chrysippus, and other leading Stoics saw their own time - the century after Alexander's conquests - as morally depraved and politically oppressive. Man could free himself from his shackles by the purity and strength of his will; this would give him undisturbed inner peace and indifference to all that might befall him. To all intents and purposes Stoicism was a practical movement that left many important metaphysical questions unanswered. It took from all other philosophies what it needed without building itself into a new comprehensive and conclusive system.

Its philosophical and ethical bywords were materialism - sensualism (sensory perception is all) - moralism - élitism - cosmopolitanism. Much, too much, was left unconsidered [177]. So, slowly but certainly, a philosophical vacuum began to originate for the filling up of which, some centuries later, Christianity, the Gnosis, and Neo-Platonism would compete.

3. Hellenic atomism

a. Some thoughts on Atomism and the atomic theory

Speaking of a spiritual and philosophical vacuum whose existence was one of the main causes of the two doctrines of redemption, one of which, the Gnosis, became the largest dualistic movement in all Antiquity, we should certainly pay attention to Epicureanism. But since the philosophy and ethics of Epicurus and his school can only be understood in the specific context of the work of Democritus in particular, we must turn our attention first of all to the Atomist school. This school was founded in the fifth century B.C. by Leucippus and Democritus.

To-day we speak of 'atomic theory' rather than of Atomism; we assume that atomic theory belongs to the realms of physics and technology rather than to philosophy. In Antiquity this was different, for then

'Atomism' was primarily a philosophical notion. Both notions find their common ground in Van Melsen's definition : "Atomism may be defined as the doctrine that material reality is composed of simple and unchangeable minute particles, called atoms" - the Greek word 'atomos' signifying 'indivisible'. Its "historical development shows a gradual shift from philosophical to scientific considerations" [178].

Philosophical atomism deserves a place in this work since it has a destabilizing effect. Because of this it plays a role in the process of demythification that in the end led to the rise of movements that promised a totally different interpretation of reality. People did not nor do they believe now that the key to physical reality, and perhaps to all reality, is to be found in the existence of myriads of infinitely small particles that arrange and rearrange themselves into shapes of their own accord. Still less do they delight in the idea that human inventiveness may be able to intervene in what is seen as the most fundamental stratum of reality.

Even in our scientific age, when so many people have acquired at least a smattering of basic physics, they are afraid of atomic power, even of peaceful nuclear energy. I remember that during the exceptionally bad summer of 1945 in the Netherlands, Dutch farmers told me that this was the effect of the dropping of the two atomic bombs on Japanese cities. From a scientific point of view this is sheer nonsense of course, but it expresses a very deep seated fear of all mankind : that penetrating into and handling the most fundamental patterns and forces of nature must needs have disastrous results of cosmic dimensions because it is felt to be sacrilegious. The Chernobyl catastrophe in May 1986 has vigorously fortified this notion.

Few people would believe to-day what Lancelot Whyte so confidently wrote in 1961 : "The conception of atomism has been the spearhead of the advance of science. Atomic ideas have led to the highest adoptive precision which the human brain has yet achieved" [179]. With a sleight of hand he brushes away all objections against modern atomic theory : "It is hard for us to-day ... to realize what passions the doctrine of atomism evoked long before the atom was discovered by exact scientists"[180]. But seeing where it has led us, it becomes less hard to understand.

What counts is that people feel that it was and is "wrong to tear beautiful things to pieces, instead of accepting, enjoying, and using them as they were"[181]. But there is still more to it. What people really believe in is harmony, order, coherence, wholeness, meaningfulness. The God, or the gods, they venerate are principles of order. Destruction, disturbance is the work of evil spirits, of demons, of the Devil. Although nuclear scientists tell them that atoms are grouped together in regular patterns and that their movements are governed by laws, people believe that the atomic world is inexplicable, mysterious, inscrutable, and above all, fraught with danger.

Our present mental attitude is not really so much different from that of the ancient Greeks. Hellenic atomists saw the atomic world as the realm of chance and devoid of any divine design. Their conceptions ran counter to the basic Hellenic belief that the universe is a 'cosmos', a well-ordered whole, and that it is purposeful and meaningful. So from the very first beginning a dualistic opposition developed between the general ideological concept of Greek society and the doctrines of the small world of early Atomists.

b. What is Atomism?

In the broadest sense, Atomism is the reduction of complex phenomena to fixed unitary factors[182]. It has always exercized a strange fascination on the western mind because it "appears to be the only policy for intellectual exploration discovered so far which can be pursued systematically, as a method. Atomism is the pre-eminent intellectual method"[183].

c. Pluralism, monism, and dualism

In Greek intellectual thought we can distinguish two main lines of argument, the monist and the pluralist. Hellenic thinkers gave differing answers to the question of what comes first, the One or the Many, or, related to this initial problem, whether there really is a One, perhaps to the exclusion of the Many, or the reverse, that there is only the Many to the exclusion of the One [184]. A Presocratic scholar in the pluralistic line was, for instance, Empedocles whose theory was a thinly disguised pluralism [185]. He is the father of the doctrine of the Four Elements [186], or 'roots'.

Another early pluralist was Anaxagoras who said that "the first principles were infinite in number" [187]. In his system there seems to be no room for a One. Anaxagoras needed this infinite plurality in order to account for change. He maintained, in the words of Van Melsen, that "the primitive beings are an unlimited number of qualitatively different primitive substances, which he called seeds. These seeds are eternal and incorruptible." He gave them the name of 'homoiomerics'. Change is the result of the alternating commingling and separation of these homoiomerics [188].

It will be clear that we are coming close to an atomic theory here. Indeed the Dutch historian of science Dijksterhuis dubs doctrines such as these 'corpuscular theories' [189]. Attention should be paid to the fact that, in the thinking of this author, such theories contribute to the the mechanization of the world picture - a process that began very early in time and that did not fill everybody with joy.

At first sight the monist line could not be further apart from the pluralist way of thinking. The most eminent monist was Parmenides who posited 'Being' as the One, the only subject worthy of the philosopher's attention and, indeed, veneration. The Many belongs to the world of Seeming which, because it is all flux and change, cannot be expressed in terms of definite propositions. Nevertheless, the two lines converge at a point in the far distance.

Being was to Parmenides and other thinkers of the Eleate School [190] indivisible. Although miles apart from the Eleate essentialism, thinkers like Anaxagoras, Empedocles, and later the Atomists concurred with the Eleates that the last word in the study of reality was not change but permanence. They too found there must be a stable element.

Heraclitus, with his doctrine of change as the fundamental characteristic of reality, remained a solitary thinker [191]. In Empedocles the stable fundament of reality was the four elements, in Anaxagoras the homoiomerics, and in Atomist theory the atoms which, just like being, were indivisible and eternal [192].

d. Leucippus

Of the life of the first Greek Atomist, Leucippus, we know precious little : born at Elea, died either at Abdera or at Milete, pupil of Zeno (the Eleate), this is all the biographical detail that Diogenes has to offer [193]. It is so little that some have doubted his historical existence [194]. However, on the authority of Aristotle we are entitled to assume that there really was a philosopher called Leucippus [195]; he may have 'flourished' in the years 450-420 B.C. [196].

He has two works to his name, 'On Mind' and the 'Great Cosmology' [197]. Of these works only one single quotation remains. We may, however, be satisfied that in the writings of Leucippus' disciple Democritus we rediscover the substance of the Leucippean doctrine; very probably Leucippus was the original genius and Democritus the faithful expositor of his master's views [198].

e. Democritus

Although we know little more of Democritus' life than of that of Leucippus, nobody doubts his existence. He was born in Abdera [199] and later migrated to Athens where he remained virtually unknown. He travelled widely for many years, visiting Egypt, Babylonia, Persia, and even, it is said, Ethiopia [200]; he himself thought he was the most widely travelled man of his time [201]. He reached a high age, perhaps ninety years; his life may have spanned the period between 460 and 380 or 370 B.C. According to a catalogue composed by Thrasyllus [202], he was the author of some sixty books of which only fragments remain [203].

f. Being and change

These first Atomists, according to Aristotle, attacked the Eleatic viewpoint that there is no change, or that change should be disregarded. "Some ancient thinkers (i.e. the Eleates - F.) held that 'what is' must necessarily be one and immovable, for they argued that the void does not exist" - the typical Greek 'horror vacui' - "... nor again could there be a multiplicity of things, since there is nothing which keeps them apart" [204]. Aristotle means here that if separate objects exist, they must remain separate from each other by means of a void; since, however, the Eleatic concept of being does not admit of a void, the existence of multiple things becomes impossible.

Leucippus' thesis was that "from that which is truly one, a multiplicity could never come into being" [205]. This means that he rejected the monist (the Eleatic) position. But he equally rejected the pluralist position, for it is impossible, he thought, that a One could come 'from the truly many" [206]. "The main weakness of the current pluralistic theories was that they destroyed the fundamental 'One' " [207].

Leucippus set out to find a middle term between monism and pluralism; he wanted to construe a theory that would combine the One and the Many. If he had succeeded in this, he would have dealt monism as well as dualism a deadly blow. First of all, he postulated that there is a void [208]. In asserting this he takes to account one of the last Eleates and followers of Parmenides, Melissus who, like Descartes, was a military man (an officer) as well as a philosopher (he 'flourished' around 440-430 B.C.). This scholar had categorically declared that "there is no void; in effect, the void is nothing, and that which is nothing cannot exist" [209]. He introduces this as a new element into the discussion since Parmenides, as far as we know, had not mentioned the void.

Leucippus was subtle enough not to deny what Melissus had brought forward. Who could reasonably argue that the void is something [210]? He agrees with Melissus that the void is 'not being' [211]. Nevertheless, it seems to me that Leucippus is contradicting himself because, in nearly the same breath, he declares that the void is 'not being' and that there is a void [212]. "That what is, in the proper sense of the word, is the completely full." But before one might think that this 'completely full', which is the only really existent, is identical with the Eleatic One, Leucippus quickly moves away from the monist position by declaring that this fulness "is not one but many things of infinite number, and invisible owing to the minuteness of their bulk" [213]. In this way Leucippus introduced the atomic concept.

g. The problem of the void

How does Leucippus solve the paradox that the void 'is not' (does not exist) and 'is' (exists) at the same time? First of all, he needed the void very urgently because his atomic particles must have room for manoeuvring. They do not constitute an immovable solid mass but they "are carried along in the void ..., and when they come together, they cause coming-to-be and when they dissolve, they cause passing-away ..., dissolution and passing-away taking place by means of the void, and likewise also growth" [214]. In this way Leucippus accounts for change; without the void, no change. According to Aristotle, "Leucippus and his disciple Democritus hold that the elements are the Full and the Void" - other elements, therefore, than the four well-known ones of Empedocles -; "they call the one 'what is' and the other 'what is not' ". Next these philosophers boldly assert that "what is not is no less real than what is, because Void is as real as Body (= Matter)" [215].

Bailey defends Leucippus against the charge that this ingenious solution may seem to us 'something of a quibble'. "In effect, Leucippus had introduced a new conception of reality, ... a new idea of existence, something non-corporeal, whose sole function is to be where the fuller reality is not, an existence in which the full reality, matter, can move and have its being" [216]. The semantic and ontological problem, however, is that Leucippus did not posit the void as a lesser reality or as something incorporeal but categorically as 'not being' and as such opposed to 'being' (what is = matter) [217].

But does this really mean that the void (or space) is not material? There is much confusion among scholars on this point, a confusion that very probably originates with Leucippus himself. Burnet, for one, thought that it was a strange achievement for the founder of the great materialist school of Antiquity to have been "the first to say distinctly that a thing might be real without having a body" [218]. Strange it surely is as long we think of space as something that is wholly immaterial. But do we? Don't we think of space, however empty it may be, as of something that is somehow substantial, like a kind of enormous empty box? Didn't the Greeks think likewise when they saw space hemmed in by the frontiers of the cosmos? Furthermore, Aristotle called the Atomists' 'Void and Full' 'elements'. We do not know whether the Atomists themselves used the term 'stoicheion", but if they did, then they thought of the void as of something that is not immaterial. For elements are material things, just as Empedocles' four elements possess a material nature.

h. The main outline of Atomism

"The main outline of the atomic theory", writes Bailey, "is handed on from Leucippus to Democritus without substantial alteration, but its statement is at once more systematic, and in some respects more elaborated " [219]. It is, therefore, perfectly defensible to make Democritus the spokesman for the older Atomists. He seems to have realized that his master had worked himself into an impasse with his notion of the void, for while he (Democritus) calls the atoms 'ta onta' = the real things, or even 'den' = thing, he describes the Void simply as 'ouden' = nothing [220]. This would evidently be a dualistic distinction.

What did the philosopher mean by 'nothing'? Since it is impossible for the human mind to imagine nothing, what did he have in mind when using this term? In his terminology the 'nothing', or the void, sometimes is different from space [221] when the void seems to be something that envelops space. But sometimes void and space clearly are identical [222]. To all intents and purposes the notion that was uppermost in Democritus' mind was not to define very subtle distinctions between void and space but, tuning down Leucippus' idea of the void somewhat, to make the atomic doctrine unequivocally (and monistically) materialistic. If this is true, than the original Leucippan position had to be cleared of all traces of dualism. For that reason every supposition that the void, as being incorporeal, might resemble something spiritual had to be cancelled [223]. If this is correct, then the Democritean void must at least have a material side to it.

In several texts 'void' and 'fulness' are posited as a pair of opposites. According to atomistic theory, all existing things, consisting as they do of atoms, are constantly moving between being and non-being, since they are incessantly originating and falling apart, without ever attaining the full ontological status of being, and without ever disappearing into Nothingness. Void and fulness, therefore, may be seen as ontological elements, as 'archai' or 'first principles' from which everything proceeds. Since the void has a material side, it may, in view of the atomic processes, be defined as a material cause.

Aristotle says that "it is possible (for all things) both to be and not to be, and this possibility is the matter (what he means is the material cause - F.) in each individual thing" [224]. And still more telling : "It must therefore be by nature that such (i.e. finite) things at one time exist and at another do not. In things like that ... one and the same potentiality is the potentiality of opposite states, and the matter is the cause of things both being and not being" [225]. The philosopher seems to be coming very near to the Democritean position here.

Anyhow, his words prove that the Democritean void may be conceived as a material cause, as the 'principle of individuation and structure' without which the atoms can neither be separate from each other nor brought together to form objects. The void might be thought of as 'spatial extension'. This interpretation of the meaning of void, space and 'non-being', leaves the materialistic character of the Atomic doctrine unimpaired [226]. But the question remains whether the original problem that, in a materialistic doctrine, the Void is nevertheless conceived of as being incorporeal, is really solved by postulating that it is a material cause. It seems to me that Democritus too did not succeed in making the theory unequivocally monistic. This whole argument emphasizes the extreme difficulty of making a monistic position entirely consistent and shows how easily it slips into some form of dualism.

j. Psyche and matter

As may be expected, psyche, or soul, is something material too in atomistic philosophy. Like fire, it is made up of very small and round particles. "Democritus argues that the soul is a form of heat ... Forms and atoms being countless, he calls the spherical ones fire and soul"[227]. The soul-atoms are dispersed throughout the whole body[228], even in such a way that psychic and bodily atoms alternate[229]. The soul-particles have to be small and rounded in order to penetrate into every nook of the human body; this is necessary because "the soul is that which imparts motion to living things"[230].

That Democritus was a materialist does not mean that body and soul are all one to him. On the contrary, he regards the soul as far more excellent than the body, so much so that he sometimes compares the body to a tent in which the soul has chosen her abode[231]. "Whosoever chooses for the goods of the soul chooses for the godlike one; those who choose for the goods of the body opts for what is human"[232]; "it is fit for human beings to take the soul in account rather than the body"[233].

In utterances such as these there is a touch - and more than a touch - of the soul-body dualism that is so persistent in Greek philosophy from Pythagoras to Plato and later. In order that his soul-theory should not conflict with his materialism Democritus viewed the psychic atoms as not only different in size and shape from the bodily ones but also in properties and qualities; in consequence the soul could be seen as more sublime than the body.

To materialist philosophers (who, after all, are 'thinkers'), it has always proved a tricky problem to explain the phenomenon of thought. In the nineteenth century Moleschott categorically proclaimed that "without phosphor (there is) no thought"[234], thus explaining that thinking is a chemical process. The Greek philosopher's idea that the soul-particles are fiery is something similar. According to him, the soul consists of two parts, one mindless and dispersed through the body, the other thinking and located in the brain or in the heart [235].

k. Death

What happens at the moment of death? Then the atomic structure that forms a human or animal shape falls apart, that is to say, the atoms disperse into the void. The soul-atoms disconnect themselves from the bodily ones [236] but do not stick together as a separate psychic structure [237]. As a consequence, there is no doctrine of immortality or metempsychosis in Democritus; he even speaks scathingly of people who live immorally but fear the punishment that awaits them after death. If they only knew that human nature will be totally dissolved [238]! This should not be taken to mean that this philosopher thought it indifferent whether people behaved morally or immorally [239].

l. The fate of the gods in Atomism

The atomistic doctrine, as far as we have considered it now, forebodes little good for the gods. "That he (Democritus) could not share his people's belief in the gods will be obvious" [240]. Not that he flatly denied their existence! Hardly anybody did so in the fifth century B.C. "But in Democritus' conception of the universe, personal gods would seem excluded a priori : the atoms, their movements, and empty space" are his basic postulates [241]. Greek popular religion was to him sheer superstition caused by the fear of overwhelming natural phenomena like thunder and lightning. "Men in the old days seeing the occurrences in the sky, such as thunder and lightning and the conjunctions of the sun and the moon, dreaded the gods believing that they were the cause of these things" [242]. The philosopher does not call these beings 'gods' but 'idols' ('eidola'). Zeller concludes that these idols are nothing else than the demons of popular belief; Democritus must, therefore, be regarded as the first one who, "wanting to mediate between philosophy and popular belief, took the road that later became so common of degrading the gods to demons" [243].

m. Summing up

Let me, at the end of this section, stress a few points. First, in Democritus' materialistic system there is no real room for a genuine spiritual world. For him, being is equivalent to matter. Although it proved difficult to him and Leucippus to keep away from the seduction of dualism, their, and in particular Democritus', doctrine, is a monistic one. This means that it did not strike a mean between the notions of Unity and Plurality by combining these into a coherent system. Since as I stated earlier, monistic systems are not the true opposites of dualistic ones, and since monism, because of its onesidedness, is apt to generate dualism, it might be expected that Democritus' categorical materialism would one day be opposed by a purely spiritual system.

Secondly, Democritus' materialistic system may also be called mechanistic; it operates automatically, like a well-ordered, computer-directed machine, or better still, like a kind of perpetuum mobile. "The term 'mechanistic' ", says Dijksterhuis, "intends to express that the movements of the atoms are controlled by laws of mechanics that acknowledge no other forces than those exercized by the mutual contact of two bodies" [244]. The consequence is that there is no finality, in other words, there is no special reason why atomic 'collocations' are formed. Why our world, and we ourselves, are as they are cannot be explained. The number of worlds is infinite; it is theoretically perfectly possible that yet another world exists that is similar to ours in every detail.

It should not be surmised, however, that the process of generation is ruled by chance. On the contrary, chance is emphatically excluded. "Nothing comes into being without plan but everything with reason and according to necessity" [245]. This is all the philosophical, intellectual, or scholarly explanation the Atomists had to offer of the most important existential questions. From a philosophical point of view the atomistic doctrine must have appeared very shallow to more inquiring minds.

This brings me to a third point. Not only as a philosophy but as a cosmology this doctrine shows grave deficiences. Who or what brings about the atomic mass? Who or what put it in motion? Why are the configurations shaped as they are? If they are the product of necessity, what is meant by this? If by 'necessity' inexorable physical laws are meant, who was the lawgiver then? The answers that Atomism (just like modern evolutionism) failed to provide were, nevertheless, advanced by other schools of classical philosophy, and more particularly, in mystical and mythical religions, in quasi- and pseudo-religions, and in fantastic explanations, many of which would assume a thoroughly dualistic character.

Lastly, the system's atheistic nature must be emphasized. It may have seemed satisfying to some purely scientific minds but it leaves all those who were religiously inclined in the cold. Atomism does away with all the great metaphysical tenets, with the gods, with immortality, with metempsychosis, with divine guidance, and with the soul as a separate entity. This was asking for a reaction, and the more categorical the denial, the stronger the new affirmations would be. Religion would not prove itself contented with an ideology as jejune as this one.

There is, of course, no telling how influential atomism was. But the fact that it could arise at all, that it founded a philosophical school of importance, that it possessed its teachers and its canonical works, that there was a kind of atomistic, rather rigid, atomistic 'orthodoxy, that the works of this school were read and copied throughout Antiquity, and finally, that in the fourth century B.C. the standard could be taken up by another eminent thinker, Epicurus, all this proves that it must have had a not inconsiderable following, especially among intellectuals.

Dissatisfied with the real or supposed superstitions of the Olympian religion, they tried to find solace in an utterly non-religious system. This not only estranged them from the broad mass of the Hellenic population but it still further undermined the position of orthodoxy. When at last a reaction occurred it proved an over-reaction since it was utterly anti-scientific and even a-rational. What I mean to say is that Atomism too was one of the stepping-stones on the road to the Gnosis with its categorical dualism.

4. Epicureanism

a. The life and the school of Epicurus

The philosopher Epicurus was born in 341 B.C., in all probablity in the island of Samos that was then under Athenian control. However, he himself was not a Samian but an Athenian citizen since his parents were members of a noble Athenian family [246]. Part of his youth he spent at Athens but after his parents had settled at Colophon, he followed them there. It is not known who were his teachers in philosophy but it is evident that he was influenced by Democritus and by Aristotle. When he was thirty years old, he began to teach himself, first in Greek cities of Asia Minor but from 306 B.C. onward in Athens, still the capital of philosophy.

Epicurus bought a house in Athens with a beautiful garden, that became the headquarters of a new philosophical school, apart from the already existing Academy and the Peripatic School. Living in this house with some close friends Epicurus established a kind of fraternity that reminds one of the Pythagorean society. Some liberated slaves formed part of the community, together with some women, wives of colleagues and also some courtesans [247]. The presence of such ladies naturally gave rise to malevolent rumors in the town about the kind of life that was led in the school - the more so because the 'Garden School' acted as a 'closed shop' and sealed itself against the uneducated vulgus.

b. Epicurean dogmatism

Not only does this dualistic element recall the Pythagorean fraternity, but still more the fact that Epicurus was the venerated and infallible head of the school. "The members of the school were bound together by their unconditional belief in the redemptive power of the doctrine of their master no less than by the way they put the rest of the world at its proper distance" [248]. There even is a story that one Colotes, after having heard a lecture by the great sage, threw himself at his knees before him, embraced his knees, and in this way paid him the homage due to a god or a deified person. Epicurus did not show himself wholly averse to this [249]. His birthday was celebrated annually by the whole community in the style of a quasi-religious occasion while in his testament he stipulated that on the twentieth of every month a memorial service should be held for himself and for his favourite disciple Metrodorus (the only one whom he considered a 'sage' like himself) [250]. It seems that his followers stuck to this custom for centuries [251].

To his disciples Epicurus "was a founder of religion and a prophet rather than a scientific professor" [252]. His philosophy ranked as a dogmatic doctrine; it must be taught, studied, and transmitted but was not presented in order to be discussed and developed. He compelled his students and even his associates to learn excerpts of his treatises by heart [253]. They had a lot to memorize since he was a prolific writer. Diogenes lists thirty-two works which he considered the best, but his production is said to have amounted to about three hundred scrolls [254]. Only fragments are extant but the complete text of three letters by Epicurus has been preserved by Diogenes [255].

It will astonish nobody that Epicurus held all philosophers, whether his predecessors or his contemporaries, in the deepest contempt. "The quotations given in Plutarch's Essay against Colotes are a perfect mine of scurrilities directed against every eminent thinker of the past who had in any way strayed from the path of rigid orthodoxy as understood by Epicurus" [256]. He called Nausiphanes who probably had been his own first teacher a 'mollusc, a boor and a quack'; Platonists were 'Dionysius (or Dionysus') lickspittlers', Plato was 'that thing of gold' (which did not signify praise), Aristotle a rake and a mountebank, Heraclitus a muddler. Worst of all, he also heaped scorn on his own philosophical ancestry, the Atomists, in particular on Democritus [257].

Calling this "wholesale abuse of all thinkers who had gone before him ... the ugliest feature in the character of Epicurus", Taylor states that this philosopher was the only one to do so; even Aristotle who had no mean idea of his own capacities and was often highly critical of his fellow-thinkers never abused them [258]. Partly, of course, this supercilious attitude is the product of arrogance; it helped him to pose as "the one and only revealer of the way of Salvation" [259]. Proud as he was of his own achievements, he stated, doubtless referring to himself, that "some people arrive at truth without anybody's help and pave their own road" [260]. But in another respect this vanity served as a smoke-screen to camouflage the undeniable fact that Epicurus, neither a deep nor an original thinker, was heavily dependent on his predecessors. Cicero points an accusing finger at him : "What is there in the physics that is not from Democritus?" [261], and he adds : "Where Epicurus alters the doctrines of Democritus, he alters them for the worse" [262].

Having long been in bad health, Epicurus died at the age of seventy in 271 B.C. He never married.

c. The esoteric character of the School of the Garden

A word must be said on the esoteric character of the Epicurean scholastic society, since this represents an important stage in the growing tendency towards mysticism, mysteriosophy, and esoterism in the Hellenistic world, and also because life in the Garden of Epicurus showed dualistic features. This is also substantiated by the fact that we rediscover the old partition of mankind into three that was also a feature of the Pythagorean fraternity [263]. The venerated leader of the school was, of course, Epicurus whose authority went undisputed. He sported the title of 'hegemon' = commander, leader, guide [264]. He did not refer to himself as 'philosopher' but as 'sophos' = the Sage [265]. Teaching ex cathedra [266], "he showed what was the Chief Good (i.e. Pleasure, not Plato's Supreme Good) to which we all move, and pointed the way, that straight and narrow path by which we might run thither without turning" [267]. Thus Epicurus by himself alone occupied the inner ring of three concentric circles.

In the second circle we find his three deputies or associate leaders, with the title of 'kathegemones' [268]. Their master unflinchingly relegated them to a lower place in the intellectual scale for, he said, "they are persons who need the help of others (sc. of the Sage); they don't progress where nobody takes the lead but are prepared to follow". Mentioning one of the three by name, Metrodorus, he assigned him to this second class : 'a brilliant mind but of the second rank' [269]. Of these three only Hermarchus survived to succeed him as head of the school. To this group, of lower rank but still within this cycle, the teachers belong, the 'kathegetes'. Most of them taught classes but some of the more able seem to have tutored single students [270]. In Epicurus' eyes, taking account of the haughty character of the man, the difference between the first and second cycles was of a dualistic sort, that between genius and talent; however talented his favourites might be, they could never aspire to genius [271].

The third circle was that of the students. They were of different ages, some of them even adults. Using an anachronism, we could say that the Garden was a comprehensive school. Part of them lived as residents in the Garden, others in town. Most of them were grouped together in classes. A curious trait of the school, clearly pointing in the direction of mysticism, were "the mystical nocturnal sessions which took place at regular intervals" [272]. All pupils committed themselves on oath to unswerving loyalty to the Master and his doctrine : "I will be faithful to Epicurus according to whom it has been my choice to live" [273]. Therefore, they should "do everything as though Epicurus were watching you" [274]. Big Brother obviously had his forerunners!

Within the Garden, therefore, three circles existed, that of the Prophet, that of the initiated, that of the aspirants. Whereas the distance between the first and second cycles was unbridgeable - Epicurus for once and for all remaining the sole Prophet -, that between the second and third circles was only relative, since an aspirant in due course could become an adept.

But there was yet another partition into three, first the Prophet, then the initiated and the aspirants, and finally the mass of the ignorant and uninterested. Here we find a second dualistic distinction, that between those who knew and those who did not and did want to know. In this context it is intriguing to note that the initiated members of the sect were dubbed 'gnoorimoi', literally 'those in the know' [275].

Taylor describes the moral atmosphere in the School of the Garden as not entirely healthy. Very probably Nietzsche was right in saying that it was decadent. The main leaders, in particular the Master himself, were unbearably self-adulatory; there was far too much mutual admiration. The adepts shrank from assuming offices in the polis; this was only needless excitation. Epicurus himself remained 'unkown in Athens where he lived a hidden life" [276]. Compare this to Socrates' daily presence on the agora! All the adepts desired was to have a peaceful and undisturbed existence in their secluded Garden from where they could safely despise all those who busied themselves in practical life [277].

d. Ridding mankind of fear

During the lifetime of Epicurus the Greek scholarly class became submerged by an enormous mass of new scientific data 'concerning the geography, the flora and fauna, and the divergent wisdoms of Persia and India' [278]; these were the results of Alexander's expedition which was as much a voyage of discovery as a military campaign. This fresh information was studied in Epicurus' institute too. But the curious thing is that the Epicureans did not study the new data out of a purely scientific interest. They neither intended to present the world, so to speak, with an up-to-date encyclopaedia of knowledge nor were their ends practical, helping people to master nature and teaching them to live more comfortably and more safely.

Their real aim was to rid mankind of its two overriding fears, that of the gods and that of death. It was, therefore, necessary to prove that all natural phenomena have natural causes [279]. Or to put it in Robin's words : "The conquest of salvation preceded knowledge" [280]. Zeller even goes so far as to state that the Sage utterly despised all scientific work done for its own end. "(The Epicureans) promised to make known the art of living; therefore, Epicurus said that philosophy is an exercise for realizing the happy life by means of reasoning" [281]. Partly this Epicurean aversion to pure science may have been an Epicurean principle, but in another respect it can have been meant to camouflage the philosopher's insufficient education [282].

The Epicureans made a virtue out of their ignorance by declaring that " there is no need for the aspirant to philosophy to be a scholar at all" [283]. This may serve to show that the Greek scientific spirit was losing ground in favour of a brand of (mostly bogus) mysticism. Epicurean convictions of this kind also put a canonical seal on the ideas of later fundamentalists, ignoramuses with scholarly pretensions, and members of esoteric sects. They all throve on a dualistic distinction between sound scholarship and what they consider real wisdom.

e. Epicurus' 'All'

Epicurus starts from a premise that was common in Greek thought, viz. that 'nothing comes from non-being' [284]; there is no 'creatio ex nihilo'. This leads to the law of the preservation of matter, for "if that which disappears were destroyed into non-being, all things would be destroyed" [285]. This means that matter is eternal. "The All" (Epicurus does not say the cosmos but 'to pan') "was always such as it is now and always will be such. For there is nothing into which it changes. For there is nothing besides the All that by entering into it would make the change" [286].

This effectively rules out the gods as creators and governors of the world. In contrast to Parmenides, Epicurus acknowledges change, i.e. generation and destruction in the 'totality' (the All, that is), but differing from the great Eleate he "views it (the All itself) as the unchanging ground of all generation and destruction and therefore assigns to it everlasting duration of past and future" [287]. It will be clear that the banished divine principle enters again by the backdoor, for this uncreated, unchanging, and eternal 'All' shows divine properties.

f. Epicurus' Atomism

Epicurus too was an Atomist : his two first principles ('archai') are void and bodies. "Besides void and bodies no third nature can be left self-existing in the sum of things" [288]. "For whatsoever things are said to be, you will either find them to be properties of these two (i.e. of void or bodies) or you will find them to be accidents of the same" [289]. This amounts to a declaration of intent : all phenomena, of whatever kind, are natural, have natural causes, and must be explained naturally. The only reality is the physical, the corporeal one, or to use a modern word, it is corpuscular, for it consists of atoms. "It is impossible to conceive the incorporeal as of itself existing, with the exception of the void" [290]. The void is necessary to make the movements of the atoms possible without which there would be no change. "If the void did not exist, things could in no way move" [291]. In that case the atoms would remain packed together in one solid block [292].

The grouping and regrouping of the atoms into structures is a process that has gone on from all eternity [293]. This leads Epicurus to the same conclusion as that of the earlier Atomists : that the number of worlds must be infinite; some of them are similar to ours, others dissimilar [294]. Our world, therefore, is only one among innumerable others. Notions like these must give people a sense of loneliness and of being wholly accidental. The idea that it is possible that another world exists that is identical to ours suggests to people that they are superfluous. Why should I take all this trouble while somewhere in the universe someone is doing exactly the same thing as I am doing now? The origin of the human race and its subsequent growth to higher civilization are explained in the same naturalistic vein.

g. Epicurus on the soul

It is wholly in accordance with the classical corpuscular theory that the soul should be considered as a body composed of subtle particles and dispersed through the whole organism. It is just like a breath, said the philosopher [295]. He follows Democritus in arguing that that part of the soul which is dispersed through the body is irrational, whereas its rational part is located in the breast [296]. At the moment of death the whole structure is dissolved; the soul is released from the body and is then dispersed [297]. There is not the slightest reason for fearing death. "Become accustomed to the belief that death is nothing to us. For all good and evil consist in sensation but death is deprivation of sensation ... There is nothing terrible in not living ... So death, the most terrifying of ills, is nothing to us, since so long we exist, death is not with us; but when death comes, then we do not exist" [298].

For a summing up we must resort to Copleston. "The world is, therefore, due to mechanical causes, and there is no need to postulate teleology. On the contrary, the Epicureans rejected the anthropocentric teleology of the Stoics and would have nothing to do with the Stoic theodicy" [299].

h. Epicurus and the gods

This brings us to the position of the gods in Epicurean philosophy. Does it acknowledge gods? In one of his witty and realistic 'characters' Theophrastus depicts to us the man who lives in constant fear of supernatural beings. "Living in fear of supernatural beings ... would seem to be some kind of cowardice with respect to the divine" [300]. Now, contrary to what we may expect, Epicurus took part in many of the ceremonies and rituals to which Theophrastus' godfearing person also so assiduously devotes himself. The philosopher is even said to have been initiated into 'the mysteries of the town' and other mysteries (by mysteries of the town hardly anything else can be meant than the Eleusinian mysteries) [301].

Philodemus epitomizes the philosopher's religious attitude in these words : "It seems that Epicurus faithfully observed all the customs of the (public) cult and that he prescribed to his friends to observe them, not only because of the laws but for natural reasons" [302]. Cicero adds to this, obviously without a trace of irony : "Epicurus (did) actually think that the gods exist, nor have I [303] ever met anybody more afraid than he was of those things which he says are not terrible at all, I mean death and the gods" [304]. Is it really a far-fetched conclusion to think that Epicurus, when combating the general fear of the gods, was first of all fighting his own fears? Be this as it may, we must pay attention to the fact that he prescribed observance of the cult for 'natural', in Greek 'physikas', reasons. This term does not suggest a really religious mind but rather a philosophical attitude.

Although a regular observant of the public cult, Epicurus was highly critical of popular belief. "What the multitude believes about the gods is truly impious. For the utterances of the multitude about the gods are not true preconceptions but false assumptions" [305]. Does the public believe in divine Providence? Sheer nonsense! This is 'nothing but a myth' [306]. The philosopher's real problem was with theodicy, with divine justice that is. "For he saw the good always struck by an adverse fate, by poverty, troubles, banishments, loss of their beloved; the bad are against the good, they grow in might, and for them honours galore! He saw innocence in danger but crimes go unpunished" [307], and so on, and so on.

j. The problem of evil

It is evident that Epicurus sees himself confronted here with the problem of evil, perhaps less with the fact of its existence than with its origin. Mankind has always tortured itself by it, the Greeks not excepted, and no Greek philosopher had ever profferred a satisfying solution. But I have the impression that in post-Platonic and post-Aristotelian philosophy the problem was growing more and more painful. The other side of the coin was that pleasure was becoming ever more meaningful as the aim of life. I suppose that these phenomena are linked with the weakening of the fabric of Hellenic life, above all with the highly diminished importance of the polis.

From what is said above it appears that, according to Epicurus, the origin of evil should not be imputed to the gods; they have nothing at all to do with it. He does not tell us how, when, and where, evil has originated. Perhaps this is a consequence of the fragmentary state of his writings but it is equally possible that he simply did not know. Anyhow, there is an unbridgeable gulf - a dualistic distance - between the Epicurean gods and evil. In a later period Lucretius, reasoning in the truest Epicurean vein, even wrote that "the world was certainly not made for us by divine powers so great are the faults with which it stands endowed" [308].

We have come a long way from the Homeric creed according to which the gods were by no means exempt from evil; they committed crimes themselves - Zeus' frequent adulteries! - and wilfully did malevolent things to people [309]. How many loud and angry complaints have we not heard in Greek lyric and tragedy about the arbitrariness and malice of the gods [310].

k. Why Epicurus needed gods

To return now to the Epicurean gods, why does this materialist philosopher postulate them at all? As Zeller says, an open avowal of atheism was no longer as dangerous as it was in the fifth century B.C. The Sage seems to have been impressed by the fact that belief in the gods is general [311] : "Verily there are gods and the knowledge of them is manifest ..., the notion of a god (is) indicated by the common sense of mankind". It is intriguing that for 'knowledge' the word 'gnosis' is used in this quotation. However, "they are not such as the multitude believes" [312]. Once again that haughty contempt of 'the multitude' [313].

There is also his 'aesthetic-religious' wish to see his ideal of blessedness realized in the gods : "The acme of bliss is enjoyed by the gods" [314]. It is for this reason that they have a human shape just like the Olympian divinities; they even are male and female. In Cicero the anti-Epicurean Cotta insinuatingly suggests : "You must see what the consequence of this will be" [315]. It must have been a relief for the Hellenes to hear that the gods speak Greek [316]. In contrast to the Olympian godhead and to man they are eternal [317].

The gods are entirely free of sorrow. "A blessed and eternal being has no trouble himself ... (and) is exempt from every movement of anger and goodwill" [318]; they are the perfect model of apatheia. "The godhead is entirely free from all ties of occupation; he toils not neither does he labour but takes delight in his own wisdom and virtue, and knows with absolute certainty that he will enjoy pleasures at once consumate and everlasting" [319]. About the world and its inhabitants they could not care less; they are 'der Welt abhanden gekommen', "far removed and separated from our happiness" [320]. Caring about human beings or the fate of the world would spoil their joy [321].

In consequence, "it is impossible that ... any holy abode of the gods exists in any part of the (= our sublunar) world ... Their abode ... must be different from our abodes" [322]. They live 'between two worlds' [323], between the sublunar world and the world beyond the heavens, that is "in their peaceful abodes, which no winds ever shake nor clouds besprinkle with rain, which no snow congealed by the bitter frost mars by its white fall, but the air ever cloudless encompasses them and laughs with its light spread abroad" [324]. This enchanting picture painted by Lucretius must not make us forget that the Epicurean gods are impersonal and bear no names; their number being legion [325] they cannot be differentiated from each other. For people with a religious mind this must have been a depressing message. It is one more stage in the ongoing process of making the gods more abstract.

Of course the divine beings would be unable to live high up in the air if they had bodies like ours. Instead, their physique is composed of the lightest atoms. "Their form ... only resembles bodily substance" [326], they are 'volatile and transparent' [327], 'with the winds blowing through them' [328]. They can only be pereceived as shapes [329].

It does not necessitate much philosophical perspicacity to see that, regarding the eternity of the gods, the Epicureans land themselves in insoluble difficulties. In their doctrine the atoms alone are eternal; all atomic configurations are perishable. Since the divinities too are composed of atoms, how can they be everlasting? Broadsides of criticism were fired in Antiquity with regard to this point which the Epicureans were unable to answer [330]. My own idea is that the Epicureans may have been somewhat aghast at the consequences of their own doctrine : that of an entirely godless world [331]. The spectre of a cosmos consisting of whirling atoms forming fortuitous configurations is neither attractive nor anodynic.

So, in spite of their unforgiving dogmatism, they brought in gods of their own making. To imagine a world wholly deprived of gods, would have been too much to be stomached by most, probably all, Hellenes. It would have been because of this that the Epicureans did not want to distance themselves from the public cult. In their polemic with the Stoics the Epicureans prided themselves on the fact that their gods, contrary to the pale shapes of the Stoa divinities, were just as anthropomorphic as those of the Olympian religion and even more polytheistic [332].

1. Epicurean epistemology

A word or two must be said on Epicurean epistemology. Since the sage should only be concerned with the good of his soul [333], Epicurus was, as Robin writes, never really interested in logic or, we may add, in science [334]. Our judgments are not formed by means of abstract thought but must be based on evidence; this is supplied by our senses and by our affective state. This is our fundamental, or to use a modern expression, our existential certitude. To state otherwise is to walk with head down and feet up; it destroys 'the foundations upon which our life and our salvation rest' [335]. Attention should be paid to the use of the word 'salvation' [336]. What modern scholar would contend that using our sense-based awareness and our feelings of pain or pleasure could 'save' us? This notion seems to reduce truth to a personal and subjective affair, with a salvific significance (truth is what one feels to be true, and that will save him).

The knowledge that Epicurus honoured was not of the scientific kind. Quite the contrary. "Hoist all sail ... and steer clear of all culture" [337]. "There is nothing in the risings and settings and solstices and eclipses that contributes to our happiness" [338]. For this reason we should feel confused when there appear "manifold causes for their (i.e. of celestial phenomena) occurence and manifold accounts ... if all be explained by the method of plurality of causes" [339]. This, of course, is not the true scientific spirit. "This leaves us free", concludes Robin, "to believe whatever we want on the size of the stars (etc.). What is really important is to cut down these imposing phenomena to the proportions of our more familiar experiences." With this decision Epicurus affirms "that the quest of salvation takes precedence over knowledge" [340].

In this context it should be noted that the philosopher invariably uses the word 'gnosis' [341] in a redemptory sense. "A right understanding ('orthè gnosis') that death is nothing to us makes the mortality of our lives enjoyable" [342]; "the knowledge ('gnosis') of the gods is manifest" [343]. And especially this : "Remember that ... knowledge ('gnosis') of celestial phenomena ... has no other end in view than peace of mind and firm conviction" [344].

m. Epicurean pleasure

It is well-known that for the Epicureans the supreme aim of life was pleasure ('hēdonē') [345]. This has led to much mudslinging as though they have preached that 'anything goes' as long it satisfies the baser human lusts. Undiscriminating opponents identified 'pleasure' solely with the urges that are situated below the midriff. These accusations stuck for my dictionaries tell me that an 'epicure' is a gastronomist, and an 'epicurean' a person devoted to pleasure, especially refined sensuous enjoyment; he is a gourmet, he has a taste for luxury, he is prurient, and he is a carouser. Excusez du peu!

Now it must be admitted that the Epicureans laid themselves open to such charges. Plutarch reports that Epicurus' disciple Metrodorus wrote to his brother Timocrates that he had learned from his master "how to gratify the belly properly"; "the belly", he adds, "is the region that contains the highest end" [346]. "What else is the good of the soul but a permanent healthy condition of the flesh?" [347]. The prophet himself is even reported to have said that "the beginning and root of all good is the pleasure of the belly, and even wisdom and all that is extraordinary depend on it" [348].

What made the Epicureans express themselves in such extravagant language by which they exposed themselves to the opprobrium of their opponents? Possibly it is true, as Taylor says, that men like Epicurus and Metrodorus, both being dyspeptics, were speaking nostalgically of what was denied to them [349]. But another guess might be that the Epicureans heartily loathed the exalted and in their eyes abstract ideas of the Academics on the Good; they wanted to stress that a human being has a body, and that this body has its justified claims. Anyhow, they had no great confidence in the virtues of ascetism.

Epicurus was by no means so categoric about pleasure as it may seem. Sometimes pleasure is a positive good; sometimes it is only freedom from pain. "The end of all our actions is to be free of pain and fear." We need not only health of the body but also tranquillity of mind, "seeing that this is the sum and end of a blessed life". "Not all pleasure is choiceworthy"; some of our desires are groundless [350]. Another time he states unequivocally that "the greatest good is prudence ('phronêsis')" [351].

5. Scepticism

a. What is a 'Sceptic'?

The cause of objective truth had already become undermined by the Epicureans but a torpedo with a powerful explosive charge was launched against it by the Sceptics. No longer did the old question of 'what is true?' form the centre of philosophical discussion, not even 'what is Truth?', but 'does Truth exist?'. The word 'sceptic' is derived from the Greek adjective 'skeptikos' which in its turn comes from the verb 'skeptomai' = to look about carefully, and later 'to examine, to consider'. The original meaning of 'skeptikos, therefore, might be rendered as 'inquirer'.

When we take this word in a general sense, then every scholar or philosopher is or ought to be an 'inquirer'; the word 'sceptical' still can denote somone with a critical turn of mind, somebody who is not credulous or complacent. But already in Antiquity it came to mean something more specific. "(Philosophical sceptics) have questioned whether any necessary or indubitable information can actually be gained about the real nature of things ... Extreme skepticism questions all knowledge claims that go beyond immediate experience, except perhaps those of logic and mathematics ... Some skeptics have held that no knowledge beyond immediate experience is possible, while others have doubted whether this much could definitely be known" [352]. Although some aspects of this more specific scepticism are already apparent before Pyrrho, this philosopher is considered the true founder of the school or mode of thought that is called 'scepticism', and sometimes, after him, 'Pyrrhonism'.

b. Pyrrho

Pyrrho was a Peloponnesian from Elis; since he was born there ca. 360 B.C. and died in ca. 270 B.C., he was a contemporary of Epicurus. It is a miracle that he lived up to the age of about ninety, for he was a reckless man taking every possible risk. It is said that he began his professional career as a painter, but then joined the army of Alexander and served in the expeditions to Iran and in India; there he made the acquaintance of Persian Magi and Indian gymnosophists, of Hindu ascetic thinkers that is. After his return he lived poorly in Elis although he was a respected citizen in that city. The philosophical school he founded in his father-city did not survive him. He was what biblical scholars call a 'word prophet' since all his utterances were oral. He left nothing in writing. Neither had he progeny; he never married [353].

c. Timon

Since we know so disappointingly little of Pyrrho's teaching, it is impossible to conjecture what made him adopt his position of extreme doubt. What we know of his thought has been handed down to us by his disciple Timon who was a native of Phlius on the Peloponnese. Born there in 320 B.C., and after a period during which he earned his bread as a rope-dancer, he later lived in Elis with Pyrrho whom he fervently admired. After having worked as a teacher of philosophy in Chalcedon he moved to Athens where he died about 220 B.C., he too being about ninety years old [354]. With Timon the independent school of scepticism already came to an end [355].

d. Greek forerunners of scepticism

Some sceptic philosophers used to venerate Homer as their patron saint; Homeric verses were constantly on Pyrrho's lips [356]. Others saw certain Presocratics and Democritus as their spiritual ancestors. This may sound strange because Eleates like Parmenides and Zeno were fiercely dogmatic. But on closer inspection we see that it was Parmenides with his 'iron ontology' who said that our sensory knowledge is utterly deceptive. An unbridgeable abyss yawns between what is intelligible (Being = Truth) and what is perceivable by the senses (Seeming = our world) [357]. According to Zeno the Eleate, the appearances offered to us by our senses are 'nothing but contradiction and absurdity [358]. Now just cut out the concept of Being and Truth will have vanished.

Then came the Sophists who taught the art of defending every thinkable thesis and its exact opposite in an equally convincing way [359]. Here the winner was the most agile debater rather than Truth. A very important role in the development of Scepticism was played by the philosophers of the Megarian School. This school was founded by Euclides (ca. 450-380 B.) of Megara [360] and counted a number of scholars none of whom acquired great fame. Euclides too started from the opposition of intelligible and sensible knowledge. The senses, according to him, offer no proper, really trustworthy knowledge but only changing and nascent phenomena. Real Being (and Truth) is only to be found in the realm of the immaterial; he denied every form of ontological status to the corporeal and material world.

Once again we must state that dualism and monism are not opposites, for here we see Platonic dualism being turned into a form of monism. Actually, Euclides even went so far as to deny categorically that becoming and change existed at all. Anyhow, it could not be a subject of scientific inquiry. The only subject worthy of study and contemplation was the One (of Parmenides) and the Good (of Plato), which Euclides considered to be one and the same thing.

This founder of the school was also the first great pastmaster of 'Megarian dialectics' which in practice meant that the Megarians polemically attacked the positions of their opponents. This offered a wide field to the disputatious and ambitious members of this school and led to much 'streetfighting' with other schools. The favourite method of these dialecticians was to show that the theses of their opponents were absurd because their opposite could be defended equally well. For instance, one of these philosophers was able to prove that movement did not exist. The helpless victim of such dialectical tricks was, of course, objective Truth [361].

Democritus the Atomist too put in a word. "We do not know reality (what is)", he said, "but only what comes to us through the disposition of our body, and through what goes into it and presses against it" [362]. Sextus who reports this saying finds it strange since Democritus was perfectly ready elsewhere to have faith in the senses. This same Sextus who wrote a substantial work on Pyrrhonism was well aware of the differences between the Atomist and Sceptical Schools [363]. His comment on Plato that he did not become a sceptic by simply uttering "some statements in a sceptical way " [364] was, according to him, equally applicable to Democritus.

e. Pyrrhonic apatheia

Although the field had been prepared by others, the true and only father of Scepticism is Pyrrho [365]. Pleasure, or perhaps rather bliss or beatitude, was his main interest too, no less than of many other thinkers. It was to be found in an even life, a life without troubles, pure 'ataraxia' [366]. All those things that seem so important to most people, like health and wealth, he held to be of equal value [367] or rather as equally worthless. In his opinion, "the wise man does not perceive these things with his senses"; Cicero called this unfeelingness 'apatheia' [368]. He loved quoting Homer 'on the unstable purpose, vain pursuits, and childish folly of man' [369].

The Ancients had many anecdotes to tell of this Pyrrhonic apatheia, how he sustained surgery and cauterization of a wound without even so much as frowning, and how on board a ship during a storm he told the distracted passengers, while pointing to a pig that undisturbedly went on eating, that "such was the unperturbed state in which the wise man should keep himself" [370]. There is only one Good in life, he taught, Moral Worth [371]. From this it follows that the only Evil is Wickedness. There is nothing in between; this is a radical, a dualistic opposition, the more so because Good and Evil excluded each other.

It does not become quite clear whether by Moral Worth Pyrrho meant something positive, the Good, or something passive, apatheia, ataraxia, adiaphora, or whatever it is named. One thing, however, is certain : his 'euthymia', this desirable state of mind, can only be attained by the use of reason and the study of philosophy [372]. Only in this way can a man become wise. But it remains to be seen what Pyrrho understood by 'philosophy'. The fact remains, however, that he situated himself squarely within the élitist tradition of the Academy, the Stoa, and the Epicureans. No wonder that Epicurus greatly admired Pyrrho and regularly asked for information about him [373]. Pyrrho's ex cathedra announcement that he would speak 'a word containing the right rule' [374] earned him the reproach of being (somewhat) dogmatic [375].

f. How to be wise

Who is really wise? The beginning of wisdom is to realize that things in themselves are nothing; they are uncertain and indiscernible. This entails the failure of our senses and our judgments to teach us what is right and wrong. In consequence, we should foster no opinions at all. Deny nothing, affirm nothing. Doubt everything, be indifferent to everything. This causes one first to attain the state of 'aphasia' in which nothing is stated, and then that of 'ataraxia' in which the mind is not disturbed by anything [376]. "The Sceptic determines nothing, not even the proposition 'I determine nothing'". In saying this, he is 'not making any confident declaration, but just explaining his own state of mind" [377].

Pyrrhonists dub themselves 'zetetics' because they are always seeking ('zētein' in Greek) truth, and also 'aporetics' because they will never find it [378]. "They were constantly engaged in overthrowing the dogmas of all schools, but enuntiated none themselves" [379]. Nevertheless, a Sceptic must not be seen as a person who lives according to his whims, as somebody "in such a frame of mind that he would not shrink from killing and eating his own father if ordered to do so" [380]. Quite the contrary! When Timon says that "he has not gone outside what is customary' [381], he means that the wise man should be true to the laws and religion of his country [382].

g. Neither truth nor probability

In the texts of the Ancients we find a great many references to 'academic scepticism'. We may describe this, with Naess [383], as 'negative dogmatism' which basically means in this context that a philosopher wants to determine what is true or false a posteriori and not a priori. But, this scholar continues, for every hundred references to this academic scepticism there is scarcely one to Pyrrhonism. The reason is that true sceptics do not speak of Truth in general; they do no state whether or not true knowledge is possible or whether or not Truth exists. Because a sceptic "only throws in particular arguments against particular knowledge claims, he is not counted a real philosopher ... The sceptic of the pure Pyrrhonist community ventures no proposition whatsoever that includes a truth or probability claim. And surely a person who is propositionally mute places himself outside the philosophical community" [384].

The Pyrrhonists turned against every philosophical doctrine that had been developed thus far, because each one of them proposed statements of a general character considered to be true, or statements about Truth itself. "If we accept for anything to be philosophy that it must contain at least one proposition, or at least one doctrine, claimed to be true or probable, then scepticism is not a philosophy" [385].

My own point here is that Pyrrhonism postulates a dualistic separation of the thinker from Truth. The question of Truth, of the possibility of Truth in general, and how to attain and recognize it, is consigned to the waste-paper basket; Truth is not even thought important enough to be formally denied. So, at this stage, we have reached the point at which at least some Hellenic thinkers began to neglect the main issue of Greek philosophy.

h. Resignation

Living in seclusion as he did, Pyrrho did not take part in the intellectual debates of his time; he never measured swords with philosophers and scientists. He was simply not interested because he found the science of his contemporaries vain. "Tired of the eternal discussions in which (they) took pleasure, Pyrrho preferred to state : I know nothing ... He only thought of living quietly and happily" [386]. Brochard says that "his philosophy ... was one of resignation, or rather of total renouncement" [387]. His favourite catchword seems to have been this line of Homer : "As leaves on the tree is the life of man" [388].

This gives us the impression that, at this juncture of their intellectual history, the Greeks became fed up with their own achievements which certainly constitutes a loss of nerve and a lack of pluck. For Pyrrho was by no means an isolated phenomenon, although there never originated a real School of Scepticism. His fellow-citizens of Elis greatly admired him; they made him high priest of their city, "on his account voted that all philosophers should be exempt from taxation", and after his death honoured him with a statue [389].

j. The Pyrrhonist method

The method of Pyrrho consisted in checking the propositions of the philosophers and their schools, and also the statements and judgments of other scholars [390]. Eusebius compares Pyrrho and his followers to wrestlers in the arena, because they too are bare, 'stripped of every truth', he says [391]. Pyrrho used to compile two series of arguments, pro and contra, and to weigh them against each other; he then argued that they were of equal value (or equally without value). The final conclusion invariably was that it is impossible to make a true statement about Being, since Being cannot be defined [392]. What we know are not the things in themselves [393]. In consequence, there can be no criteria of Truth [394].

k. The happiness of not knowing

How is it possible that this philosophy - if it is one - of not knowing can make people happy? Don't we count uncertainty as the worst of moral evils [395]? Don't we all seek certitude of some kind, however illusory? But no, the Pyrrhonist retorts, it is exactly this uncertainty that is so satisfying, since it makes all reality appear equally unimportant [396]. This will liberate us from 'the servitude of opinions and the vain wisdom of the sophists' [397]. Like Pyrrho himself, we must not be 'puffed up' [398], viz. with pride in our idle wisdom.

Once again we detect a dualistic [399] distinction, that between happiness and reality. It is not ordinary life, however morally pursued, that is conducive to final salvation nor is it science nor scholarship nor philosophy of whatever school. It is only by turning one's back resolutely on reality in all its aspects that happiness may be attained. In the future reality itself will be subjected to a philosophical critique [400].

6. The Middle Academy [401]

Although after the death of Timon there was no longer a proper School of Scepticism, this does not mean that this trend itself was dead. It lived on in other schools. The 'unopinionated life-style', as inaugurated by Pyrrho, had already become too much of an ideal. Pyrrho's "personal example inspired those who knew him or read about him to set the values which he embodied on a firm theoretical foundation" [402]. For many a scholar it now became a "radical conviction that to suspend assent and to resign oneself to ignorance is not a bleak expedient but, on the contrary, a highly desirable intellectual achievement" [403]. The result was an 'epistemological mind-clearing' [404]. This development was occasioned by the growing destabilization of the Hellenistic world - the political and social features of which were portrayed in Chapters I and II - to which it, in its turn, also contributed. Individualism took the place of communal sense; "the individual stood alone opposite a world the sense of which he did not understand, not knowing which aims could be realized" [405].

a. Arcesilaus, the trustee of Scepticism

Shortly after 270 B.C. Arcesilaus (or Arcesilas) became head of the Academy at Athens; with him the period of the Middle Academy (or Second Academy) begins. Arcesilaus was born ca 315 B.C. at Pitane in Asia Minor, at some distance to the north of Smyrna. He began with studying mathematics but became more and more attracted to philosophy. He migrated to Athens, was for some time a student of Theophrastus but then transferred to the Academy. Later he became its principal by universal consent and remained in this position until his death in 241/240 B.C., when he was about seventy-five years old. He lived a secluded life and did not marry; he was much praised for his even temper and his mild and friendly character. He too was a 'word prophet' leaving no writings behind [406]. It was this philosopher who became the true heir of Pyrrhonic Scepticism.

b. The impossibility of notional assent

"Arcesilaus took position against all that the Stoa had taught" [407]. We know - it has been expounded in these pages too - that Zeno saw an enormous difference between knowledge and opinion, the first being the preoccupation of the wise and the latter of the fool. Opinions are based on representations prompted by exterior objects and offered to us by our senses; they can be true or false, and for this reason form no secure basis for certain knowledge. Whosoever trusts solely to his senses is a fool. But it is by no means necessary to confide in the senses alone, since the mind possesses a safe criterion by the help of which a wise and sensible person can sift the true from the false and so arrive at sure knowledge. This criterion is called 'katalêpsis' or 'apprehension' and is an integral category of the mind. It enables us to give our assent or to withhold it from what sensory perceptions propose to us [408].

The main thrust of Arcesilaus' attack on the Stoic theory of knowledge was directed against this notion 'katalêpsis', the instrument that empowers us to give our assent to a true proposition. There simply exists no katalêpsis, he declares, which signifies that "between knowledge, limited to the sage, and opinion, limited to the fool, there is no intermediate reality, and that apprehension (katalepsis) as an intermediate between them is only a word" [409].

This makes the distance between knowledge and opinion, or between the wise and the fool, insuperable. The possibility we all have, fools though we may be, for arriving at the truth by using the faculty of apprehension that is common to all of us, is invalidated by Arcesilaus [410]. In his opinion the Stoics were incapable of providing an incontestable proof that apprehension functions as infallibly as they said it does. The result is that the wise will remain wise, and the fool foolish, and never the twain will meet [411]. Once again we find the idea that wisdom is a kind of charisma, or a heavenly gift, rather than something that we can acquire by human means.

c. The withdrawal of reality

An important sceptic argument against the Stoics is that katalêpsis only includes our thoughts and abstract concepts rather than our observations of reality [412]. Now Stoic comprehension of reality was already at one remove from the object world, because apprehension does not refer to reality itself but to the observations we have of it. But the Middle Academy believes we cannot be sure of our observations either. "Arcesilaus ... pressed the point at issue (e.g. the Stoic doctrine that presentations of objects can be true and false) further in order to show that no presentation proceeding from a true object is such that a presentation from a false might not also be of the same form" [413]. When it comes to sorting out the correct from the wrong presentations, we are utterly helpless. This puts the individual mind and objective reality still more radically and dualistically apart than already was the case in Stoic philosophy.

The inescapable consequence is that it is impossible to know anything whatsoever for certain [414]. "There is nothing that can be known, not even that residuum of knowledge that Socrates had left himself" - viz. that he knew that he knew nothing -, "so hidden in obscurity did he believe (e.g. Arcesilaus) that everything lies, nor is there anything that can be perceived or understood" [415]. I for one should think that this makes an end of all philosophy and scholarship. But no, Arcesilaus loved philosophical argument. "He made it a rule that those who wished to hear him should not ask him questions but should state their opinions; and when they had done so he argued against them [416], ... always controverting every position, but setting out all the possible arguments on either subject in every argument" [417].

It goes without saying that it is a very useful exercise for a student of any matter to look at it from both sides, the pro and the contra. But Arcesilaus outstripped almost all other teachers by emphatically stating that "no one must make any positive statement or affirmation or give the approval of his assent to any proposition" [418]. The philosopher, as far as I know, never denied that Truth or reality exists, but he declared them utterly unattainable. The only attitude that behoves the true philosopher is suspension of judgment, 'epochè' in Greek [419].

The main objection of the Stoics and the Epicureans against Arcesilaus was that, if we know nothing for certain, or better, if we know nothing at all, it will be impossible to act [420]. But, says Arcesilaus, acting is not only possible but necessary. We do not need certain knowledge in order to act. There is another, much more useful criterion by the help of which we will be able either to choose or to reject; this criterion is the 'eulogon'. "Who acts according to this criterion will act well ... A right action is one that, being accomplished, proves itself to be 'eulogos'. Who recurs to the 'eulogon' will act rightly and will attain happiness ... In effect, happiness results from the use of prudence" [421]. This whole passage turns on the meaning of 'eulogos'. It signifies 'reasonable or 'probable'. What Arcesilaus is saying is that probability must be our criterion. In fact, it is the only choice left to him between not acting at all and acting at random. 'Prudence' ('phronèsis') is used here in the sense of 'practical wisdom'.

Let me explain what this means in Kantian terms. We doubtless are in the possession of 'reine Vernunft', of the faculty of abstract reasoning. But this faculty does not help us at all when it comes to acting rationally, since there is no connection between abstract thought and the object world (the world outside us). Luckily we also have 'praktische Vernunft', practical wisdom, and this may guide our actions. However, practical wisdom is of a far lesser quality than abstract thought since it is not infallible. The fact that Arcesilaus made use of a circular argument proves that he had manoeuvred himself into a quandary : prudence will teach us to act rightly; that we have acted in the right way proves that we have used prudence. The overall conclusion, in the words of Zeller, is that 'probabiblity' is the highest norm for practical life [422].

d. Arcesilaus' popularity

Arcesilaus did not keep his cloud of unknowing to himself; on the contrary, he let many others shelter under it. Being highly eloquent [423], 'most effective in argument' [424], and "very fertile in invention, he could meet objections acutely or bring the course of discussion back to the point at issue, and fit it to every occasion" [425]. He seems to have considered himself a second Socrates. Contrary to the real Socrates he was wealthy and entertained lavishly which made him very popular and at the same time the butt of ridicule [426]. He was much lionized by the scholarly community of his days if only because of the opulence of his table.

His school lacked pupils who, "although somewhat in terror of his pungent wit, willingly put up with that, for his goodness was extraordinary" [427]. It is true that he could not really convince all of them, but more than Pyrrho he made scepticism into an established doctrine. It became a fashionable trend 'not to know anything'. This may seem an innocent game for intellectuals (who, living off their knowledge, probably did not really believe in it). But it opened the door to all kinds of cranks, would-be prophets, and intellectual charlatans who did not want to be burdened by erudition; it also brought to the front people who, although sincere, trusted to their intuition rather than to solid factual knowledge. Not only Truth disappeared further down the horizon, this sceptical onslaught made even the possibility of objective knowledge seem remote.

7. The New Academy

a. Carneades, the founder

Carneades is usually seen as the founder of the New (or Third) Academy. With him we are already a century after Arcesilaus; thus he was not this philosopher's direct successor. He came from Cyrene in what is now Libya where he was born about 213 B.C. He studied philosophical literature so intensely that he forgot to have his hair cut and to pare his nails. His favourite author was Chrysippus; "without Chrysippus where should I have been", he would often exclaim [428]. Later he emigrated to Athens where he not only became the head of the Academy but also a citizen of the town. The Athenians were obviously much pleased with their new fellow-citizen, for in 156/155 B.C. they sent him on an embassy to Rome, together with two other philosophers, in order to negotiate with the Senate on account of the Roman devastation of the city of Oropus.

This visit caused a great stir in Rome, because Carneades gave a convincing proof of his dialectical dexterity by speaking one day for justice and the next day against it. The jeunesse dorée and the modernists were much impressed by his sophistry, but the establishment, under the moral leadership of Cato the Elder, became so upset that the Senate made great haste with the affair in order to get rid of such dangerous people as soon as possible [429]. His oratory is characterized as 'rapid and violent' [430]; he had such a booming voice that the neighbours once "sent to him and requested him not to shout so loud" [431].

He showed himself a worthy successor of Arcesilaus, for "his talent for criticizing opponents was remarkable, and he was a formidable controversialist" [432]. He brought the Academy great fame; when he died in 129/128 B.C., "the moon is said to have been eclipsed, and one might well say that the brightest luminary in heaven next to the sun thereby gave token of her sympathy" [433]. This is more than will happen to you or me. Carneades was another 'word prophet'; except for a few letters, "everything was compiled by his pupils; he himself left nothing in writing" [434].

b. The demolition of the notion of the divine

An important part of Carneades' doctrine is his theology [435] - if an argument the aim of which is to deny the existence of gods may be called theology. Stoics and Epicureans used to refer to the 'consensus gentium' as a a proof that there are gods. But does this really prove anything, so the sceptic asks? Do we really know then what 'all peoples' believe? And even if we did, would the opinion of so many uneducated, and even barbarian, people constitute a decisive argument? Philosophers like Diagoras and Protagoras have already argued to the contrary [436]. Perhaps we should think of a cosmic god, in the line of Stoic pantheism according to which the Universe is a living, divine, and rational being, the cause of order and finality in the world. But, the Sceptic retorts that he does not observe much purpose in the world. If god really made the world for our sake, why are there so many fatal and pernicious things in earth and sea [437]?

Referring to the widely shared popular belief that sees gods in everything and divinizes even inanimate objects, Carneades [438] uses a 'sorites', or chain-argument : if Zeus is a god, then, of course, his brother Poseidon too; if Poseidon, who is the god of the waters, is a god, then the Nile too; if the Nile, then every river, stream, or rivulet. And if the sun is a god, then the day too, for day is nothing else than the sun above the earth. But the month and the year are also gods since they are compositions of days. And if the day is a god, then naturally dawn and midday and evening too, for they are parts of the day. And why not include bulls, snakes, cats, and crocodiles, like the Egyptians do. And so on ad infinitum. All this is stark nonsense so that the conclusion must be : there are no gods [439].

With equal gusto Careneades attacked the philosophers' notions of god, especially those of the Stoics. God is a living being, you say? Good, but then he must have sensations, and some of these sensations must be vexatious to him. And if this is the case, "god is subject to change for the worse, and thus also to decay. Therefore, god is perishable. But this is contrary to the general conception of him. Therefore the divine does not exist" [440]. Again, if god exists, then he must either be incorporeal or have a body. But since the incorporeal is inanimate and insensitive and is incapable of action (this according to Stoic doctrine), god cannot be incorporeal. However, if he has a body, he is "subject to change and perishable, whereas the divine is imperishable; so then, the divine does not exist" [441].

It is not necessary to present all the Carneadean arguments against the existence of gods; they are all meant to be equally devastating [442]. But it will certainly interest the reader to hear how Carneades exploded the Epicurean argument that the gods speak Greek. If god is capable of speech, he must have organs of speech. "But this is absurd and borders on the fairy-tales of Epicurus. And if god converses, he must do so in some tongue." Why should he prefer Greek to a barbarian dialect? And if he really speaks Greek, which dialect would he prefer, Ionian, Aeolic, or some other? Furthermore, if god (in case he speaks Greek - F.) wants to address barbarians, he must use an interpreter. How absurd! "We must say, then, that the divine does not employ speech, and on this account it is non-existent" [443].

His audience will have found this way of reasoning highly amusing, and will not have paid too much attention to the blatant defectiveness and superficiality of some of his arguments. But will his hearers also have noticed that the master fobbed them off with empty hands? For in Carneades' doctrine there is neither a cosmology nor an explanation of the origin and meaning of the universe.

c. The attack on justice

Perhaps Cato, that self-appointed custodian of morals, was not wholly wrong in wishing to see the last of Carneades in Rome. For the philosopher consciously unsettled the notion of justice on which the whole body politic as well as the relations between private persons should be built. To be honest, it was not Carneades' intention to prove that there should be no justice but rather that the classical arguments in favour of it were defective [444]. For instance, 'justice is sanctioned by nature', and for this reason all men should unequivocally practise it. But justice is by no means the same for everybody. Far from it! The Cretans, for instance, find raids and forays permissible; the Gauls see nothing reprehensible in mowing the cornfields of others. What is lawful in one place is punishable in another; what one people finds right is injustice to another. Are there not tribes that find it most pious to bring human sacrifices [445]? The only possible solution is that there is no natural law.

But, it will be retorted, you are arguing against natural law; however, the idea of natural justice should be defended. Really? Nothing could be more foolish [446]! Natural justice would mean that a perfectly just person should care for others and give every living being its due. Does one realize that, if justice is 'natural', we should also give the beasts what is their due, we should not kill wild or obnoxious animals, we should not tame animals, subject them to our will and use them for our purposes [447] - to say nothing of making other people serve our ends [448]?

When a state or a private person would exercise natural justice, they would cause great damage to themselves by losing sight of their own advantage and, instead, they would favour the interests of others. But does not this selfsame Nature teach us to promote our own wellbeing first and foremost [449]? Of course, states and individuals cannot do without justice. Carneades is not advocating the law of the jungle. But there can only exist positive justice, that is that kind of justice - with the laws that are based on it - that has its origin either in force or in a treaty [450]. Its principle and guide must be usefulness, but what is useful is differently assessed in different times and cultures.

If natural justice really existed, no state could be intent on its own development; in particular the Romans who govern the whole world would have to return to their huts if natural justice guided their behaviour [451]. Perhaps somebody might indignantly object that this is not justice but injustice; the answer is that states and inviduals can only prosper when they build their lives on such injustice [452]. "Recht ist was dem Volke nützt", where did I hear that one before?

Of course, Carneades was playing a game trying to 'épater le bourgeois' in which he succeeded extremely well. If we took him to task, he would smilingly answer that he was no dogmatist. But to many unscrupulous people who did not break their heads over philosophical subtleties and probabilities his words must have been - and indeed were [453] - 'gefundenes Fressen'. On the one hand, it was a sanctioning of existing practices, especially in Hellenistic power politics; on the other, it was a new factor in the destablization and demoralization of society.

8. The tendency to eclecticism

The Hellenistic philosophical scene showed a number of strands that nearly all were based on a kind of university. The Aristoteleans assembled in the Peripatetic School, the Platonists in the Academy, the Epicureans in the School of the Garden, the Stoics in the Stoa. Every school produced important scholars who, as philosophers have always done, lustily fought one another. Perhaps we might say : the more their philosophies resembled each other, the more acrimonious the discussion. In this chapter I have possibly distinguished the schools from each other somewhat more precisely than the actual situation warrants; I did this for the sake of better understanding.

There was, however, a growing tendency during the Hellenistic period to blur the distinctions between the several philosophies. Scholars ever more readily borrowed from one another and from their predecessors, in particular from such famous thinkers as Pythagoras, Plato, and Aristoteles. We call this process 'eclecticism'; it is a distinctive feature of the Hellenistic period. However, this does not mean that philosophers were consciously striving after the establishment of the one generally accepted doctrine. If there sometimes appears a philosopher who pretends to outphilosophize all others of past and present with the one 'absolute philosophy', someone like Hegel or Heidegger, he is soon forced to admit, much to his chagrin, that the philosophical world does not agree with him.

The increasingly forceful tendency to eclecticism was in itself a sign of the times; Hellenistic scholars were subjected to growing pressure. The situation is normal and usual circumstance enough. Whereas the founders of the schools were geniuses intent on bringing forward their ideas with the greatest precision and clarity, their successors who were no geniuses tended to blunt the sharp edges of their philosophies. As Zeller said, their scientific spirit was fagging, and they were ready to make concessions and to adapt their ideologies to those of other schools. The climactic element in this development, it goes without saying, was that the Sceptics so loudly proclaimed that there is no certain knowledge. So why bother about shades and distinctions [454]?

The great shock came when the Romans made the acquaintance of Greek philosophy. Pythagoreanism had been at home in southern Italy [455]; from there some knowledge of it may have reached Rome. But the real introduction of the Romans to Greek thought only occurred when, in the second century B.C., they started penetrating ever farther into the Hellenistic world. A decision of the Roman Senate in 161 B.C. banned (Hellenic) philosophers and rhetors from Rome. An edict of the censors of some time afterward mentions unfavourably 'a new kind of training' that was frequented 'by our young men'; "these innovations in the customs and principles of our fathers do not please us nor seem proper" [456]. I have already described a similar panicky reaction on the occasion of Carneades' visit to Rome in 156 B.C. Not that it helped very much! Greek scholars came flocking to Rome in growing numbers or were imported as slaves and employed as private teachers for the scions of Roman society. The number of young Romans that travelled to Hellas to study there was not small either.

As a consequence the Romans became acquainted with all the Hellenistic schools of philosophy. Initially, of course, the Romans felt themselves to be the pupils of those learned Greeks. But after some time a retroactive element became discernible. It was not that the Romans now began to make an original contribution to Greek scholarship. But they exerted a modifying influence. They were an eminently practical people, impatient of the niceties, subtleties, and minutiae that are the delight of philosophers. They saw the most treasured philosophical theses as fit for nothing but 'fashionable conversation', to quote Zeller. Their most pertinent question was : what is the use of philosophy for the practical conduct of life, in particular for the education of the young. Members of the Roman 'jeunesse dorée' were not destined to become scholars and philosophers but orators and politicians, governors and generals. To them the battles of the schools were of no importance;

the distinctions between the several schools did not interest them at all [457].

This point of view was unambiguously expressed by Lucius Gellius, a proconsul, who in 93 B.C. called a meeting of philosophers in Athens and seriously advised them to settle their differences and no longer waste their time in argument; "he promised his own best efforts to aid them in coming to some agreement". This naive proposal, as Cicero adds, "has often raised a laugh" [458]. This notwithstanding, the practical spirit of the Romans fortified the tendency to eclecticism; they saw Hellenistic philosophy as a kind of supermarket from the shelves of which they could select what they wanted while neglecting all the rest.

Zeller rightly points out that people, when making this selection, tacitly acted on the assumption that they inwardly knew what is right and wrong, true and false. The criterion of truth, so the Stoics held, is implanted by nature into man. What this means is, as Zeller explains in his excellent exposition of this trend, that "fundamentally the final decision on questions of philosophy fell to the unphilosophical consciousness" [459]. In other words, the criterion of truth shifted from the objective to the subjective. This loss of rationality represents one more stage in the development into the direction of the Gnosis. To quote Zeller once again : all this "had the effect that human thought began to look more and more for a source of knowledge outside thought itself and outside the existing scholarship - a source that was sought partially in the inner revelation by the godhead, partially in religious tradition" [460].

9. The Middle Stoa [461]

a. Boethus

The Middle Stoa really begins with Boethus [462], a philosopher of whose life very little is known [463]. Born at Sidon, he 'flourished' in the second century B.C., and was, perhaps, head of the School at Athens [464]. He was a highly unorthodox member of it and threw some cherished Stoic concepts overboard. According to Von Arnim he gave up the 'monistic psychologism' of Chrysippus in favour of a dualistic conception. Chrysippus had held that there is only one standard of truth, the katalêpsis, or "the apprehending presentation, i.e. that which comes from a real object". But Boethus "admits a plurality of standards, namely intelligence, sense-perception, appetency, and knowledge" [465]. It seems that two pairs of dualistic oppositions are meant, intelligence ('nous', rationality) and appetency ('orexis', desire as a natural impulse); as a second pair, knowledge ('epistêmê') and sense-perception ('aisthêsis') [466]. This means that to Boethus the mind and the natural impulses were opposed but equally valid sources of knowledge.

What a pity that we know so little of the thought of this shadowy figure! Why did he so radically oppose two kinds of knowledge that he considered equivalent? Whatever the answer to this riddle may be, it seems to me that Boethus was one of those who wanted to give subjective knowledge a status of its own, and what is more, one that is irreconcilable with objective knowledge.

b. Panaetius, the mainstay of the Middle Stoa

Yet another philosopher, Panaetius, is seen as the true founder of the Middle Stoa. He was born in 185 B.C. at Lindos in the island of Rhodes as a member of a wealthy and noble family. After studying for some time at Pergamum, he went, then about thirty years old, to Athens where he joined the Stoa. At some time later he travelled to Rome where he made the acquaintance of Scipio Africanus the younger in whose house he lived for a considerable time. Later, in 140/139 B.C., Scipio took the philosopher with him when he made a long fact-finding tour through the Middle East. Panaetius also met the famous historian Polybius.

But finally he returned to Athens and there became scholarch of the Stoa in 129 B.C. Under his inspiring leadership the school prospered. Students came from all parts of the Hellenistic world [467]. Towards 110 B.C. he seems to have retired. He died in 110 or 109 B.C. at the zenith of his fame [468]. The titles of six books written by him are known but very little else [469].

Zeller states that "the Stoic system underwent not inconsiderable changes under his hands" [470]. In fact, Panaetius jettisoned 'some of the cargo of Stoic orthodoxy' [471]. He was famous, he knew that he was famous, and he loved to be famous. He felt good, he was happy. In consequence, he had little sympathy for the Stoic ideal of 'apatheia', of indifference to all feelings, enthusiasm and euphoria not excluded. He expressed his views on this subject in a little book that was very un-Stoically called 'On Cheerfulness' [472]. It is not that he totally rejected the ideal of 'ataraxia', the moral duty of remaining undisturbed in all circumstances, but he pleaded for enjoyment of life [473].

Perhaps he was so popular in Rome because he was less 'idealistic' than the orthodox Stoics [474]. Of course, he maintained the ideal of the wise man, but in his eyes a wise man was a practical rather than a theoretical person. He acknowledged the duty to be successful, to make headway in life. This must have suited the practical instincts of the Romans better than the abstract Stoic ideal of the 'sophos'.

A consequence of this practical attitude was that he took the psychology of everyday life far more into account than his teachers had done. But whether his sollicitude for the purely human advanced the cause of objective knowledge is another question. For Panaetius roundly declared that the aim of life is 'to live according what is presented to us by the impulses of nature' [475]. Although he never denied that objective knowledge exists, he was, nevertheless, taking an important step in the direction of the subjectivisation and individualisation of knowledge; it means that the claims of the strictly personal and the irrational are also acknowledged. This view is confirmed by another fragment that is conserved by Cicero : " The force and the nature of our spirits is dual (duplex); one part of it is to be found in impulses (this is 'hormê' in Greek) that force a person hither and thither; the other part is reason that teaches us what we should do and not do" [476]. "Thought is occupied chiefly with the discovery of truth; impulse prompts to action' [477]. In the same breath it is added that we should keep our impulses under control.

The distinction of the soul into two parts can easily give rise to the supposition that, in his anthropology, Panaetius was a dualist. The two parts are of a different order, the rational part being valued more than the instinctive one. That it is said that the ratio should control the impulses means that there is no real harmony in man. Panaetius is deviating here from the traditional Stoic doctrine that the soul is one; in the older Stoics there is no division of the soul into 'psyche' and 'phusis' [478]. That Panaetius, however, made a clear distinction into two is testified by Nemesius : "The generative principle does not form part of the soul but of the (physical) nature" [479]. Other faculties that this philosopher attributes to our physical nature are the nutritive faculty and the faculty of growth. We must, therefore, agree with Van Straaten that "the anthropology of Panaetius has a dualistic tendency. It is clearly not possible to have doubts that he separates the phusis from the psyche". Differently from Plato, "he considers certain functions in man as excluded from the action of the soul; they operate independently of the soul" [480]. It remains of course true that Panaetius saw the human person as a unity but it is a unity that is not without its tensions.

c. Posidonius, traveller, historiographer, philosopher

Panaetius had a highly gifted pupil, Posidonius. This man was born ca. 135 B.C. at Apamea in Syria. It is not certain whether he was a native Greek or a Syrian, or whether he was of mixed descent. Yet if he was not originally Hellenic, he became so by adoption. He migrated to Athens where he studied with Panaetius. Perhaps stimulated by his master who had travelled widely with Scipio, Posidonius embarked on his travels into the world. In all probability he visited Egypt, Asia Minor, Mesopotamia, and Palestine [481]. That he visited the west too is an asecertained fact; the opportunity was provided by the Roman conquests. He first spent some time in Rome and then wandered northward to Etruria (the present-day Toscana); he crossed through Liguria (roughly the Italian Riviera) and penetrated into Gallia (southern France). His first stop was Massilia, now Marseille, an important Greek cultural and commercial centre.

But his unquenchable thirst for knowledge drove him into the wild country where the uncouth Celts lived, in what now is the French Midi. As a good fieldworker he shared their life for some time. He then proceeded to Spain and he traversed it from the Pyrenees to Gades (Cadiz) where he stayed for a month. He went back by ship (the trip lasted full three months) and took the opportunity to visit Sicily. At this time Posidonius must have been about forty years old.

On his return to Greece he obviously felt that he should settle somewhere. The place he chose was Rhodes where he founded a school of his own that soon became very famous. Greeks and Romans came to hear him. It even became a must for illustrious Romans to pay a visit to Rhodes when travelling to Asia Minor. Lucullus came along, perhaps Julius Caesar too, certainly Brutus in 58 B.C., and most renowned of all, Pompey the Great in 66 B.C. In his last years Posidonius suffered severely from the gout. He is said to to have been 84 years of age when he died about ca. 50 B.C. He was not married [482].

It is highly deplorable fact that not one complete work of this versatile scholar is extant. For he was a great system-builder, a truly universal and cosmopolitan mind such as the Hellenistic age had not produced so far. He reminds one of Alexander von Humboldt and his book 'Kosmos. Entwurf einer physischen Weltbeschreibung' (5 volumes, 1845-1862). To Posidonius the universe is an organic whole, a living unity. All parts of it are interrelated by 'sympathy'. "The continuum of the world's nature is constituted by the cyclic transmutations of the four kinds of matter. For earth turns into water, water into air, air into aether, and the process is reverse ... Thus the parts of the world are connected by the constant passage up and down, to and fro, of these four elements of which all things are composed" [483]. The whole cosmos is beautifully structured in layer after layer, from the minerals deep in the earth to the sphere of the Divine [484]. "The structure of the world is such that it could not have been better in point of utility or beauty ...;

given the existing elements, the best that could be produced by them has been produced" [485].

Man too forms an integral part of creation. It is an ancient Hellenic notion that the world has been created in the interest of gods and men; this put human beings to some degree over against nature. Posidonius does not deny this but proves the regularity of nature by showing that man too is structured according to a most perfect plan. There is, however, no real community between man and the lower echelons of nature : "it does not at once follow that, if there exists a spirit which pervades us and them, there (also) exists some form of justice between us and the irrational animals ..., (and likewise) we have no relations of justice with plants and stones" [486]. But there is a special relationship between the gods and man which human beings express by venerating the gods; "we possess that reason which reaches out to one another and the gods" [487]. "Deity possesses an excellence and pre-eminence which must of its own nature attract the worship of the wise" [488].

The fundamental fellowship of all organic beings is explained by the fact that they all share in the same life-giving element. "Every living thing ..., whether animal or vegetable, owes its vitality to the heat contained in it. From this it must be inferred that this element of heat possesses in itself a vital force that pervades the whole world" [489]. We know this life-giving element only in its Latin rendering by Cicero, 'vis vitalis'. Reinhardt, the great expert in Posidonian philosophy, says that the original Greek must have been 'zootikê dunamis' (which reminds one of Bergson's 'élan vital'), but we have no fragment containing this term. The element of heat that is mentioned is the fiery 'pneuma'. The vis vitalis is a new term; neither Aristotle nor the Stoa before Posidonius used it. Reinhardt even says that it is un-Stoic [490]. This all-pervading vital force makes the world into one great living being.

Like many Greek philosophers of his days, Posidonius did not have much use for the traditional Greek divinities. The difference between his idea of the godhead and the Zeus of popular creed was too great. Nevertheless, the belief in gods was found politically useful since the moral behaviour of the populace depended on their fearful belief in the gods. As was usual in intellectual circles, Posidonius did not refuse to take part in the official cult as long as it was not supposed to have any religious significance [491]. But after all, it was no more than superstition to him.

However, Posidonius was no atheist. It will not surprise us that he acknowledges only one godhead - which is not equivalent to stating that he was, therefore, a monotheist. A monotheist would not call the godhead 'amorphous' as Posidonius did [492]. To him the godhead is a pneuma, a fiery breath that is thinking but has no definite shape; "it changes itself according to its wish and becomes one with every shape that is" [493]. Although he is not really a pantheist, god and the world in his view are bound together into an essential unity. Even when he did not write "the cosmos is the specific shape of the all-containing being", his idea of the unity of god and world did not differ from this [494].

Posidonius is one of those philosophers who see the world as "one and finite, having a spherical shape ... The world has no empty space within it, but forms one united whole. This is a necessary result of the sympathy and tension which bind together things in heaven and earth ... The world is a living being, rational, animate, and intelligent, ... and it is endowed with soul" [495]. It will strike the reader that the godhead has no name; there is no 'Zeus' or any other personal divinity in Posidonius.

That he is leaving the Olympian gods behind him does not mean that a highly personal god like the Jahve of the Old Testament will take their place. It was a trend in Hellenic religious philosophy - I have mentioned this before - that theology moved into the direction of an ever greater abstraction. This did not make things easier for people : it is difficult to venerate or to pray to an impersonal god. Perhaps we might call such an idea of god 'deistic'.

So far so good. Posidonius' philosophy makes a unified, if not a monistic impression, at least on the surface of it. For there is a snake in the grass. In a sense I have already drawn attention to this by pointing out that there is a far closer kinship between gods and humans than between human beings and animals. Now there is a remarkable passage in Cicero that ticks like a bomb under the fabric of Posidonian cosmology. "In the heavens ... there is nothing of chance or hazard, no error, no frustration, but absolute order, accuracy, calculation and regularity. Whatever lacks these qualities, whatever is false and spurious and full of error, belongs to the region between the earth and the moon (the last of all the heavenly bodies), and to the surface of the earth. Anyone therefore who thinks that the marvellous order and incredible regularity of the heavenly bodies, which is the sole source of preservation and safety for all things, is not rational, cannot be deemed a rational being himself" [496].

This is strong language and wholly unambiguous at that. But, unequivocal as it may be, this powerful assertion of Posidonian dualism did not go unchallenged. The attack was opened in 1921 by Karl Reinhardt. He stated that this Ciceronian passage says more, and is of a different nature, than "the usual dualistic distinction between the heavens as the realm of the pure and perfect, and the terrestrial as the realm of the imperfect, impure, and sinful" [497]. Some years later, Paul Schubert, taking his cue from Reinhardt, added that this allegedly Posidonian notion had undergone a profound transformation in its rendering by Cicero; Posidonius is supposed to have stated his meaning 'more thoroughly and clearer'. How does he know, in the absence of a literal Posidonian text? The supposed opposition of celestial and terrestrial, says this scholar, hangs on the slender peg of these few words 'what is false and spurious and full of error' : "this really does not say very much" [498]. I wonder which expression could say more.

Once again we meet the vitium originis that since the days of Christian Wolff bedevils every discussion of this kind : that a monistic system never admits of any form of dualism. As a proof Schubert cites another passage of Cicero saying that "the moon ... roams in the same courses of the sun" [499]; on this ground he concludes that Posidonius "does not draw dualistic boundaries in the construction of the universe nor does he want to have them drawn". The quoted words prove this 'with all desirable clarity' [500]. In his eyes the Posidonian theology is a 'grandiose, monistic-immanent system' [501].

But the cited words prove nothing of this kind. For the passage on the disorder of the terrestrial world expressly places it below the moon, whereas the moon itself belongs to the heavenly bodies, although being the last (lowest) and, perhaps, also the least of them. It is only when one, going downwards from the sun, has passed the moon, that he reaches the realm of inferiority.

To return now to Reinhardt. He does not deny that an opposition is mentioned - "the words admit of no doubt" -, but they do not refer to an opposition between good and bad or beautiful and ugly. The opposition that is meant is between rational and irrational. But, first of all, who spoke of sinful and impure and ugly? Not Cicero! And next, cannot an opposition between rational and irrational be quite as dualistic as any other? Do we not meet here another original sin in the discussion on dualism - this one originating in the days of Thomas Hyde -, namely, that as long as an opposition is not between good and evil it is not dualistic? Reinhardt himself, however, states in as many words that "in the cosmos the realm of rational and irrational falls apart" [502].

The dualism we observe in the macrocosm repeats itself in the microcosm, that is in man. The imperishable upper world and the perishable nether world are 'bound together in man who is the bond between them'. From this it follows that man is just as much part of the imperishable as of the perishable world. His faculty of knowledge makes him akin to the godhead, but on the other hand he is physical too, like animals and inanimate objects. "Just as man from the corporeal viewpoint is the highest grade, so, conversely, from the spiritual viewpoint he is the lowest grade" [503].

It is at this point that an opposition announces itself. Man "has been given a certain disinguished status by the supreme god who created him", for "since there is nothing better than reason, and since it exists both in man and god, the first common possesion of man and god is reason" [504]. But by the same token, man, on account of his material constitution, forms part of the animal world. This is a severe hindrance to his faculty of understanding. "Since the universe is wholly filled with the Eternal Intelligence and the Divine Mind, it must be that human souls are influenced by their contact with divine souls. But when men are awake their souls, as a rule, are subject to the demands of everyday life and are withdrawn from divine association because they are hampered by the chain of the flesh" [505].

This passage accuses the body of being the enemy of the soul. The soul-part of man obviously is unable to reach for higher things as long as the bodily impulses are not silenced. "How great is the power of the soul when it is divorced from the bodily senses, as it is especially in sleep, and in times of frenzy and inspiration ... The souls of men, when released by sleep from bodily chains ..., see things that they cannot see when they are mingled with the body." Cicero, whom I am quoting here, states that Posidonius has dug 'into question as deep as any man can' [506]. This quotation makes it clear that, much as Posidonius extols human reason, it is not really by means of his reason that man comes into contact with the godhead.

d. Conclusion

Other names of the Middle Stoa and of other schools might be mentioned, but we know very little of them, and they are not important for our subject. I end this chapter at the same point where I ended Chapters I and II : when the Romans take over. For the next great names in the history of philosophy are those of Cicero, Varro, and Seneca.

NOTES TO CHAPTER III

1. See Vol. III, Ch. III.11.
2. Life in DL 8.86-91; see also Guthrie, Hist.Gr.Phil. V (1978), 447/448.
3. Vol. III, Ch. III.25b (p. 191) : "that there is a 'chorismos', an (unbridgeable) gap between the Forms and the objects that exist because of the Forms".
4. Zeller, Phil.d.Gr. III.1. 1039.

5. Ar., Met. 991.13-20; Alexander Aphrodisiensis in Ar. Met. Comm. 97.14.
6. Guthrie, Hist.Gr.Phil. V (1978), 453.
7. See for a full discussion of this subject, together with that of the way Aristotle used the quotations from Eudoxus, Gosling/Taylor, Greeks on Pleasure.
8. Ar., EN 1172.9-15.
9. Plato, Rep. 505C and 509A.
10. 'Ek tou enantiou'.
11. Ar., EN 1172.b9-72; also 1101.b27-34.
12. Life in DL IV.1-5. Most recent edition of the fragments by Leonardo Tarán, Speusippos (see Bibliography).
13. DL IV.2.
14. DL 4.1.14.22
15. Ar., Met. 1072b30.
16. Clem., Al., Stromata 2.22.133.4.
17. Guthrie, Hist.Gr.Phil. V (1978), 466.
18. 'epistēmonikē'.
19. Sext.Emp., Adv.math. 7.145; Proclus, Comm. Eucl. 179.
20. Ar., Met. 1086a2-5.
21. Vol. I, Ch. I.10.
22. Ar., Met. 1069a33 speaks of philosophers (doubtless amongst others also Speusippus is included) who recognize only the objects of mathematics as universal and separate substances. See also Zeller, Phil.d.Gr. IV.459.
23. Zeller, Phil.d.Gr. II.1, 1006.
24. Vol. I, Ch. I.13, p. 29.
25. Zeller, Phil.d.Gr. II.1, 995.
26. See Vol. I, Ch. I.14. I hope critics will note that I am not saying that Speusippus was a Gnostic or even a proto-Gnostic.
27. Cic., Acad. 1.4.17; he does not exclude Aristotle himself from this censure.
28. Now the Turkish town of Kadiköy.
29. DL 4.6-15.
30. DL 4.7.
31. Dl 4.11-14.
32. Most recent edition of the fragments by Isnardi Parente (see Bibliography).
33. Heinze, Xenokrates, fr. 1 = Sext.Emp., Adv.Dogm. 1.16.
34. Dörrie s.v. 'Xenokrates', PW IXA2 (1967), 1518/1519.

35. Dörrie s.v. 'Xenokrates', PW IXA2 (1967), 1517.
36. See Vol. III, Ch. III,4.
37. Heinze, Xenokrates, fr. 5 = Sext.Emp., Adv.math. 7.147-149.
38. Heinze, Xenocrates fr. 5 = Sext.Emp., Adv.math. 7.149.
39. Heinze, Xenocrates fr. 30 = Proclus, Comm.Parm. 888/889; X. says that this cause is 'choristê kai theia'.
40. Ar., Met. 1083b2. Ar., who is an 'absolute philosopher' in this sense that he does not readily admit having had predecessors and colleagues, does not mention Xen. by name here, but Guthrie whom I quote between the brackets in the main text, thinks that the citation stems from Xen. indeed, on the strength of what Ar.'s Greek commentators say, Guthrie, His.Gr.Phil. IV, 473.
41. Heinze, Xen. fr. 15 = Stobaeus, Ekl. 1.62 = Aëtius, Placita 1.7.30.
42. At least his Greek commentators say so. Aëtius (Placita 1..3.23 = Stobaeus, Ekl. 1..3.23 = Heinze, Xen. fr. 28) and Theodoretus (Graecarum Affectionum Curatio = Heinze, Xen. fr. 28) both use the term 'hulê' when speaking of X.' second principle.
43. See Vol. I, Ch. I.11, p. 28.
44. Theophrastus, Met. 3.12.
45. See for this subject the rightly famous work of Arthur Oncken Lovejoy, The Great Chain of Being : a Study of the History of an Idea (Cambridge, Mass., 1936).
46. Dörrie s.v. 'Xenokrates', PW IXA2. 1520.
47. Plut., On the Gen. of the Soul in the Timaeus, 1012D-E = Heinze, Xen. fr. 68.
48. Plut., On the Gen. of the Soul in the Timaeus 1012E.
49. Guthrie, Hist.Gr.Phil. IV 472. Ar., Met. 1028b25-28; Ar. says that 'some' hold this but there is no doubt that this refers to Xen. and his followers.
50. Zeller, Phil.d.Gr. II.1 1021.
51. Plutarch, Plat.Quest. 1007F = Heinze, Xen. fr. 28.
52. Heinze, Xen. fr. 75 and 76.
53. Cicero, De nat.deor. 1.13.34 = Heinze, Xen. fr. 17.
54. Laurentius Lydus, De mensibus 36 = Heinze, Xen. fr. 58. I was unable to check this quotation.
55. Heinze, Xen. fr. 15 = Aetius, Placita 1.7.30 = Stobaeus, Ekl. 1.36.
56. Dörrie s.v. 'Xenokrates', PW IXA2 (1967) 1524.
57. Heinze, Xen. fr. 24 = Plut., De Is. et Os. 360D-E.
58. Heinze, Xen. fr. 23 = Plut., De defectu oraculorum 416C.
59. In Antiquity nobody seems to have doubted its authenticity, perhaps with the exception of Diogenes who throws some doubt on its authorship by writing that "it was said that Plato was the

author", DL 3.37, followed in this by some Byzantine scholars like Suidas, and above all by Proclus who found that such an obscure text could not be the work of a master mind, Proclus, In Plat.Rem publ.Comm. 170 and 185 (of this work a medieval Latin translation by William of Moerbeke exists). It was only in this century that Plato's authorship began to be doubted. Many modern scholars are now satisfied that Plato is not the author, to quote only Lamb who is 'aware of contact with an inferior mind'. According to him the Epinomis was intended to serve as an appendix to Plato's Laws, Plato, Epinomis, ed. Lamb, XII. As in Vol. III, Ch. III.2, I am following Guthrie who is convinced that "the Epinomis was not written by Plato", Guthrie, Hist.Gr.Phil. V (1978) 321 and 385. See for the history of the argument Des Places, Epinomis 97-109.

60. Zeller, Phil.d.Gr. II.1 1040.
61. Epin. 973A.
62. Epin. 973A.
63. Epin. 976D, 992D.
64. Epin. 974B, 976D, 979D, 980A.
65. Epin. 991B.
66. Epin. 977A.
67. Epin. 984E-985A.
68. Epin. 986D.
69. Epin. 992D.
70. Epin. 974D, C.
71. Epin. 974D-E.
72. Epin. 975A and 974B.
73. Epin. 975A-976C.
74. Epin. 977A.
75. Epin. 977B.
76. Epin. 977C-D.
77. Epin. 978B.
78. Epin. 982C-D.
79. Epin. 983E-984A.
80. Epin. 987D-988A.
81. Epin. 990C-E.
82. Epin. 992C-D.
83. Epin. 985A.
84. Epin. 989A.
85. Epin. 977C.
86. DL.7.168-176.
87. Hossenfelder, Phil.d.Ant. 3.44.

88. DL.7.178-202.
89. For a thematic treatment of the Stoa the reader should consult the work of Max Pohlenz, Die Stoa (see Bibliography).
90. Vol. I, Ch. II.6.
91. Hunt, Phys.Interpr. 17.
92. Pearson fr. 51 = Stob., Ekl. 11.5a. What Zeno says here is repeated by Chrysippus, DL.7.150.
93. Hunt, Phys.Interpr. 18.
94. Dl.7.150.
95. Adkins, Many to One 219. Stoic sources in Arnim, Fragmenta, and in Hülser, Fragmente, see Bibliography.
96. See Vol. I, Ch. I.12.
97. DL 7.140.
98. Stob. 1.392, from Chrysippus.
99. "Of the somethings (tinoon), they (the Stoics) say, some are bodies, others are incorporeal; and of the incorporeal they sum up four forms, that what is thought (lekton), and void, and place, and time", Sext.Emp., Adv. Math. 10.218.
100. Hülser 808 = Stob., Ekl. 1.260 = Arrii Didymi epitomes fr. phys. 26 (DG). See Goldschmidt, Syst.Stoic. 47-49, and also Hossenfelder, Phil.d.Ant. 3, 80/81.
101. Galenus Methodi med. 2.7 = SVF (Arnim) II.322.
102. SVF (Arnim) II.329 = Alex.Aphrod. comm. in Ar. Topica 4.155a; Hossenfelder, Phil.d.Ant. 3.81.
103. Hunt, Phys.Interpr. no 23 = Cic., ND 2.18. Hunt 31 says that this is 'Zeno's own doctrine'.
104. Cic., ND 2.82.
105. The title of Ch. 2 in Hunt, Phys.Interpr.
106. DL 7.134.
107. Hunt, Phys.Interpr, no 5 = SVF (Arnim) II.303 = Seneca, Ep. 65.2.
108. Copleston, Hist.Phil. I.2, 132.
109. Hunt, Phys.Interpr. 21.
110. DL 7.134.
111. SVF (Arnim) I.85 = Aetius 1.3.25, and Achilles Tatius, Isagoge 124E.
112. Vol. I, Ch. II.5.
113. For instance in Zoroastrianism, see Vol. IV, Ch. IV.9 and Vol. V, Ch. I.4.
114. SVF (Arnim) II.323 = Galenus, De qualitatibus in corporeis 5.

115. 'Materiam mundialem a deo separatam', SVF (Arnim) I.155 = Tert., Ad nationes 2.4.
116. SVF (Arnim) I.87 = Epiphanius, Adversus haereses 1.5.
117. SVF (Arnim) I.87 = Chalcidius, In Timaeum 294 : "deum esse quod silva (matter) sit".
118. DL.7.137.
119. Tertullian, Ad nationes 2.4.
120. SVF (Arnim) I 161 = Epiph., Ad.haer. 1.5.
121. It re-emerged in Teilhard de Chardin's evolutionist theology.
122. Aristocles, Ap.Eus.praep.ev. 816d : 'archas hulēn kai theon'.
123. DG 410 = Aet., Plac. 4.20.2, in Plut., De Placitis Epitomes 4.20. The same in Cic., Academica (a lost work) 1.39, quoted by Hunt, Phys.Interpr. no 17.
124. SVF (Arnim) I 153 = Galenus, Hist.phil. 16.
125. Moreau, Âme du monde 161.
126. Moreau, Âme du monde 163.
127. Hunt, Phys.Interpr.
128. SVF (Arnim) II 135 = Sext.Emp., Adv.Math. 9.75.
129. See Vol. III, Ch. III.27.
130. See Vol. I, Ch. II.6, p. 69.
131. SVF (Arnim) I 98 = Aristocles, Ap.Eus.praep.ev. 15.816; idem SVF I 157 = Aetius, Plac. 1.7.23, and Augustinus, Adv.Acad. 3.
132. SVF (Arnim) I 154 = Cic., ND 1.36 and Academ. 2.126; Tertullianus adv. Marcionem 1.13; Minucius Felix 19.10.
133. Cic., ND 2.28.
134. Cic., ND 2.32 = Rufus Ephesius, De part.hom. 44 : " Zeno said that heat and soul (pneuma) are the same". The Stoic position is very close to the 'hylozoism" of the Ionian philosophers, see Vol. I, Ch. II.5.
135. DL 7.142; also SVF (Arnim) I.110 = Sext.Emp., Adv.Math. 9.107.
136. SVF (Arnim) I.160 = Tertullianus, Apol. 21. The extant texts do not permit us to conclude with certainty whether the Logos is wholly identical with the godhead or that it is an effect or an emanation from it.
137. Hunt, Phys.Interpr. 29.
138. Cic., ND 2.58.
139. Rist, Stoic Phil. 123.
140. Cic., De Fato 20.
141. Rist, Stoic Phil. 125 : 'anangkē heimarmenēs'.
142. On the authority of Diogenianius apud Eus.Praep.ev. 6.8.1.
143. Rist, Stoic Phil. 127.

144. Hülser I, 327A = Eus., Praep.Ev. 15.14.2.
145. SVF (Arnim) II.975 = Hippolytus, Phil. 21.
146. My eye fell on these lines in Rodis-Lewis, Mor.Soic. 114, in her chapter V 'Liberté et ordre du monde". The verse is quoted by Epictetus in dispersed order in several places in his Dissertationes and at the end of his Manual (53), see SVF (Arnim) I.527. The translation is by Long/Sedley, Hell. Phil. I, no. 62B.
147. DL 7.121. The notion that the wise are free and the stupid slaves is treated at some length by Cicero in his fifth Stoic Paradox 33-41, Cic.Par.Stoic.
148. DL 7.122-125.
149. Dl. 7.127.
150. Dio Chrys. 14.17-18, ed. Cohoon.
151. SVF (Arnim) I.374 = Galenus de Hipp. et Plat. decr. 7.2.
152. SVF (Arnim) II.294 = Sext.Emp., Adv.math. 2.6.
153. SVF (Arnim) I.413 = Cic., Acad.priora 2.129.
154. So in SVF (Arnim) I.201 where Plut., De virt.mor. 2 states that Zeno called epistēmē phronēsis.
155. Do the two texts quoted by Arnim, by Clem. Al. and Gal. (index under 'gnosis'), really refer to Stoic positions? Hülser in his more recent edition does not print them. There is a chapter (12) on 'knowing and willing' in Rist, Stoic Phil.
156. Just like Kirilov in Dostojevski's 'The Devils'.
157. Rist, Stoic Phil. 233.
158. Plut., De comm.not.adv.Stoic. 1063 D.
159. Plut., De Stoic.rep. 1039 E.
160. DL 7.130.
161. Edelstein, Meaning, Ch. III.
162. Aulus Gellius, Noctes 7.1.1-4.
163. Copleston, Hist.Phil. I.2, 134 and 136.
164. Plut., De Stoic.rep. 1051C.
165. Hülser III.1000 = Aetius, Plac. 1.27.3 = Plut., De plac.phil. 884F; in this passage anankē and heimarmenē are not seen as identical.
166. Plut., De Stoic,rep. 1051C-E.
167. Aulus Gellius, Noctes Atticae 7.1.8.
168. Plut., De Stoic.rep. 1051C.
169. Stob., Ekl. 2.92 = Aulus Gellius, Noctes Atticae 9.5.5 : "neutrum, neque bonum neque malum, quod ipse Graeco vocabulo adiaphoron appellavit".
170. In Stob., Ekl.2.198 even called 'two races of human beings", as though they were biologically different.

171. Plut., De recta rat.aud. 25C.
172. SVF (Arnim) III.658 = Al.Aphrod, On Fate, ed. Sharples. 78.
173. Plut., Virt.profectus 75.
174. Plut., De comm.not. 1062B.
175. Plut., Stoic.abs. 1057E-D. It is part of the elitist way of thinking of the Stoics that only the sage, i.e. the Stoic, is considered beautiful, or has the right to be beautiful. "The wise man in a moment or second of time changes from the lowest possible depravity to an unsurpassable state of virtue; and all his vice, of which he has not in long years succeeded in removing even a small portion, he suddenly leaves behind for ever", Plut., In virt.prof. 75D.
176. Copleston, Hist.Phil. II.1, 135.
177. Zeller, Phil.d.Gr. III.1, 370-373.
178. A.G.M. van Melsen s.v. 'Atomism' in Enc. of Phil. I; see also Van Melsen s.v. 'Atomtheorie' in Hist.Wörterbuch d.Phil. Bd. 1, 603-606.
179. Whyte, Essay 3.
180. Whyte, Essay 16.
181. Whyte, Essay 16.
182. Whyte, Essay 12.
183. Whyte, Essay 13; his underlining.
184. See Vol. I, Ch. I.11.
185. Bailey, Gr.Atom. 27.
186. See Vol. I, Ch. II.9.
187. Ar., Met. 984a.
188. Van Melsen, From Atomos to Atom 24/25.
189. Dijksterhuis, Mechaniz. 7-9.
190. See Vol. I, Ch. II.8.
191. See Vol. I, Ch. II.6.
192. Dijksterhuis, Mechan. 7/8; see for this passage also Furley, Two Studies, Ch. 4 The Eleatic concept of an indivisible being, and ch. 5 Zeno.
193. DL 6.30.
194. The first to write him off was Epicurus who categorically stated that "the philosopher Leucippus had never existed", DL 10.13.
195. DK II.67.6,7 and 9 gives the quotations from Ar. in which Leucippus' name occurs.
196. E.R.Lloyd s.v. 'Leucippus and Democritus', in Enc. of Phil. 3 and 4 (1967).

197. Attributed to him by Theophrastus, but by Thrasyllus to Democritus, DL 9.46.
198. Zeller, Phil.d.Gr. I.2, 1038-1046.
199. Some say in Milete.
200. DL 9.34-36.
201. Clem.Al., Strom. 11.69.
202. Preserved in DL 9.46.
203. We find a large collection of texts regarding Dem. in Luria, Democritea (see bibliography); this is a Russian work the first part of which, however, gives the texts in Greek and Latin. See for those referring to his Vita pp. 14-20. See also the critical discussion in Zeller, Phil.d.Gr. I.2, Note 1, 1043-1054. See for a full treatment of the Democritean doctrine Guthrie, Hist.Gr.Phil. II, 386-507.
204. Ar., De gen. et corr. 325a.
205. Ar., De gen. et corr. 325a35/36.
206. Ar., De gen. et corr. 325a37.
207. Bailey, Gr.Atom. 71.
208. Ar., De gen. et corr. 325a31/32.
209. DK I.30B7.7 (p. 272).
210. Melisso, Test. 428 "Infatti (Leucippo) presuppone proprio la dottrina del vuoto quale è formulata da Melisso"; Reale whom I am quoting adds that Mel,. is not polemizing here against the Atomists.
211. Ar., De gen. et corr. 325a27.
212. He utilizes both the particle and the infinitive of the verb 'einai'.
213. Ar., De gen. et corr. 325a29-31.
214. Ar., De gen. et corr. 325a31-66.
215. Ar., Met. 985b5-10.
216. Bailey, Gr.Atom. 75.
217. Burnet, Early Gr. Phil. 337 defends L. by saying that "he hardly ... had words to express his discovery (namely that space is not real, i.e. corporeal, but nevertheless exists - F.), for the verb 'to be' had hitherto been used by philosophers only of body". Really? Wasn't Parmenides' 'to on' the exact opposite of all that is physical? And didn't, in view of the Eleatic position, Leucippus choose for his 'lesser existence' exactly that term that would expose him to profound misunderstanding?
218. Bailey, Gr.Atom. 76 who is quoting here from Burnet, Early Gr. Phil. ,second edition 389; I was unable to detect this passage in the third edition.
219. Bailey, Gr.Atom. 217.

220. Ar., Phys. 188a; Plut., Adv.Col. 1109A. 'Den' is an artificial word coined on the analogy of 'ouden'; Einarson and De Lacy in Loeb Class. translate it with 'aught', and DK still more pregnantly with the no longer used German word 'Ichts" as opposed to 'nichts'. Plut. adds that Dem. means that "space like body has a real existence of its own". The question may arise whether in Democritean doctrine 'space' and 'void' are identical.

221. As very probably may be concluded from Simpl. in Ar. Phys. CAG 9.571.13-29.

222. Simpl. in Ar.Phys. CAG 9.394/395, and especially 533.17/18 where he quotes D. as saying that the void is space. We might agree with Zeller, Phil.d.Gr. I.2, 1069, Note 1, who says that "wahrscheinlich ... Demokrit seine Ansicht noch nicht so genau formuliert hatte".

223. In view of D.'s basic (and monistic!) materialism I do not understand how van Melsen, From Atomos 20 can speak of the 'metaphysical aspect of Democritus' atomic theory'.

224. Ar., Met. 1032a20-22.

225. Ar., De caelo 283b5-6.

226. For this passage I am much indebted to two fine treatises by Rudolf Löbl, Demokrits Atome, in particular II Das Leere (218-224), and Demokrits Atomphysik, in particular Teil 2, Das Leere und der Raum (131-139). See Bibliography.

227. Ar., De an. 404a1-3.

228. Ar., De an. 409b5 : "The soul exists in every part of the sentient body".

229. Lucr., De rer.nat. 372-374 : "The first beginnings of body and soul are placed one beside one alternately in pairs".

230. Ar., De an. 404a6-9.

231. Aelian, On Animals 12.17 = DK II.68(55)A152.

232. DK II.68(55)B13.37 = Ael., On Animals.

233. DK. II.68(55)B187.

234. Jacob Moleschott (1822-1893), Der Kreislauf des Lebens (1852) : "Ohne Phosphor kein Gedanke". Moleschott, who was Dutch, had to abandon his chair of physiology at Utrecht State University because of his materialism; later he became a professor in Rome where he died.

235. DK II.68(55)A105 = Aët., Plac. 4.4.6, but it is possible that this location is more Epicurean than Democritean, Zeller, Phil.d.G. I.2, 1116/1117.

236. DK II.68(55)A109 = Aët., Plac. 4.7.4 : "Epicure says that the perishable (sc. the soul) is dispersed at the same moment as the body".

237. Stob., Ekl. 1.924.

238. DK II68(55)B297 = Aët., Plac. 4.34.62.

239. DK II68(55)B39 : "One should either be good or imitate somebody who is good", and ib. 40 : "Neither body nor money can make us happy but rightmindedness and fulness of understanding".
240. Zeller, Phil.d.Gr. I.2, 1157.
241. Drachmann, Ath. 24.
242. Sext.Emp., Adv.Math.9.24.
243. Zeller, Phil.d.Gr. I.2, 1161.
244. Dijksterhuis, Mech. 12.
245. DK II67(54)B2; this is the only literal fragment of Leucippus that we possess; there is no reason to suppose that this was not Democritus' opinion too.
246. Life in DL 10, the longest after that of Zeno.
247. DL 10.7. Taylor, Epic. 11 Note 1 remarks that "the form of the names stamps the ladies in question as 'demi-mondaines' ". Some of them are known by name indeed, Hedeia, Erotion, Nicidion, which Taylor renders by 'Maimie, Chérisette, and Désirée'.
248. H. von Arnim s.v. 'Epikuros' in PW VI (1909), 135.
249. Plut., Adv.Col. 1117A-C.
250. DL 10.18; Pliny, NH 35.5.
251. At least Pliny gives this piece of information in the present tense.
252. H. von Arnim s.v. 'Epikuros' in PW VI (1909), 135.
253. DL 10.12, and the letter by Epicurus himself to a certain Herodotus in DL 10.36 and 82-83.
254. DL 10.26-28.
255. DL 10.35-135.
256. Taylor, Epic. 23.
257. DL 10.8; I use the renderings presented by Taylor, Epic.11. Although Diog. says that people who allege such things against Epic. are 'stark mad', there can be no doubt that Epic. spoke scathingly of other philosophers and that he was most ungrateful to his own teachers, Taylor, Epic. 23/24; H. von Arnim s.v. 'Epikuros' in PW VI (1909), 135.
258. Taylor, Epic. 24/25.
259. Taylor, Epic. 23.
260. Seneca, Epist. 52.3.
261. Cic., ND 1.73; De Fin. 1.16 : "His doctrines are those of Democritus, with very few modifications".
262. Cic., De fin. 1.21.
263. See Vol. I.Ch.I.5.
264. DL 10.20.
265. Plut., Adv.Col. 1117C.

266. He reminds one of Wittgenstein who solely pronounced infallible utterances but did not bother about arguments and did not like discussion. The difference is that W. was a far greater mind than E.
267. Lucr., De rer.nat. 6.26-28.
268. Philod. nr. 22 (p. 49).
269. Seneca, Epist. 52..3.
270. DeWitt, Epic. 94.
271. Curiously enough, Wittgenstein made the same distinction.
272. DeWitt, Epic. 96.
273. DeWitt. Epic. 94 citing from Philod., On Frankness fr. 45.9-11.
274. Seneca, Epist. 25.5.
275. DL 10.9; DeWitt, Epic. 102.
276. Seneca. Epist. 79.15.
277. Once again a comparison with Wittgenstein obtrudes itself since he, while spending a considerable part of his equally unmarried life in a secluded hut on a Norvegian fjord, believed that the true philosopher is not interested in politics and social planning, let alone does he engage in them. Nevertheless, W. served courageously as a soldier in the Austrian army during World War I.
278. DeWitt, Epic. 10.
279. Boyancé, Epic. 18.
280. Robin, Pensée gr. 18.
281. Sext.Emp., Adv.Math. 11.169.
282. Sext.Emp., Adv.math. : "The followers of Epicurus seem to have conducted their polemics against the scientists in a more general manner ... affirming that science is no help at all for the perfect fulfilment of wisdom ...; thus they believe to have found an efficient camouflage for their ignorance (Epicurus in effect is accused of being uneducated)". According to Cic., De fin. 1.20 he condemned the study of mathematics.
283. Cic., De fin. 2.12.
284. DL 10.38.
285. DL 10.39.
286. DL 10.39.
287. Asmis, Epic.' Method 236.
288. 'Rerum in numero', Lucr., Rer.nat.1.445/446.
289. Lucr., Rer.nat. 1.449/450.
290. DL 10.67.
291. Lucr., Rer.nat. 1.335/336.
292. Asmis, Method 241.

293. Cic., De fin. 1.17-18.
294. DL 10.45.
295. DL 10.63.
296. DL 10.66.
297. DL 10.64-66.
298. DL 10.124-125.
299. Copleston, Hist.Phil. II.I.149.
300. Theophrastus, Char. 16.1-25. The Greek word Theophrastus employs is 'deisidaimonia" which is certainly not translated correctly with 'superstitiousness' (as in the in the Loeb Class. edition), see Festugière, Epicure.
301. Usener fr. 169 = Philodemus, Peri eusebeias 2.109.3. For the Eleusinian mysteries see my Vol. I, Ch. IV.8. The 'other mysteries' may have been the Anthestêria, Usener fr. 157 = Phil., Peri eus. 2.75.25.
302. Usener fr. 13 = Phil., Peri eus. 2.110.
303. The spokesman is a certain Cotta.
304. Cic., ND 1.31.86. Of course, Epicurus who was known as a materialistic Atomist was accused of hypocrisy because of this : "Out of fear for public opinion he (Epicurus) goes through a mummery of prayer and obeisances that he has no use for and pronounces words that run counter to his philosophy ... This is the comedy Epicurus thinks we should play, and not spoil the pleasure of the multitude or make ourselves unpopular with them by showing dislike ourselves for what others delight in doing", Plut., Pleasant life imposs. 1102B.
305. DL 10.123.
306. Plut., De def.or. 420B.
307. Lactantius, Div.Inst. III.17.
308. Lucr., Rer.nat. 5.196-199.
309. See Vol. I, Ch.IV.3.
310. See Vol. I, Ch. III and Vol. III, Ch. I.
311. Zeller, Phil.d.Gr. III.1, 447.
312. Dl 10.123-124.
313. 'Hoi polloi'.
314. DL 10.121; Zeller, Phil.d.Gr. III.1, 447.
315. Cic., ND 1.34.95.
316. Or a language much akin to it, Usener fr. 356 = Philod., De victu deorum 6.13. This makes me think of what the Dutch professor of philosophy Beerling once said of Being, viz. that it preferably speaks German.
317. DL 10.123.

318. DL 10.139.1.
319. Cic., ND 1.19.51.
320. Lucr., Rer.nat. 2.648.
321. Drachmann, Ath. 105/106.
322. Lucr., Rer.nat. 5.146-155.
323. Cic., De div. 2.17.40.
324. Lucr., Rer.nat. 3.18-22.
325. Cic., ND 1.19.50.
326. Cic., ND 1.18.49.
327. Cic., ND 1.27.75.
328. Cic., ND 2.23.59.
329. Cic., ND 2.23.59.
330. Drachmann, Ath. 106.
331. A separate work has been devoted to the inconsistencies in Epicurean doctrine by Bonelli, Aporie etiche (see Bibliography). It lists among others the Epicurean attitude to death, to the gods, and to pleasure.
332. Zeller, Phil.d.Gr. III.1, 451 with the quotation from Philod., Peri eus. 84 in Note 4, 451/452. Bailey, Gr.Atom. 469 thinks that "Philodemus was in concession to popular prejudice working out the anthropomorphic idea further than his master would have approved", but Rist, Epic. 152 says that "there are indications at least that Philodemus is following his master fairly closely".
333. DL 10.122.
334. Robin, Pensée gr. 390.
335. Lucr., Rer.nat. 4.471-472 and 500-506.
336. 'Salus' in the version by Lucr.
337. DL 10.6.
338. DL 10.79.
339. DL 10.79 and 87.
340. Robin, Pensée gr. 394.
341. Seven times.
342. DL 10.124.
343. DL 10.123.
344. DL 10.35.
345. The Epicurean texts with regard to the subject of pleasure have been collected, translated, and commented upon by Bollack, Pensée (see Bibliography).
346. Plut., Pleas. life imp. 1098D.
347. Usener fr. 345 = Clem.Al., Strom. 2.21.

348. Usener fr. 409 = Athen., Deipn. 12.546f.
349. Taylor, Epic. 87.
350. DL 10.128-129.
351. DL 10.132.
352. Richard H. Popkin s.v. 'Skepticism' in Encyclopedia of Philosophy 7, New York/London (1967), 449.
353. DL 9.61-69.
354. DL 9.109-116. See also Brochard, Scept.gr. 77-91, and W. Capelle s.v. 'Timon' in PW VIa (1936), 1301-1303.
355. Texts Caizzi, Pirrone Testimonianze, and De Vogel, Gr.Phil III, Ch. XXII.2 (for both consult Bibliography).
356. DL 9.71.
357. See Vol. I, Ch. II.8.
358. Brochard, Scept.gr. 5.
359. See Vol. III, Ch. II.1a.
360. Not to be confounded with Euclides the mathematician.
361. See for this passage Zeller, Phil.d.Gr. II.1,, 244-275.
362. Sext.Emp., Adv.Math. 7.136.
363. Sext.Emp., Pyrrh. 1.213-214.
364. Sext.Emp., Pyrrh. 1.223; see Brochard, Scept.gr. 9/10.
365. Goedeckemeyer, Gesch.gr.Szept. 4.
366. Caizzi fr. 62 = Sext.Emp., Adv.Math. 9.20.
367. Cic., De fin. 3.3.11.
368. Cic., Ac. 2.42.130.
369. DL 9.67.
370. DL 9.67-68; Plut., Virt.prof. 82F.
371. Cic., De fin. 3.4.12.
372. Plut., Virt.prof. 82F.
373. DL 9.64.
374. Caizzi fr. 62 = Sext.Emp., Adv.Math. 9.20.
375. Numenius spoke of 'dogmatisai', DL 9.68.
376. Caizzi fr. 53 = Aristocles in Eus., Praep.ev. 14.8.1-4 and 7.
377. Sext.Emp., Pyrrh. 1.197.
378. DL 9.70.
379. DL 9.74.
380. DL 9.108.
381. DL 9.105.
382. Brochard, Scept.gr. 59.

383. Naess, Sceptic. 28.
384. Naess, Sceptic. 28/29, his underlining.
385. Naess, Sceptic. 29; his underlining.
386. Brochard, Scept.gr. 67.
387. Brochard, Scept.gr. 71.
388. DL 9.67 quoting from Il. 6.146.
389. DL 9.64; Brochard, Scept.gr. 71.
390. Dox. 591.5 = Epiph., Adv.haer. 3.18.
391. Caizzi fr. 26A = Eus., Praep.ev. 14.2.4.
392. DL 9.106; Eus., Praep.ev. 14.18.13 quoted by Goedeckemeyer, Gesch.gr.Skept. 12 Note 3.
393. Long, Hell.Phil. 8 : "Pyrrho removes the external world as a subject of philosophical discussion.
394. Caizzi fr. 76 = Lucianus, Bis accusatus 25 : "(Pyrrho) does not acknowledge any criterion of Truth".
395. "L'incertitude est de tous les maux le plus difficile à supporter", Alfred de Musset, La confession d'un enfant du siècle (1836).
396. Caizzi fr. 58 = Eus., Praep.ev. 14.18.28-19 quoting from Aristocles and Timon.
397. DL 9.65 quoting from a poem by Timon.
398. The word is 'atuphos', Caizzi fr. 23 = Eus., Praep.ev. 14.18.27 (Aristocles).
399. The following quotation from Del Pra very nicely demonstrates how easily a duality can develop into a dualism : "La critica democritea della conoscenza sensibile diviene con Pirrone avvertimento delle difficoltà che investono tutta (his underlining) la conoscenza. Tali difficoltà hanno come presupposto la dualità di realtà, cioè la concezione che pone, al di là della nostra percezioni delle cose, una realtà, una realtà in se, esterna al mondo delle nostre percezioni e da esso independente", Del Pra, Scett.gr. I, 80.
400. Stough, Gr.Scept. 30/31 very aptly writes that "the seeker of well-being philosophize(s) in order to give up philosophy ... The Pyrrhonist's goal of well-being is not the traditional ideal of the philosopher. Speculation as such is incompatible with an untroubled spirit."
401. DL 4.28 says : "with him (Arcesilaus) begins the Middle Academy"; he was followed in this by Sext.Emp., Pyrrh. 1.220. Others take the Middle and New Academy together and call it the "New Academy'.
402. Sedley, Motiv. 15.
403. Sedley, Motiv. 10.
404. Thus I paraphrase somewhat Hossenfelder's 'erkenntniskritischer Kahlschlag', Hossenfelder, Phil.d.Ant. 3, Gesch.gr.Phil. III, 193.
405. Hossenfelder, Phil.d.Ant. 3, Gesch.gr.Phil. III, 193.

406. Vita in DL 4.28-51, see also Von Arnim s.v. 'Arkesilaos' in PW II (1896), 1164-1168, and Zeller, Phil.d.Gr. III.1, 508/509, Note 1.
407. Sext.Emp., Adv.Math. 7.153; see also Cic., Ac. 1.144 : "It was entirely with Zeno ... that Arcesilaus set on foot his battle".
408. Cic., Ac. 2.40-42. See for this subject for instance Robin, Pyrrhon 49/50, and Del Pra, Scett.gr. 129-131.
409. Couissin, Stoic. 32.
410. Sext.Emp., Adv.Math. 7.150-157.
411. Sext.Emp., Adv.Math. 7.153.
412. Sext.Emp., Adv.Math. 7.154 : "toon gar axioomatoon eisin hai sunkatatheseis".
413. Cic., Ac. 2.24.77.
414. Sext.Emp., Adv.Math. 7.155 : " panta estai akatalêpta".
415. Cic., Ac. 1.12.45.
416. Cic., De fin. 2.1.2.
417. Cic., De fin. 5.4.10; DL 4.28.
418. Cic., Ac. 1.12.45
419. DL 4.28 says that Arcesilaus "was the first to suspend his judgment ("epischoon tas apophaseis'). Although DL sows some confusion by also stating that Pyrrho's philosophy took 'the form of not-knowing and suspension (epochê) of judgment', DL 9.61, it is, nonetheless, "un fait que tous nos témoins ... sont unanimes à présenter Arcésilas comme l'initiateur dans la philosophie de la notion dont il s'agit", Robin, Scept.gr. 56. Another problem is that Couissin believes that 'epochê' is less a philosophical theorem of Arcesilaus himself than a reductio ad absurdum by him of the Stoic theory of knowledge. Sextus concludes the passage in which he is disserting on the Arcesilaic notion of epochê (Adv.math. 7.155-157) with this conclusion that he clearly holds to be that of A. : "So the Sage will suspend judgment on everything" (157). From the future tense ('ephexei') Couissin concludes that this would be the consequence of Stoic scepticism. But wouldn't Sextus, speaking for A. here, not have used the conditional if he really meant this : "If this were true, the sage would have to suspend etc.". I cannot understand why Couissin argues in this way since Sextus, still speaking for Arcesilaus, says that "everything is inapprehensible in consequence of the non-existence ('dia tên anuparxian') of the Stoic criterion" (156). In my opinion Couissin is misinterpreting Sextus here, for if the Stoic criterion, viz. katalêpsis, were valid, we would be able to arrive at sure knowledge. Anyhow, he (Couissin) too holds that A. strongly propounded the necessity of epochê.
420. Zeller, Phil.d.Gr. III.1, 513 Note 1.
421. Sext.Emp., Adv.Math. 7.158.

422. Zeller, Phil.d.Gr. III.1, 513; Goedeckemeyer, Gesch.gr.Skept. 43 Note 2 objects to the translation of 'eulogos' with 'probable'; his rendering is 'wohlbegründet'. But he conveniently forgets that in sceptic doctrine sure knowledge is not possible.
423. Cic., Ac. 2.18.68).
424. DL 4.30.
425. DL 4.37.
426. According to DL 4.42 some called him 'a friend of the mob who courted popularity'.
427. DL 4.37.
428. DL 4.62.
429. That this event made a great impression is shown by the fact that it is mentioned at least ten times in ancient sources, Lact., Inst.5.-125; Gellius, NA 6.14,8 and 17.21.48; Plin., HN 7.30.112, and no less than four times by Cic., Ac. 2.137, de Or. 2.155, Tusc. 4.5, Ad Att. 12.23, the longest description being that of Plut., Cato 22 who says that "the charm of Carneades ... filled the city, like a rushing mighty wind, with the noise of his praises".
430. Gell., NA 6.14.10.
431. DL 4.63.
432. DL 4.63.
433. DL 4.65.
434. DL 4.65.
435. See for a full treatment of this subject Pieri, Carneade 52-79.
436. Cic., ND 1.6263.
437. Cic., Ac. 2.120.
438. There is no doubt that this is indeed an argument of Carneades himself since Sext.Emp., Adv.Math. 9.182, expressly states that it was recorded by Carneades' friend Clitomachus.
439. Sext.Emp., Adv.Math. 9.182-190; Cic., ND 3.43-52.
440. Sext.Emp., Adv.Math. 9.138-143. Carneades is expressly cited by Sextus.
441. Sext.Emp., Adv.Math. 9.151.
442. Cic., ND 3.29-37 gives them too, citing Carneades as his source. See also von Arnim s.v. 'Karneades', PW X (1919), 1972-1975. Goedeckemeyer, Gesch.gr.Skept. 72-81 presents a clear exposition of C.' doctrine. He also was, of course, a strongly-worded opponent of divination, mantics, fortune-telling, and astrology.
443. Sext. Emp., Adv.Math. 9.178-179.
444. Cic., Rep. 3.7.
445. Cic., Rep. 3.8-11.
446. Cic., Rep. 3.12.21.

447. Cic., Rep. 3.11.19.
448. Cic., Rep. 3.24.36.
449. Cic., Rep. 8.24.36.
450. Cic., Rep. 3.13.23.
451. Cic., Rep. 3.12.21.
452. Cic., Rep. 3.20.31 and 24.36.
453. Goedeckemeyer, Gesch.gr.Skept. 86.
454. Zeller, Phil.d.Gr. III.1, 548/549.
455. See Vol. I, Ch. I.16.
456. Suetonius, Rhet. 1. See Zeller, Phil.d.Gr. III1., 552/553.
457. See for this passage Zeller, Phil.d.Gr. III.1, 557-560.
458. Cic., De leg. 1.20.53.
459. Zeller, Phil.d.Gr. III.1., 563.
460. Zeller, Phil.d.Gr. III.1, 564.
461. The term 'Middle Stoa' admittedly is controversial. The scholar who introduced it was August Schmekel with his 'Die Philosophie der mittleren Stoa in ihrer geschichtlichen Zusammenhange dargestellt', Berlin 1892 (photostatic reprint Hildesheim-New York 1974). Max Pohlenz in his book on the Stoa (see bibliography) says on p. 191 : "der Ausdruck führt insofern irre, als er die Vorstellung weckt, alsob damit eine geschlossene Gruppe gemeint sei". But he would not object to speak of 'a middle period of the school'. Heinrich Dörrie, in Der kleine Pauly 5 (1975) s.v. 'Stoa', 377 says : "Da der Terminus 'mittlere Stoa' uneinheitlich verwendet wurde, ist es ratsam auf diesen Terminus ganz zu verzichten." But is there really such ad difference between 'Middle Stoa' and 'the middle period of the Stoa'?
462. Of the successors of Chrysippus, Zeno of Tarsus and Diogenes of Seleucia, hardly anything is known with certainty.
463. Mentioned by DL 7.54.143, 148-149, but no vita; see Von Arnim s.v. 'Boëthos', PW III (1899), 601-603.
464. William David Ross s.v. 'Boethus', Oxf.Class.Dict. (1970), 171.
465. DL 7.54.
466. Von Arnim s.v. 'Boethus' in PW III (1899), 601.
467. Among them his compatriot Stratocles who wrote a history of the Stoa of which not much is extant.
468. No vita. For his life see Schmekel, Phil. 1-7; Pohlenz, Stoa I, 191-194; Zeller, Phil.d.Gr. III.1, 577-580.
469. Schmekel, Phil. 8/9; Zeller, Phil.d.Gr. III.1, 579, note 3. The fragments have been edited in recent times by my compatriot Modestus van Straaten, see Bibliography. The modern editions replace those by F.G. van Lynden (1802) and H.N. Fowler (1885).

470. Zeller, Phil.d.Gr. III.1, 580.
471. Copleston, Hist.Phil. I.II, 165.
472. 'Peri euthumias', DL 9.20.
473. M. Pohlenz s.v. 'Panaitios', PW XVIII (1949), 434 and 438.
474. Copleston, Hist.Phil. I.II, 165.
475. Clem., Al., Strom. 2.129.4.
476. Cic., De off. 1.28.101.
477. Cic., De off. 1.36.132.
478. Van Straaten, Pan. 98.
479. Nemesius, De natura hominis 15 = Van Straaten, Pan. fragm. 96.
480. Van Straaten, Pan. 101
481. We have no direct testimony for this, but his descriptions of these countries are such that they must be based on his visiting them, Pohlenz, Stoa 209, and Malitz, Hist. 14.
482. For his life see first of all Reinhardt s.v. 'Poseidonios', PW XXII (1954), 558-826; Pohlenz, Stoa 208-211; Malitz, Hist. 5-33. Reinhardt also wrote a monograph on him, called 'Poseidonios' (1921, see Bibliography). A more recent book is by Marie Lafranque, Poseidonios d'Apamée (1964, see Bibliography). Reinhardt does not present a vita but Lafranque does, Ch. II Vie et formation. There exists a collection of fragments by my compatriot Janus Bake, Posidonii Rhodii reliquae doctrinae. Lugduni-Batavorum 1810 (photostatic reprint Osnabrück 1972). A later collection is that in FGrH II A (1926), nr. 87.
483. Cic., ND 2.33.84.
484. Copleston, Hist.Phil. I.II, 166/167.
485. Cic., ND 2.34.87 and 86.
486. Sext.Emp., Adv.Phys. 1.130.
487. Sext.Emp., Adv.Phys. 1.131 and 124.
488. Cic., ND 1.41.116.
489. Cic., ND 2.9.24.
490. Reinhardt, Pos. 243. In its Greek form the term only turns up in the first century B.C.
491. Heinemann, Pos.' Metaph.Schr. I, 116-118.
492. Diels, Dox.Gr. 458.8.
493. Diels, Dox.Gr. 302/303, b 19.
494. DL 7.138; Schmekel, Mittl. Stoa 243; Heinemann, Pos.' Metaph.Schr. I, 110, note 2.
495. DL 7.140 and 143.
496. Cic., ND 2.56.
497. Reinhardt, Pos. 246.

498. Schubert, Esch. 51.
499. Cic., ND 2.103.
500. Schubert, Esch. 52.
501. Schubert, Esch. 53.
502. Reinhardt, Pos. 246/247.
503. Copleston, Hist.Phil. I.II, 167.
504. Cic., De leg. 1.7.22-23.
505. Cic., De div. 1.49.110.
506. Cic., De div. 1.56.129-130.

CHAPTER IV

PRAECURSORIA GNOSTICA

1. How the Greeks profited from Alexander's triumphs

Great and lofty had been Alexander's achievement, great and lofty his plans. But such a man was too high-powered to fit into the normal patterns of history and to be quietly accepted, either as a boon or as a plague, by common people. Chapter I related what happened to his empire, greater than the world had ever seen before; it told how it became dismembered into a number of smaller kingdoms under the hands of his ambitious, greedy, and pitilessly cruel generals and their equally vicious and criminal successors. None of them had a vision larger than that of the narrow circle of his own dynastic interests. In the course of the decades by far the larger part of the Alexandrian conquests, every scrap of territory beyond the Euphrates, was lost to the Asiatics who became an ever mounting threat to the remaining Hellenistic kingdoms and later to the Roman Empire.

The creation of the Alexandrian Empire opened up incredible and totally unexpected vistas, for the Greek world certainly but still more for mankind. If the fabric of the new realm would have been strong enough, its political impetus might have triumphed over the isolationist particularity of Egypt, over the imperialist aspirations of the past, those of Sumer and the Akkadian Empires, and, most powerful of all, of the Persians, and also over the particularism of the Greeks.

The possibility presented itself that, within the orbit of the new empire, slowly but certainly, and in the course of the centuries, a new people would emerge from the populations of Greece and Macedonia, of Egypt and Western Asia. A truly Hellenistic civilization might have originated, one to which Hellenes and Macedonians, Lydians and Egyptians, Mesopotamians and Iranians would have contributed equally, a culture that would have absorbed the older elements and, at the same time, sublimated them. A common, perhaps syncretistic religion could have become the foundation-stone of the whole edifice. If these possibilities had been realized, the history of the world would have taken a totally new turn. But, as Chapter II has amply shown, they were not realized.

Surely in no small measure the Greeks profited from the opportunities that were offered to them. Taking everything together, I believe that the Hellenes drew far more profit from the new situation than the Egyptians and Asiatics. The Greek geographical horizon was widened to an incredible extent; the Hellenes now established themselves in regions beyond the Indus, strange lands of which up to then they had known very little or even nothing at all, territories that had been the playground of their fertile mythical imagination [1]. The Greeks had become ubiquitous; they were found along the Nile, in the foothills of the Caucasus, in the mountains of Lebanon, in the valleys of Afghanistan, and even in the Indian plain, at a distance of sixteen hundred miles from Athens as the crow flies. The Greek tongue was heard everywhere; Greek influence radiated from many centres; countless barbarians adopted the Hellenic way of life. At least for a time, and often till the Romans took over, Graeco-Macedonian royal houses ruled over large parts of the former Persian Empire. Hellenic interests seemed to be safely protected everywhere.

2. The reverse of the coin

I assume, however, that Chapter II has copiously shown how this picture that brought many modern historians to lyrical enthusiasm about the final triumph of the Greek way of life was more shadow than substance.

We should not wholly concentrate, as so often is done, on these few brilliant centres of Hellenic art and learning, such as Antioch and Alexandria. Let us rather pay attention to the innumerable Greek settlements deep in the interior, often hardly more than stockaded villages with a mixed population of Graeco-Macedonians and Asiatics. Nearly all of them, after a precarious existence of a few decades or centuries, disappeared without leaving a trace, not even a name to remember them by.

In the northern half of Asia Minor and between the Euphrates and the Indus, whatever was Greek was drowned in the mounting Asiatic flood. The old patterns of Hellenic, Egyptian, and Asiatic historical life proved to be too inveterate to be overcome and replaced by new and rather vague ideals. The Akkadian-Persian imperialism to which the Parthians, and later the Sasanians, became the heirs, the invincible Greek particularism, and the equally invincible Greek contempt of the barbarians were destructive of the Alexandrian ideals, and became, by the same token, the constitutive elements of the situation that finally prevailed, that in which the Euphrates was the frontier between 'Europe' and 'Asia'.

3. The demise of the polis

Murray argues that the decay of the city state had already begun in 404 B.C. with the defeat of Athens at the hands of Sparta even if this city did not prove capable of replacing her. "The city state had concentrated upon herself all the loyalties and aspirations of the Greek mind. And in the fall of Athens it had failed"[2]. The downward slope became a steep incline in 338 B.C., when the last Athenian coalition was beaten at Chaeronea by King Philip II of Macedonia; thereafter he took the affairs of Greece into his own hands.

In the Hellenistic kingdoms every polis lost its sovereign rights to the royal ruler; it became dependent on the policy, not to say on the whims, of an often arbitrary and capricious monarch. The Diadochs who became the political heirs of Philip and Alexander virtually took the place of the city state; "the polis (was) turned into an individual", as Burckhardt graphically described this process [3].

The polis paid very dearly for the great change in Hellenic history [4]. "Previously the doings of the world had been, so to say dispersed (e.g. over the sovereign poleis - F.), as they were held together by no unity of initiative, result, or locality; but ever since this date (e.g. Rome's victory over Hannibal - F.) history has been an organic whole, and the affairs of Italy and Africa have been interlinked with those of Greece and Asia, all leading up to one end (e.g. the establishment of Roman rule - F.)" [5]. Polybius whom I am quoting here sees world-history as following one fixed line from the Macedonian triumph at Chaeronea to the foundation of the Imperium Romanum, with, as the consequence of these developments, the steady diminution of the polis till it floundered into utter insignificance and oblivion.

4. The rise of individualism

Since the ideological, social, and moral foundations of the polis were more and more sapped, the unavoidable result was the rise of individualism. Perhaps one might call this the emancipation of the individual [6], so long as one keeps in mind that this emancipation was translated into their own terms by the lesser elements of society. The example was given by such forceful personalities as Alexander himself who arbitrarily killed his friend Clitus and married several wives, or like Demetrius I with his five wives (even though he married them at various times), a man who, in every respect shifted his allegiances very easily, or like Pyrrhus of Epirus who married three times. The Ptolemaeans of Egypt as a rule wedded their own sisters, a custom which was also prevalent in the Seleucid dynasty [7]. All this ran counter to traditional Greek ideas of morality.

It will surprise nobody that the lesser elements readily followed their rulers' example. The polis no longer produced outstanding political personalities, and this left ample room for the ambitions of greedy and unscrupulous men. Only too frequently it was the rabble that took over, in particular in the newly founded towns without any tradition; here abandoned and disabled soldiers, displaced persons, fortune-hunters, and barbarians flocked together. Often there was "a deliberate selection of the worst men, the most god-forsaken and the greatest corruptors of the nation" [8]. In this violent outburst Polybius is speaking of the Achaeans but there is no doubt that this judgment also applies to the whole of the Hellenistic world.

This does not mean that honourable citizens necessarily led an unhappy life. Since the Hellenes had spread over three continents, new economic opportunities were offered from which many knew how to profit. A new class of wealthy and prosperous people made its appearance. Furthermore, cultural life was by no means extinct. In the foregoing chapter many flourishing philosophical schools were mentioned, together with important and productive centres of Hellenic culture. For those who studiously abstained from politics, the times probably were not so bad.

But, by the same token, this signifies that the general atmosphere was one of indolence and not exactly conducive to the creation of great works of art and thought. "It was a society", says Bradford Welles, "that is doing (economically) well and that ... does not know real problems - or at least no problems of which it wished to be reminded" [9]. Chapter III will have shown that there were no longer great philosophers, thinkers of the stature of Plato and Aristotle. Also great literature was no longer created. It is a telling fact that nearly everything that was written in this period has almost completely disappeared.

Every Greek polis that respected itself had a theatre in which tragedies and comedies were performed. Already in the fourth century B.C. the great tragedies of the fifth century B.C. were considered 'classics'. This great tradition had a sequel since new tragedies were written and performed. But what remains of them is little enough, a number of titles and names of authors, and further only fragments varying in length from a few lines to some words or even only one word [10]. Very probably their contemporaries did not judge these works important enough to go on transcribing them. After 300 B.C. the genre died out [11]. I guess that the extinction of the tragic genre was a consequence of that 'loss of nerve' that was so characteristic of the Hellenistic period. The deep-seated contradictions in human existence that were mirrored in the tragedies of the fifth century certainly had not become less in the subsequent decades. But now people preferred not to pay attention to them. Whereas the public of the great classical age dared confront the risks of life squarely, that of the following age turned its gaze away.

5. The complacency of Hellenistic comedy

Probably this is also the reason why we know a lot more about Hellenistic comedy. Farce can bite but is rarely dangerous. The so-called Old Comedy was mainly characterized by the great name of Aristophanes [12]. The Middle Comedy must be situated between 400 and 320 B.C. An anonymous work 'On Comedy' lists 57 poets (among them three sons of Aristophanes) and 607 plays, but Lesky says there must have been more [13]. This is a very considerable output that testifies to a brisk cultural life. However, not one play has been handed down to us in its entirety. The fragments are very numerous [14].

Since a number of these fragments are somewhat long - up to sixty-five lines - and even contain short scenes, they can give us an impression of what Middle Comedy was like. This impression is not particularly positive. "No ancient who has come down to us ever made a selection of passages to illustrate the wit and the dramatic capabilities of the 'Middle' Comedians", so Rose [15]. The most probable reason for this blank is that wit and dramatic capabilities were nowhere to be found. The characters are stereotyped, the caterer or cook and the fishmonger being the favourite butts of raillery. It was in this period that the word 'parasite' came to mean 'sponger' (orginally it meant no more than just 'guest') [16]. This is not the material out of which to create poignant comedy.

The period of the 'New Comedy' is connected with the name of Menander (343/342-292 B.C.); he was a born Athenian who always remained faithful to his city. This author was a most prolific writer who is said to have turned out one hundred and five plays or even more. A great number of fragments has been handed down to us, but more important, five nearly complete plays [17]. Rather than Aristophanes, he was the precusor of modern comedy. This does not signify that he was really a great author. "If we compare him to the greatest modern of his own class, Molière, the advantage is certainly not with the Athenian. Rather, he was a good second-rate author ... He was not and did not try to be a particularly funny writer. He wished rather to draw pictures of ordinary human nature, acting under violent stress, and in this he succeeded" [18]. There is not the slightest trace in his plays, nor in those of later authors of the New Comedy, of the great upheavals and commotions of the Hellenistic period [19].

There is a dramatic distance between the sound and fury of the Hellenistic political scene and the petty bourgeois life that was shown on the stage. There also yawns a chasm between the public of the fifth century B.C. that dared to look straight into the abyss, and their successors, Hellenic and Hellenized, that preferred to bake in their complacency. But they were in for a surprise. The great questions which they dodged would be sprung upon them from two sides, the Christian and the Gnostic.

6. Individualism in Hellenistic philosophy and science

The rise of individualism is particularly discernible in the realm of philosophy and science. There it is closely connected with rationalism, with faith in human reason, especially one's own reason. Dodds states that 'for Zeno, man's intellect was not merely akin to God, it was God (his underlining), a portion of the divine substance in pure or active state" [20]. "Zeno of Kittion states that what is sacred must not necessarily be at home with the gods, but that the divine resides in individual reason, and that the godhead rather leads reason" [21]. In such a contention, "Greek pride in human reason attains its most confident expression" [22].

There is no reason for believing that these dogmatic rationalists, with all their trust in human reason, in their own individual reason, that is, were great psychologists. Élitists as they were, they were not interested in the thoughts and feelings of their fellow-men, especially those of the uneducated sort. Their ideal was the 'sophos', the really wise man who had become wise by the study of philosophy. "Without philosophy there can be no goodness", they thought [23].

This predilection for rationality is very clearly expressed by their rejection of the passions. On this point the different schools agreed. What is not strictly rational is contemptible and cannot be a subject of philosophical enquiry. It goes without saying that people who give in to their passions are equally contemptible. The ideal of the wise man was 'ataraxia', to remain unmoved by anything; the vicissitudes of normal life are only 'adiaphora', indifferent things that should not disturb a sophos. In all probability the philosophers, their disciples and their followers saw this attitude as heroic and praiseworthy; what it really meant is that they refused to brave the dangers of life. Most of them spent their lives in the secluded buildings of their schools. It was in fact that same complacency, but in an intensified and sophisticated form, that we detected already, an aversion of being confronted with all that life implied in those noisy Hellenistic times.

7. Following the trail to the Gnosis

The loss of the significance of the polis as the organism that for so long had shaped the lives of Hellenic citizens and given meaning to their social, and even personal existence, caused the rise of individualism which, more often than not, led to complacency and indifference. Taken as a whole, the situation in growing measure spelled destabilization and demoralization. I do not mean by this last term that people in general grew more and more immoral and criminal. No, not that, but rather their moral fibre weakened. They became less ready, less fit also to shoulder the usual burdens of life.

In the following sections I shall recapitulate a number of issues that were treated in Chapter III. I shall not first of all revert to our usual isssue, viz. dualism, but, instead, follow the trail that leads to the Gnosis - which, after all, was the most important dualistic ideology of Antiquity. Here a warning is fit! I am not saying that during the Hellenistic age there was something like a pre-Gnosis or a proto-Gnosis. I do not want to call down the ire of the great Gilles Quispel upon my head. He uses to protest that there was either Gnosis or no Gnosis - in which he is right of course. However, it is not be imagined that such an important and extensive spiritual movement like the Gnosis suddenly sprang into full bloom like Athena who stepped from the head of Zeus as an adult person. It is to be expected that there were precursory stages and preliminary phases. Of these, and not of the Gnosis or of a supposed proto-Gnosis, the next section will testify.

8. The influence of philosophy

We must now see to what extent the general attitude of the Hellenistic public was mirrored in and by philosophy, and what effect this philosophy had on this public. This last question is hard to answer. In no period of western thought are we able to assess exactly how far the influence of philosophers reached. We may be certain that Nietzsche made a great impression on intellectuals. It is equally not to be doubted that Sartre had a large audience among scholars, students, and artists. But how well their intentions were understood, and how far they were assimilated by their real or would-be followers, that is another question. And it is still more difficult to determine the influence of these thinkers on the less educated members of this public.

Nevertheless, I believe that we are entitled to expect that when philosophers focus and systematize the mental trends and sentiments of their time, this will not remain without influence. With regard to the Hellenistic period, we have a few indications that some philosophers were widely read and much admired.

9. A new goal for life

The demoralization of Hellenistic society, its failure of nerve, is exemplified by the replacement of the Good by Pleasure as the goal of life. After all, the Good was essentially something divine, only to be attained by great exertion of thought and an ascetic way of life. Pleasure, on the the other hand, was far more easily obtainable, for instance by eating and sleeping well. It sometimes sounds like the Pappatacci ideal in Rossini's 'L'Italiana in Algieri'. In other words, Pleasure as an ideal was only a banal thing compared to the lofty goals of the Pythagorean Fraternity or of Plato's own Academy.

But already his deputy Eudoxus equated Pleasure with the Good and made it into an end in itself. Plato's successor Speusippus did not differ from Eudoxus in this; he "was easily overcome by pleasure" which shows that he was far from ascetic. For the Epicureans, Pleasure was so important that 'Epicurean', used in malam partem, became a byword. They manoeuvred themselves onto this slope by speaking somewhat loosely about the gratifications of the belly.

One need not be a psychoanalyst to suspect that there lurks an anguish behind such self-indulgent statements. Pleasure often enough is a negative thing in these ideologies. To Speusippus, to begin with, happiness was identical with freedom from disturbance. Eudoxus too opposed pleasure to pain. The Stoic ideal, however, seems more exalted than that of other Hellenistic schools of thought, for it is 'eudaimonia', the wellbeing of the soul, which state can only be attained by the practice of virtue. True enough, there was only one absolute Evil, depravity. But with regard to the normal things of life, whether good or bad, the Stoics were 'stoical', stolid. Not only poverty, illness, pain and death were 'adiaphora' to them, but also health, riches and honours [24].

Even the Epicureans who propagated the enjoyment of life came no further than that pleasure is freedom from pain. We find this same attitude in scepticism where very frequently the Good, which is equivalent to moral worth, is something neutral or negative. Remaining unmoved is the desirable state of mind for which preferably the word 'apatheia' is used. It may be clear that most philosophers kept themselves as far as possible from the less pleasurable aspects of life. Their abhorrence of pain and unpleasantness was so great that it may be dubbed dualistic.

10. The problem of Evil

This brings us to the important issue of Evil. Why does Evil exist, where does it come from? These are questions with which mankind, not only the professional thinkers, has plagued itself from the beginning. To Xenocrates with his 'Chain of Being', Evil presents a nasty problem. The line begins in the sphere of the divine and runs straight down into the physical world; this unbroken homogeneous line leaves Evil no opportunity to intrude itself upon the universe. But Evil exists, and Xenocrates is unable to explain how and where it originated. But of one thing he is sure : the fact of its existence may not be imputed to the gods.

We detect a similar difficulty in Stoic philosophy. The godhead has ordered everything for the best, but in spite of this there is Evil. Once again, Providence is absolved. Chrysippus suggested that there might be malevolent spirits who brought Evil into the world. The first outline of a dual world, with a good half and a bad one, is already sketched here. Nor did Epicurus remain exempt from this problem. No more than his fellow-thinkers did he know where Evil originated, but he absolved the gods from any responsibility. All those thinkers saddled posterity with a great problem, that of the origin of Evil. If the godhead was not the cause of its existence, where then did it originate?

11. Hellenistic theology

We must now turn to theology. There was no atheism proper in those days; philosophers and scholars virtuously took part in the public cult. But not one of them had any use for the traditional twelve Olympian gods or their mythology. If they did use the personal name of one of these gods, mostly that of Zeus, they did so in an abstract or metaphorical sense. Stoic philosophy makes the universe into a self-directed physical system; it precludes the idea of a Creator God. Their idea of the divine was pantheistic; they postulated a force within the world that suffuses all things. This leads to the notion of a 'cosmic god' who is nameless, impersonal, and purely metaphysical, although, rather incongruously, the divine principle is also defined as Fire.

The Atomists came closest to sheer atheism; their doctrine left no room at all for the divine. Democritus devaluated the Olympians to idols. That Atomism became fairly popular not only shows that the grip of the established religion on the Hellenic population, especially on the more educated class, was steadily waning. It mirrors equally the state of society in which kingdoms and invididuals seemed whirling around aimlessly like atoms, forming configurations at random and wholly by accident.

Epicurus and his school equally rule out the Olympian gods, together with divine providence and the afterlife. The Epicurean gods are impersonal and far more abstract than the Olympians. It goes without saying that dogmatic religion meant nothing to the Sceptics; with equal ease they could argue for and against the existence of gods. It is not knowing alone that makes people happy, not a firm belief in the gods. In the second half of the second century B.C. Carneades was bold enough to destroy the notions of the divine held by the Stoics and the Epicureans and to declare that it did not exist at all. Finally, Posidonius, the last noteworthy scholar of this period, did away with the old gods too; being no atheist, his one god was more or less identical with the cosmos and just as impersonal.

What must strike us in this short overview is that, at least for the philosophers, their schools, and their follwers, the Olympian religion had lost its significance completely. This created a widening vacuum that was not adequately and satisfactorily filled with new religious insights. There was a strong tendency to make the gods ever more abstract and impersonal. Sometimes the god were placed in the supralunar world, at a very great distance from mankind; sometimes there remained only one godhead that was hardly or not at all distinguishable from the cosmos.

Ironicallly enough, whereas the Olympians were far from perfect and occasionally even vicious, now the different schools of thought were at one in exonerating the godhead for any responsibility for Evil.

12. Mysticism, esoterism, and elitism

It would be, however, wholly mistaken to assume that the philosophical atmosphere was coldly intellectual. There was a distinctive touch of mysticism - the same mysticism that is present in the doctrines of Pythagoras and Plato. We heard, for instance, how Speusippus, by means of his own Theory of Numbers, sought to come into contact with 'the essence of things'. Xenocrates allotted his three modes of cognition to the three Moirai or Fates; it is not accidental that he chose Fates to stand guard over his modes of the intelligible. His vision of the cosmos was distinctly mystic which is also proved by the fact that in his system the sublunar world is peopled with demons. Finally, there is the unintellectual aversion to pure science and his advocacy of holy ignorance that are so characteristic for Epicurus. A last element is the dominant role that Fate had begun to play and to which we shall have to return. This tendency was especially pronounced in Stoic philosophy. "Fate is the logos of the cosmos", Speusippus said.

Our attention must also be directed to the élitism, and the accompanying esoterism, that were rampant in these philosophical schools. In itself this was nothing new. We find it already in the Pythagorean Fraternity while Plato and his Academy kept themselves studiously apart from the turmoil of political and social life in Athens. Xenocrates too, the custodian of the Platonic heritage, led a secluded life, not even deigning to write for the general public. In his view the only really wise men were those who were thoroughly grounded in astronomy; they alone could be happy. Knowledge of astronomy was purely esoteric since it remained the privilege of a few. The distance of those who were thus blessed was so great that it must be called dualistic. It is the dualistic division of mankind into those who know and those who do not.

In Stoicism we meet a similar distortion, this time between the wise and the unwise, equally dualistic in character. The Stoics felt entitled to speak of the folly of mankind and to consider the far greater part of it as fools and even as being bad. The chasm that separated the enlightened few from the ignorant many was exemplified by the fact that transition from the bad to the virtuous state happened all of a sudden and was wholly inexplicable - another touch of mysticism.

In respect of contempt for 'the multitude', the Epicureans did not remain behind the Stoics. They were dogmatic to the extent that they claimed to know and to understand everything better than anybody else. The School of the Garden, with its own special rituals, showed a highly esoteric, even mystical character. Mysticism, elitism, and esoterism, we will find them all back in the Gnosis.

13. The fate of objective Truth

Another milestone on the road to the Gnosis was the decline of objective Truth and the glorifying of subjectivity. This too began with Speusippus who held that everyone should live in accordance with his nature. He underpinned this philosophically by stating that there are two roads to Truth, that of reason and that of sense-perception. The Stoics proceeded much further along this road. Like the materialists that they were, they only believed in the results of sense-perception.

The cause of objective Truth was utterly lost in Scepticism. Sceptics believed in doubt and in taking two sides at the same time, but not in objectivity. Neither reason nor sense-perception could lead to Truth. By denying any possibility of notional assent, the Middle Academy dealt the death-blow to objective Truth. This also meant that man can have no sure knowledge of what is real. In this way the individual mind and objective reality were separated from each other.

Later Panaetius proclaimed that man should live according to the impulses of his nature. He divided thought from action, and action, according to him, was governed by natural impulses rather than by reason. Xenocrates did not deny the possibility of true knowledge, although he thought that it was only found in the supralunar world.

14. The issue of knowledge and wisdom

This brings us to the particularly important issue of knowledge and wisdom. The pseudo-Platonic treatise, the 'Epinomis', gave a special meaning to wisdom that distinguished it from plain knowledge - a wisdom that is given from above and to a few only; it is not the result of common knowledge of life or of scientific enquiry. It is especially at home with the astral gods. For this kind of knowing the anonymous author mostly uses forms of the verb 'gignooskein' (but not the substantive 'gnosis').

To the Stoa too 'knowledge' had a special, a specialized meaning; it did not use the word 'gnosis' but, instead, 'epistêmê' and 'prhonêsis'. What is decisive in this respect is that these substantives connote a higher knowledge that is only to be found amongst the wise. However, the ignorance of the unwise is called 'agnoia'. The Epicurean divinities are knowable by means of 'gnosis'. Here this term is used in a theological context.

It must not be overlooked that there was also talk of salvation. Knowledge is sometimes seen not as an end in itself but as a means of salvation. The Epicureans despised normal scientific work; scholarship, like money, did not make men happy nor could it lead to salvation. The need of being saved was far more important than the thirst for (common) knowledge and practical wisdom. The Epicureans really used the word 'salvation'.

15. A short overview of the mental situation

Summing up now, we may be able to describe the general mental situation. Negative factors were the growing destabilization and demoralization of society. The loss of the organic coherence of polis existence caused a feeling of being 'atomized' which made Atomism as an ideology so popular. It also led to individualism, which gave expression to the feeling of being thrown back upon oneself. The corollary of this individualism was subjectivity which, in mental matters, meant that Truth was what one felt to be true. A climactic element in the mental make-up of the Hellenistic mind was the demise of the notion of objective Truth.

In this context mention should also be made, not only of Atomism but also of Scepticism and Materialism. It looks as though in the centre of the Hellenistic mind a 'black hole' had appeared into which the notion of objective Truth and the belief in the Olympian gods were drained away, not to appear again. The lacuna that resulted was filled either with abstract, and therefore, unattractive divinities or with nothing at all. To unsophisticated Hellenes philosophers must have seemed people who shrug their shoulders when confronted with essential questions and who patted one's back with the consoling words that the best thing was not knowing anything at all.

Of course, candidates presented themselves to fill up the gap. The most successful of these, Christianity and the Gnosis, only came forward in Roman times; they therefore fall outside the scope of this volume. They both aspired to quench the thirst for a knowledge that led to salvation; both of them had an explanation for the origin of Evil. They disagreed in this respect that, whereas Christianity was open and ready to accept everyone, the Gnosis was élitist, esoteric, and secretive.

Several factors operated as conducive to the origination of the Gnosis. One of these is the quest for Pleasure; already at this junction it was sometimes rendered as 'salvation'. Then there was the blatant élitism, with the accompanying idea that true knowledge is only the prerogative of the happy few. Another element of this élitism was esoterism, its tendency to keep away from the unknowing multitude; the schools guarded their semi-secret knowledge as a hoard that must not be contaminated by the eyes of the many. It should also be mentioned that the gods and Evil were totally separated from each other. The philosophers did not know how and where Evil originated but, anyhow, not with the gods. Highly important, of course, is that the terms 'knowledge' and 'wisdom' were filled with such a special significance when Truth was mentioned.

16. Dualistic elements

We must not omit paying due attention to the dualistic elements in Hellenistic philosophy. These are, of course, the stock-in-trade of this work, but at the same time they present yet another link with the Gnosis since this ideology, the third component of the western cultural tradition as it is sometimes called, was the most successful and extensive dualistic movement of Antiquity, and perhaps of all times.

First of all, there is the radical separation of the spheres of Pleasure and pain, and second, Posidonius' opposition of body and soul. Fairly general is the incisive difference between the wise and the unwise, between those who know and those who are ignorant, between the happy few and the foolish multitude. We must not forget the dualistic split of the individual mind and objective reality in Stoicism and Scepticism. Finally, it must be pointed out that Xenocrates came very near to a dualistic bipartition of the cosmos into supralunar and sublunar worlds.

The elements that were summed up and shortly described in the foregoing sections do not add up to one coherent ideology, let alone to something like the Gnosis. But let us not forget that, in the course of time, the different doctrines began to resemble each other more and more. If I may use a theatrical metaphor, a player was standing in the wings, waiting for his cue.

We must now see how the Hellenistic world coped with the situation, in particular with regard to religion.

17. What to do with the Olympian gods?

This question was effectively answered by the Hellenistic thinkers who obviously no longer had any use for them. But they offered hardly anything to meet what Festugière calls 'the needs of the spirit in a sophisticated society' [25]. Although the new modes of thought encroached upon the old religion, this was by no means a thing of the past. The public cult in the cities went on for centuries; as we have seen, even the most incredulous scholars took part in it. It was only many centuries after the birth of Christ that Roman emperors abolished the last rituals of the pagan religion. We may be sure that it continued to have many faithful adherents, and not only among the uneducated classes.

Perhaps we may compare the situation to that of Western Europe after the Age of Enlightenment. During the nineteenth century agnosticism and scepticism, later also downright atheism, slowly spread among the educated, and hardly perceptibly filtered downward. It was only in the twentieth century, in particular after World War II, that having no religion at all and not belonging to a church became the rule rather than the exception among all classes (but far less in the USA than in Europe).

In the course of two centuries the new Hellenic way of thought made steady progress. Dodds, for instance, writes that "in third-century Athens a scepticism once confined to intellectuals had begun to affect the general population". However, "while rationalism, of a limited and negative kind, continued to spread from above downwards, antirationalism spreads from below upwards and eventually wins the day". This antirationalism showed itself in a pseudo-scientific literature, the authors of which often claimed to have received a divine revelation [26]. Such 'revelations' formed part of the urge for mysticism.

It was, of course, very difficult for ordinary people, who in every age tend to look up to their more learned contemporaries, to withstand on the long run the onslaught on religion that the scholars had inaugurated. As Nilsson expresses it, "not one stone was left upon another in the edifice of the old religion. It became a total ruin in the Hellenistic period" [27]. The decay of the official religion becomes apparent, for instance, in the loss of the authority of the oracles. The treasure house of the Delphic Oracle was thoroughly looted by the Phocians during the Holy War of 356-346 B.C., a telling proof of profound disrespect. The oracle never recovered from this blow, the more so because it became the mouthpiece of Philip II of Macedonia, and later of several Hellenistic rulers. Of other once famous oracles hardly anything is heard during the subsequent centuries. Probably many of them, like the Oracle of Ammon, no longer existed [28]. That people had stopped consulting the oracles means that they had ceased to have confidence in the gods.

18. Euhemerism

To many citizens it must have seemed that the gods to whom they sacrificed were quite powerless. A clear proof of the decline in the position of the old gods is the spread of an idea that is called 'Euhemerism'.

Euhemerus was a Greek author who is assumed to have lived in the period 340-260 B.C. He came from the town of Messene, either that in the Peloponnese or the one in Sicily. Of his life very little is known [29]. He was a friend of King Cassander of Macedonia (316-297 B.C.). Whether or not he made one or more long voyages by order of this Macedonian king is a matter of conjecture. What is really important is that he wrote a novel of travel, the 'Hiĕra Anagraphĕ', the contents of which are wholly fictitious. Of this book probably appeared around 298 B.C. only fragments remain [30].

The author describes how he, sailing from Arabia through the Indian Ocean, landed on a legendary island with the name of Pancheia. Its inhabitants were very pious people who had dedicated their island to the gods. Situated on the slopes of an exceptionally high hill he found a sanctuary of Zeus Triphylius, erected by the god himself when he lived amongst men and was king of the whole world. Inside the temple stood a pillar of gold with an inscription commemorating the deeds of Uranus, Kronos, and Zeus. Uranus was the first king, Kronos the second, and Zeus the third. Zeus was greatly honoured by everybody and called a god [31].

From this Euhemerus drew the conclusion that the gods had once been human beings who had been deified after their death. He "declared that those counted as gods had been certain men of power, because of which they were deified by the rest and reputed to be gods" [32]. This is the origin of what we call 'Euhemerism', the notion that divine beings were nothing but divinized humans in fact. What Euhemerus did not explain was why people were not content with considering such men as shining examples of humanity but, instead, raised them to a divine status. Where then did this notion of divinity come from?

Euhemerus' idea was not wholly brand-new. Xenophanes and others had already criticized the anthropomorphism of the Hellenic religion [33]; Sophists had brought forward the notion that religion, with its gods, was a human invention [34]. For the Stoa the authentically divine element was the 'pneuma' that permeates the whole world. Not wishing to do away with the old gods entirely, this philosophical school degraded them to a species of subgods, manifestations or aspects of the one pneuma. Many of these subgods were supposed to be deified heroes [35]. The line that runs from Xenophanes to Euhemerus is succinctly sketched by Schippers in this way : from "the gods are far too human" to "the gods are (nothing but) human" [36].

Euhemerism became popular in the Hellenistic world, mainly because it constituted a half-way house between the old, largely disregarded Olympian religion and sheer atheism. As Drachmann states, it was radical in assuming that the Olympian divinities did not exist (as autonomous divine beings). But it softened the blow by declaring that, at least, they had once existed. This scholar says that the theory under consideration "is no doubt the last serious attempt in the old pagan world to give an explanation of the popular faith", although Euhemerism in itself is sheer atheism [37]. We may add that it provided sceptics and unbelievers with a good reason to continue taking part in the official cult.

Euhemerism perhaps proved a sop to sophisticated minds at odds with the old creed but it cannot have been a solace for really religious persons. What Euhemerists offered was in fact a piece of historicism, of the kind that again became popular in the nineteenth century, viz. the notion that religion, its cult and its creed, must be explained historically, its origin, its shape, its modifications all being due to specific, that is entirely human circumstances. For religiously minded persons the gap between what they wanted and what they got was not bridged by Euhemerus but rather widened.

19. The ruler-cult

For Hellenistic rulers, however, the idea of the divinization of human beings came in very handy. If the kings of former times had been deified, why not they themselves too? Someone had to take the place of the old city-gods, and the new rulers were perfectly ready to assume this role. The ruler-cult is yet another token of the individualization and personalizing and, at the same time, the secularization of religion. Let us listen to what the historian Demochares had to tell about the conduct of the Greeks towards Demetrius Poliorcetes, the erratic king of Macedonia (294-287 B.C.) [38].

The Thebans went so far as to erect a temple to Aphrodite Lamia, Lamia being a mistress of Demetrius. The Athenians welcomed him with offerings of incense and processional choruses. They sang and danced repeating the refrain that he was the true god, whereas - and this is extremely revealing for the prevailing state of mind! -"all the others were asleep or making a journey or non-existent". In former times there had been what the Germans call 'Götterburleske', mockery of the gods, [39]. It was, however, quite unprecedented that a whole populace should openly deny the existence of the gods. Demetrius, they sang, "was preeminent in beauty and embracing all in his benevolence".

Duris of Samos, in Book 22 of his 'Historiai' [40], has preserved for us the paean sung in praise of Demetrius [41]. "O son of the most mighty god Poseidon and Aphrodite, hail! For other gods are either far away, or have not ears, or are not (sic!), or heed us not at all; but thee we can see in very presence, not in wood and stone, but in truth, and so we pray to thee." Duris scathingly adds : "This was the song sung by the victors of Marathon, not merely in public, but even in their homes ..., the heroes who had slaughtered countless myriads of barbarians!".

To exonerate Demetrius it must be said that "some of these things ... annoyed him ... (He) was amazed at these actions, and declared that not a single Athenian of his time had shown himself great and fine in soul" [42]. And, indeed, never before had such things happened. Of old a cult like this went against the grain with the Greeks. Heroes, indeed, were deified, but these were legendary persons of long ago. Living men, however famous, could not qualify for divinization. But although Demetrius showed himself somewhat wary of the divine honours bestowed on him ' - probably he was still too much a Hellene of the old block -, the Hellenistic rulers soon enough became quite used to it.

The first sign of what was to come was, of course, the proskunêsis, the prostration demanded by Alexander of all those who ceremoniously approached him, although this was refused by the Macedonians with scorn. Alexander's claim to divinity was based on his contention that the Ammon Oracle had proclaimed him 'Son of Zeus'. The Hellenistic rulers, as the successors of the conqueror, claimed to share not only in his right of conquest but also in his divinity [43]. "The divine right of the founder of the empire devolved on the dominions of the successors" [44].

The ruler-cult was a constitutive characteristic of the Ptolemaic monarchy in Egypt; this will cause no surprise since Egyptian Pharaohs had always been gods. It is also to be found in the Seleucid dynasty; of old Mesopotamian monarchs had shared in the divinity of the celestial beings. Ptolemaeans and Seleucids, therefore, were heirs to an old tradition, but we find it too in Pergamum and elsewhere, even in Macedonia.

One remark is necessary here. It is possible that these monarchs were not considered gods in the fullest sense of the word. A title like 'epiphanes' would rather say that its bearer was a manifestation of the godhead and its excellency - this always with the exception of Egypt.

Summing up, Wilamowitz does not ascribe much positive value to the ruler-cult. This scholar thinks that 'theos' was rather a title (like 'Holy Father') than the expression of a full divine status [45]. But there was a strongly negative side to it - negative from the standpoint of true religion. Men were seen as equal to the gods, and these human beings were not holy, ascetic, prophetic persons but cruel, greedy, and arbitrary potentates. This might elevate the rulers but by the same token it was a slight on the gods [46]. Another negative aspect is that the "ruler-cult ... (is) primarily ... (an) expression of helpless dependence; he who treats another human being as divine thereby assigns to himself the relative status of a child or an animal" [47].

20. Tychè, the new goddess

The demise of the Olympians left room for other divinities and an alternative religion. "It was", as Drachmann remarks, " as if the old gods could not keep pace with (the) violent process of expansion" [48]. A new goddess stepped into the empty circle driving the old gods still further back. She was Tychè, or Fate. She brought a few advantages with her that were dear to the people of the Hellenistic age. She presented, to quote Drachmann again, "a wider and more comprehensive religious concept to answer the changed conditions" [49]. And further, Fate seemed to be able to fit into a more or less understandable pattern happenings at once unexpected and inexplicable .

She was, of course, not wholly new. Of old, even the Olympians had been somewhat scared of her [50]. When we are reading Thucydides who did not allow the gods to play a role of any importance in the events of his day, we get the impression that to him the dominating factor was Fate [51]. But one result of the disorder prevailing in the Hellenistic world "is the sudden and enormous spread of Fortune" [52]. There is every reason for speaking of a Hellenistic Tychè-religion.

Let us call upon Pliny the Elder to take the floor since he, probably drawing on Hellenistic sources, gives a fine description of the state of affairs, even if we admit that there is Plinian rhetoric in it [53]. He begins with stating that the Tychè-religion occupied an intermediate position between belief in the traditional gods and sheer atheism or indifference. He then continues like this. "Everywhere in the whole world at every hour by all men's voices Fortune alone is invoked and named, alone accused, alone impeached, alone pondered, alone applauded, alone rebuked and visited with reproaches; deemed volatile and indeed by most men blind as well, wayward, inconstant, uncertain, fickle in her favours and favouring the unworthy. To her is debited all that is spent and credited all that is received, she alone fills both pages in the whole of mortals' account; and we are so much at the mercy of chance that Chance herself", - and now follow the really revealing words - "by whom God is proved uncertain, takes the place of God" [54]. Even when religious thought seems to take a monotheistic turn and to assume an highly personal tone, as is the case in Cleanthes' great 'Hymn to Zeus' [55], in yet another Cleanthes-text it appears that, after all, Zeus is put on a par with Destiny and even identified with it. "Lead me, o Zeus, lead me, thou Destiny, by whatsoever path you have ordained. I will not flinch" [56].

What Pliny wrote is strikingly illustrated by Polybius the historian (ca. 200-ca.118 B.C.). He concludes the long exposition of the plan of his work with the following words. "Such is the plan I propose, but all depends on Fortune granting me a life long enough to execute it" [57]. There is no invocation of the gods. But it is not only Polybius as a private person who honoured Fortune, as an historian too he wants to be her servant. "Fortune having guided almost all the affairs of the world in one direction and having forced them to incline towards one and the same end (i.e. the establishment of the Roman Empire), a historian should bring before his readers under one synoptical view the operations by which she has accomplished her general purpose" [58]. What a windfall for an historian that Fortune was kind enough to map out his route so neatly!

It is, of course, not accidental that a Tychê-cult originated in the fourth century B.C. Very probably the first temple dedicated to her was erected in Thebes when Epaminondas in 371 had crushed the Spartan phalanx, obviously an incredible piece of luck [59]. We hear that in the year 334/333 B.C. the Athenians offered a sacrifice to Agathê Tychê, the Good Fate. Slowly but certainly her cult gained ground and became general. She not only was a general divinity but also became city-goddess of many towns and a personal one for countless individuals, in this sense that many people believed that they had their own Tychê [60].

But once again it must be doubted whether Tychê was capable of alleviating the cravings of the really religious soul. Although she could act as a personal goddess, she was essentially an abstract, impersonal deity. And she was utterly unreliable! We heard what Pliny had to say of her and her fickleness.

21. Faith in the stars

Then there was astrology. In the same text that I cited already Pliny goes on in this way. "Another set of people banishes Fortune also, and attributes events to its star and to the laws of birth (i.e. to the constellation at the moment of one's birth), holding that for all men that ever are to be God's decree has been enacted once for all, while for the rest of time leisure has been vouchsafed to him. This belief begins to take root, and the learned and unlearned mob alike go marching towards it at the double" [61]. Please take note that astrology assigns only a minimal role to the godhead!

There had always been some astrology in the Greek world but its full deployment only came in the second century B.C. The fact that Babylonia where from time immemoria astrology had been at home, had for a considerable period formed part of the Hellenistic world may have meant something in this respect. In the general climate of instability that characterized the later stages of the Hellenistic period, it must have been a consolation for many people that at least the heavenly bodies followed fixed and preordained courses. And these courses were calculable! Small wonder that many hoped and believed that such utterly reliable phenomena - far more reliable than Fate! - had a decisive influence both on the course of events and on the lives of individuals.

22. Astrology as a pseudo-religion

Just as a religious or quasi-religious faith in the goddess Tychê, astrology was a form of fatalism and determinism. It was for this reason that Dodds wrote his section on astrology under the chapter-heading of 'The

Fear of Freedom'. It was only around 280 B.C. that the Greeks became acquainted with it by means of the work of Berossus. Berossus (or Berosus) was a Babylonian and a Baal-priest who, during the reign of Antiochus I (281-261 B.C.), wrote a chronicle of Babylonian history in three books, called the 'Babyloniaca' or 'Chaldaeica' [62]. This book contained a good deal of astrology but did not cause 'any great excitement' [63]. It was effectively countered by the prevailing scepticism and by the criticisms of Carneades [64].

But a hundred years later the idea suddenly began to spread like wildfire. The second century spawned an imposing series of astrological handbooks, for instance, 'The Revelations of Nechepso and Petosiris', the 'astrologers' Bible' [65]. Dodds gives us the reasons why it happened 'then and not sooner'. The first reason is to be found in the political conditions. "In that troubled half-century that preceded the Roman conquest of Greece, it was particularly important to know what was going to happen." The second reason is that "for a century or more the individual had been face to face with his own intellectual freedom, and now he turned tail and bolted from the horrid prospect - better the rigid determinism of the astrological fate than that terrifying burden of daily responsibility" [66].

23. Occultism

Yet another irrational doctrine, occultism, was closely linked with astrology, and connected with magical medicine and alchemy. Its basis was the Stoic notion of the organic unity of all that exists. This means that there was also a connection, a 'sympathy', between the stars and nature. "Each planet had its representative in the animal, vegetable, and mineral kingdoms" [67]. But whereas the celestial bodies were cold, immovable, and indifferent to prayer, the natural world could be manipulated by means of magic. The theory was that occult forces were at home in plants and animals and other natural objects.

The great prophet of this new pseudo-science was another charlatan of the kind that proliferated in the last two centuries before the

Christian era, a certain Bolos the Democritean who came from Mendes in the Egyptian Delta. He wrote his many works around 200 B.C. and published them under the pseudonym of 'Democritus'. The genre became highly popular; many others followed in his footsteps [68]. In the first century B.C. Bolos became the great authority on natural science and was considered the equal of Aristotle.

For the connection between the decline of rationalism and true science on the one hand, and the rise of occultism and obscurantism, and at the same time the origination of the Gnosis, on the other, we should closely attend to what Festugière has to say on this point. "This decadence of the scientific spirit had as its corollary ... the growth, not of true piety ..., but rather an exaltation of piety, and something like a perversion of piety ... By a fatal reaction, Greek rationalism, after having ruined its own fundament, now reposed in the irrational, in something that was above, or below, or at least beyond the scope of reason, on the level of mystical intuition, or of theosophical mysteries, or of the fascination of magic, and often of all of these together" [69].

24. Conclusion

There was a good deal of dualism in the new mentality. God and nature had grown very far apart, since Nature had come to be seen as an assembly of occult forces that could be manipulated by man. A great distance had arisen between rational science and philosophy on one side, and, on the other, the new pseudo-science that reached even greater proportions in the hands of freaks and fantasts. Logic and reason seemed to have been banished from human considerations, to be replaced by intuition, arbitrariness, and sheer phantasy.

But the most important ingredient of this increasing dualism was the sentiment that the cosmos was splitting up into supralunar and sublunar worlds. Between these worlds an enormous difference in quality existed, the sublunar being evil and utterly contrasted to the sublime higher world. The climactic question for countless people became : how to set oneself free from this evil world [70]. To many anguished persons their world seemed such an awful mess that they desired to escape from it.

NOTES TO CHAPTER IV

1. For this subject see the fascinating work by Ballabriga, Le soleil (bibliography).
2. Murray, Five Stages 106.
3. Burckhardt, Gr.Kult.gesch. IV 443.
4. Burckhardt, Gr.Kult.gesch.
5. Pol., 1.3.3-4.
6. Loenen, Mens en cultuur 92.
7. Burckhardt, Gr.Kult.gesch. IV, 450/451.
8. Pol. I.3.3-4.
9. Bradford 556.
10. Augustus Nauck, Tragicorum Graecorum Fragmenta. Leipzig, 1889 2 (1856 1).
11. Lesky, Gesch.gr.Lit. 678-680.
12. See Vol. III, Ch. I.7.
13. Lesky, Gesch.gr.Lit. 680/681.
14. These fragments were first edited by Augustus Meineke, Fragmenta Comicorum Graecorum. Berlin, 1839-1857 (photostatic reprint Berlin 1970), then by Theodorus Kock, Comicorum Atticorum Fragmenta. Leipzig, 1880-1888, and finally by John Maxwell Edmonds, The Fragments of Attic Comedy. Leiden, 1957-1961.
15. Rose, Handbook 242.
16. Rose, Handbook 242/243.
17. 'The Arbitrants', 'The Girl from Samos'. 'The Girl who gets her hair cut short', 'The Hero', 'The Peevish Fellow'. A Greek edition is that by F.H.Sandbach, Menandri Reliquiae selectae. Oxford, 1972. There are two Loeb Classical editions : 1. Menander. The Principal Fragments. Ed. Francis G. Allinson. Cambridge (Mass)-London, 1964; 2. Menander. Ed. W.G. Arnott. Cambridge (Mass)-London (Vol. I 1979).
18. Rose, Handbook 246.
19. Lesky, Gesch.gr.Lit 700.
20. Dodds, Gr. and Irr. 238.
21. Arnim, SVF I 146 = Epiphanius adv.haer. 3.2.9.
22. Dodds, Gr. and Irr. 238.

23. Dodds, Gr. and Irr. 240.
24. Zeller, Phil.d.Gr. III.1, 218/219.
25. Festugière, Vie spir. ..
26. Dodds, Gr. and Irr. 245.
27. Nilsson, Hist.Gr.Rel. 201..
28. Drachmann, Atheism 96/97.
29. We find all we want to know in the doctoral thesis of my compatriot Herman Franke van der Meer, Euhemeros van Messene. Amsterdam, 1949.
30. Published by G. Vallauri, Euhemero di Messene con introduzione e commentario, 1956, and earlier in FrGHist I 63 (p. 300-313).
31. Fr.GH. I 63F2 = Diod.6.1.
32. FrGH I 63T4b = Sext.math.9.51.
33. See Vol.I, Ch.II.7.
34. See Vol.III, Ch.II.2d.
35. A useful summary of older opinions is to be found in the doctoral thesis of my compatriot J.W. Schippers, De ontwikkeling der euhemerische godencritiek in de Christelijke Latijnse literatuur (with an English summary). Groningen/Djakarta, 1952.
36. Schippers, Ontw. 1.
37. Drachmann, Atheism 112/113.
38. A fragment of Democrates' 'Historiai', Bk. 20 and 22, is quoted by Theopompus in his 'Hellenica', Bk. 9, quoted in his turn by Ath., Deipn. 6.253 = FHG (Müller) II.449.
39. See Vol.I, Ch.IV.5.
40. Quoted by Ath., Deipn. 6.253 = FHG (Müller) II.476/477.
41. The author of the hymn was the poet Hermocles.
42. Demochares 20 = Ath., Deipn, 6.253 = FHG (Müller) II.449.
43. Bianchi, Rel.gr. 289/290.
44. Kaerst, Gesch.d.Hell.II, Beilage V, 380.
45. Wilamowitz, Glaube der Hell. II, 269.
46. Wilamowitz, Glaube der Hell. II, 270.
47. Dodds, Gr. and Irr. 242.
48. Drachmann, Atheism 93.
49. Drachmann, Atheism 93.
50. See Vol.I, Ch.IV.3.
51. See Vol.II, Ch.III.1.i.
52. Murray, Five stages 165.
53. Drachmann, Atheism 95.
54. Pliny, NH 2.5.22.

55. SVF (Arnim) I.537.
56. SVF (Arnim) I.527. 'Destiny' is R.D.Hicks' translation of the Greek 'peproomenē', from the verb 'poroo'; this form indeed means 'ordained, fated, destined. See for the role of Tychē also Greene, Moira, Ch. XX Fate and Providence.
57. Pol. 3.5.7.
58. Pol.1.4.1.
59. See Vol.II, Ch.II.4f.
60. See for this passage Wilamowitz, Glaube der Hell. II,298-309, and Kern, Rel.d.Gr. III, 74-78.
61. Pliny, NH 2.5.23.
62. Schwartz s.v. 'Berossos', PW III (1899), 309-316.
63. Dodds, Gr. and Irr. 245.
64. Des Places, Rel.gr. 282.
65. Dodds, Gr. and irr. 245.
66. Dodds, Gr. and Irr. 246.
67. Dodds, Gr. and Irr. 247.
68. Festugière, Rév. I, 196-200.
69. Festugière, Rév. I, 5 and 13.
70. Dodds, Gr. and Irr. 248.

APPENDIX A

PLUTARCH, DE ISIDE ET OSIRIDE
Isis and Osiris. Translated by Frank C. Babbitt. Moralia VI. Loeb Classical Libary 306. 4th impression. London/Cambridge (Mass.), 1936 1.

351F-352A. "Isis is a Greek word, and so also is Typhon, her enemy, who is conceited, as his name implies, because of his ignorance and self-deception. He tears to pieces and scatters to the winds the sacred writings, which the goddess collects and puts together ... The name of her shrine also promises knowledge and comprehension of reality."
355F "On the third day Typhon was born, but not in due season or manner, but with a blow on his mother's side and leapt forth."
361D "Prompted by jealousy and hostility, (Typhon) wrought terrible deeds and, by bringing utter confusion on all things, filled the whole Earth, and the ocean as well, with ills ..."
363D "Some relate that, after his escape (from Egypt), (Typhon) became the father of sons, Hierosolymus and Judaeus, ... attempting to drag Jewish traditions into the legend." (Tac., Hist. 5.2 "Some hold that in the reign of Isis the superfluous population of Egypt, under the leadership of Hierosolymus and Judaeus, discharged itself on the neighbouring lands.")
363D "Let us now begin over again, and consider first the most perspicuous of those who have a reputation for expounding matters more philosophically ... And thus among the Egyptians such men say that Osiris is the Nile consorting with the Earth, which is Isis, and the sea is Typhon into which the Nile discharges its waters and is lost to view and dissipated, save for that part which the earth takes and thereby becomes fertilized."
363E "The Nile ... which runs from the south and is swallowed by the seas in the north, is naturally said to have its birth on the left (= the south) and its dissolution on the right (= the north). For this reason the priests religiously keep themselves aloof from the sea, and call the sea 'the spume of Typhon', and one of the things forbidden to them is to set salt on the table ..."
364A "But the wiser of the priests call not only the Nile Osiris and the sea Typhon, but they simply give the name of Osiris to the whole source and faculty creative of moisture, believing this to be the cause of generation and the substance of life-producing seed; and the name of Typhon they give to all that is dry, fiery, and arid in general and antagonistic ('polemion')."
367C-D "The Egyptians ... think that by Typhon is meant the solar world, and by Osiris the lunar world; they reason that the moon ... has a light that is generative and productive of moisture ... The Egyptians regularly call Typhon 'Seth' which, being interpreted, means 'overmastering and compelling'."
368A "The terrestrial universe ('perigeios kosmos') ... is never completely exempt either from dissolution or from generation."
369A "The origins of the universe are not to placed in inanimate bodies, according to the doctrines of Democritus and Epicurus, nor is the Artificer of undifferentiated matter, according to Stoic doctrine, one

Reason and one Providence which gains the upperhand and prevails over all things." (Vide DL 7.134 on the active and passive principles).
369B-E "It can be traced to no source, but it carried a strong and almost indelible conviction, and is in circulation among barbarians and Greeks alike, not only in story and tradition but also in rites and sacrifices, to the effect that the Universe is not of itself suspended aloft without sense or reason or guidance, nor is there one Reason which rules and guides it by rudders as it were, or by controlling reins but inasmuch as Nature brings, in this life of ours, many experiences in which both good and evil are commingled, or better, to put it very simply, Nature brings nothing which is not combined with something else. We may assert that it is not the keeper of two great vases (vide II.24.527-528) who, after the manner of a barmaid, deals out to us our failures and successes in mixture but it has come about as the result of two opposed principles and two antagonistic forces, one of which guides us along a straight course to the right while the other turns us aside and backward, and so is also the universe, and if this is not true of the whole of it, yet it is true that this terrestrial universe, including the moon as well, is irregular and variable and subject to all manner of changes. For it is the law of Nature that nothing comes into being without a cause, and if the good cannot provide for us a cause for evil, then it follows that Nature must have in herself the source and origin of evil, just as she contains the source and origin of good. The great majority and the wisest of men hold this opinion : they believe that there are two gods, rivals as it were, the one the Artificer of good, and the other of evil. There are also those who call the better one a god and the other a daemon, as, for example, Zoroaster the Magos ..."

APPENDIX B

HYDE, Thomas
HISTORIA RELIGIONIS VETERUM PERSARUM, EORUMQUE MAGORUM. Oxonii, MDCC.

Cap. IX Persarum principia duo, unum aeternum, alterum creatum : cum utriusque nominibus. Haec Zoroastres vocavit Lucem & Tenebras.
163 "Autor magis accurate distinguendo, exponit quod ... secundum opinionem ... magorum **dualistarum**, apud quos horum prior habetur ... Agens Bonum ... posterior .. Agens Malum."
164 "Dualistas meliore sensu accipit laudatus autor : nam alias dualistas diaboli coëternitatem afferunt. Sunt enim ex Indo-Peris & dualistis Manichaeis aliisque haereticis ... qui opinantur diabolum a seipso procecisse ... i.e. aeternum fuisse, & malos angelos sibi creasse; sed est Haeretica opinio, eaque ignorantium quorundam hominum qui peculiariter vocantur ... Thanavia, i.e. dualistas seu ... domini duorum scil. assertores seu autores duorum principiorum; qui Lucem & Tenebras seu Deum & Diabolum statuunt duo principia coëterna."

BAYLE, Pierre
DICTIONNAIRE HISTORIQUE ET CRITIQUE

ed. 1697 1 : no entry
ed. 1702 2 3079/3080 s.v. 'Zoroastre' quotes "Mr. Hyde dans son excellent traité de la religion des ancients Perses", then gives 3081 Note F, Nr. V, Hyde's words "Dualistas diaboli ... principia coëterna", and goes on to say "Je vais citer ce qui concerne les dualistes qui tiennent encore la coëternité du diable, et qui demandent d'une manière très importune d'où le mal a pu venir, si le mauvais principe n'est pas éternel?".

LEIBNIZ, Gottfried Wilhelm von
THEODICEE. Essais sur la bonté de Dieu, la liberté de l'homme, et l'origine du mal. 1710.

Partie II, par. 136 :... Zoroastre avait enseigné ... de deux principes intelligents de toutes choses, l'un bon, l'autre mauvais."
par. 137 "Il paraît qu'il considérait la lumière comme le bon principe; mais il ajoutait le mauvais, c'est à dire l'opacité, les ténèbres, le froid."
par. 138 (quoting Hyde) "Les deux principes (sc. of Zoroaster) ont partagé l'empire du monde."
par. 144 "Il (Bayle) avoue que les dualistes (comme il les appelle avec M.Hyde), c'est à dire les défenseurs de deux principes, auraient bientôt été mis en fuite par des raisons a priori, prises de la nature de Dieu, mais il s'imagine qu'ils triomphent à leur tour quand on vient aux raisons a posteriori, prises de l'existence du mal."
par. 152 "M. Bayle fait combattre Mélisse, philosophe grec, défenseur de l'unité de principe, et peut-être même de l'unité de substance, avec Zoroastre, comme avec le premier auteur de la dualité."

WOLFF, Christian
PSYCHOLOGIA RATIONALIS. 1734.

Sect. I, Cap. I, par. 39 "Dualistae sunt, qui & substantiarum materialium, & immaterialium existentiam admittunt, hoc est, & corporibus realem extra ideas animarum concedunt, & animarum immaterialitatem defendunt. Communem esse hanc sententiam, quae inter nos obtinet, nemo ignorat, ut **Dualismus** sit dominans & Monismus ideo exosus habeatur."
par. 43 "Dualistae sunt philosophi dogmatici ... Dualistae affirmant animam esse substantialem immaterialem a corpore prorsus diversam & corpora extra ideas ejus realem existentiam habere ... Dogmatici vel monistae sunt, vel dualistae." (Par. 40 "Dogmatici sunt qui veritatis universales defendunt, seu quid affirmant, vel negant vel negant in universali." Par. 32 "Monistae dicuntur philosophi, qui unum tantum modo substantiae genus admittunt.")
Sect. III, Cap. I, par. 555 "Commercium animae et corporis dari admisso dualismo certum est."
Sect. IV, Cap. I, par. 665 "Propositionis hujus praeclarus est usus in defendenda autoritate scripturae sanctae, quae spiritus contingentis dari & eos ortum suum a Deo ducere docet. Utilis etiam est ad evertendum principia atheismi, cum athei dualistae vel idealistae animas spiritus

necessarios faciant, quod earum ortus distincta notione explicare non valeant."

ENCYCLOPÉDIE, OU DICTIONNAIRE RAISONNÉ DES SCIENCES, DES ARTS ET DES MÉTIERS
Ed. D.Diderot. Tome V. Paris, 1755.

1151/1152 "Dualisme ou Dithéisme : (Théol) Opinion qui suppose deux principes, deux dieux, deux êtres, indépendens & non créés, dont on regarde l'un comme principe du bien & l'autre comme principe du mal ... La première origine de ce système vient de la difficulté d'expliquer l'existence du mal dans le monde ... Cet article est pour la grand partie tiré des papiers de M.Formey, historiographe de l'Académie Royale de Prusse."

KANT, Immanuel
KRITIK DER REINEN VERNUNFT. 1781.

A367 "Nun sind alle äusseren Erscheinungen von der Art : dass ihr Dasein nicht unmittelbar wahrgenommen werden kann, sondern auf sie, als die Ursache gegebener Wahrnehmungen, allein geschlossen werden kann : also ist das Dasein aller Gegenstände zweifelhaft. Die Ungewissenheit nenne ich die Idealität äusserer Erscheinungen und die Lehre dieser Idealität heisst Idealism, in Vergleichung mit welchem die Behauptung einer möglichen Gewissheit von Gegenständen äusserer Sinne, der Dualism genannt wird."

BIBLIOGRAPHY

I ORIGINAL SOURCES

A COLLECTIONS

FRAGMENTA COMICORUM GRAECORUM. Berlin, 1839-1857 (photostatic reprint Berlin, 1970).

COMICORUM ATTICORUM FRAGMENTA. Ed. Th. Kock. III. Leipzig, 1880-1888.

THE FRAGMENTS OF ATTIC COMEDY. Ed. John Maxwell Edmonds. Leiden, 1957-1961.

DOXOGRAPHI GRAECI, coll. H. Diels. Berlin, 1958 3 (photostatic) reprint of first edition 1879).

FRAGMENTA HISTORICORUM GRAECORUM, ed. Carolus Müllerus. Vol. II. Parisiis, MDCCCXLVIII (cited as FrHG).

TRAGICORUM GRAECORUM FRAGMENTA. Ed. Augustus Nauck. Leipzig, 1889 2 (1856 1).

DIE FRAGMENTE ZUR DIALEKTIK DER STOIKER. Neue Sammlung der Texte mit deutscher Übersetzung und Kommentar. 4 vols. Ed. Karlheinz Hülser. Stuttgart/Bad Canstatt, 1987-1988.

DIE GEOGRAPHISCHEN FRAGMENTE DES ERATOSTHENES, ed. Hugo Berger. Amsterdam, 1964.

THE HELLENISTIC PHILOSOPHERS. Vol. I Translations of the principal sources with philosophical commentary. Edited by A.A. Long and D.W. Sedley. Cambridge (UP), 1987.

HISTORIKER, DIE FRAGMENTE DER GRIECHISCHEN --, herausgegeben von Felix Jacoby. Teil IIB. Berlin, 1929 (cited as FGH).

STOICORUM VETERUM FRAGMENTA, collegit Joannes ab Arnim. 4 vols. Stuttgart 1968 (photostatic reprint of first edition 1924).

SUIDAE LEXICON, ed. A. Adler II. Leipzig, 1931.

VOGEL, Cornelia de, Greek Philosophy. A Collection of Texts with notes and explanations. Vol. III The Hellenistic-Roman Period. Leiden, 1959.

DIE FRAGMENTE DER VORSOKRATIKER. Griechisch und Deutsch von Hermann Diels. Herausgegeben von Walther Kranz. Vol. I. Unveränderter Nachdruck der sechsten Auflage 1951 (1903 1). Vol. II. Unveränderter Nachdruck der sechsten Auflage 1952. (Cited as DK).

B INDIVIDUAL AUTHORS

AELIAN
On the Characteristics of Animals. Vol. III. Translated by A.F. Schofield. Loeb Classical Library 449. London/Cambridge (Mass.), 1959.

ALEXANDER APHRODISIACUS
De Fato. Translation by R.W. Sharpless of Alexander of Aphrodisias, On Fate. London, 1983.

APPIAN
Roman History, with a translation by Horace White. Loeb Classical Library 2 and 3. London/Cambridge (Mass.), 1955 (1912 1) (contains also The Syrian Wars).

ARISTOTLE
De anima. With an English translation by W.S. Hett. Loeb Classical Library 288. Cambridge (Mass.)/London, 1975 (1936 1).
Ars rhetorica. Ed. Adolphus Roemer. Lipsiae, 1898.
De caelo. With an English translation by W.K.C. Guthrie. Loeb Classical Library 338. London/Cambridge (Mass.), 1971 (1939 1).
Metaphysica. Metaphysics. With an English translation by H. Tredennick. Loeb Classical Library, 271 and 287. London/Cambridge (Mass.), 1975 and 1979.
De generatione et corruptione. Translated by E.S. Forster. Loeb Classical Library 400. Cambridge (Mass.)/London, 1978 (1955 1).
Nicomachean Ethics. Translated by H.R. Rackham. Loeb Classical Library 73. London/Cambridge (Mass.), 1975 (1926 1).
Physics I. With an English translation by Philip H. Wicksteed and Francis M. Cornford. Loeb Classical Library 228. Cambridge (Mass.)/London, 1970 (1929 1).

ARRIAN
Anabasis of Alexander. Translated by P.A. Brunt. Loeb Classical Library 236 and 269. London/Cambridge (Mass.), 1976 and 1983 4.

ATHENAEUS
The Deipnosophists. Translated by Charles Burton Gulick. Loeb Classical Library . London/Cambridge (Mass), 1928 1.

CICERO
Academica. Translated by H. Rackham. Loeb Classical Library 268. London, 1961 7 (1933 1).
Ad Atticum. Translated by E.O. Winstedt. Loeb Classical Library 97. London/Cambridge (Mass.), 1918 1.
De divinatione. Translated by W.A. Falconer. Loeb Classical Library 154. London/Cambridge (Mass.), 1923 1.
De Fato. Translated by H. Rackham. Loeb Classical Library 348. London/Cambridge (Mass.), 1942 1.
De finibus. Translated by H. Rackham. Loeb Classical Library 40. London/Cambridge (Mass.), 1914 1.
De legibus. Translated by Clinton W. Keyes. Loeb Classical Library 213. London/Cambridge (Mass.), 11970 9 (1928 1).
De natura deorum. Translated by H. Rackham. Loeb Classical Library 268. London/Cambridge (Mass.), 1933 1.
De officiis. Translated by Walter Miller. Loeb Classical Library 30. London/Cambridge (Mass.), 1913 1.
De Oratore. Translated by E.W. Sutton and H. Rackham. Loeb Classical Library 348. London/Cambridge (Mass.), 1942 1.
Cicéron. Les Paradoxes des Stoïciens. Ed. Jean Molager. Paris, 1971.
De Re Publica. Translated by Clinton W. Keyes. Loeb Classical Library 213. London/Cambridge (Mass.), 1970 9 (1928 1).
Tusculan Disputations. Translated by J.E. King. Loeb Classical Library 141. London/Cambridge (Mass.), 1945 6 (1927 1).

CLEMENS OF ALEXANDRIA
Stromata. Les Stromates. Texte et traduction de Marcel Casier and others. Series : Sources chrétiennes 38, 278, 279. Paris, 1954-1981.

CURTIUS Rufus, Quintus
Geschichte Alexanders des Grossen. Ed. Konrad Müller. Deutsche Übersetzung Herbert Schönfeld. München, 1954.

DEMOCRITUS
Salomo Luria, Democritea. Leningrad, 1970.

DIO CHRYSOSTOMUS
Discourses Vol. II Translated by J.W. Cohoon. Loeb Classical Library 339. London/Cambridge (Mass.), 1961 (1939 1).

DIODORUS SICULUS
Library of History Vol. IX. With an English translation by Russell M. Geer. Loeb Classsical Library 377. London/Cambridge (Mass.), 1967.
Vol. XI. Translated by Francis R. Walton. Loeb Classical Library 409. London/Cambridge (Mass.), 1957.
Vol. XII. Translated by Francis R. Walton. Loeb Classical Library 423. London/Cambridge (Mass.), 1967.

EPICTETUS
The Encheiridion. Translated by W.A. Oldfather. Loeb Classical Library 218. London/Cambridge (Mass.), 1928 1.

EPICURUS
Jean Bollack, La pensée du plaisir. Épicure : textes moraux, commentaires. Collection Sens commun. Éditions du minuit (1978).

EUHEMERUS
G. Vallauri, Euhemero di Messene. Con introduzione e commentario. 1956.

EUSEBIUS OF CAESAREA
Praeparatio evangelica. La préparation évangélique. Ed. Jean Sirinelli and others. Series : Sources chrétiennes 206, 228, 262. Paris, 1974-1979.

GELLIUS, Aulus
Noctes Atticae. The Attic Nights of --. Ed. John C. Rolfe. Vol. II. Loeb Classical Library 200. Cambridge (Mass.)/London, 1948 (1927 1).

HIPPOLYTUS
Philosophoumena, or Refutatio omnium haeresium. Ed. Miroslav Marcovich. Series : Patristische Texte und Studien. Bd. 25. Berlin/New York, 186.

ISOCRATES
Antidotis. Isocrates II. Ed. George Nolin. Loeb Classical Library. London/Cambridge (Mass.). 1962 (1929 1).

JOSEPHUS, Flavius
Vol. II and III. The Jewish War. Translated by H.St.J. Thackeray. Loeb Classical Library 203 and 219. London/Cambridge (Mass.), 1927 and 1928 5.
Vol. VII Jewish Antiquities. Translated by Ralph Marcus. Loeb Classical Library 365. London/Cambridge (Mass.), 1943 6.

JUSTINUS
Justini Epitoma historiarum Philippicarum Pompei Trogi. Ed. F. Ruehl. Bibliotheca Teubneriana. Leipzig, 1886.

LACTANTIUS
Divinarum Institutionem Liber III. Ed. J.C. Firmiani. Paris, 1836.

LIVY
Vol. VIII. Translated by F.G. Moore. Loeb Classical Library 381. London/Cambridge (Mass.), 1949 5.
Vol. IX. Translated by Evan T. Sage. Loeb Classical Library 295. London/Cambridge (Mass.), 1935 5.
Vol. XII. Translated by E.T. Sage and A.C. Schlesinger. Loeb Classical Library 332. London/Cambridge (Mass.), 1938 5.

LUCRETIUS
De rerum natura. Ed. W.H. Rouse. Revised by Martin Ferguson Smith. Loeb Classical Library 181. Cambridge (Mass.)/London, 1975 (1924 1).

MELISSUS
Melisso. Testimonianze e frammenti. A cura di Giovanni Reale. Biblioteca di Studi Superiori L. Firenze (1970).

MENANDER
Menandri reliquiae selectae. Ed. F.H. Sandbach. Oxford, 1972.
Menander. Translated by W.G. Arnott. Loeb Classical Library 132 etc. London/Cambridge (Mass.), 1979 (replacing the edition 1921 1 in LCL by F.C. Allinsor).

MINUCIUS FELIX, Marcus
Octavius. Translated by G.H. Rendall. Loeb Classical Library 230. London/Cambridge (Mass.), 1931 1.

PANAETIUS
Panaetii Rhodii fragmenta collegit tertioque edidit Modestus van Straaten. Editio amplificata. Leiden (1962). (This is an enlarged edition of the same collection that was published in 1952.)

PAUSANIAS
Description of Greece Vol. I and IV. Translated by W.H.S. Jones and H.A. Ormerod. Loeb Classical Library 93 (1918 7) and 297 (1935 5). LondonCambridge (Mass.).

PHILODEMUS
Volumina rhetorica. Ed. Siegfried Sudhaus. 1892 1 (reprographischer Nachdruck Amsterdam, 1964).

PLATO
The Republic. Translated by Paul Shorey. Loeb Classical Library 237 and 276. London/Cambridge (Mass.), 1969 and 1070 (1930 and 1935 1).
Epinomis. Ed. Edouard des Places, Platon. Oeuvres complètes. Vol. XII. Paris, 1956.

PLINIUS
Natural History
Vol.II Translated by H. Rackham. Loeb Classical Library 352. London/Cambridge (Mass.), 1942 4.

PLUTARCH
Moralia. Translated by Frank C. Babbitt.
Vol. I 1. De recta ratione audiendi. 2. Quomodo quis suos in virtute sentiat progressus. Loeb Classical Library 197. London/Cambridge (Mass.), 1960 (1927 1).
Vol. IV On the Fortune or Virtue of Alexander the Great. Loeb Classiccal Library 305. London/Cambridge, 1936 4.

Vol. V De defectu oraculorum. Loeb Classical Library 306. London/ Cambridge (Mass.), 1957 (1936 1).
Vol. VI On Moral Virtue. Translated by W.C. Helmbold. Loeb Classical Library 337. London/Cambridge (Mass)., 1939 1.
Vol. X Translated by H.N. Fowler. Loeb Classical Library 321. London/Cambridge (Mass.), 1936 4.
Vol. XI De placitis philosophorum. Translated by Lionel Person and P.H. Sandbach. Loe Classical Library 426. London/Cambriidge (Mass.), 1965.
Vol. XIII Part 1. On the Generation of the Soul in the Timaeus. 2. Platonic Questions. Translated by Harold Cherniss. Loeb Classical Library 427. London, 1967. Part 2. De Stoicorum repugnantiis. Compendium argumenti stoicos absurdiora de communibus dicere. Notitiis adversus Stoicos. Translated by Harold Cherniss. Loeb Classical Library 470. Cambridge (Mass.)/London, 1976.
Vol. XIV 1. Adversus Colotem. 2. That Epicurus actually makes a pleasant Life impossible. Translated by Benedict Einarson and Philip de Lacy. Loeb Classical Library 428. London/Cambridge (Mass.), 1967.
The Parallel Lives. Translated by B. Perrin.
Vol. II Cato Major. Loeb Classical Library 47. London/Cambridge (Mass.), 1914 1.
Vol. VI Aemilius Paulus. Loeb Classical Library 98. London/Cambridge (Mass.), 1918 5.
Vol. VII Alexander. Loeb Classial Library 99. London/Cambridge (Mass.), 1919 6.
Vol. VIII. Eumenes. Loeb Classical Library 100. London/Cambridge (Mass.), 1919 4.
Vol. IX Demetrius, Pyrrhus. Loeb Classical Library 101. London/ Cambridge (Mass)., 1959 (1920 1).
Vol. XI Aratus. Loeb Classical Library 103. London/Cambridge (Mass.), 1926 5.

POLYBIUS
The Histories. Translated by W.R. Paton. Loeb Classical Library. London/Cambridge (Mass.).

PORPHYRIUS
Porphyrius ad Marcellam. Porphyrii opuscula selecta. Ed. A. Nauck. Leipzig, 1886.

POSIDONIUS
Posidonii Rhodii reliquae doctrinae. Ed. Janus Bake. Lugdunis Batavorum (Leiden), 1810 (photostatic reprint Osnabrück, 1972).

PROCLUS
A Commentary on the First Book of Euclid's Elements. Translated by Glenn R. Morrow. Princeton NJ, 1970.
In Platonis Rem publicam commentarii. Ed. W. Kroll. Amsterdam, 1965.
De Providentia et Fato. Procli philosophi opera inedita. Ed. Victor Cousin. Parisiis, 1864 (unveränderter Nachdruck. Frankfurt a.M.,).

PYRRHO
Fernando Decleva Caizzi, Pirrone. Testimonianze, a cura di --. Series Elenchos V. 'Bibliopolis' (1981).

SENECA
Epistulae morales LI. Translated by R.M. Gummere. Loeb Classical Library 75. London/Cambridge (Mass.), 1917 1.

SEXTUS EMPIRICUS
Translated by R.G. Bury.
Adversus Mathematicos. Loeb Classical Library 382. London/Cambridge (Mass.), 1971 (1949 1).
Adversus Physicos. Loeb Classical Library 311. London/Cambridge (Mass.), 1936 1.
Outline of Pyrrhonism. Loeb Classical Library 273. London/Cambridge (Mass.), 1933 1.

SIMPLICIUS
Simplicius in Aristotelis Physicorum Libros. Ed. H. Diels, Commentaria in Aristotelem Graece IX. Berolini, 1882 (photomechanischer Nachdruck 1960).

STOBAEUS, Ioannes
Eklogai. Anthologium. Ed. Curtius Wachsmuth and Otto Hense. Berolini, 1884.

STRABO
Geography. Translated by Horace L. Jones. Vol. I. Loeb Classical Library 49. 1917 1.

SUETONIUS
De rhetoribus. Suetonius. Ed. J.C. Rolfe. Loeb Classical Library 38. London/Cambridge (Mass.), 1949 11 (1914 1).

TERTULLIANUS
Apologia. Translated by T.R. Glover. Loeb Classical Library 250. London/Cambridge (Mass.), 1931 1.
Adversus Marcionem. Ed. Ernest Evans. Oxford Early Christian Texts. Oxford, 1972.
Ad nationes. Ed. A. Schneider. Neuchâtel, 1968.

THEOPHRASTUS
The Characters. Translated by J.M. Edmonds. Loeb Classical Library 225. London/Cambridge (Mass.), 1967 (1929 1).
Metaphysics. Eds. W.D. Ross and F.H. Fobes. Hildesheim, 1967.

XENOCRATES
Isnardi Parente, M., Senocrate-Ermodoro. Frammenti. Napoli, 1981.

(XENOPHON)
Constitution of the Athenians. Translated by Glen W. Bowersock. Loeb Classical Library 183. London/Cambridge (Mass.), 1968.

ZENO
A.C. Pearson, The Fragments of Zeno and Cleanthes. With introduction and explanatory notes by --. London, 1891 (photostatic reprint New York, 1973).

II SECONDARY WORKS

A   WORKS OF REFERENCE

The Oxford Classical Dictionary. Edited by N.G.L. Hammond and H.H. Scullard. Oxford, 1970 2 (1948 1).

Glossarium Epicureum (Hermannus Usener). Ed. M. Giganti and W. Schmid. Lessico Intellettuale Europea XIV. Roma, 1977.

Historische Wörterbuch der Philosophie. Bd. 1. Darmstadt (1971).

Der kleine Pauly. Lexicon der Antike. Herausgeber Konrat Ziegler und Walther Sonntheimer. Stuttgart, 1964-1975.

The Encyclopedia of Philosophy. Vol. 1, 3, 4, 7. New York/London (1967).

Paulys Real-Encyclopädie der classischen Altertumswissenschaft. Neue Bearbeitung von Georg Wissowa. Stuttgart (cited as PW).

B   MONOGRAPHS

ADKINS, A.W.H., From the Many to the One. A Study of Personality and Views of Human Nature in the Context of Ancient Greek Society, Values and beliefs. London (1970).

ALTHEIM, Franz,
1. Alexander und Asien. Geschichte eines geistigen Erbes. Tübingen, 1953.
2. Weltgeschichte Asiens im griechischen Zeitalter. 1. Bd. Halle, 1947.

ASMIS, Elizabeth, Epicurus' Scientific method. Cornell University Press. Ithaca and London (1894).

BAILEY, Cyril, The Greek Atomists and Epicurus. New York, 1964.

BALDRY, H.C., The Unity of Mankind in Greek Thought. Cambridge, 1965.

BALLABRIGA, Alain, Le soleil et le Tartare. L'image mythique du monde en Grèce archaïque. Éditions de l'École des Hautes Études en Sciences Sociales. Paris (1986).

BELOCH, Julius, Griechische Geschichte. Vol. III. Strassburg, 1904.

BERVE, Helmut, Das Alexanderreich auf prosopographischer Grundlage. Vol. II. München, 1926.

BIANCHI, Ugo, La religione greca. Torino, 1975.

BONELLI, Guido, Aporie etiche in Epicuro. Collection Latomus Vol. 163. Bruxelles, 1979.

BOYANCÉ, Pierre, Épicure. Presses universitaires de France. Paris, 1969.

BRADFORD WELLES, C., Die hellenistische Welt. Propyläen Weltgeschichte 3. Berlin/Frankfurt/Wien (1962).

BROCHARD, V., Les sceptiques grecs. Patris, 1959 2 (1887 1).

BUDGE, E.A. Wallis, A History of Egypt from the End of the Neolithic Period to the Death of Cleopatra II B.C. 30. Vol. VIII Egypt under the Ptolemies and Cleopatra VII. London, 1902.

BURCKHARDT, Jacob, Griechische Kulturgeschichte. Berlin/Leipzig, 1930 (1889 1).

BURNET, John, Early Greek Philosophy. Photostatic reprint of the fourth edition 1930. London (1975) (1892 1).

CARDINALI, Giuseppe, Il Regno di Pergamo. Ricerche di diritto pubblico. Roma, 1906.

CARY, M., A History of the Greek World from 323 to 146 B.C. London (1951 2, 1913 1).

COPLESTON, Frederick, A History of Philosophy. Vol. I Greece & Rome, Part II. Image Books Edition. New York, 1962 (1944 1).

COUISSIN, Pierre, The Stoicism of the New Academy. In : The Sceptical Tradition. Ed. Myles Burnyeat. Major Thinkers Series. Berkeley/Los Angeles/London (1983).

DES PLACES, Édouard , La religion grecque. Dieux, cultes, rites et sentiment religieux dans la Grèce antique. Paris, 1969.

DeWITT, Norman Wentworth, Epicurus and his Philosophy. University of Minnesota Press. Minneapolis (1964 2, 1954 1).

DIJKSTERHUIS, E.J., De mechanisering van het wereldbeeld. Amsterdam, 1950. The Mechanization of the World Picture. Oxford, 1960.

DODDS, E.R., The Greeks and the Irrational. Berkeley/Los Angeles/London (1973 8) (Sather Classical Lectures, Vol. 25, 1925 1).

DRACHMANN, A.B., Atheism in Pagan Antiquity. Chicago, 1957 (photostatic reprint of the edition London, 1922; this was the English translation by G.F. Hill of the original Danish publication of 1919).

DROYSEN, J.G., Geschichte des Hellenismus. Vol. I. 1836 1. Vol. III 1877 2.

EDELSTEIN, Ludwig, The Meaning of Stoicism. Martin Classical Lectures Vol. XXI. Cambridge (Mass.).

FERGUSON, William Scott,
1. Hellenistic Athens. An historical essay. London, 1911.
2. The Leading Ideas of the New Period. Cambridge Ancient History VII. Cambridge (1928).

FESTUGIèRE, A.-J.,
1. Épicure et ses dieux. Series : Mythes et religions. Paris, 1968 2 (1946 1).
2. La Révélation d'Hermès Trismégiste. I l'astrologie et les sciences occultes. Paris, 1983 (photostatic reprint of 1950 edition).
3. La vie spirituelle en Grèce à l'époque hellénistique, ou Les besoins de l'esprit dans un monde raffiné. Paris (w.d.).

FONTINA, Marcello, Cassandro, Re di Macedonia. Torino, 1965.

FURLEY, David J., Two Studies in the Greek Atomists. Princeton N.J., 1967.

GHIRSHMAN, R., Iran from the earliest times to the Islamic conquest. Penguin Books A 239. (1954, 1951 original French version).

GOEDECKEMEYER, Albert, Die Geschichte des grichischen Skeptizismus. Leipzig, 1905 (photostatischer neudruck, 1968).

GOLDSCHMIDT, Victor, Le système stoïcien et l'idée du temps. Paris, 1969 2 (1953 1).

GOSLING, J.C.B., and TAYLOR, C.C.W., The Greeks on Pleasure. Oxford, 1984 (Paperback reprint of first edition 1982).

GRANT, Michael, From Alexander to Cleopatra. The Hellenistic World. London (1982).

GUTHRIE, W.K.C., A History of Greek Philosophy.
Vol. II The Presocratic Tradition from Parmenides to Democritus. Cambridge University Press. Paperback Edition, 1978 (1965 1).
Vol. IV Plato. The Man and his Dialogues. Cambridge UP, 1975.
Vol. V The Later Plato and the Academy. Cambridge UP, 1978.

HAARHOFF, T.J., The stranger at the gate. Aspects of exclusiveness and co-operation in ancient Greece and Rome, with some references to modern times. London, 1948.

HABICHT, Gottmenschentum und griechische Städte. München, 1956.

HAMILTON, J.R., Alexander the Great. Pittsburgh, 1979 2 (1973 1).

HAMPL, Franz, Alexander der Grosse. Series : Persönlichkeit und Geschichte IX. Göttingen, 1958.

HANSEN, Esther V., The Attalids of Pergamum. Second Edition, Revised and Expanded. Ithaca and London, 1971 (1946 1).

HEINEMANN, J., Poseidonios' Metaphysische Schriften I. Breslau, 1921 (photostatic reprint Hildesheim, 1968).

HEINZE, Richard, Xenokrates. Darstellung der Lehre und Sammlung der Fragmente. Hildesheim, 1965.

HOFFMANN, O. and DEBRUNNER, A., Geschichte der griechischen Sprache I. Bis zum Ausgang der klassischen Zeit. II. Grundfragen und Grundzüge des nachklassischen Griechisch. Sammlung Göschen 111. Berlin, 1969.

HOPP, Joachim, Untersuchungen zur Geschichte der letzten Attaliden. München, 1977.

HOSSENFELDER, Malte, Stoa, Epikuerismus und Skepsis. Reihe : Philosophie der Antike Vol. 3. München, 1985.

HUNT, H.A.K., A Physical Interpretation of the Universe. The doctrines of Zeno the Stoic. Melbourne University Press, 1976.

JONAS, Hans, The Gnostic Religion. Boston, 1963 2 (1958 1). Dutch translation : Het Gnosticisme. Utrecht/Antwerpen (1969).

JOUGUET, P., L'impérialisme macedonien et l'Hellénisation de l'Orient. Paris, 1926.

JÜTHNER, Julius, Hellenen und Barbaren. Aus der Geschichte des Nationalbewusstseins. Reihe : Das Erbe der Alten. Neue Folge. Heft VIII. Leipzig, 1923.

KAERST, I, Geschichte des Hellenismus Vol. II. Berlin. 1926.

KERN, Otto, Die Religion der Griechen. 3. Bd. Von Platon bis Kaiser Julian. Berlin, 1938.

KINCAID, C.A., Successors of Alexander the Great. Chicago, 1969.

LAFFRANQUE, Marie, Poseidonois d'Apamée. Essai de mise au point. Paris, 1964.

LAUFFER, Siegfried, Alexander der Grosse. München, 1978.

LESKY, Albin, Geschichte der griechischen Literatur. Bern/München (1963 2, 1957/1958 1).

LIEBERT, Jakob, Alexander der Grosse. Darmstadt, 1972.

LÖBL, Rudolf,
1. Demokrits Atome. Eine Untersuchung zur Überlieferung und zu einigen wichtigen Lehrstücken in Demokrits Physik. Hobelts Dissertationsdrucke. Reihe Klassische Philologie. Heft 24. Bonn, 1976.
2. Demokrits Atomphysik. Erträge der Forschung Bd. 252. Darmstadt (1987).

LOENEN, D., Mens en cultuur van Hellas. Amsterdam (1960 2, 1947 1).

LONG, A.A., Hellenistic Philosophy. Stoics, Epicureans, Sceptics. London, 1974.

MALITZ, Jürgen, Die Historien des Posidonius. München, 1983.

McSHANE, Roger, The Foreign Policy of the Attalids of Pergamum. Urbana, 1964.

MEER, Herman Franke van der, Euhemerus van Messene. Amsterdam, 1949.

MELSEN, Andrew G. van, From Atomos to Atom. The History of the Concept. (Translated from the Dutch by Henry J. Koren). Duquesne Studies. Philosophical Series 1. Pittsburgh (Pa.), 1952.

MEYER, Eduard, Blüte und Untergang des Hellenismus in Asien. Berlin, 1925. Reprinted in 'Der Hellenismus in Mittelasien". Eds. Franz Altheim und Joachim Rehork. Wege der Forschung, Bd. XCI. Darmstadt, 1969.

MOMIGLIANO, Arnaldo, Alien Wisdom. The Limits of Hellenization. Cambridge, 1975.

MOREAU, Joseph, L'âme du monde de Platon aux Stoïciens. Hildesheim, 1965 (photostatic reprint of first edition Paris 1939).

MURRAY, Gilbert, Five stages of Greek religion. Oxford (1930, 1925 1).

NAESS, Arne, Scepticism. International Library of Philosophy and Scientific Method. London/New York (1968).

NARAIN, A.K., The Indo-Greeks. Oxford, 1957.

NIESE, Benedictus, Geschichte der griechischen und makedonischen Staaten seit der Schlacht bei Chaeronea. 3. Teil Von 188 bis 120 v.Chr. Gotha, 1903.

NILSSON, Martin,
1. Geschichte der griechischen Religion. Zweiter band. Die hellenistische und römische Zeit. München, 1950.
2. A History of Greek Religion. Oxford, 1925 (Swedish edition 1921).

PÉDECH, Paul, La géographie des Grecs. Presses universitaires de France (1976).

PETIT, Paul, La civilisation hellénistique. Paris, 1965.

PIERI, Stefania Nonvel, Carneade. Padova, 1978.

PIERSON, Allard, Geestelijke voorouders. Studiën over onze beschaving.
Vol. IV. A. Pierson and K. Kuiper, Het Hellenisme. Haarlem, 1913 2.

POHLENZ, Max, Die Stoa. Geschichte einer geistigen Bewegung. 2 Bde. Göttingen, 1979-1980.

PRA, Mario del, Lo scetticismo greco. Series Universale Laterza 327. Edizione riveduta ed aggiornata. Roma/Bari, 1975 (Milano, 1950 1).

PRÉAUX, Claire, Le monde hellénistique. Grèce et l'Orient de la mort d'Alexandre à la conquête romaine de la Grèce (323-146 av. J.-C.). Vol. II. Paris, 1978

RADIN, Max, The Jews among the Greeks and Romans. Philadelphia, 1915 (photostatic reprint New York, 1973).

REINACH, Thédore, Mithridates Eupator, König von Pontos. Deutsche Übersetzung von A. Goetz. Leipzig, 1895 (Paris, 1890).

REINHARDT, Max, Poseidonios. München, 1921.

RIST, J.M., Stoic Philosophy. Cambridge (UP), 1969.

ROBIN, Léon,
1. La pensée grecque. Les origines de l'esprit scientifique. L'évolution de l'humanité. 1e section. III.V. Paris, 1963.
2. Pyrrhon et le scepticisme grec. Presses universitaires de France (1944). (Photostatic reprint New York & London, 1980).

RODIS-LEWIS, G., La morale stoïcienne. Paris, 1970.

ROSE, H.J., A Handbook of Greek Literature from Homer to the time of Lucian. London, 1954 4 (revised edition) (1934 1).

ROSTOVZEFF, M.
1. A History of the Ancient World I. Oxford, 1930.
2. The Social and Economic History of the Hellenistic World. Oxford, 1941.

SALLET, Alfred von, Die Nachfolge Alexanders des Grossen in Baktrien und Indien. Berlin, 1879.

SCHIPPERS, J.W., De ontwikkeling der euhemeristische godencritiek in de Christelijke Latijnse literatuur. Groningen/Djakarta, 1952.

SCHMEKEL, August, Die Philosophie der mittleren Stoa in ihrem geschichtlichen Zusammenhange dargestellt. Berlin, 1892 (photostatischer Nachdruck Hildesheim/New York, 1974).

SCHUBERT, Paul, Die Eschatologie des Posidonius. Leipzig, 1927.

SEDLEY, David, The Motivation of Greek Scepticism. In : The Sceptical Tradition. Ed. Myles Burnyeat. Major Thinkers Series. Berkeley/Los Angeles/London (1983).

STOUGH, Charlotte L., Greek Scepticism. A Study in Epistemology. Berkeley/Los Angeles, 1969.

STRAATEN, Modestus van, Panétius. Sa vie, ses écrits et sa doctrine, avec une édition des fragments. Amsterdam, 1946.

TARÁN, Leonardo, Speusippus of Athens. A critical study with a collection of the related texts and commentary. Series : Philosophia antiqua. Vol. XXXIX. Leiden, 1981.

TARN, W.W.,
1. Alexander the Great. Vol. I Narrative; Vol. II Sources and studies. Cambridge, 1948.
2. Alexander : The Conqueror of the Far East. Cambridge Ancient History VI. Cambridge, 1927.
3. Greece : 335-321 B.C. The Cambridge Ancient History VI. Cambridge, 1927.
4. The Greeks in Bactria and India. Cambridge, 1951.
5. Hellenistic Civilization. London, 1947 4 (1927 1).

TAYLOR, Edward, Epicurus. Select Biographies Seties. Freeport NY, 1969 (1911 1).

TCHERIKOVER, Victor, Hellenistic Civilization and the Jews. Translated from the Hebrew by S. Appelbaum. Philadelphia, 1959.

VITUCCI, Giovanni, Il Regno di Bitinia. Roma, 1953.

WALBANK, F.W., The Hellenistic World. Fontana Paperbacks, 1981.

WHYTE, Lancelot White, Essay on Atomism. From Democritus to 1960. Middletown (Conn.) (1961).

WILAMOWITZ-MOELLENDORF, Ulrich von,
1. Geschichte der griechischen Sprache. Vortrag Göttingen, 27.IX. 1927. Berlin, 1928.
2. Der Glaube der Hellenen II. Berlin, 1932.

WILCKEN, Ulrich, Griechische Geschichte im Rahmen der Altertumsgeschichte. Vierte revidierte Auflage. München und Berlin, 1939.

WILL, Edouard, Histoire politique du monde hellénistique (323-30 av. J.-C.). II Des avènements d'Antiochus III et Philippe V à la fin des Lagides. Nancy, 1967.

WOODCOCK, George, The Greeks in India. London (1966).

ZELLER, Eduard, Die Philosophie der Griechen in ihrer geschichtlichen Entwicklung. Bd. I.2. 1920 6.Bd. II.1. 1922 5. Bd. III.1. 1923 1. (photomechanischer Nachdruck Hildesheim, 1963).

GENERAL INDEX

Abdera, 154
Abydos, 35, 106
Academy of Plato, 46, 121, 123, 125, 126, 163, 176, 180, 193, 234, 237
Achaean(s), 34, 36, 37, 229
Achaean League, 34, 37
Achaemenid(s), 39, 52, 65, 114
Achilles Tatius, 208
Açoka, 69
Adkins, A.W.H., 208
Adonis, 66
Aegean (Sea), 14, 19, 21, 24, 56, 61, 79, 80, 83
Aelian, 213
Aeolic, 58, 191
Aëtius, 206, 208, 213
Afghanistan, 20, 26, 45, 54, 56, 70, 71, 107, 226
Africa, 228
Agis III, 27
Ahuramazda, 67, 95
Akkadian (Empires), 225, 227
Akko, 88, 101
Albania, 9
Alcimus (Jewish High Priest), 101-102
Alcidamas, 46
Aleppo, 114
Alexander III the Great, 1, 2, 4, 5, 6, 7, 8, 9, 10, 11, 12, 14, 16, 17, 18, 19, 20, 21, 22, 25, 26, 27, 31, 33, 39, 45, 46, 47, 48, 49, 50-55, 57, 60, 64, 65, 66, 67, 68, 71, 72, 74, 75, 77, 79, 83, 86, 95, 102, 107, 108, 109, 110, 111, 112, 114, 122, 150, 167, 177, 225, 227, 228, 246

Alexander IV Aigos, 3, 5, 11, 14
Alexander V, son of Cassander, 11, 12
Alexander Aphrodisiensis, 205, 208, 211
Alexandria (in Egypt), 54, 56, 80, 88, 102, 103, 106, 107, 114, 227
Alexandria (Iskenderun), 87
Alexandria Eschatê, 57
Alexandrian(s), 54
Alexandrian Empire, 20, 225
Alexandrian House, 7, 41
Allard Pierson Museum, Amsterdam, 109
Altheim, Franz, 78, 113, 114
Amaseia, 82
Amastrine, Amastris, 52, 53
Amathe, 85
Ammon, 64, 66, 67
Ammon, Oracle of, 64, 243, 246
Ammonite(s), 89
Amphion, 85
Amsterdam, 118
Amyntas I, 5
Anaximander, 44
Anaxagoras, 153, 154
Antialcidas, 113
Antigoneia, 16
Antigonid House, 36
Antigonus I Monophthalmos, 7, 8, 9, 10, 11, 13-14, 14, 15, 16, 18, 21, 30-31, 113
Antigonus II Gonatas, 25, 32, 33
Antigonus Doson, 34
Antimachus I, 73-74, 113
Antioch, 18, 80, 84-85, 86, 88, 90, 92, 93, 101, 107, 227
Antiochus I Soter, 18, 53, 250

Antiochos II Theos, 71, 112, 118
Antiochus III the Great, 21, 22-23, 23, 34, 35-36, 71, 86-87, 87, 89, 94
Antiochus IV Epiphanes, 24, 92-96, 115, 117, 118
Antiochus V Eupator, 101
Antipater, governor of Macedonia, 4, 6, 7, 8, 10, 27, 28, 29, 53
Antipater I, son of Cassander, 11, 12, 41
Antony, Marc, 38
Apame, 53
Apamea, Peace of, 23, 38
Apameia, 110, 198
Aphrodite Lamia, 245
Apis, 64
Apollo, 96
Apollodorus of Artemisia, 72, 78
Apollodotus, 113
Apollonius, 97
Appian, 40, 42, 118
Arabia, 62, 243
Arachosia, 73
Aramaic, 63, 86
Aratus, 34
Arcesilaus, 185-188, 189, 219, 220
Archelaus, 60
Archytas, 121
Areus, 32, 33
Argos, 32
Aristocles, 209, 218, 219
Aristophanes, 230, 231
Aristotelian(s), 125, 193
Aristotle, 27-28, 44, 45, 46, 60, 108, 121, 123, 130, 134, 140, 141, 154, 155, 156, 157, 158, 163, 164, 165, 193, 200, 205, 206, 211, 212, 213, 229, 251
Armenia(n)(s), 23
Arnim, J. von, 208, 210, 214, 220, 222
Arnim, P. von, 195
Arrhidaeus see Philip III
Arrian, 40, 42, 50, 51, 109, 110, 112
Arsaces I, 101
Arsacid(s), 20, 78, 79
Arsi(i), 114
Arsinoe, 9

Artaxerxes III, 2, 52
Asclepius, 114
Asia, 2, 4, 6, 7, 8, 10, 13, 14, 17, 19, 23, 25, 30, 31, 39, 44, 45, 48, 50, 51, 52, 53, 54, 57, 60, 61, 62, 63, 65, 68, 75, 107, 108, 122, 227, 228
Asia (Roman province), 39
Asia Minor, 7, 9, 13, 14, 15, 17, 18, 19, 21, 22, 23, 24, 31, 38, 39, 45, 48, 49, 61, 63, 66, 70, 79-84, 86, 87, 106, 107, 121, 133, 134, 163, 198, 199, 227
Asianism, Asianic, 61
Asiatic(s), 3, 18, 40, 55, 57, 59, 62, 63, 83, 94, 111, 125, 225, 226, 227
Asmis, Elizabeth, 215
Assos, 133
Assyria(n)(s), 67, 105
Astarte, 66
Atheism, 236, 242, 244, 247
Athena, 233
Athenaeus, 40, 117, 218, 253
Athenian(s), 27, 28, 35, 46, 60, 85, 133, 163, 189, 227, 231, 245, 246, 248
Athenian Sea League (First), 28
Athenodorus, 58
Athens, 27, 28, 29, 31, 32, 33, 35, 37, 39, 46, 59, 80, 121, 126, 133, 154, 167, 178, 189, 195, 195, 196, 198, 227, 237, 242
Atomic Theory, 150
Atomism, Atomists, 150-162, 164, 169, 179, 212, 216, 236, 239, 240
Atropos, 127
Attalid House, Attalid(s), 21, 80
Attalos III
Attic, 58, 59, 60, 61
Attica, 29, 45
Atticism, 59
Atticists, 61
Augustine, St., 146, 209
Austrian, 215

Baal, 98, 99
Babylonia, 7
Babylon, 1, 2, 6, 7, 15, 68, 71

Babylonia(n)(s), 62, 107, 154, 249, 250
Babylonian Empire, 20
Bactra, 71, 72
Bactria, 6, 20, 23, 26, 65, 70-77, 78, 112, 114
Bactrian(s), 3, 51, 52, 53, 54, 70-77, 78, 79, 107, 113, 114
Baghdad, 114
Bailey, Cyril, 157, 211, 212
Bake, Janus, 223
Baldry, H.C., 109
Balkans, 23, 24, 25, 32, 54
Balkh, 113
Ballabriga, Alain, 252
Barbarian(s), 29, 45, 46, 49, 50, 54, 55, 56, 57, 60, 62, 66, 81, 82, 84, 85, 94, 108, 190, 191
Barsine, 2, 110
Beerling, R.F., 216
Behaviourists, 138
Belgian, 70, 112
Beloch, Julius, 51
Bergama, 114
Bergson, Henri, 200
Berkeley, George, 146
Beros(s)us, 250
Berve, Helmut, 110, 111, 112
Best, Jan, 8
Bianchi, Ugo, 253
Bible, 63, 91
Bithynia(n)(s), 21, 22, 39, 79, 82, 107
Black Sea, 9, 21, 24, 56, 79, 82, 107
Boethus, 195-196
Bollack, Jean, 217
Bolos the Democritean, 251
Bonelli, Guido, 217
Book of Ecclesiasticus, 91
Book of Daniel, 96, 118
Book of Machabees, 90, 95, 99
Bosporus, 9, 21, 125
Bowersock, G.W., 111
Boyancé, Pierre, 215
Bradford Welles, C., 38, 43, 229, 252
Brahmans, 69, 70
British-India, 62
Brochard, V., 182, 218, 219

Brutus, Marcus Iunius, 199
Budge, E.A. Wallis, 120
Buddhism, Buddhist(s), 69, 70, 74, 75
Burckhardt, Jakob, 228, 252
Burnet, John, 157, 212
Byzantine, 85, 207
Byzantium, 9, 125

Caecilius Calactinus, 62
Caesar, Julius, 18, 38, 115, 199
Caizzi, Fernanda Decleva, 218, 219
Callisthenes, 65
Cambyses, 65
Capelle, W., 218
Cappadocia, 14, 22, 79, 83, 107
Cardinali, Giuseppe, 115
Carneades, 189-193, 221, 236, 250
Carolingian, 119
Cary, M., 9, 11, 13, 16, 25, 41, 42, 43
Cassander, 4, 5, 8, 10-11, 11, 14, 15, 16, 29, 30, 31, 41, 243
Cato the Elder, 189, 191
Caucasus, 58, 62, 226
Celtic, 22
Celts, 22, 25, 63, 81, 83, 199
Central Asia, 45, 73, 76
Chandragupta Maurya, 18, 68
Charlemagne, 119
Charles Martel, 119
Chassidim, 100, 119
Chaeronea, Battle of, 19, 26, 35, 227, 228
Chain of Being, 128, 130
Chalcedon, 125, 178
Chalcidius, 209
Chanukah, 100
Chernobyl. 151
China, 72
Chinese, 71
Chrysippus, 134, 135, 141, 142, 145, 146, 150, 189, 196, 208, 222, 235
Christian(s), 139, 231
Christianity, 150, 240
Cicero, 62, 125, 141, 165, 171, 172, 180, 195, 197, 200, 202, 203, 204, 205, 206, 208, 209, 210, 214,

215, 216, 217, 218, 220, 221, 222, 223, 224
Cilicia, 17, 22, 23, 38, 45, 134
Circumcision, 98
Cleanthes, 133-134, 142, 248
Clemens of Alexandria, 205, 210, 212, 217, 223
Clotho, 127
Cleopatra, wife of Ptolemy V, 21
Cleopatra VII, wife of Ptolemy XIII, 38, 76
Clitomachus, 221
Clitus, 228
Cnidus, 121
Colophon, 163
Colotes, 164
Copleston, Frederick, 137, 145, 170, 208, 211, 216, 223, 224
Corinth, 29, 30, 31
Corinthian League, 27, 28, 30, 31, 54
Cosmopolitanism, 47-48
Corupedium, Battle of, 19
Cos, Battle of, 34
Cotta, 172, 216
Couissin, Pierre, 220
Craterus, 52, 53, 110
Cretans, 191
Curtius Rufus, Quintus, 109, 111
Cynoscephalae, Battle of, 35
Cypriote, 46, 133
Cyprus, 16, 24, 38, 46
Cyrene, 24, 45, 188

Danube, 9, 22
Dardanelles, 19
Darius III Codomannus, 2, 3, 52, 54
David's City, 97
Dead Amazon, 81
Dead Sea, 88
Debrunner, A., 61, 111
Dekapolis, 88
Delphi, Oracle of, 22, 64, 242
Demetrius I Poliorcetes, 9, 12, 16 12-13, 17, 21, 24, 30-31, 32, 113, 228, 245, 246
Demetrius I, king of Bactria, 73-74, 113

Demetrius II, king of Bactria, 73-74
Demetrius, probably another Bactrian king, 75, 113
Demochares, 245
Democritus (Democritean), 150, 154, 154-162, 163, 164, 165, 170, 178, 179, 212, 213, 214, 236
Demosthenes, 27, 33
Descartes, René, 155
DeWitt, Norman Wentworth, 215
Diadochi, 7, 8, 15, 16, 17, 18, 21, 22, 38, 53, 56, 86, 92, 94, 110, 227
Diagoras, 190
Dialectical materialism, 138
Diaspora, 101
Dicaearchus, 45
Dijksterhuis, E.J., 153, 161, 211, 214
Dio Chrysostomus, 210
Diodorus Siculus, 6, 7, 14, 15, 29, 40, 41, 42, 43, 53, 57, 58, 88, 109, 110, 111, 116, 117
Diodorus, 123
Diodotian House, 71
Diodotus I, 71, 112
Diodotus II, 71
Diogenes Laertius, 123, 125, 134, 135, 154, 163, 206-226
Diogenes of Seleucia, 222
Diogenianus, 209
Dionysios Petoserapis, 106
Dionysos, 66
Dörrie, Heinrich, 126, 205, 206, 222
Dodds, E.R., 231, 242, 249, 250, 252, 253
Dostojevski, F.M., 210
Drachmann, A.B., 214, 217, 244, 247, 253, 254
Droysen, J.G., 109, 110
Drypetis, 52
Dualism, dualistic, 2, 8, 9, 19, 20, 25, 26, 27, 28, 29, 32, 37, 40, 42, 48, 49, 53, 55, 57, 59, 61, 62, 63, 68, 73, 75, 77, 84, 85, 91, 93, 97, 98, 99, 102, 108, 116, 122, 123, 127, 130, 132, 137-138, 139-141,

143, 146, 150, 152, 157, 158, 159, 161, 162, 163, 165, 167, 168, 172, 179, 182, 183, 196, 198, 201, 202, 203, 233, 234, 237, 238, 241, 251
Dura-Europos, 78
Duris of Samos, 245
Dutch, 49, 59, 70, 111, 112, 114, 115, 151, 213, 216
Dying Gaul, 81

Edelstein, Ludwig, 145, 210
Egypt, 4, 6, 7, 9, 15, 17-18, 18, 19, 20, 24, 26, 30, 33, 34, 37-38, 56, 62, 63, 64, 66, 67, 69, 86, 87, 88, 91, 96, 102-106, 107, 108, 112, 116, 154, 198, 225, 226, 228, 246
Egyptian(s), 16, 17, 21, 23, 24, 34, 38, 62, 63, 66, 67, 87, 89, 96, 100, 102-106, 107, 109, 116, 190, 226, 227, 246, 251
Einarson, Benedict, 213
Elea, 154
Eleate School, 153, 155, 178, 211, 212
Eleazar, 99
Eleusinian mysteries, 170, 216
Elis, 177, 178, 182
Empedocles, 153, 154, 156, 157
English, 62
Enlightenment, Age of, 242
Epaminondas, 248
Epictetus, 210
Epicurean(s), 163-176, 180, 187, 191, 193, 213, 217, 234, 236, 238, 239
Epicureanism, 122, 150, 163-176, 189
Epicurus, 162, 163-176 passim, 177, 191, 211, 213, 214, 215, 216, 217, 235, 236, 237
Epinomis, 131-133, 206-207, 239
Epiphanius, 138, 139, 209, 219
Epirus, 9, 32, 228
Epirotes, 25, 33
Essalehiye, 114
Eratosthenes, 45
Ethiopia(n), 105, 154
Etruria, 198

Eucratides, 75
Eudoxus, 121-122, 123, 205, 234
Euclid (the mathematician), 218
Euclides (the philosopher), 178-179
Euhemerism, 243-245
Euhemerus, 243-244
Eumenes (general of Alexander), 14-15, 15, 21, 42, 52
Eumenes II, king of Pergamum, 80
Euphrates, 23, 40, 45, 48, 63, 68, 77, 79, 106, 107, 114, 225, 227
Euripides, 60
Europe, 1, 2, 8, 10, 11, 23, 25, 36, 40, 44, 45, 48, 53, 55, 57, 61, 63, 68, 77, 79, 106, 107, 108, 227, 241
Eurydice, wife of Philip III, 3, 4, 5
Eusebius, 183, 210, 219
Euthydemus I, 71, 72, 73, 113, 114

Feast of the Tabernacles, 102
Fergana, 71
Ferguson, William Scott, 43, 48, 66, 67, 109, 112
Festugière, A.-J., 216, 241, 251, 253, 254
Flamininus, Titus Quinctius, 35
Fortina, Marcello, 41
Fournier, Alain, 1
Fowler, H.N, 222
French, 70, 199
Fritz, Kurt von, 108
Furley, David J., 211

Gades, 199
Galatia, 22, 79, 83, 107
Galatians see Celts
Galen, 80, 136, 138, 139, 208, 209, 210
Galilee, 101
Gallia, 199
Gandhara, 69, 74, 75, 76
Ganges, 74
Garden School, 163, 166, 167, 193, 238

Gaul(s), 191
Gaza, 88
Gelder, H. van, 112
Gellius, Aulus, 210, 221
Gellius, Lucius, 195
Gerasa (Jerash), 88
German(s), 22, 213, 216, 245
Germany, 118
Geyer, F., 40
Gezerot (the Evil Decrees), 92, 98
Ghirshman, R., 72, 73, 113, 114
Gnosis (Gnosticism), 125, 128, 130, 143, 148, 150, 163, 238, 240, 241, 251
Gnostic(s), 125, 133, 143, 146, 205, 231, 233
Goedeckemeyer, Albert, 218, 219, 221, 222
Goldschmidt, Viktor, 208
Gosling, J.C.B., 205
Grant, Michael, 84, 115
Greece, 6, 7, 10, 11, 13, 19, 22, 23, 25, 26-37, 39, 40, 46, 56, 199, 226, 228, 250
Greek(s) (Hellenes, Hellenic), 6, 9, 13, 14, 17, 19, 21, 22, 23, 25, 26, 26-37, 40, Ch. II passim, 122, 129, 132, 135, 143, 148, 151, 152, 154, 155, 157, 159, 160, 167, 168, 171, 174, 176, 182, 184, 187, 190, 191, 194, 197, 198, 199, 200, 201, 212, 216, 223, Ch. IV passim
Greene, William C., 254
Gujarat, 76
Guthrie, W.K.C., 204, 205, 206, 207, 212
Gymnosophists, 177

Haarhoff, T.J., 109, 111
Habicht, Christian, 118
Hades, 129
Hamilton, J.R., 111
Hampl, Franz, 110
Hannibal, 35, 228
Hansen, Esther V., 115
Hasmon, 100, 119
Hasmonean House, 100, 101, 102, 118, 119

Hebrew, 59, 62, 67, 86, 89, 90, 91, 100
Hecataeus of Abdera, 88
Heckel, Waldemar, 110
Hegel, F.W., 193
Heidegger, Martin, 193
Heinemann, I., 223
Heinze, Richard, 129, 205, 206
Hellas see Greece
Hellenes see Greeks
Hellenic see Greek
Hellenic League, 28, 33, 34
Hellenic War, 27
Hellenism, Hellenistic, 20, 21, Ch.II passim, 193, 194, 195, 196, 199, Ch. IV passim
Hellenization, 49, 57, 63, 66, 80, 84, 86, 87, 88, 91, 93, 94, 102, 103, 106, 107, 108
Hellespont, 9
Hephaestion, 52, 53
Heracles (the hero), 64
Heracles, son of Alexander the Great, 3, 5
Heraclides, 60
Heraclitus, 134, 140, 154, 165
Hermaeus, 76
Hermarchus, 166
Hermes, 90
Hermocles, 253
Herodotus, 58, 59
Herodotus (a correspondent of Epicurus), 214
Hicks, R.D., 254
High Priest (Jewish), 87, 89, 101, 102
Hindu, 69, 77, 177
Hindu Kush, 45, 75
Hippocrates, 59, 80
Hippolytus, 210
Hittite Empire, 22
Hoffmann, O., 61, 111
Holy War, 242
Homer, 178, 180, 182
Homeric, 58, 172, 178
Hopp, Joachim, 115
Hossenfelder, Malte, 207, 219
Hülser, Karlheinz, 208, 209, 210
Humboldt, Alexander von, 199

Hunt, H.A.K, 135, 137, 139, 208, 209
Hyde, Thomas, 203
Hyksos, 103

Idumaea, 101
Illyria, 35
India(n)(s), 1, 18, 20, 45, 50, 59, 68-70, 73, 74, 75, 76, 107, 111, 113, 114, 167, 177, 226
Indian Ocean, 243
Indian Union, 62
Indus, 15, 18, 19, 62, 63, 68, 69, 70, 71, 76, 106, 107, 226
Intifadah, 92
Ionian, 44, 59, 191
Ionic, 58, 59
Ipsus, Battle of, 8, 9, 11, 16, 18, 31
Iran, 45, 95
Iranian(s), 38, 54, 62, 67, 73, 78, 113, 114, 226
Isnardi Parente, M., 205
Isocrates, 59, 111
Israel, 67, 95, 99, 100
Issus, Battle of, 3, 110
Isthmian Games, 35
Isthmian League, 28
Isthmus of Corinth, 31, 37
Italy, 32, 35, 228

Jaffa (Jafo, Joppe), 88
Japanese, 151
Jason (Joshua, Jewish High Priest), 89-90, 92, 97
Jerusalem, 87, 89, 90, 91, 92, 96, 97, 98, 100, 118
Jesus Christ, 63
Jewish, 24, 63, 85, 85-102, 115, 116, 118, 120
Jewish War, 95, 100-101
Jew(s), 24, 38, 85-102, 103, 104, 107, 116, 118, 119
Joannes Antiochenes, 119
Joannes Malalas
Johannes Hyrcanus, 102
Jonas, Hans, 67, 112
Jonathan the Machabee, 102
Jordan, 21, 101

Jordanian, 88
Joseph, a Tobiad, 89
Josephus, Flavius, 87, 115, 116, 119, 120
Joshua (Jewish High Priest) see Jason
Jouguet, P., 56, 106, 110, 120
Judaea, 24, 38, 86, 87, 88, 89, 92, 96, 98, 101, 102, 107, 116
Judaism, 103
Judas the Machabee, 38, 100-101, 119
Jüthner, Julius, 108, 111
Jumna, 75
Juppiter, 67
Justinus, 34, 40, 41, 43, 71, 74, 105, 112, 113, 120

Kabul, 113
Kadiköy, 205
Kantian, 187
Kaerst, I., 41, 253
Kshatriyas, 70
Kennedy, J.F., 61
Kern, Otto, 66, 112, 254
Khyber Pass, 74
Kincaid, C.A., 7, 40
Kipling, Rudyard, 77
Kittion, 46, 133
Knaack, 108
koinê-Greek, 60-63, 86, 103, 107
Kronos, 243
Kuiper, K., 115
Kushan Empire, 76

Lachesis, 127
Lactantius, 216, 221
Lacy, Philip H. de, 213
Lake Tatta, 83
Lamia, 245
Lamian War, 42
Lanfranque, Marie, 223
Laodice (mother of Antiochus IV), 94
Latin, 200, 207, 212
Lauffer, Siegfried, 51, 109
Laurentius Lydus, 206
Lebanon, 226

Leibniz, Gottfried Wilhelm, 146
Lenschau, 41
Lesbos, 133
Lesky, Albin, 230, 252
Leucippus, 150, 154, 155, 156, 157, 158, 161, 211, 212, 214
Libya, 24, 188
Liguria, 198
Lindos, 196
Livius, Titus, 35, 43, 117
Lloyd, E.R., 211
Löbl, Rudolf, 213
Loenen, D., 252
Long, A.A., 210, 219
Lovejoy, Arthur Oncken, 206
Lucianus, 219
Lucretius, 172, 173, 213, 215, 217
Lucullus, Lucius Licinius, 199
Luria, Salomo, 212
Lydia(n)(s), 71, 226
Lynden, F.G. van, 222
Lysias (guardian of Antiochus V), 101
Lysimacheia, 9, 41
Lysimachus (general of Alexander), 6, 8, 9, 12, 13, 14, 15, 16, 18, 19, 21, 31, 40
Lysimachus, governor of Jerusalem, 92

Macedonia, 1, 3, 4, 5, 6, 7, 8, 9, 10, 11, 12, 13, 17, 19, 20, 22, 24-25, 26, 27, 28, 29, 31, 32, 33, 34, 35, 36, 37, 39, 113, 226, 227, 243, 245, 246
Macedonian(s), 3, 4, 5, 6, 9, 11, 12, 13, 14, 15, 16, 18, 21, 25, 26, 27, 28, 32, 33, 34, 35, 36, 38, 40, 46, 50, 51, 52, 53, 54, 55, 56, 57, 60, 65, 68, 70, 78, 79, 80, 83, 84, 85, 94, 102, 104, 105, 106, 107, 108, 109, 226, 227, 228, 243, 246
Macedonian Empire, 6, 48, 63, 68
Macedonian War, 35
Magi, 177
Magnesia, Battle of, 23, 36
Malitz, Jürgen, 223
Malwa, 76
Marathon, Battle of, 245

Marduk, 66
Marmora, Sea of, 21, 78
Marseille, 199
Martini, 108
Marx, Karl, 138
Massilia, 199
Materialism, 240
Matthatias, 100, 119
Mauryan Emperors, 69
Mauryan Empire, 74
Mauthausen KZ, 118
McShane, Roger B., 115
Media(n)(s), 18
Mediterranean (Sea), 24, 38, 44, 45, 56, 83, 103
Meer, Herman Franke van der, 253
Megalopolis, Battle of, 27, 29
Megara, 178
Megarian School, 178, 179
Melissus, 155, 212
Melsen, A.G.M. van, 151, 211, 213
Memphis, 4, 65
Menander (the Indian king), 74, 92, 113, 114
Menander (the playwright), 230-231
Mendes, 251
Menelaus (Jewish High Priest), 75, 76
Mesopotamia(n)(s), 23, 40, 86, 94, 198, 226, 246
Messene, 243
Messina, 45
Metrodorus, 164, 166, 175
Meyer, Eduard, 79, 103, 114, 120
Middle Academy, 184, 186, 219, 238
Middle Comedy, 230
Middle Stoa, 195-204, 204, 222
Milete, 17, 22, 118, 154, 212
Minucius Felix, Octavius, 209
Mithras, 82
Mithridates I, 21, 77
Mithridates II, 94
Mithridates V, 39
Mithridates VI Eupator, 82, 101
Modin, 119

Moerbeke, William of, 207
Moleschott, Jakob, 159, 213
Molière, 231
Monism, monist(ic) 135, 137-138, 152, 155, 161, 179, 195, 202, 213
Momigliano, Arnaldo, 78, 114
Moreau, Joseph, 140, 209
Mosaic Law, 87, 91, 92, 99, 100, 119
Murray, Gilbert, 227, 252, 253
Musset, Alfred de, 219

Naess, Arne, 181, 219
Napoleon I, 2
Narain, A.K., 73, 112, 113, 114
Naucratis, 103
Nausiphanes, 164
Nehemia, 89, 116
Nemesius, 198, 223
Neo-Platonism, 146, 150
Netherlands, 70, 151
New Academy, 188-189, 219
New Comedy, 230
New Testament, 88
Nicaea (daughter of Antipater), 8, 9
Nicaea (city), 82
Nicomedia, 82
Niese, Benedictus, 117
Nietzsche, Friedrich, 167, 233
Nikopolis, 82
Nile, 17, 24, 37, 114, 190, 226
Nile Delta, 103, 106
Nilsson, Martin, 117, 118, 242, 253
North-Africa, 1, 45, 76
Norvegian, 215
Nubian, 106
Numenius, 218

Oceanus, 44
Octavian (Augustus), 18, 38
Old Comedy, 230
Old Testament, 62, 103, 200
Olympia, 94
Olympian(s), 129, 162, 172, 174, 201, 235, 236, 237, 240, 241-243, 244, 247
Olympias, 3, 4, 5, 14, 29

Onias, 89
Opis, 50, 55
Orchomenus, 31
Orontes, 16, 85, 88
Oropus, 189
Otto, Walter, 119

Pakistan, 26, 68
Palestine, 18, 23, 24, 38, 63, 86, 87, 88, 100, 102, 107, 198
Palestian(s), 92
Panaetius, 196-198, 198, 238
Panium, Battle of, 21
Pantheism, 139
Paphlagonia, 14
Parmenides, 124, 134, 138, 153, 155, 168, 178, 179, 212
Parthian Empire, 20, 23, 40, 70, 71, 77-79, 101
Parthian(s), 23, 71, 75, 86, 227
Parysatis, 52
Pataliputra, 74
Patna see Pataliputra
Paul (the apostle), 62
Paullus, Lucius Aemilius, 25, 36
Pausanias, 40, 41
Pausanias Damascenus, 115
Pearson, A.C., 208
Pearson, Lionel, 111
Pedech, Paul, 108
Peloponnese, 10, 29, 30, 32, 34, 45, 178, 243
Peloponnesian, 177
Peloponnesian League, 28, 32, 33
Perdiccas, 3, 4, 6, 8, 10, 14, 15, 52, 53, 57
Pergamum (city), 21, 80-81, 88, 107, 114, 115, 196
Pergamum (kingdom), 21, 22, 23, 26, 34, 39, 79, 80-81, 246
Pergamum Altar, 80, 81
Pergamum Museum, Berlin, 80
Peripatetic School, 125, 163, 193
Perseus, 25, 36
Persia(n)(s), 2, 6, 18, 19, 21, 26, 27, 31, 39, 48, 50, 52, 53, 54, 55, 59, 65, 66, 73, 76, 78, 82, 83, 86, 105, 116, 154, 167, 177, 225, 227

Persian Empire, 1, 6, 17, 19, 20, 27, 28, 48, 50, 51, 56, 66, 70, 71, 79, 226
Persian Wars, 48
Petit, Paul, 81, 83, 115
Phila, 12, 24, 53
Philip II, 3, 5, 10, 19, 25, 26-27, 31, 32, 33, 60, 227, 242
Philip III Arrhidaeus, 3, 5, 14, 29
Philip IV, 11
Philip V, 25, 34-35, 36, 227
Philodemus, 170, 215, 216
Phlius, 178
Phocians, 242
Phoenicia(n)(s), 18, 23, 46, 87, 94
Phrygia, 15, 16, 22
Phrygian(s), 62, 97
Phryne, 125
Pieri, Stefabia Nonvel, 211
Pierson, Allard, 49, 84, 85, 109, 115
Pillars of Heracles, 44
Piraeus, 32
Places, Edouard des, 207, 254
Plato, 48, 59, 108, 121, 122, 123, 124, 125, 126, 129, 130, 134, 139, 140, 143, 159, 164, 165, 179, 193, 198, 205, 206, 207, 229, 234, 237
Platonism, Platonic, Platonist(s), 128, 131, 134, 164, 179, 193, 237, 239
Pliny the Elder, 116, 214, 221, 247, 249, 253
Plutarch, 17, 31, 35, 41, 42, 43, 47, 51, 57, 109, 110, 111, 114, 128, 129, 146, 147, 164, 175, 206, 209, 210, 211, 213, 214, 216, 217, 218, 221
Pohlenz, Max, 208, 222, 223
Polybius, 36, 93, 103, 105, 112, 113, 117, 120, 196, 228, 229, 248, 252, 254
Poly(s)perchon, 4, 5, 8, 10, 14,
Pompey, Gnaeus, 38, 39, 199
Pontus, 21, 39, 79, 82-83, 94, 101, 107
Popkin, Richard H., 218
Poseidon, 190, 245
Posidippus, 60

Posidonius, 198-204, 236, 241
Possenti, G.B., 40
Pra, Mario del, 219, 220
Préaux, Claire, 110, 111
Presocratic(s), 135, 140, 152, 178
Proclus, 205, 207
Proskynêsis, 65
Protagoras, 190
Ptolemaic, Ptolemaean(s), 7, 17, 20, 21, 22, 24, 38, 83, 86, 89, 104, 116, 118, 228, 246
Ptolemais see Akko
Ptolemy I Soter, 4, 6, 8, 9, 10, 11, 13, 14, 15, 16, 17-18, 30, 69
Ptolemy II Philadelphus, 33-34
Ptolemy III Euergetes, 24, 117
Ptolemy IV Philopator, 105
Ptolemy V Epiphanes, 21, 24, 95
Ptolemy VIII Euergetes, 37
Ptolemy XIII Auletes, 38
Ptolemy XV Caesarion, 18
Punjab, 26, 68, 74, 75, 76
Purification of the Temple (Chanukah), 100
Pydna, Battle of, 25, 36
Pyrenees, 199
Pyrrho, 177, 178, 180, 182, 183, 184, 188, 219, 220
Pyrrhonism, Pyrrhonist(s), Pyrrhonic, 177, 179, 180, 181, 182, 183, 219
Pyrrhus of Epirus, 9, 12, 13, 32, 35, 228
Pythagoras, 124, 129, 159, 193, 237
Pythagorean, Pythagoreanism, 124, 125, 127, 131, 132, 143, 163, 194, 237

Quispel, Gilles, 233

Radin, Max, 93, 94, 117
Reinach, Théodore, 82, 115
Reinhardt, Karl, 200, 202, 203, 223, 224
Renaissance, 7
Rhodes, 23, 34, 45, 196, 199
Rhodian, 83
Rist, J.M., 144, 209, 210

Riviera, 199
Robin, Léon, 167, 174, 175, 215, 217, 220
Rodis-Lewis, G., 210
Roman(s), 23, 25, 26, 34-39, 51, 62, 67, 68, 70, 82, 92, 94, 95, 109, 144, 192, 194, 195, 198, 199, 204, 228, 240, 242, 250
Roman Empire, 20, 39, 40, 80, 228, 248
Rome (city), 22, 36, 40, 94, 189, 191, 194, 196, 197, 198, 213
Rose, H.J., 230, 252
Ross, William David, 222
Rossini, Giacomo, 234
Rostovzeff, M., 70, 104, 112, 120
Roxane, 3, 5, 51, 52, 110
Rufus Ephesius, 209
Russia(n), 57, 212

Sabbath, 91, 98, 100
Sais, 106
Sako-Scythian, 26, 76, 114
Sallet, Alfred von, 112
Salome, 51
Salonika, 5
Samaritans, 67
Samos, 163
Sardes, 9, 17
Sardinia, 45
Sartre, Jean-Paul, 233
Sasanian(s), 79, 227
Sceptic(s), 176-184, 236, 238
Scepticism, 176-184, 238, 240, 241
Schippers, J.W., 244, 253
Schmekel, August, 222
Schubert, Paul, 202, 224
Schwartz, 254
Scipio Africanus, 196, 198
Scythian(s), 26, 76
Sedley, D.W., 210, 219
Seleucid(s), 18, 20, 21, 22, 23, 38, 39, 53, 68, 70, 71, 77, 78, 83, 84, 85, 86, 87, 89, 92, 93, 95, 96, 101, 116, 228, 246
Seleucid Empire, 7, 18-19, 20, 21, 23, 24, 38, 77-79, 84, 87, 102

Seleucus I, 7, 11, 15, 16, 17, 18-19, 26, 53, 68, 69, 94, 110, 114
Seleucus IV Philopator, 94
Seleukeia, 78
Semitic, 86, 91, 103
Senate of Rome, 35, 36, 189, 194
Seneca, 144, 204, 214, 215
Septuagint, 62, 103
Sextus Empiricus, 179, 205, 208, 209, 210, 214, 215, 218, 219, 220, 221, 223
Shudras, 70
Sicily, 45, 121, 199, 243
Sicilian(s), 45
Sidon, 195
Silk Road, 72
Simon the Machabee, 101, 102
Simplicius, 213
Sind, 68
Sirkap, 113
Siwah Oasis, 64
Socrates, 46, 167, 186, 188
Socratic, 125
Sogdiana, 71
Soloi, 134
Sophist(s), 46, 178, 244
Spain, 199
Sparta, 27, 28, 31, 32, 33, 34, 37, 97, 227
Spartan(s), 34
Speusippus, 123-125, 125, 205, 234, 237, 238
Spitamenes, 53
Starr, Chester G., 112
Statira, 52, 110
Stähelin, 41
Stoa, Stoic School, 133-150, 180, 185, 193, 196, 200, 208, 210, 211, 222, 239, 244
Stobaeus, 208, 210, 213, 220
Stoicism, 46, 122, 123, 133-150, 241
Stoic(s), 47, 133-150, 170, 174, 185, 186, 187, 189, 190, 193, 195, 195, 196, 198, 209, 234, 235, 236, 237, 238, 250
Stough, Charlotte L., 219
Straaten, Modestus van, 198, 222, 223

Strabo, 54, 82, 110, 111, 113, 114, 115
Straits of Gibraltar, 45
Straits of Messina, 45
Stratocles, 222
Structure and antistructure, 26, 28, 29
Suetonius, 222
Suidas, 43, 207
Sulla, Lucius Cornelius, 39, 126
Sumer, 39, 225
Susa, 14, 52
Syncretism, 63-67
Syria, 4, 16, 18, 20, 21, 23, 24, 26, 34, 35, 38, 63, 84, 84-85, 86, 101, 105, 107, 112, 198
Syrian(s), 35, 85, 87, 92, 95, 97, 99, 100, 101, 102, 106, 119, 199

Table of Oppositions, 127
Tarán, Leonardo
Tarn, W.W., 28, 42, 69, 72, 73, 82, 109, 110, 112, 113, 114, 115
Tarsus, 134
Taurus, 9, 23, 45
Taxila, 69, 74, 76
Taylor, Alfred Edward, 164, 167, 176
Taylor, C.C.W., 205, 214, 218
Tcherikover, Victor, 87, 88, 89, 92, 93, 95, 98, 99, 100, 101, 115, 116, 117, 119, 120
Teilhard de Chardin, Pierre, 209
Temple (of Jerusalem), 98, 99
Temple Hill (Jerusalem), 90, 98
Tertullian, 138, 208, 209
Thebes (in Egypt), 106
Thebes (in Greece), 31, 248
Themistocles, 34
Theodoretus, 206
Theophrastus, 127, 170, 206, 212, 216
Theopompus, 253
Theory of Forms, 121-122, 124, 139, 140
Theory of Numbers, 124, 127, 131, 132, 237
Thermopylae, 30
Thessalonika (the town), 5

Thessalonike (sister of Alexander the Great), 5, 11
Thessaly, 9, 11, 35
Thessalian(s), 60
Thompson Griffith, Guy, 15, 41, 42
Thrace, 6, 8, 9, 12, 16, 18, 21, 22, 31
Thracian(s), 8, 18, 21, 54, 62, 82
Thracologist, 8
Thrasyllus, 154, 212
Thucydides, 29, 58
Tigris, 15, 18, 20, 50, 63, 78, 110
Timocrates, 175
Timon, 178, 181, 184, 219
Tobiads, 88-90, 92
Tobiah (possible ancestor of the Tobiads), 89, 90
Tobiah (head of the Tobiad clan), 89
Tomaschek W., 113
Torah, 91, 98
Toscana, 198
Trabizonde (Trebzond), 82
Triparadisus, 4, 6
Tubin, 101
Turkestan, 71
Turkey, Turks, Turkish, 17, 87, 114, 205
Tychè(-cult), 247-249, 254

Uranus, 243
USA, 242
Utrecht, 213

Vallauri, G., 253
Varro, 204
Vezin, A., 42
Vitucci, Giovanni, 115
Vogel, Cornelia de, 218

Walbank, F.W., 54, 104, 110, 115, 120
Wars of the Diadochi, 8
Wars of the Machabees, 86
Watson, John Broadus, 138
Whyte, Lancelot Law, 151, 211
Wilcken, Ulrich, 7, 33, 40, 42, 43, 113, 117

Wilamowitz-Moellendorf, Ulrich von, 62-63, 64, 111, 246, 253, 254
Will, Edouard, 116
Wisdom of Jesus Ben Sirach, 91
Wittgenstein, Ludwig, 215
Wolff, 120
Wolff, Christian, 202
Woodcock, G., 69, 70, 71, 73, 74, 75, 76, 112, 113, 114
World Soul, 127, 128, 143, 149

Xenocrates, 125-130, 206, 235, 237, 239, 241
Xenophanes, 244
Xenophon, 46
Xerxes I, 28

Yahve, 67
Yavanas, 69-70
Yüe-Chi, 26, 76, 114

Zeller, Eduard, 122, 125, 150, 160, 167, 172, 187, 193, 194, 195, 197, 204, 205, 206, 207, 211, 212, 213, 214, 216, 218, 220, 220, 221, 222, 223, 253
Zeno the Eleate, 108, 154, 178
Zeno of Kittion, 46-48, 133, 134, 137, 138, 139, 140, 141, 142, 146, 150, 185, 208, 209, 210, 214, 231
Zeno of Tarsus, 222
Zeus (Olympios), 64, 67, 94, 95, 96, 98, 127, 128, 129, 142, 172, 190, 201, 233, 235, 248
Zeus Triphylius, 243
Zschietschmann, W., 115
Zoroastrian(ism), 71, 95, 208